As a Reincarnated ARISTOCRAT, I'll Use My Appraisal Skill to Rise in the World

6

[Story] **Miraijin A**
[Art] **Natsumi Inoue**
[Character Design] **jimmy**

☆☆☆☆☆

CONTENTS

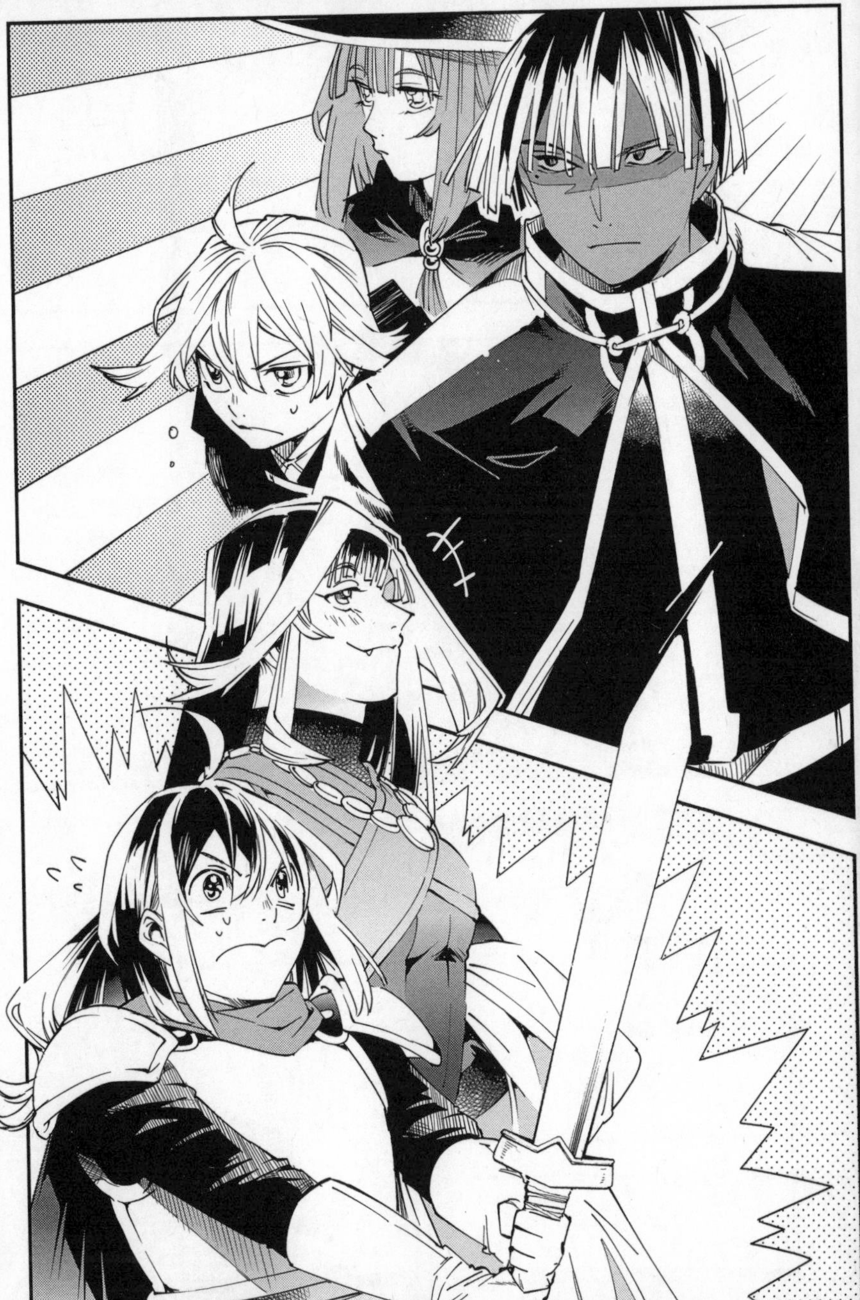

Chapter 45: The Mock Battle (2)

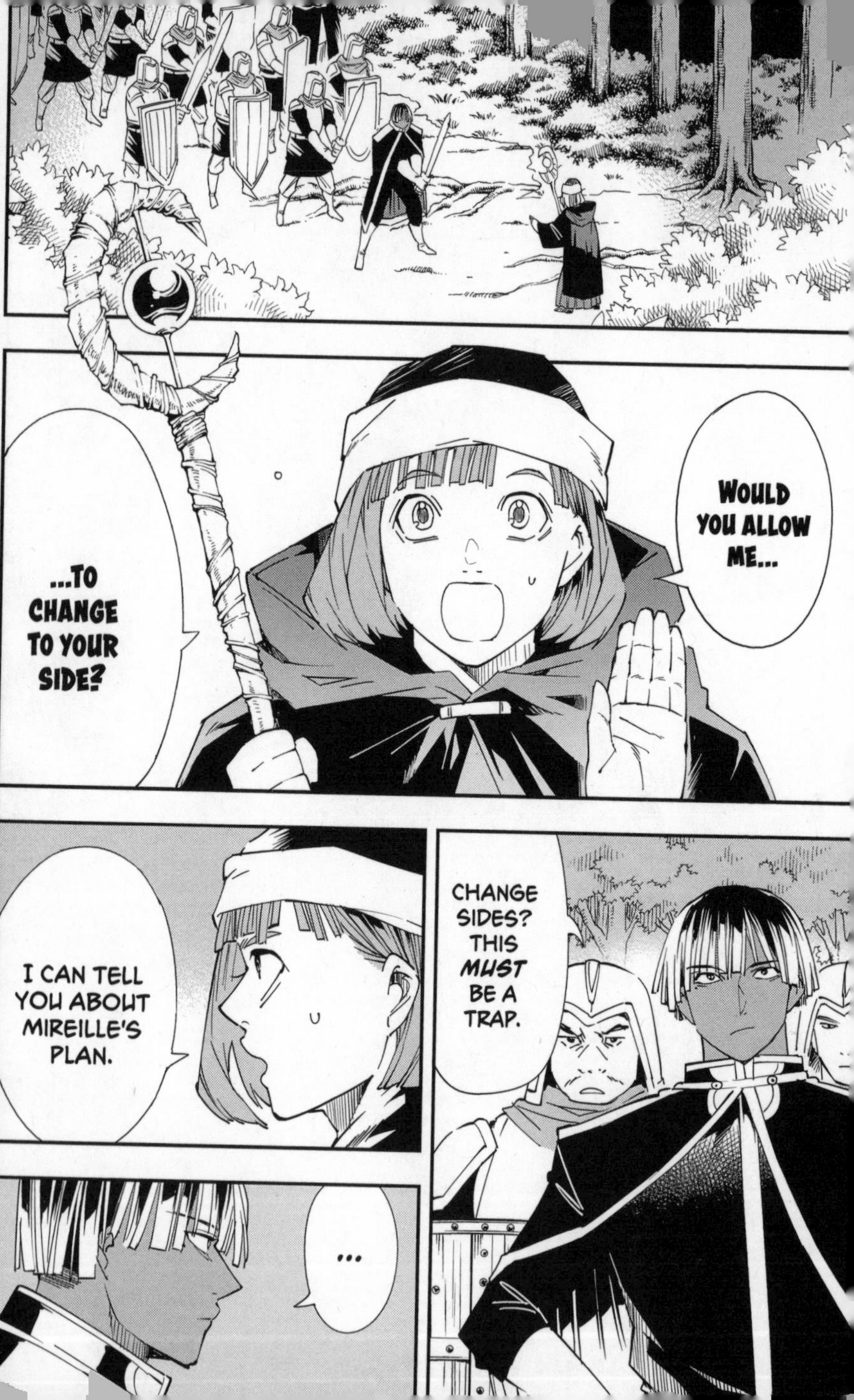
WOULD YOU ALLOW ME...
...TO CHANGE TO YOUR SIDE?
CHANGE SIDES? THIS *MUST* BE A TRAP.
I CAN TELL YOU ABOUT MIREILLE'S PLAN.
...

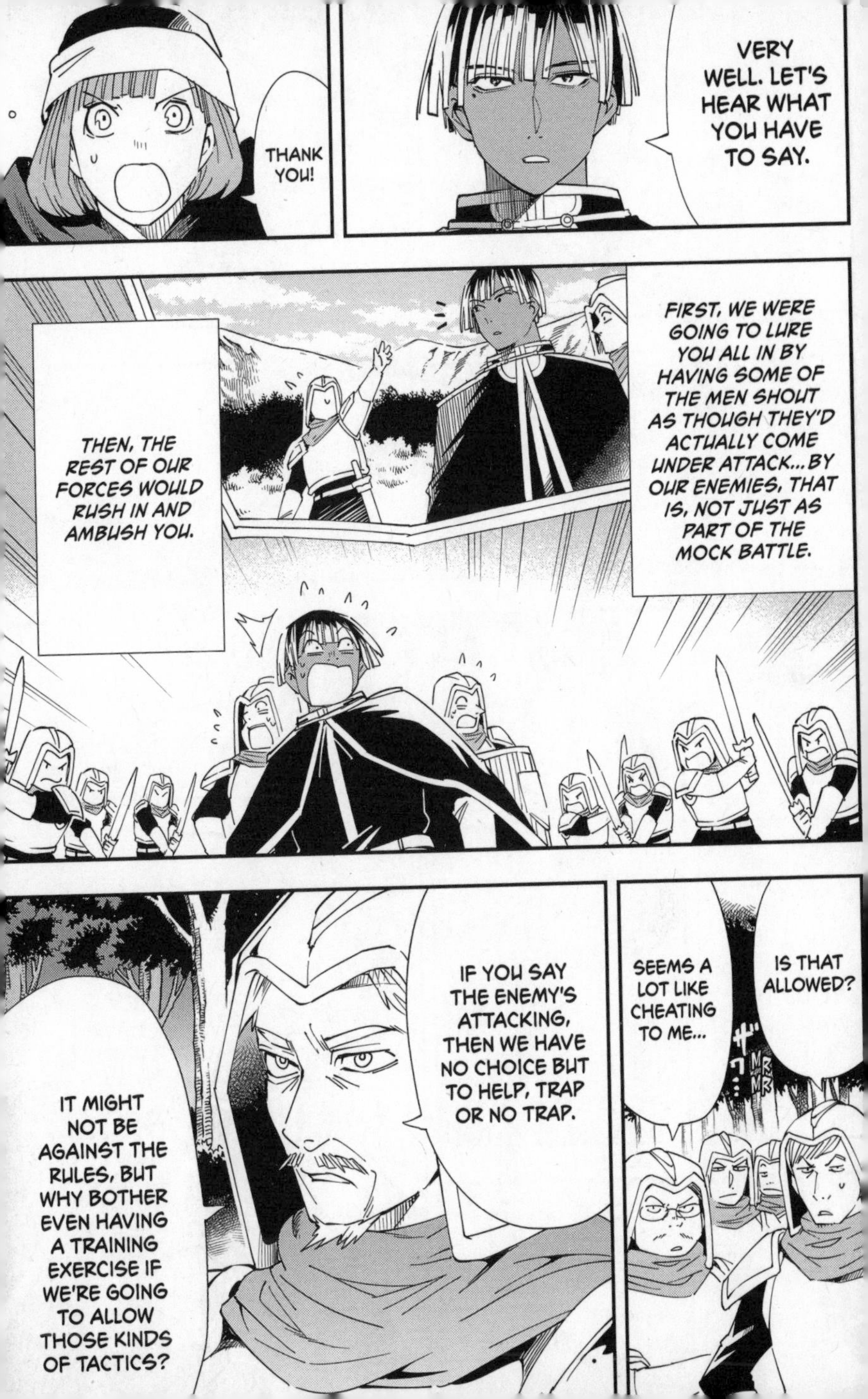
VERY WELL. LET'S HEAR WHAT YOU HAVE TO SAY.
THANK YOU!
FIRST, WE WERE GOING TO LURE YOU ALL IN BY HAVING SOME OF THE MEN SHOUT AS THOUGH THEY'D ACTUALLY COME UNDER ATTACK... BY OUR ENEMIES, THAT IS, NOT JUST AS PART OF THE MOCK BATTLE.
THEN, THE REST OF OUR FORCES WOULD RUSH IN AND AMBUSH YOU.
IS THAT ALLOWED?
SEEMS A LOT LIKE CHEATING TO ME...
ザワ
MRMR
IF YOU SAY THE ENEMY'S ATTACKING, THEN WE HAVE NO CHOICE BUT TO HELP, TRAP OR NO TRAP.
IT MIGHT NOT BE AGAINST THE RULES, BUT WHY BOTHER EVEN HAVING A TRAINING EXERCISE IF WE'RE GOING TO ALLOW THOSE KINDS OF TACTICS?

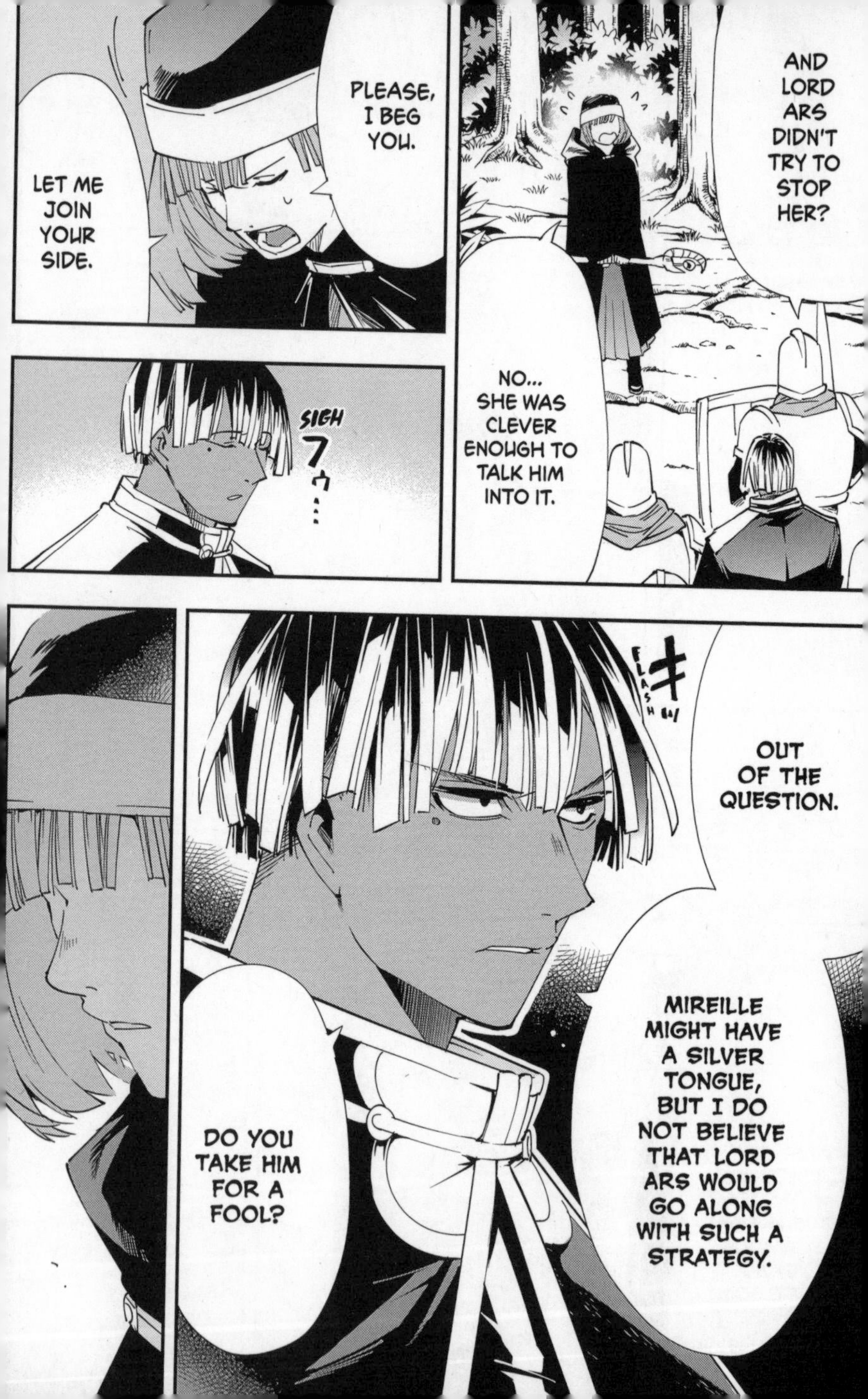
AND LORD ARS DIDN'T TRY TO STOP HER?
NO... SHE WAS CLEVER ENOUGH TO TALK HIM INTO IT.
PLEASE, I BEG YOU.
LET ME JOIN YOUR SIDE.
SIGH
FLASH
OUT OF THE QUESTION.
MIREILLE MIGHT HAVE A SILVER TONGUE, BUT I DO NOT BELIEVE THAT LORD ARS WOULD GO ALONG WITH SUCH A STRATEGY.
DO YOU TAKE HIM FOR A FOOL?

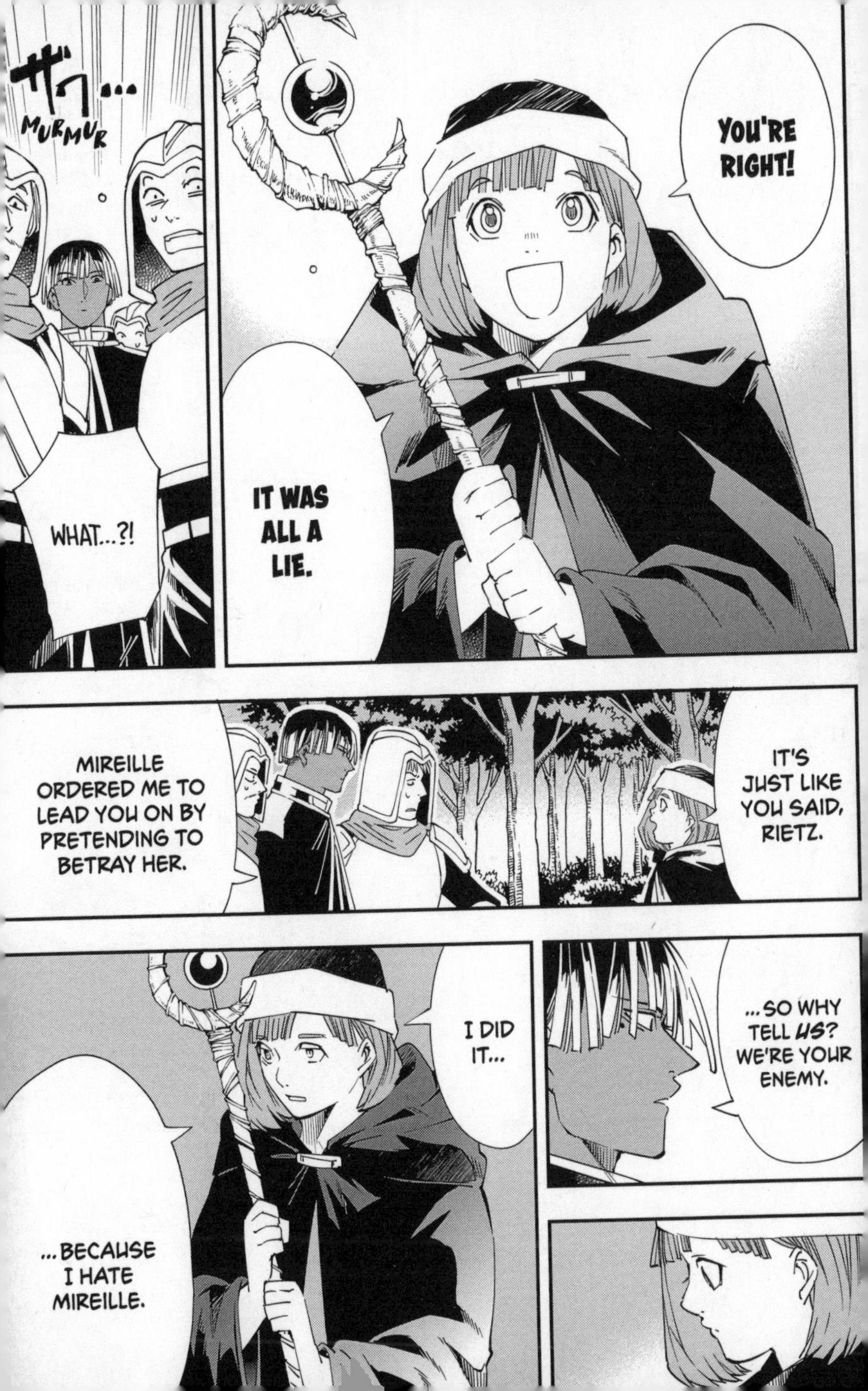

YOU'RE RIGHT!
IT WAS ALL A LIE.
ザワ...
MURMUR
WHAT...?!
IT'S JUST LIKE YOU SAID, RIETZ.
MIREILLE ORDERED ME TO LEAD YOU ON BY PRETENDING TO BETRAY HER.
...SO WHY TELL *US*? WE'RE YOUR ENEMY.
I DID IT...
...BECAUSE I HATE MIREILLE.

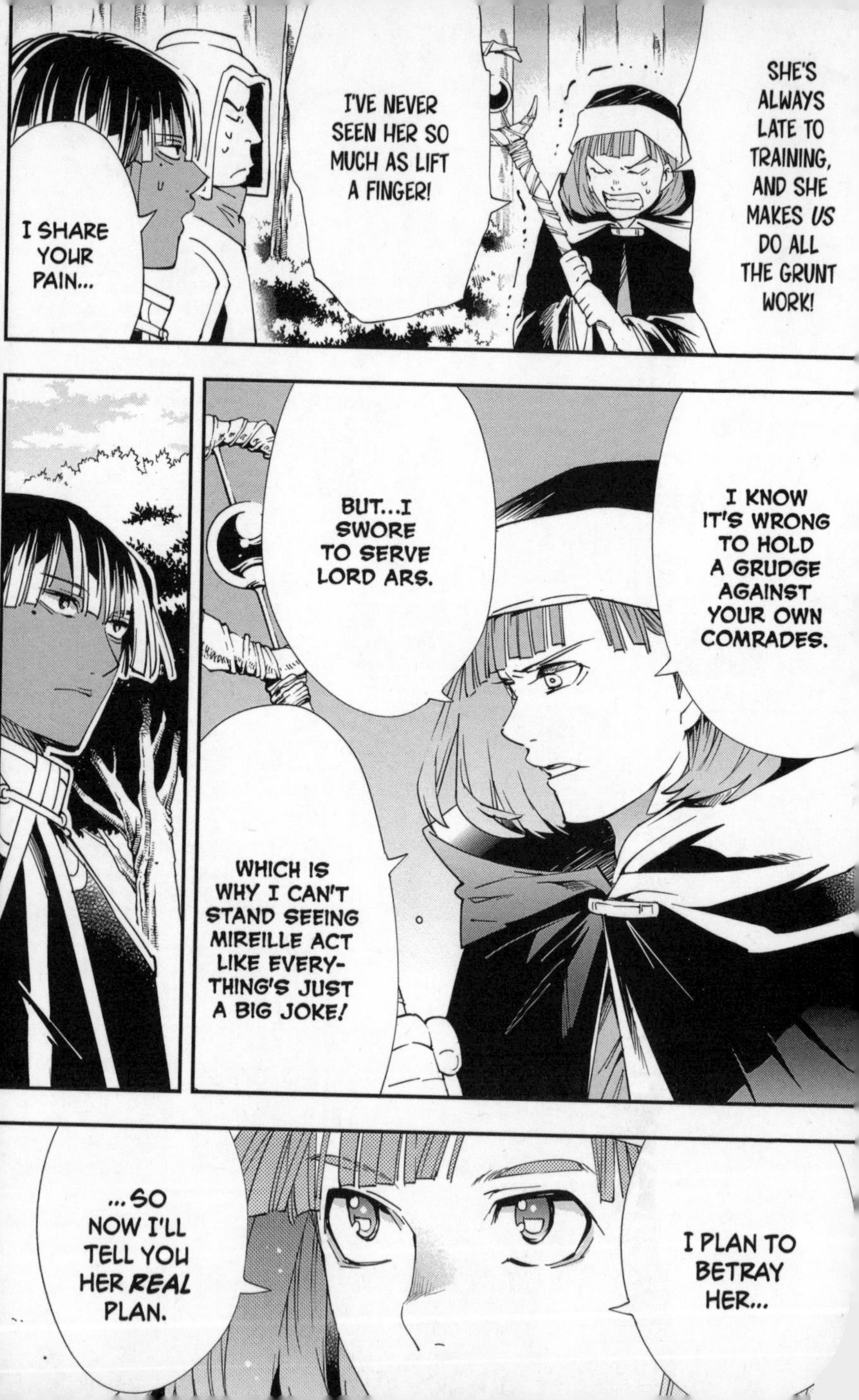
SHE'S ALWAYS LATE TO TRAINING, AND SHE MAKES *US* DO ALL THE GRUNT WORK!
I'VE NEVER SEEN HER SO MUCH AS LIFT A FINGER!
I SHARE YOUR PAIN...
I KNOW IT'S WRONG TO HOLD A GRUDGE AGAINST YOUR OWN COMRADES.
BUT...I SWORE TO SERVE LORD ARS.
WHICH IS WHY I CAN'T STAND SEEING MIREILLE ACT LIKE EVERY-THING'S JUST A BIG JOKE!
I PLAN TO BETRAY HER...
...SO NOW I'LL TELL YOU HER ***REAL*** PLAN.

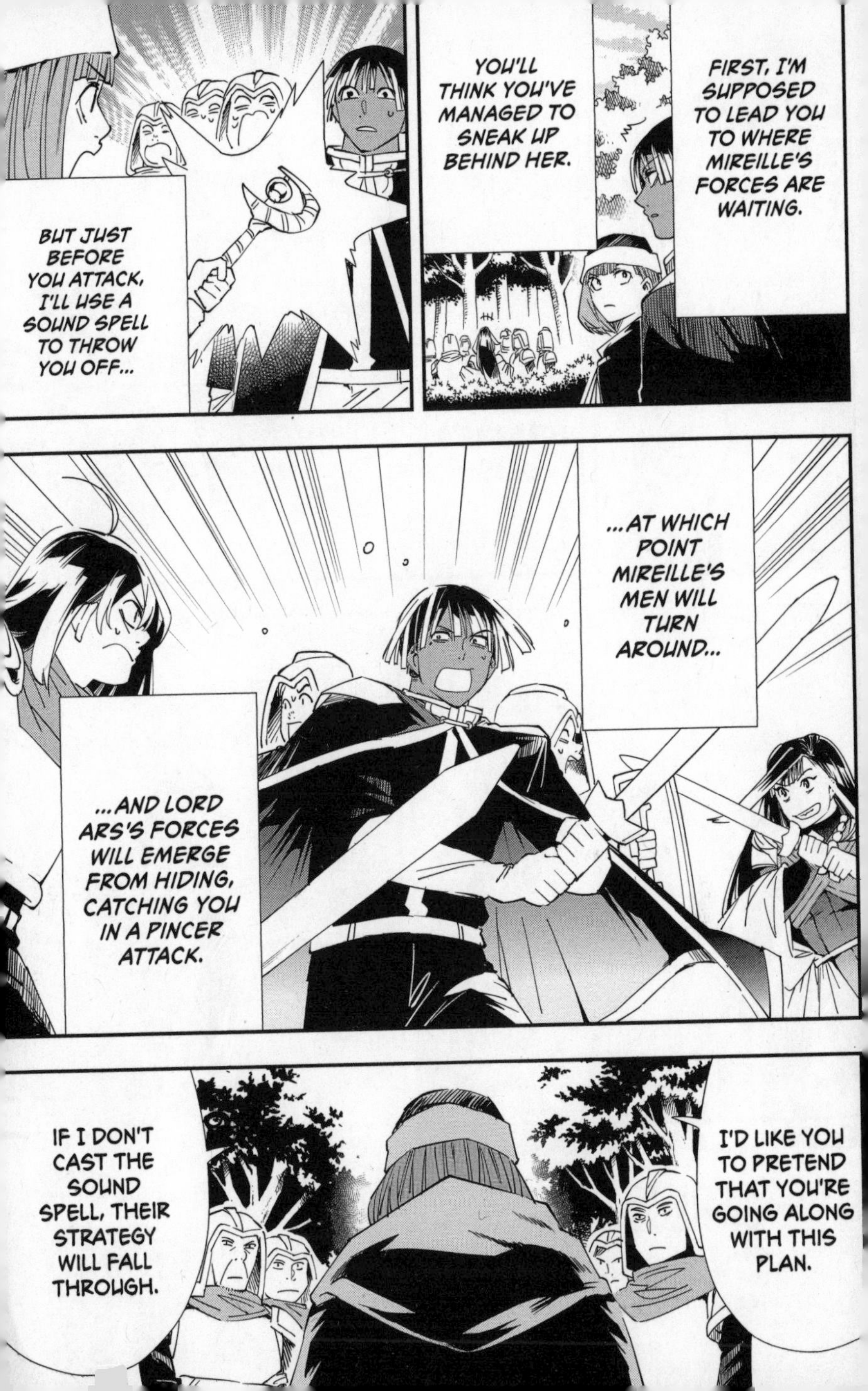
FIRST, I'M SUPPOSED TO LEAD YOU TO WHERE MIREILLE'S FORCES ARE WAITING.
YOU'LL THINK YOU'VE MANAGED TO SNEAK UP BEHIND HER.
BUT JUST BEFORE YOU ATTACK, I'LL USE A SOUND SPELL TO THROW YOU OFF...
...AT WHICH POINT MIREILLE'S MEN WILL TURN AROUND...
...AND LORD ARS'S FORCES WILL EMERGE FROM HIDING, CATCHING YOU IN A PINCER ATTACK.
I'D LIKE YOU TO PRETEND THAT YOU'RE GOING ALONG WITH THIS PLAN.
IF I DON'T CAST THE SOUND SPELL, THEIR STRATEGY WILL FALL THROUGH.

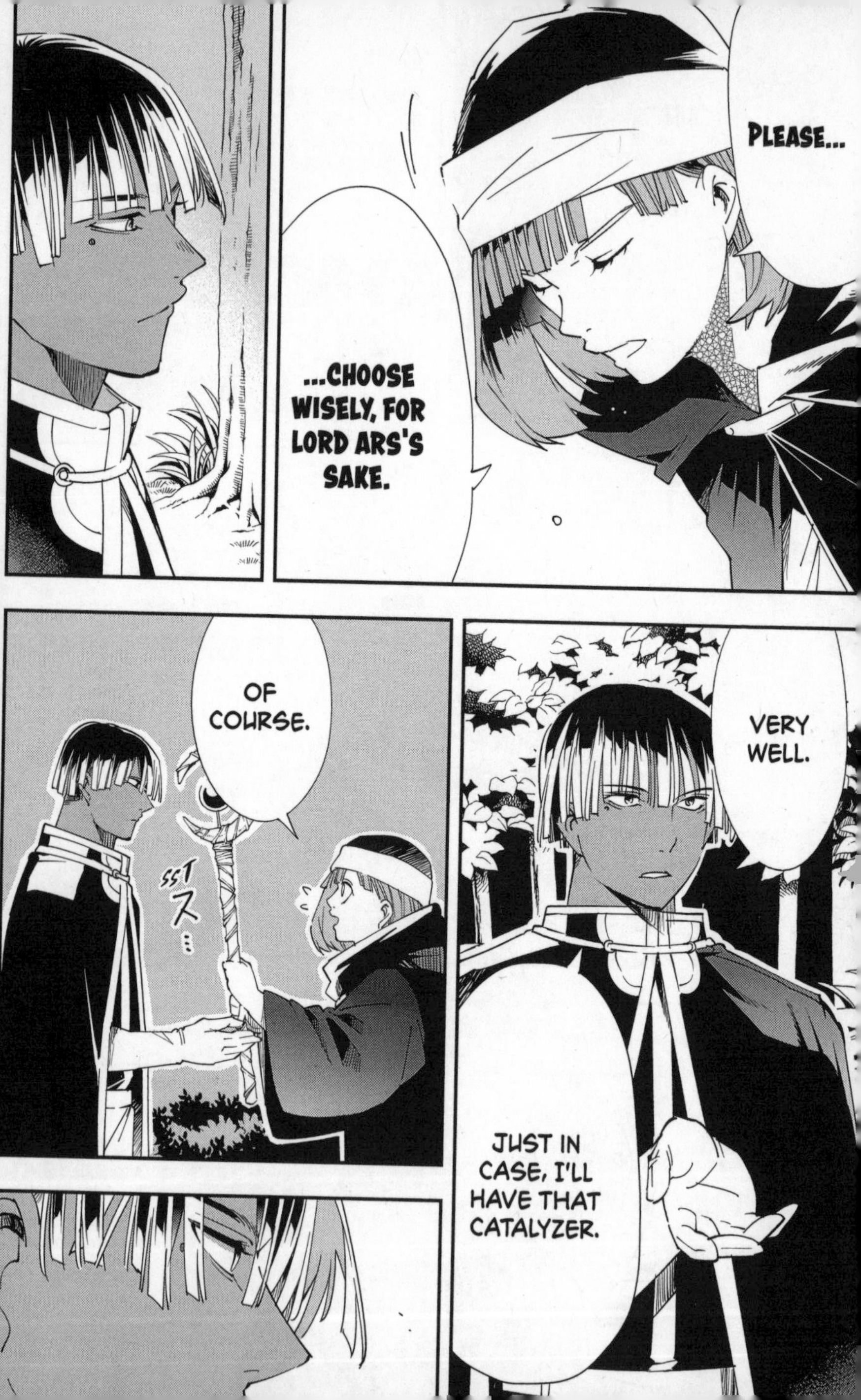
PLEASE...
...CHOOSE WISELY, FOR LORD ARS'S SAKE.
VERY WELL.
JUST IN CASE, I'LL HAVE THAT CATALYZER.
OF COURSE.
SST ス..

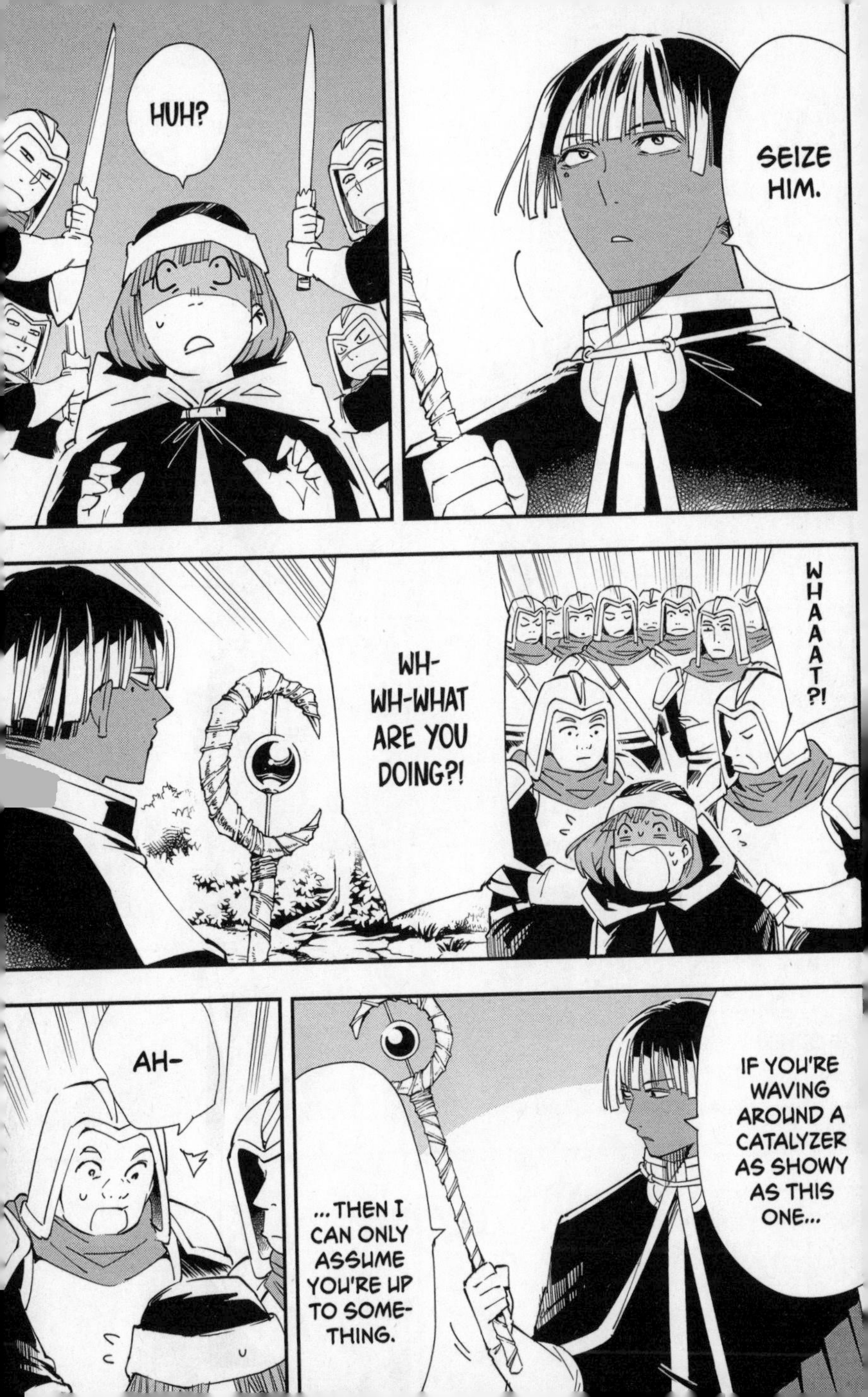
SEIZE HIM.
HUH?
WHAAAAT?!
WH- WH-WHAT ARE YOU DOING?!
IF YOU'RE WAVING AROUND A CATALYZER AS SHOWY AS THIS ONE...
...THEN I CAN ONLY ASSUME YOU'RE UP TO SOME-THING.
AH-

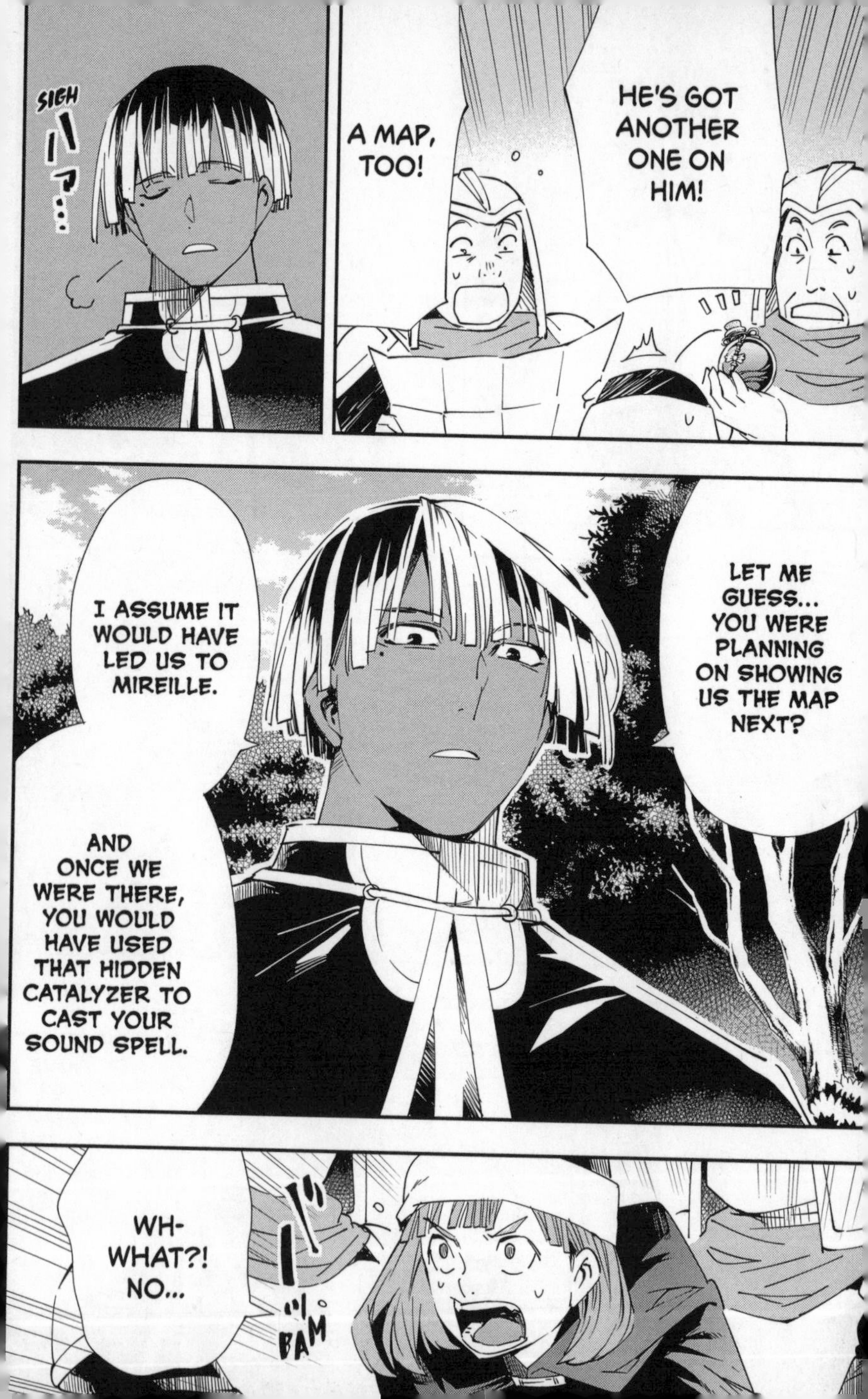
HE'S GOT ANOTHER ONE ON HIM!
A MAP, TOO!
SIGH
LET ME GUESS... YOU WERE PLANNING ON SHOWING US THE MAP NEXT?
I ASSUME IT WOULD HAVE LED US TO MIREILLE.
AND ONCE WE WERE THERE, YOU WOULD HAVE USED THAT HIDDEN CATALYZER TO CAST YOUR SOUND SPELL.
BAM
WH-WHAT?! NO...

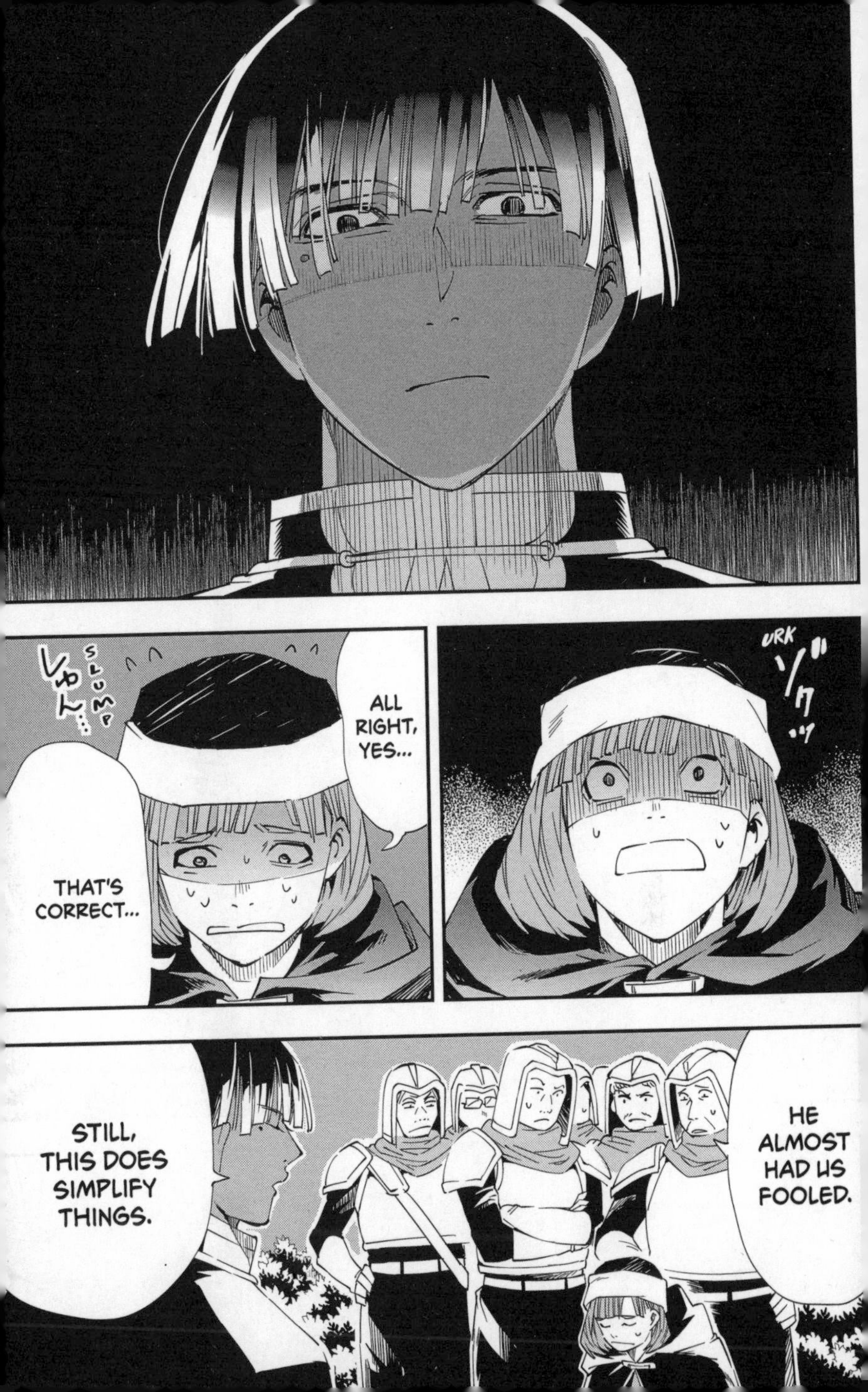
URK
ゾクッ
SLUMP
しゅん…
ALL RIGHT, YES...
THAT'S CORRECT...
HE ALMOST HAD US FOOLED.
STILL, THIS DOES SIMPLIFY THINGS.

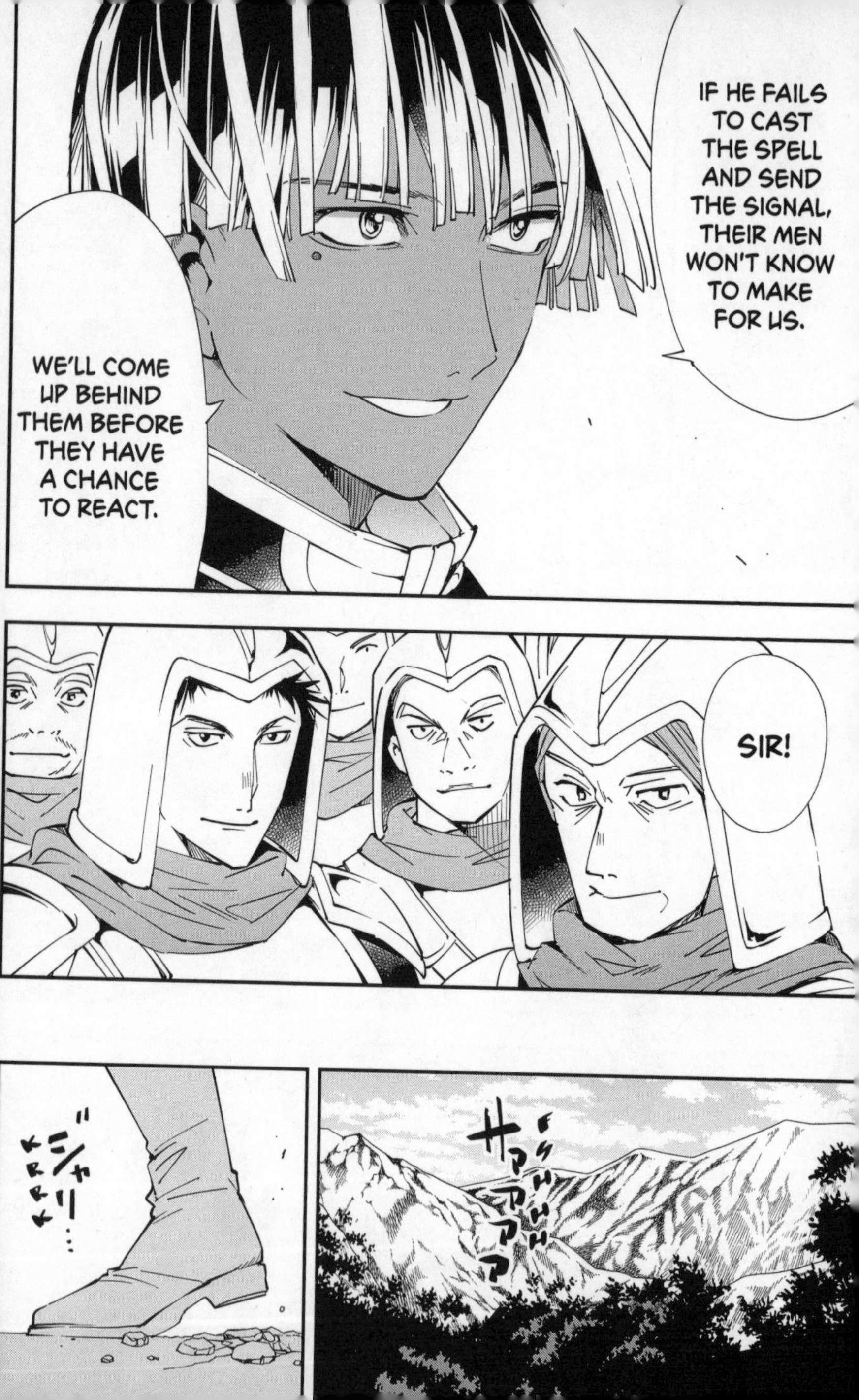
IF HE FAILS TO CAST THE SPELL AND SEND THE SIGNAL, THEIR MEN WON'T KNOW TO MAKE FOR US.
WE'LL COME UP BEHIND THEM BEFORE THEY HAVE A CHANCE TO REACT.
SIR!
サアアアア
FSHHHH
ジャリ…
KRRK

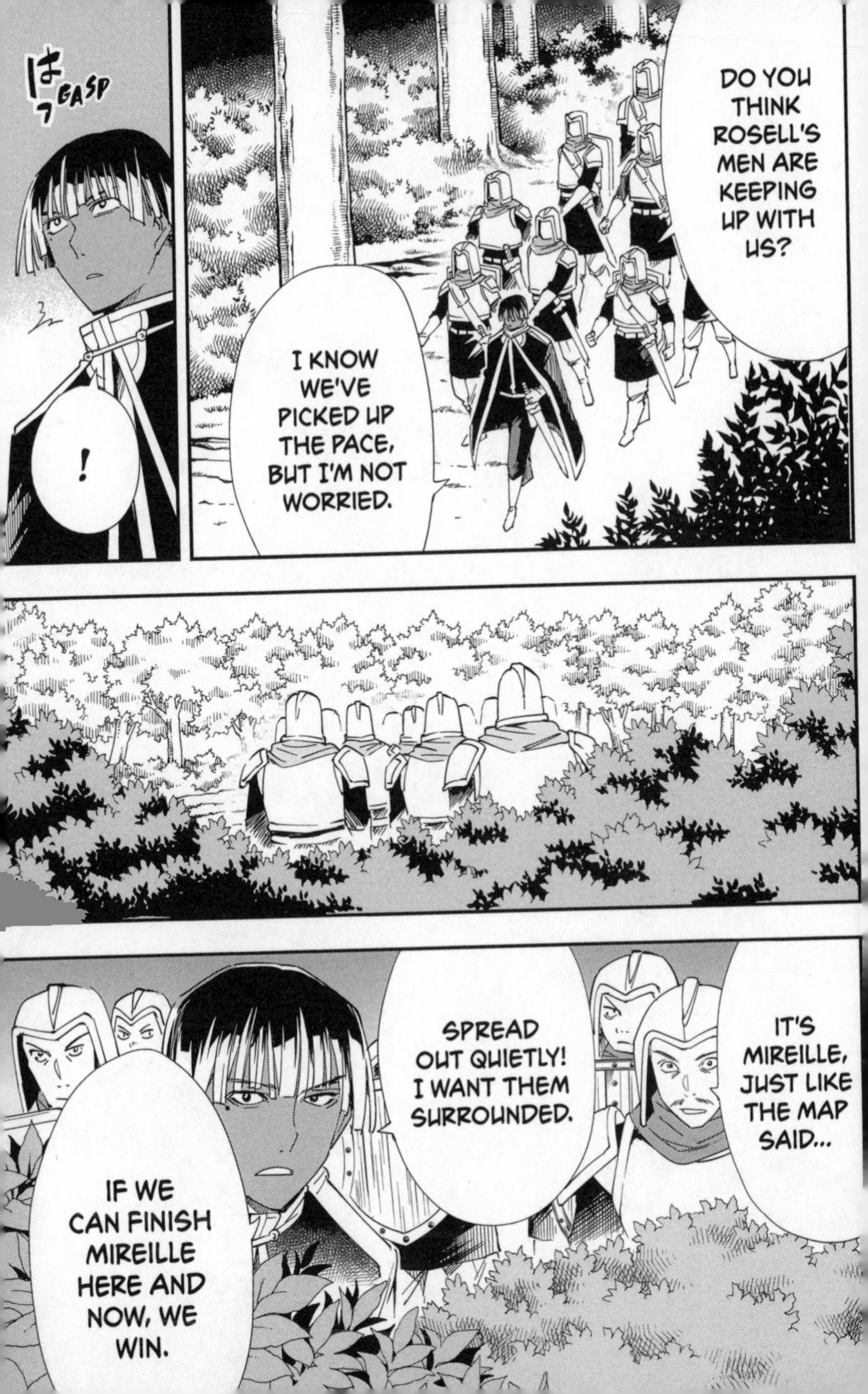
DO YOU THINK ROSELL'S MEN ARE KEEPING UP WITH US?
I KNOW WE'VE PICKED UP THE PACE, BUT I'M NOT WORRIED.
はっ GASP
!
IT'S MIREILLE, JUST LIKE THE MAP SAID...
SPREAD OUT QUIETLY! I WANT THEM SURROUNDED.
IF WE CAN FINISH MIREILLE HERE AND NOW, WE WIN.

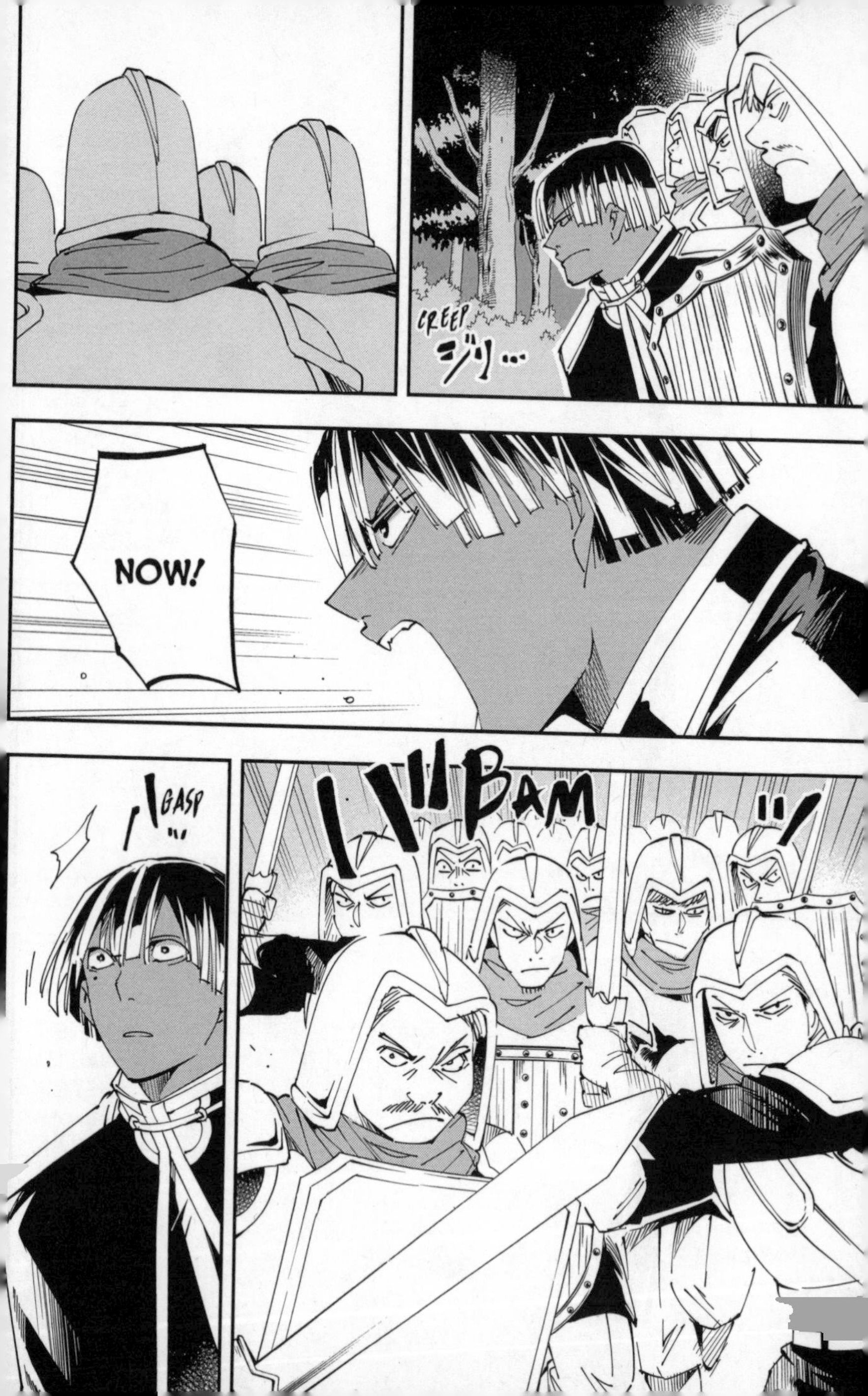
CREEP
ジリ…
NOW!
BAM
GASP

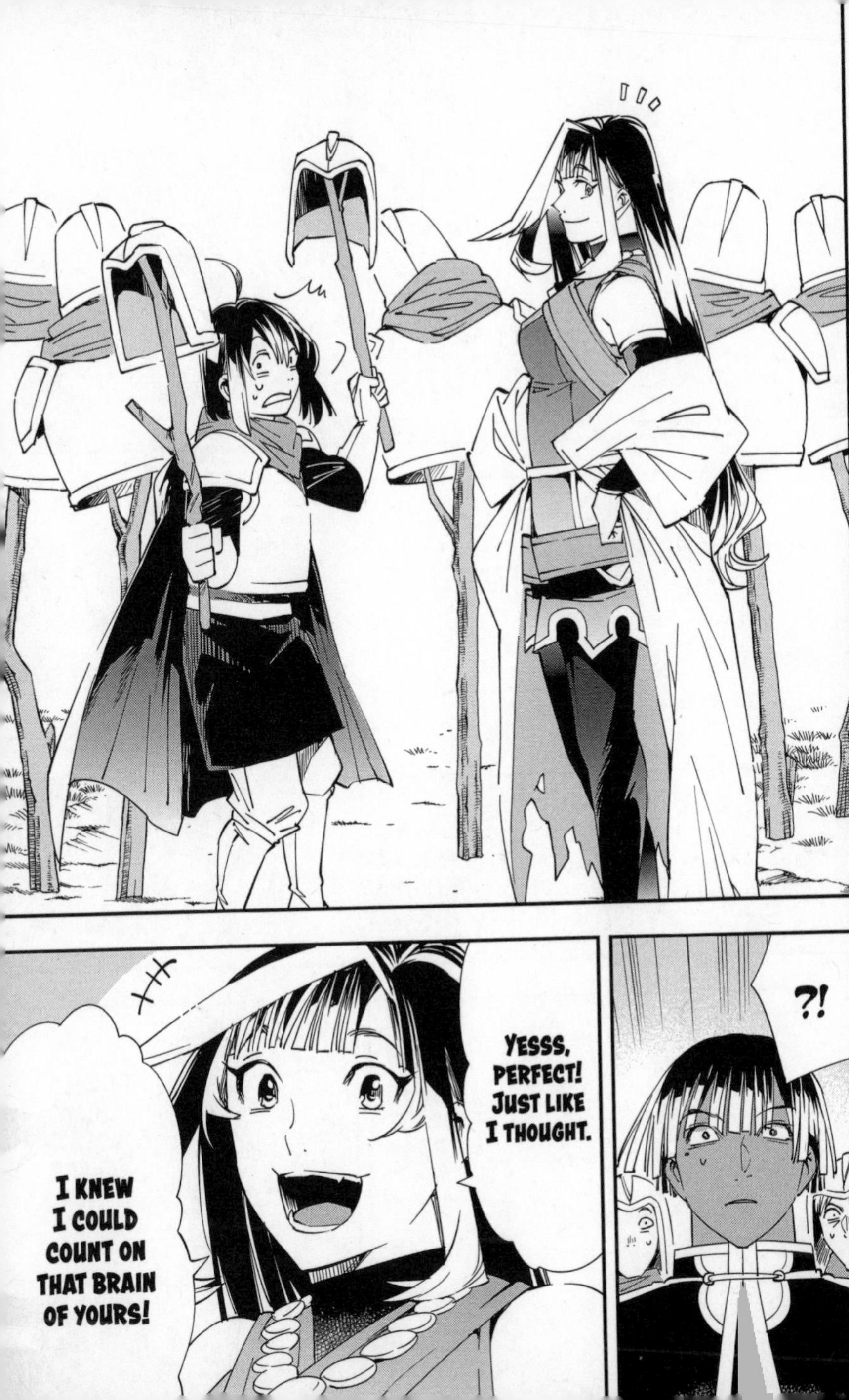
?!
YESSS, PERFECT! JUST LIKE I THOUGHT.
I KNEW I COULD COUNT ON THAT BRAIN OF YOURS!

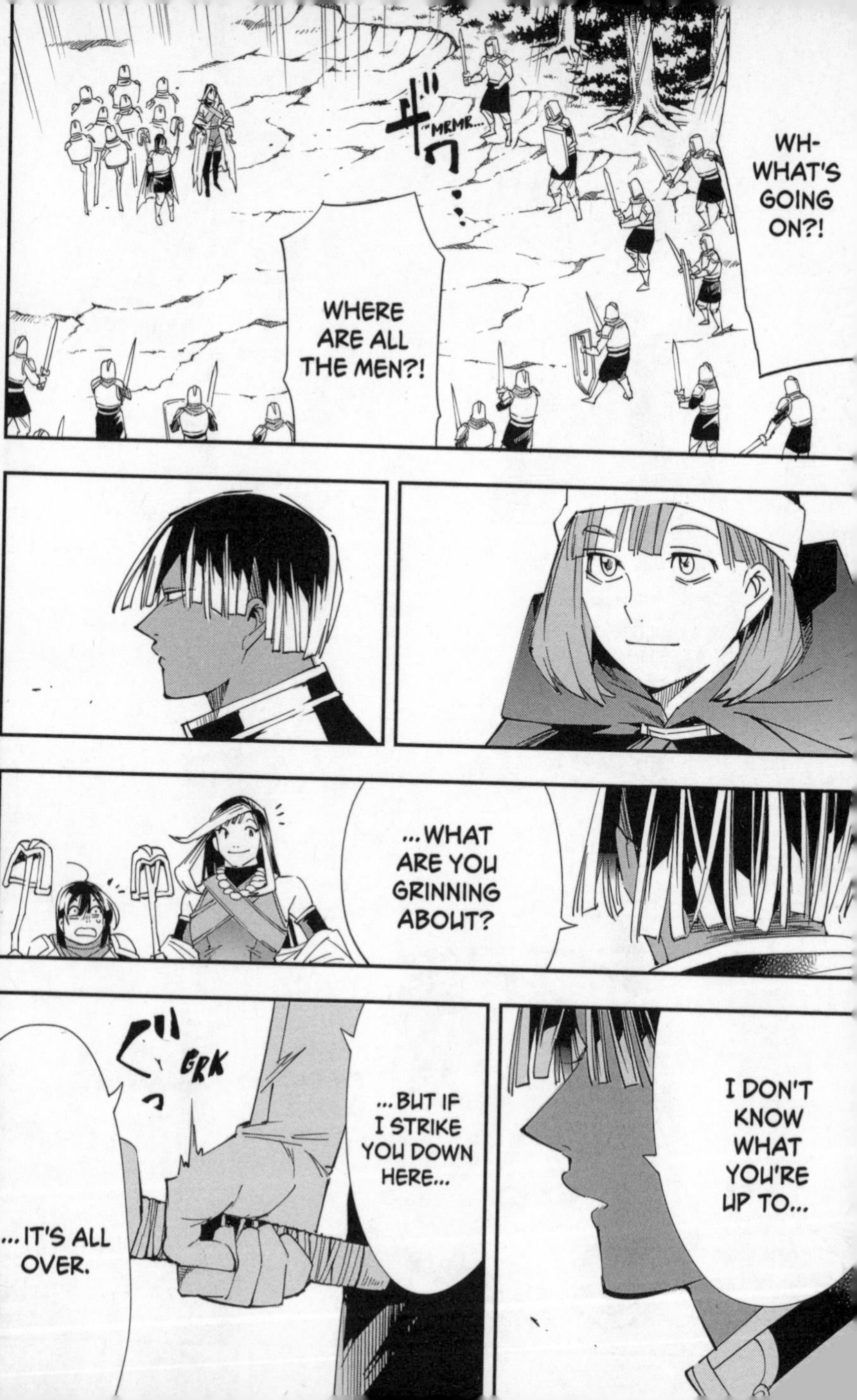
WH- WHAT'S GOING ON?!
MRMR...
WHERE ARE ALL THE MEN?!
...WHAT ARE YOU GRINNING ABOUT?
I DON'T KNOW WHAT YOU'RE UP TO...
...BUT IF I STRIKE YOU DOWN HERE...
GRK
...IT'S ALL OVER.

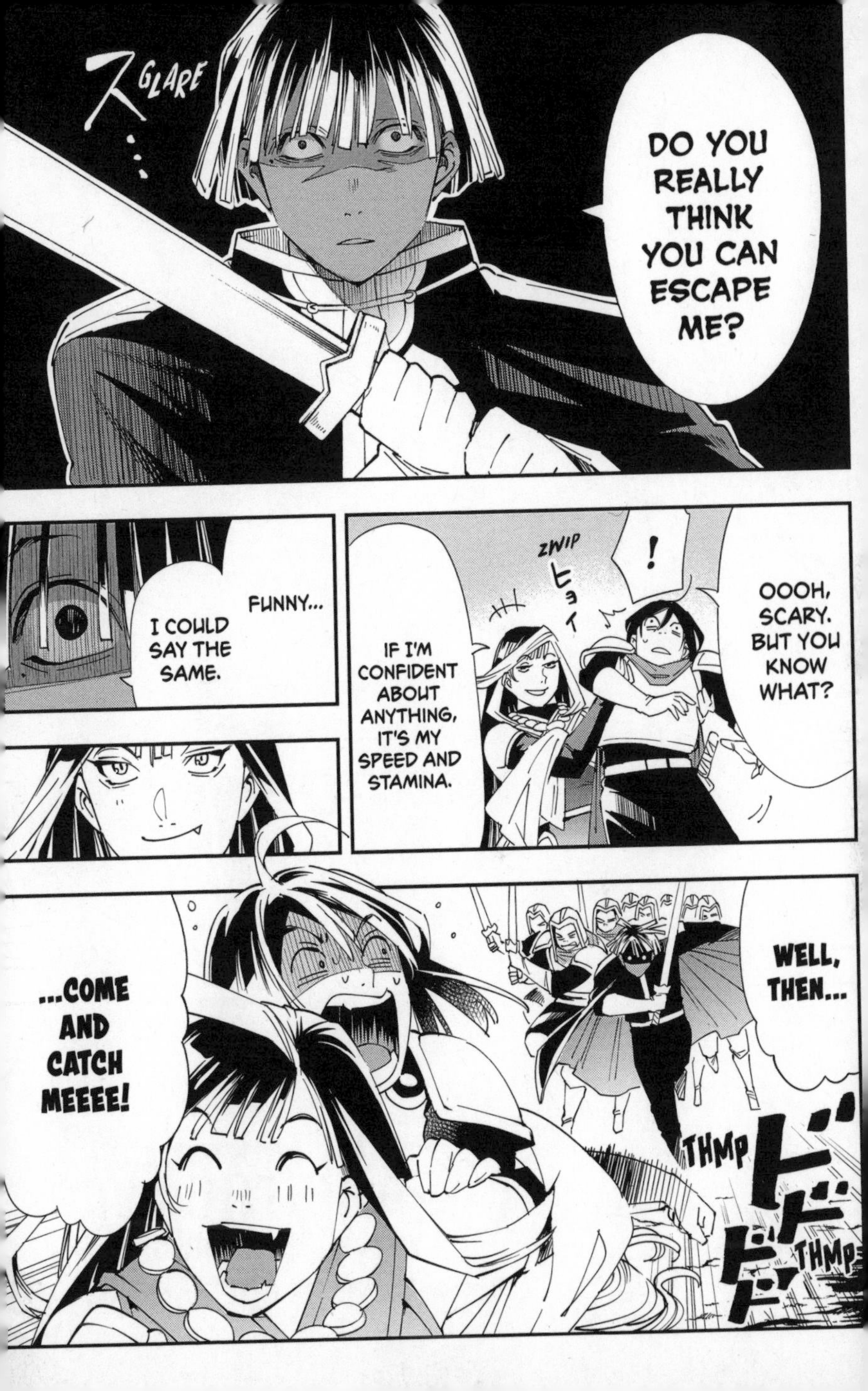
ス GLARE
DO YOU REALLY THINK YOU CAN ESCAPE ME?
!
ZWIP ヒョイ
OOOH, SCARY. BUT YOU KNOW WHAT?
IF I'M CONFIDENT ABOUT ANYTHING, IT'S MY SPEED AND STAMINA.
FUNNY... I COULD SAY THE SAME.
WELL, THEN...
...COME AND CATCH MEEEE!
THMP ドドド THMP

As a Reincarnated
ARISTOCRAT,
I'll Use My Appraisal Skill to
Rise in the World

Chapter 46: The Mock Battle (3)

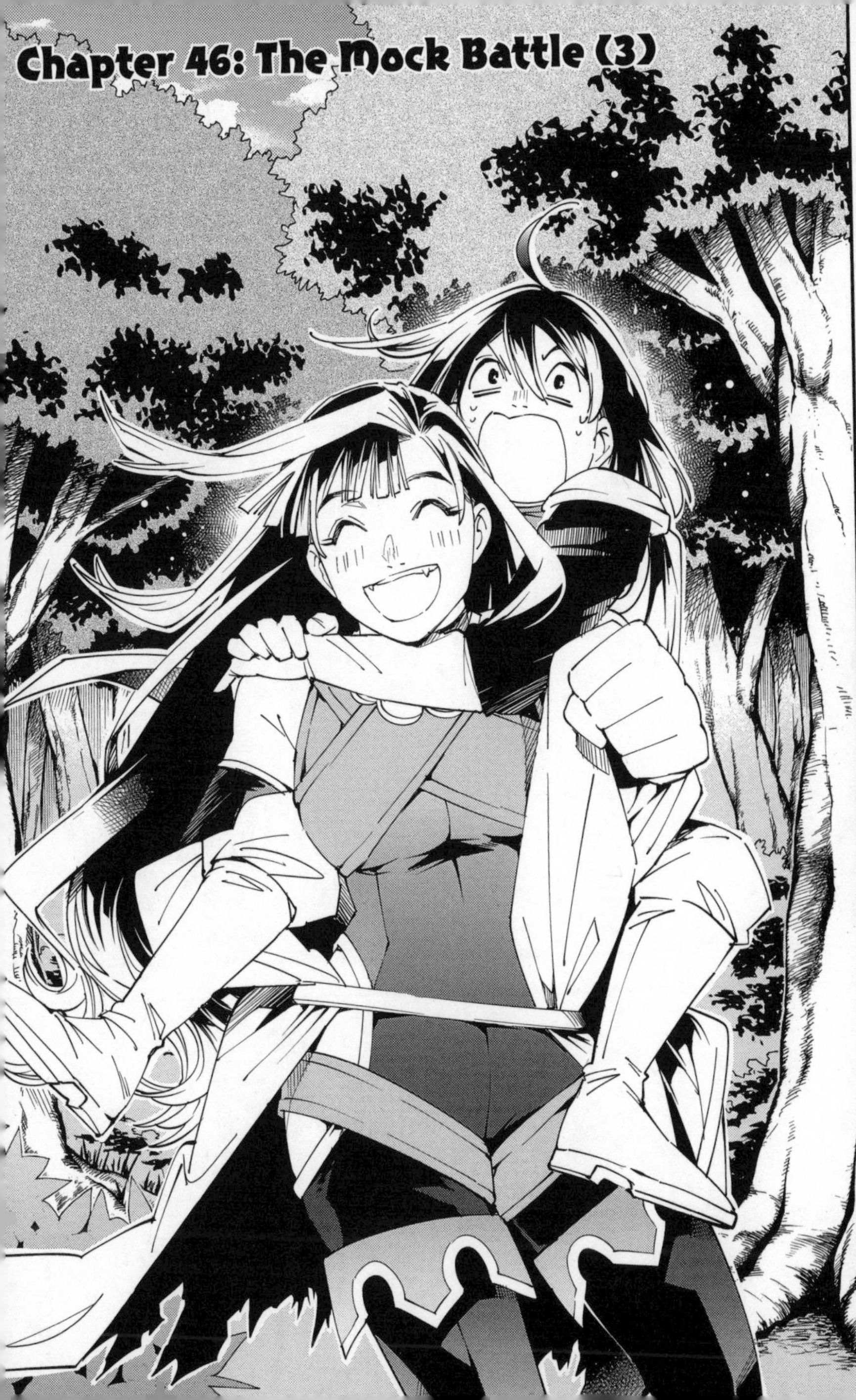

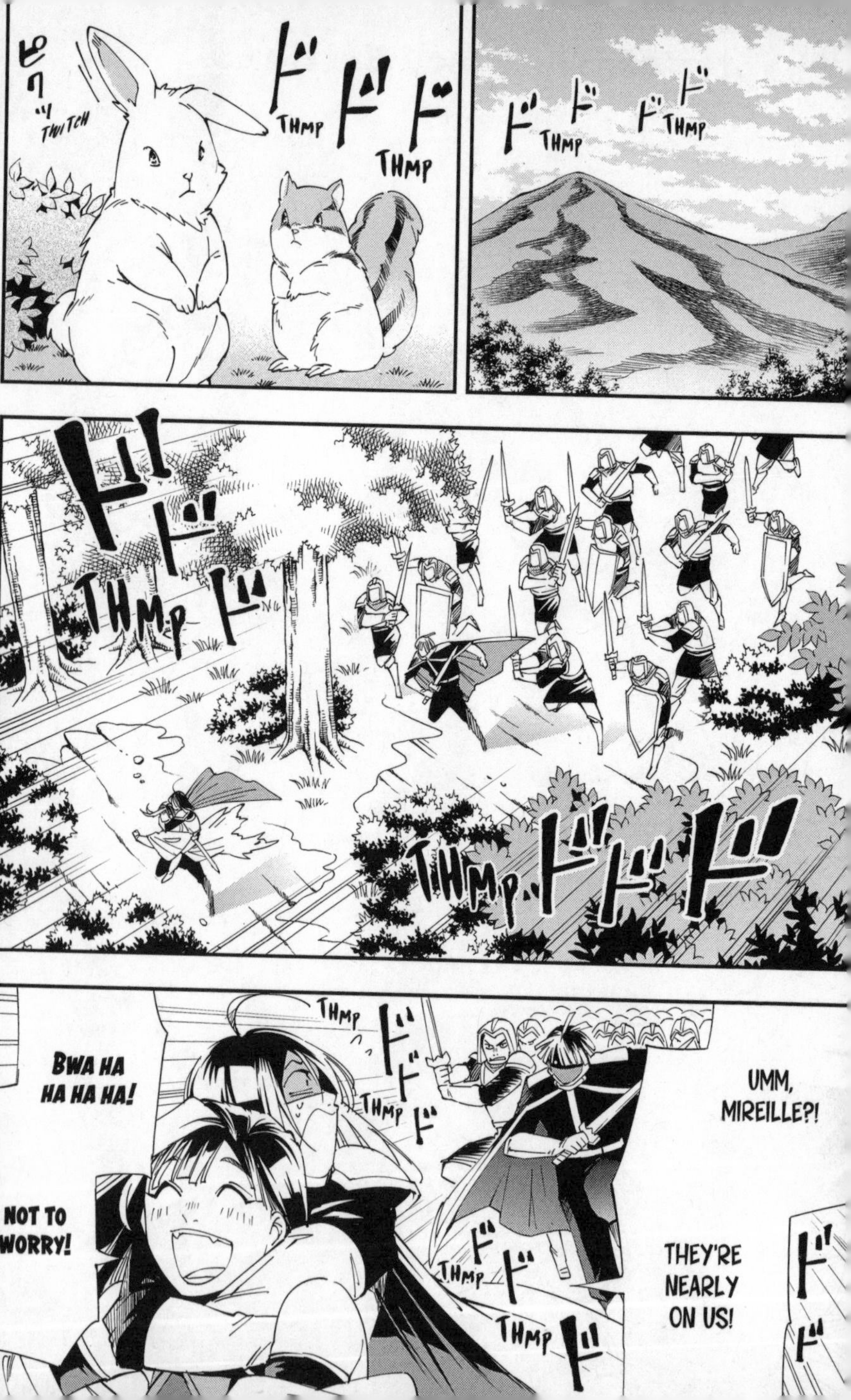

ド THMP
ド THMP
ドド THMP
ピクッ
THWITCH
ド THMP
ドド THMP
ドドドドド
THMP
THMP ドドドド
UMM, MIREILLE?!
THEY'RE NEARLY ON US!
THMP ドドド
THMP ド
BWA HA HA HA HA!
NOT TO WORRY!
ドド
THMP ドド
THMP ド

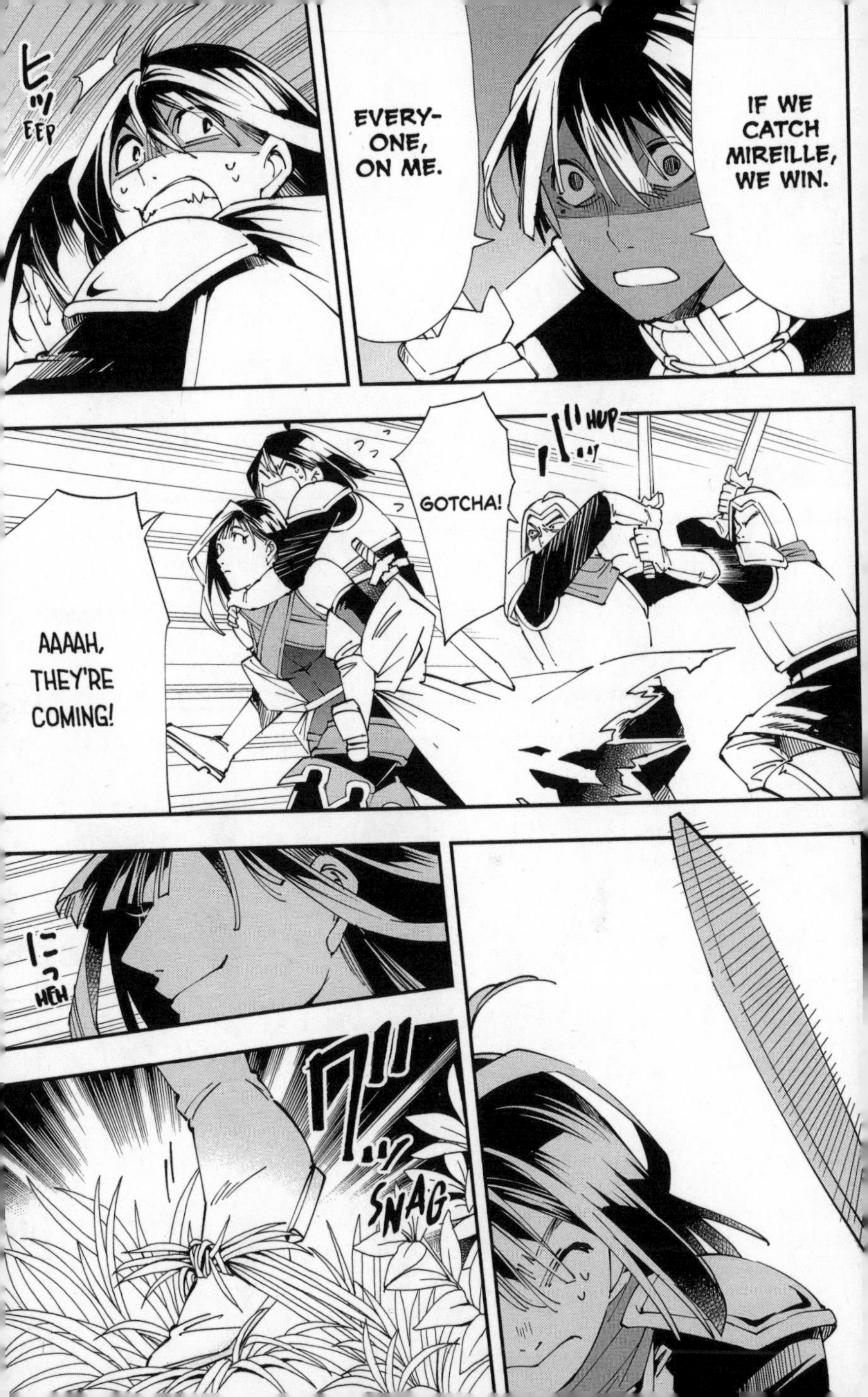
IF WE CATCH MIREILLE, WE WIN.
EVERY-ONE, ON ME.
ヒッ
EEP
HUP
GOTCHA!
AAAAH, THEY'RE COMING!
にっ
HEH
SNAG

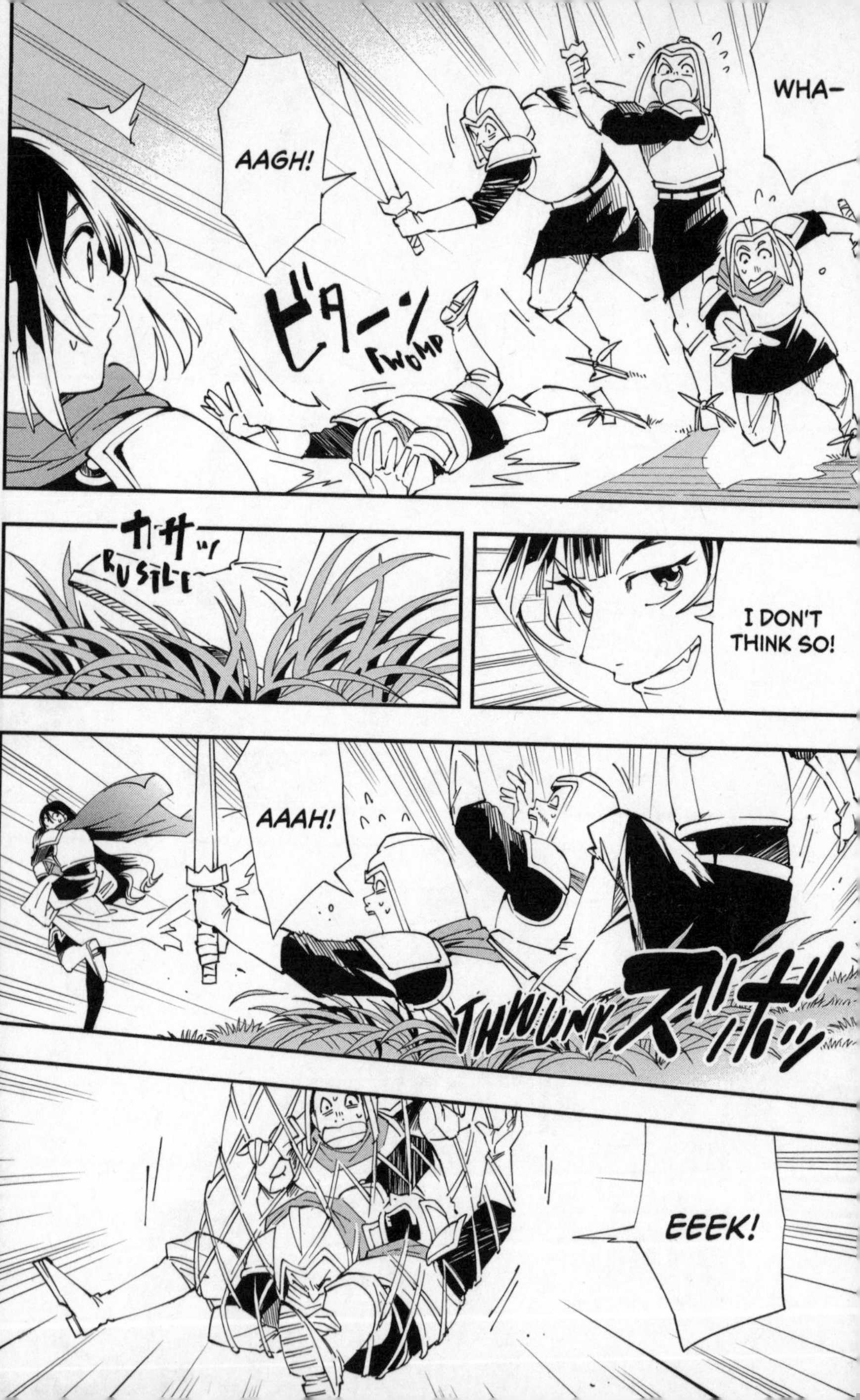
WHA–
AAGH!
ビターン
TWOMP
I DON'T THINK SO!
カサッ
RUSTLE
AAAH!
THWUNK
スポッ
EEEK!

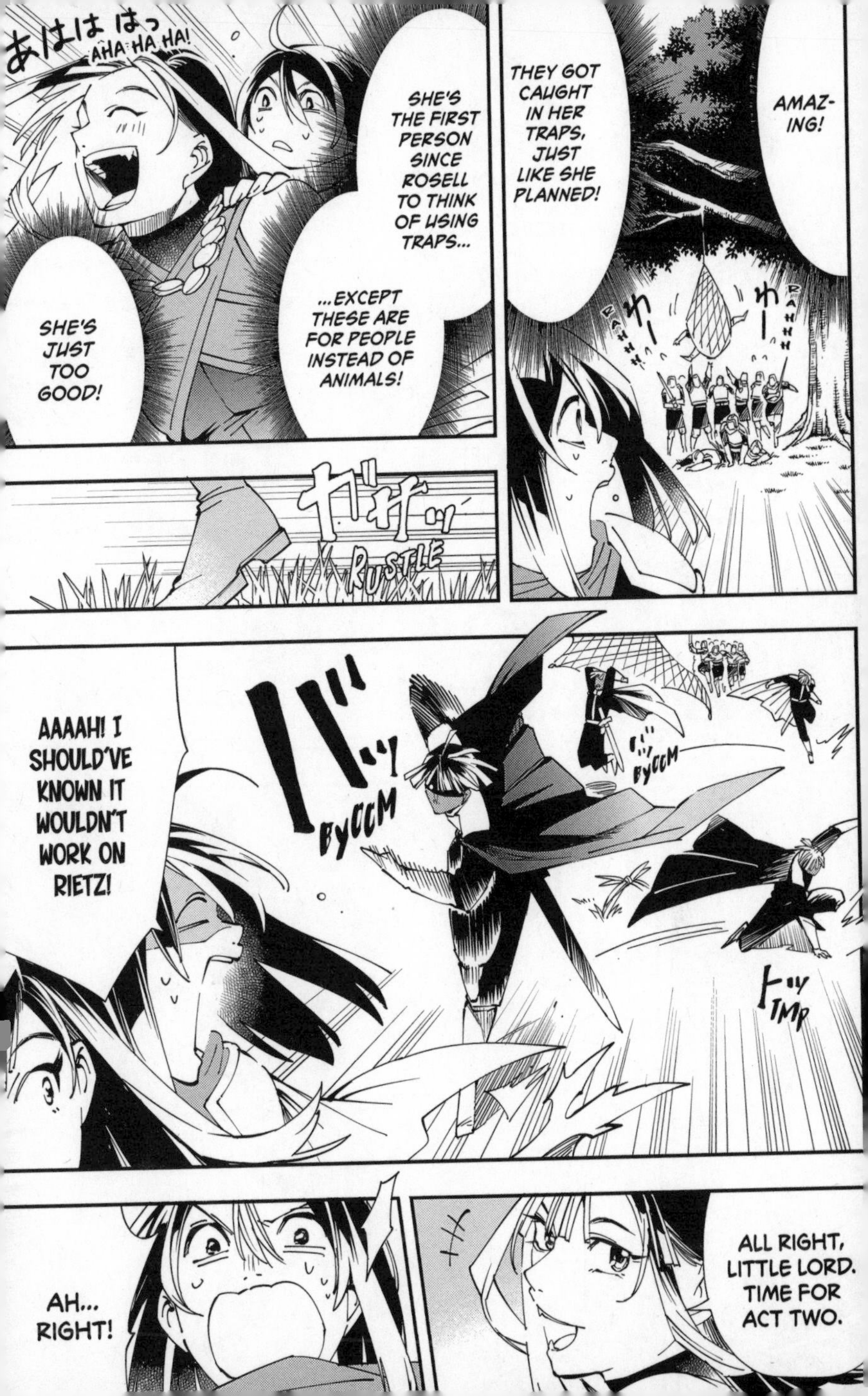
AMAZ-ING!
THEY GOT CAUGHT IN HER TRAPS, JUST LIKE SHE PLANNED!
わー RAHHH
わー RAHHH
SHE'S THE FIRST PERSON SINCE ROSELL TO THINK OF USING TRAPS...
...EXCEPT THESE ARE FOR PEOPLE INSTEAD OF ANIMALS!
あははは AHA HA HA!
SHE'S JUST TOO GOOD!
ガサッ RUSTLE
バッ BYOOM
バッ BYOOM
トッ TMP
AAAAH! I SHOULD'VE KNOWN IT WOULDN'T WORK ON RIETZ!
ALL RIGHT, LITTLE LORD. TIME FOR ACT TWO.
AH... RIGHT!

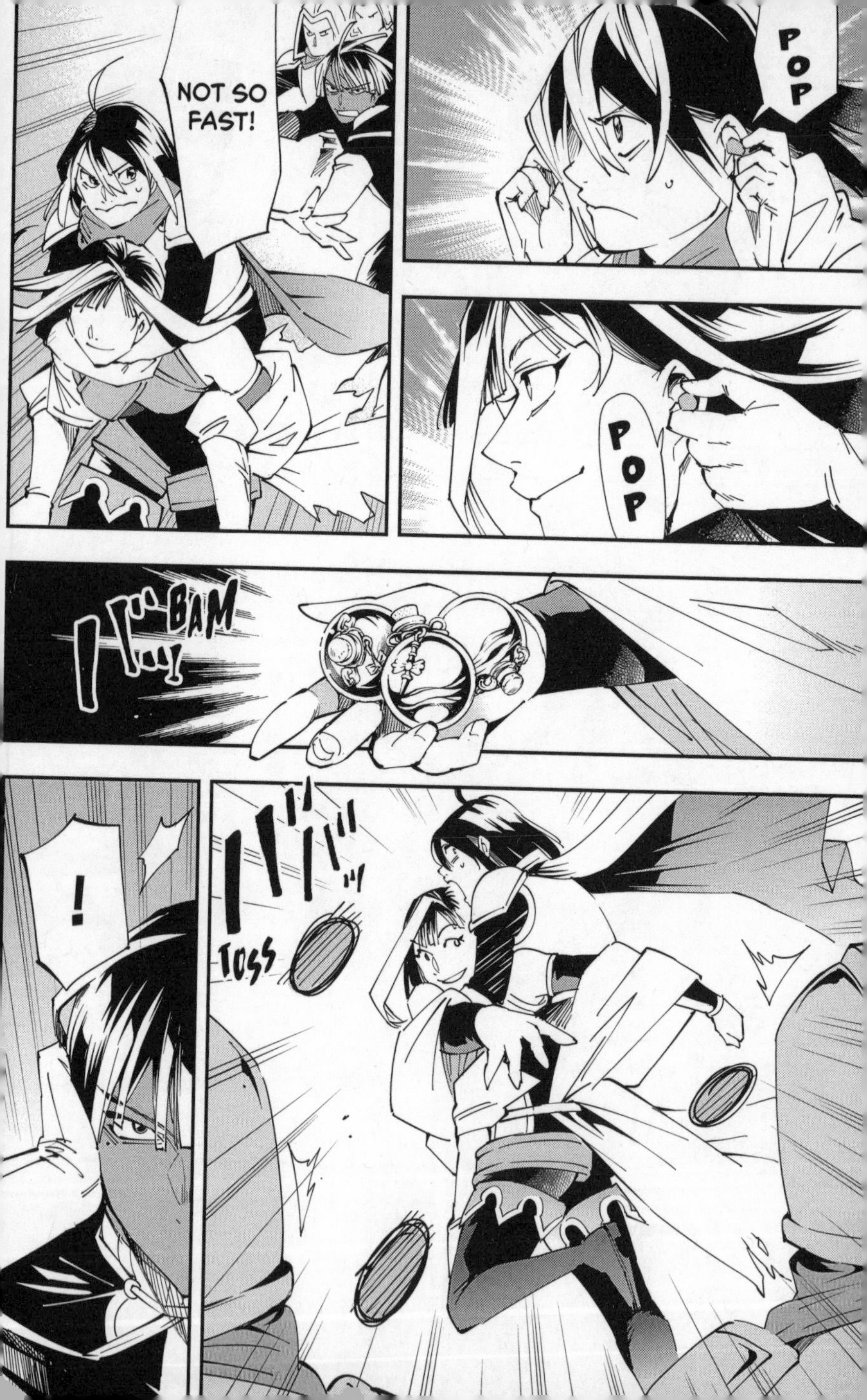
POP
POP
NOT SO FAST!
BAM
TOSS
!

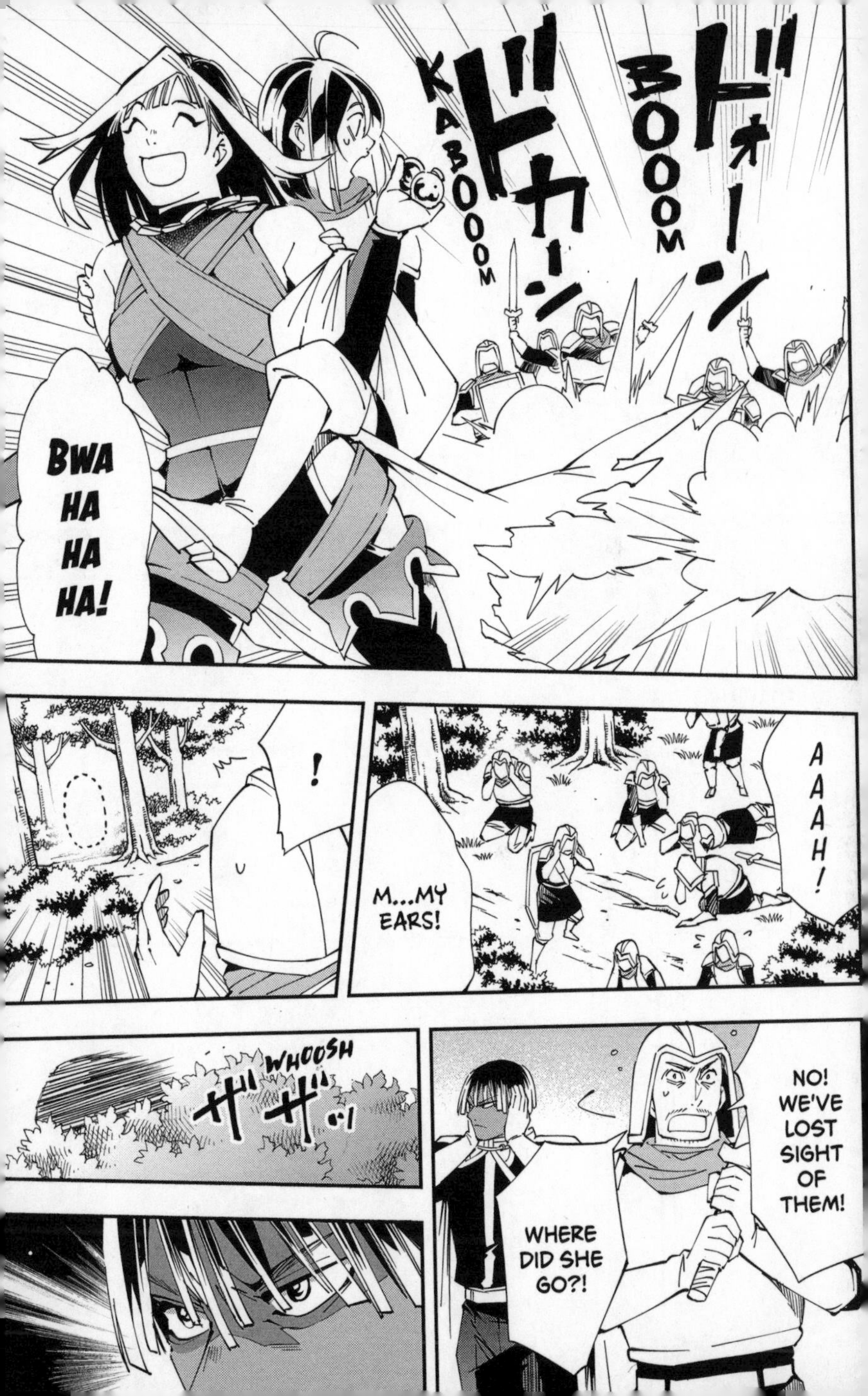
ドォーン
BOOOOM
ドカーン
KABOOOOM
BWA HA HA HA!
AAAAH!
M...MY EARS!
!
NO! WE'VE LOST SIGHT OF THEM!
WHERE DID SHE GO?!
ザッザッ
WHOOSH

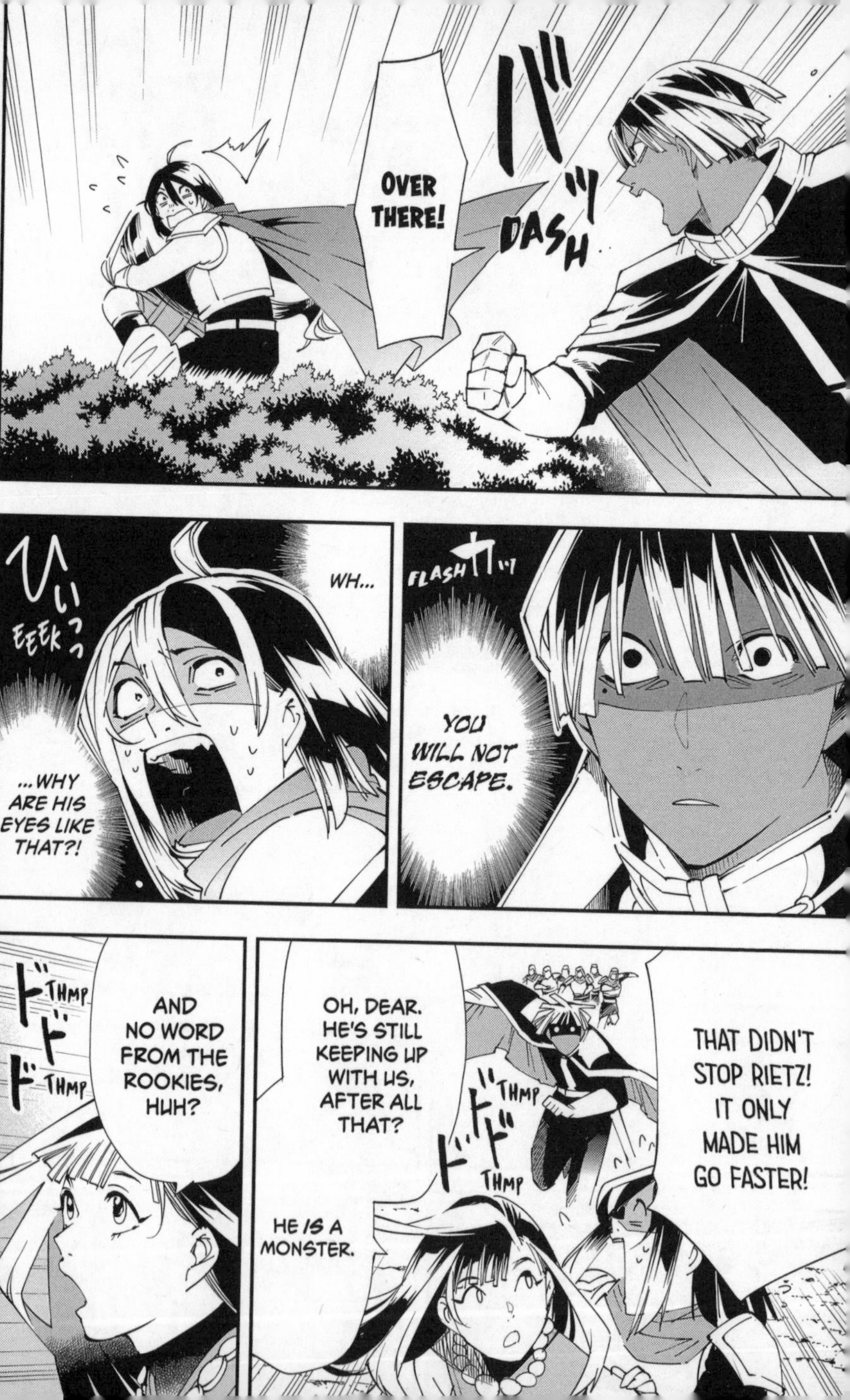
OVER THERE!
DASH
FLASH
YOU WILL NOT ESCAPE.
WH...
...WHY ARE HIS EYES LIKE THAT?!
EEEEK
THAT DIDN'T STOP RIETZ! IT ONLY MADE HIM GO FASTER!
OH, DEAR. HE'S STILL KEEPING UP WITH US, AFTER ALL THAT?
THMP
THMP
HE IS A MONSTER.
AND NO WORD FROM THE ROOKIES, HUH?
THMP
THMP

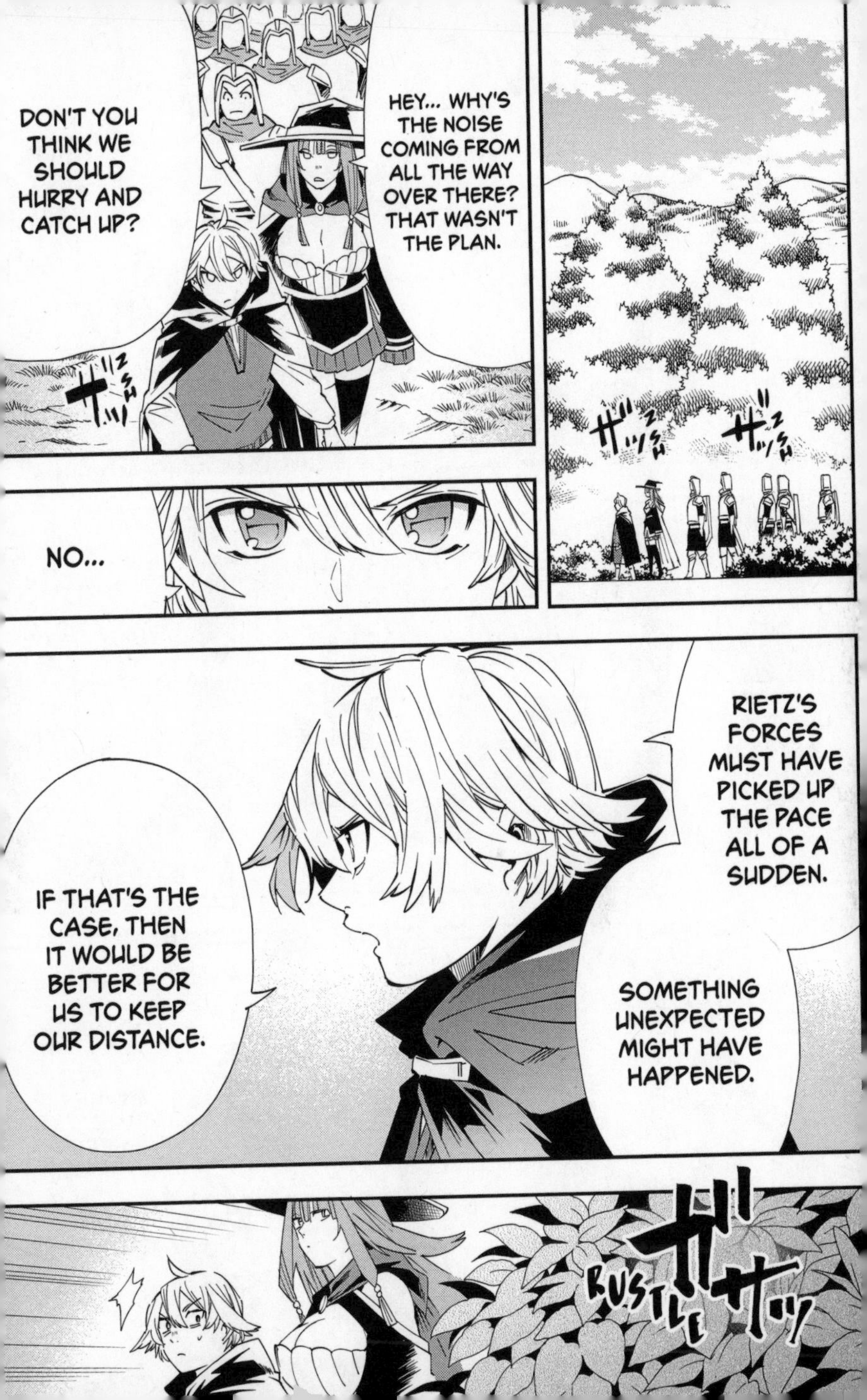
ZUSH
ZUSH
HEY... WHY'S THE NOISE COMING FROM ALL THE WAY OVER THERE? THAT WASN'T THE PLAN.
DON'T YOU THINK WE SHOULD HURRY AND CATCH UP?
ZUSH
NO...
RIETZ'S FORCES MUST HAVE PICKED UP THE PACE ALL OF A SUDDEN.
SOMETHING UNEXPECTED MIGHT HAVE HAPPENED.
IF THAT'S THE CASE, THEN IT WOULD BE BETTER FOR US TO KEEP OUR DISTANCE.
RUSTLE

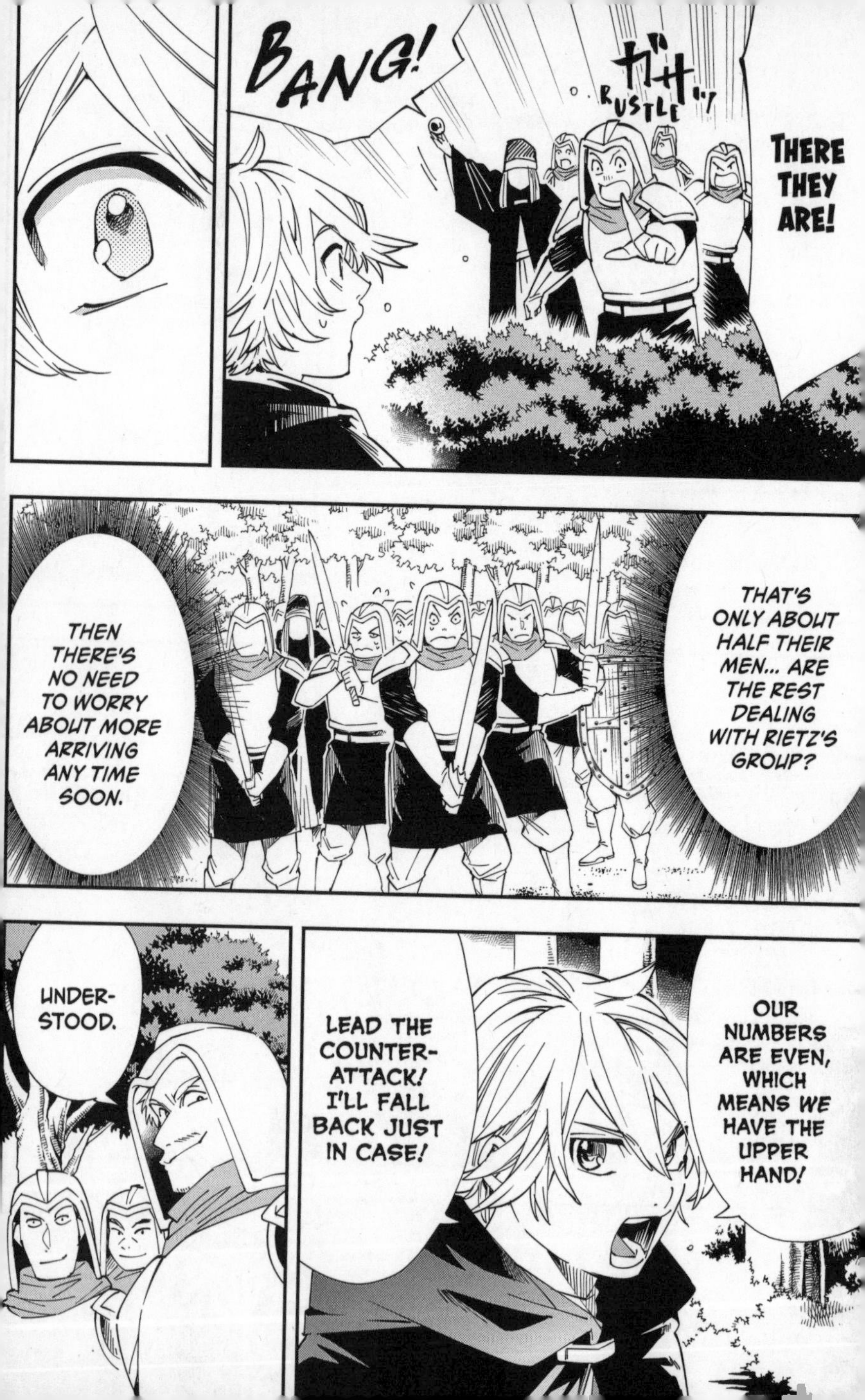
THERE THEY ARE!
ガサッ RUSTLE
BANG!
THAT'S ONLY ABOUT HALF THEIR MEN... ARE THE REST DEALING WITH RIETZ'S GROUP?
THEN THERE'S NO NEED TO WORRY ABOUT MORE ARRIVING ANY TIME SOON.
OUR NUMBERS ARE EVEN, WHICH MEANS WE HAVE THE UPPER HAND!
LEAD THE COUNTER-ATTACK! I'LL FALL BACK JUST IN CASE!
UNDER-STOOD.

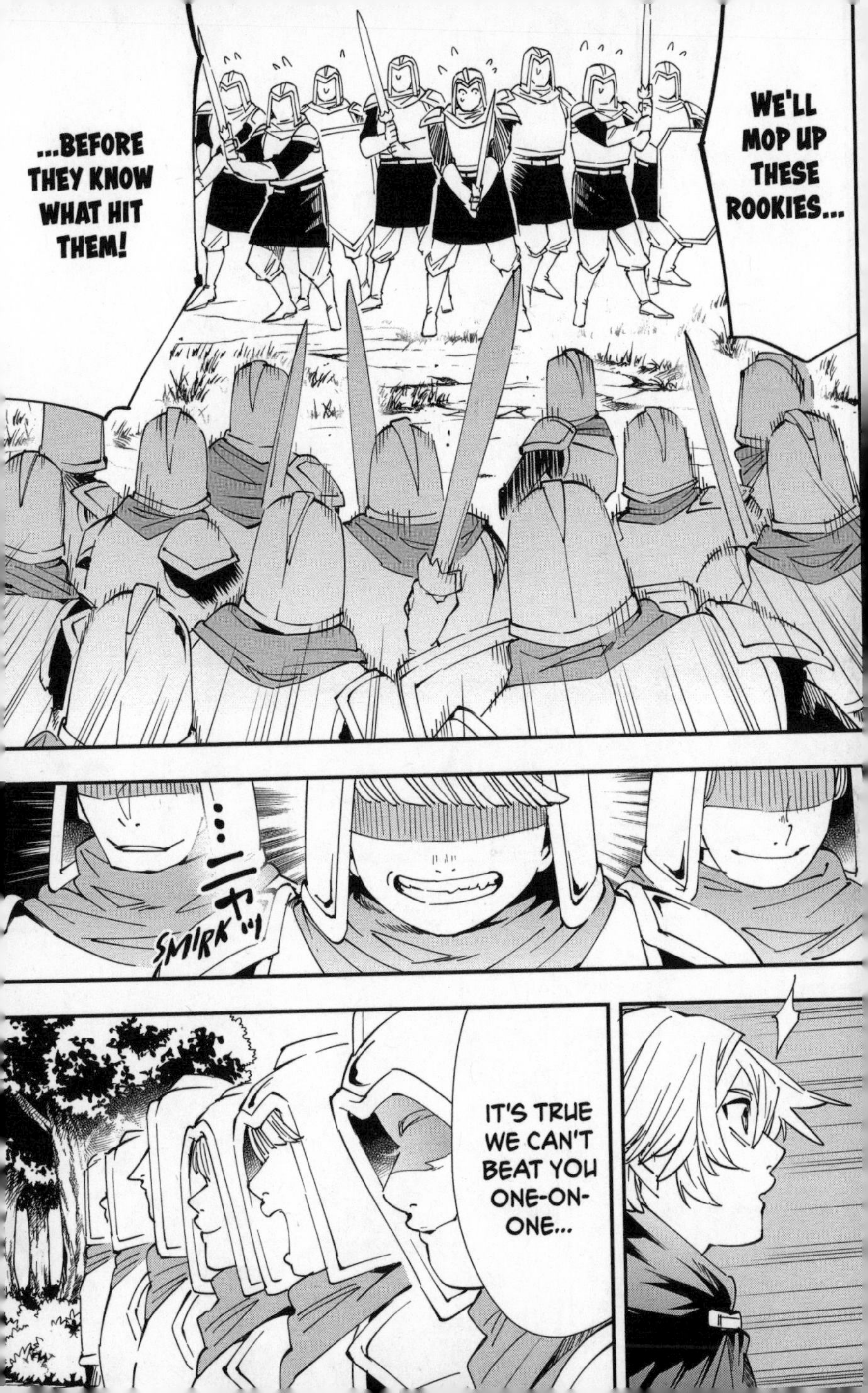
WE'LL MOP UP THESE ROOKIES...
...BEFORE THEY KNOW WHAT HIT THEM!
...
ニヤッ
SMIRK
IT'S TRUE WE CAN'T BEAT YOU ONE-ON-ONE...

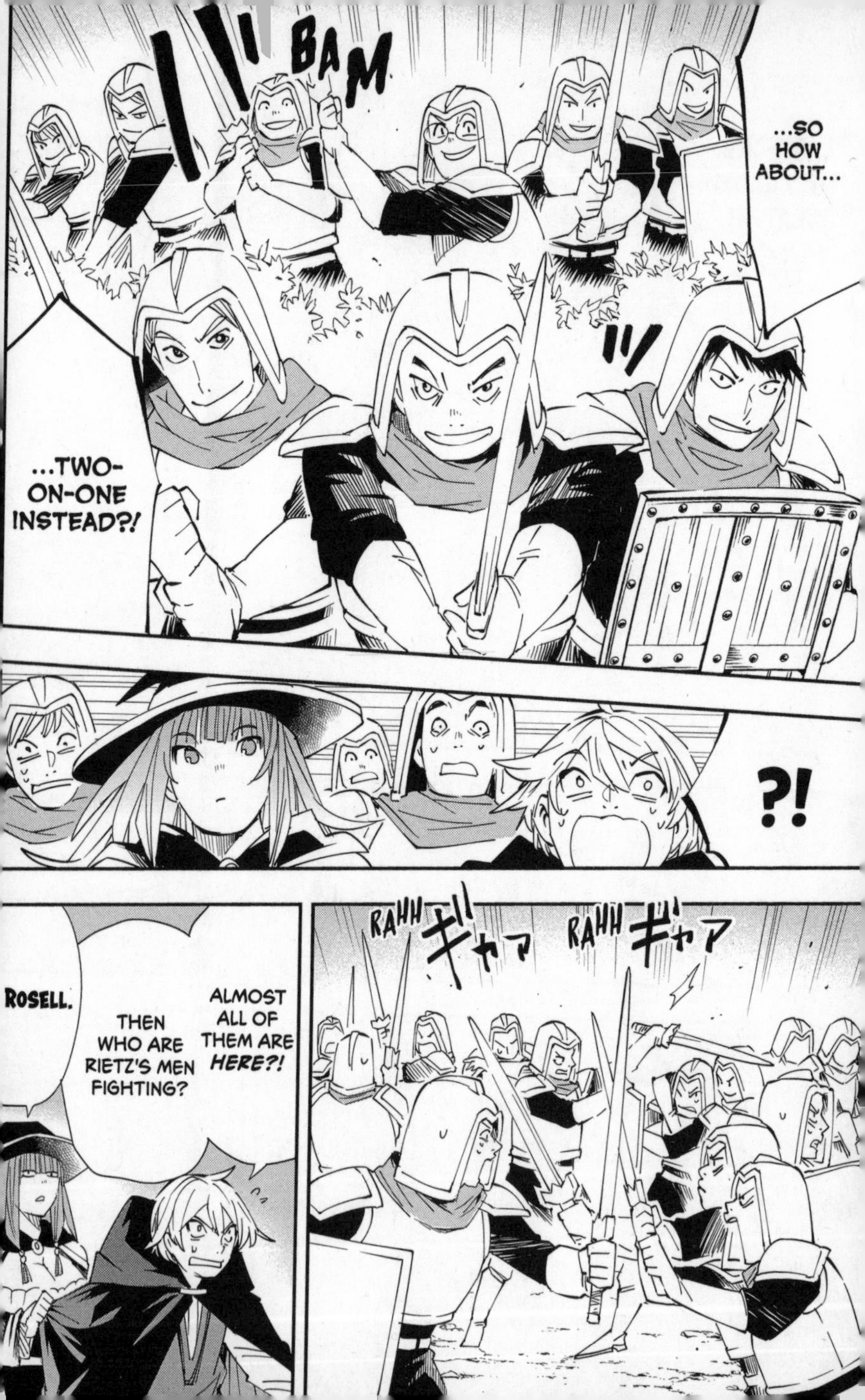
...SO HOW ABOUT...
BAM
...TWO-ON-ONE INSTEAD?!
?!
RAHH ギャア
RAHH ギャア
ALMOST ALL OF THEM ARE HERE?!
THEN WHO ARE RIETZ'S MEN FIGHTING?
ROSELL.

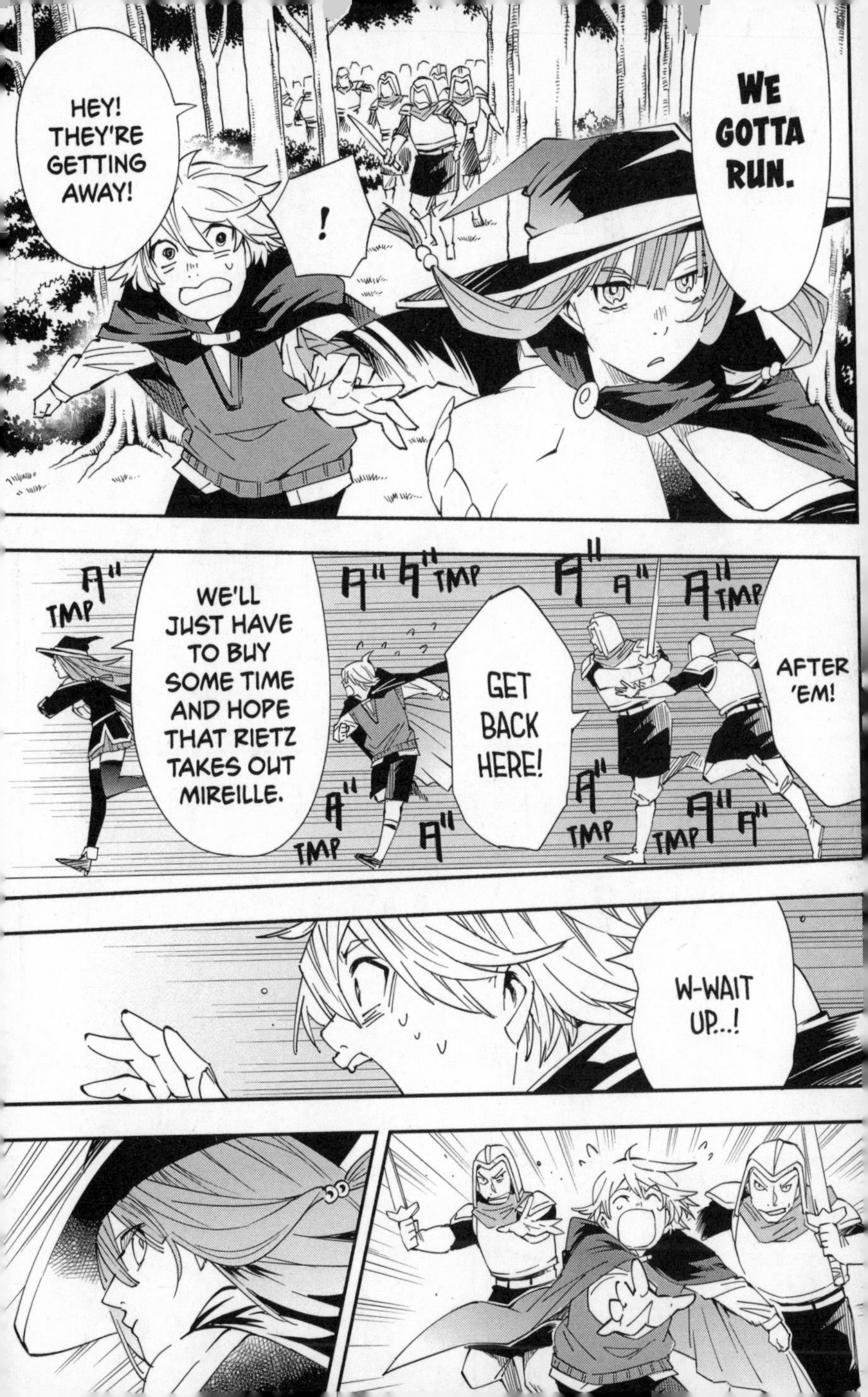
WE GOTTA RUN.
!
HEY! THEY'RE GETTING AWAY!
TMP
AFTER 'EM!
TMP
GET BACK HERE!
TMP
TMP
TMP
WE'LL JUST HAVE TO BUY SOME TIME AND HOPE THAT RIETZ TAKES OUT MIREILLE.
TMP
TMP
W-WAIT UP...!

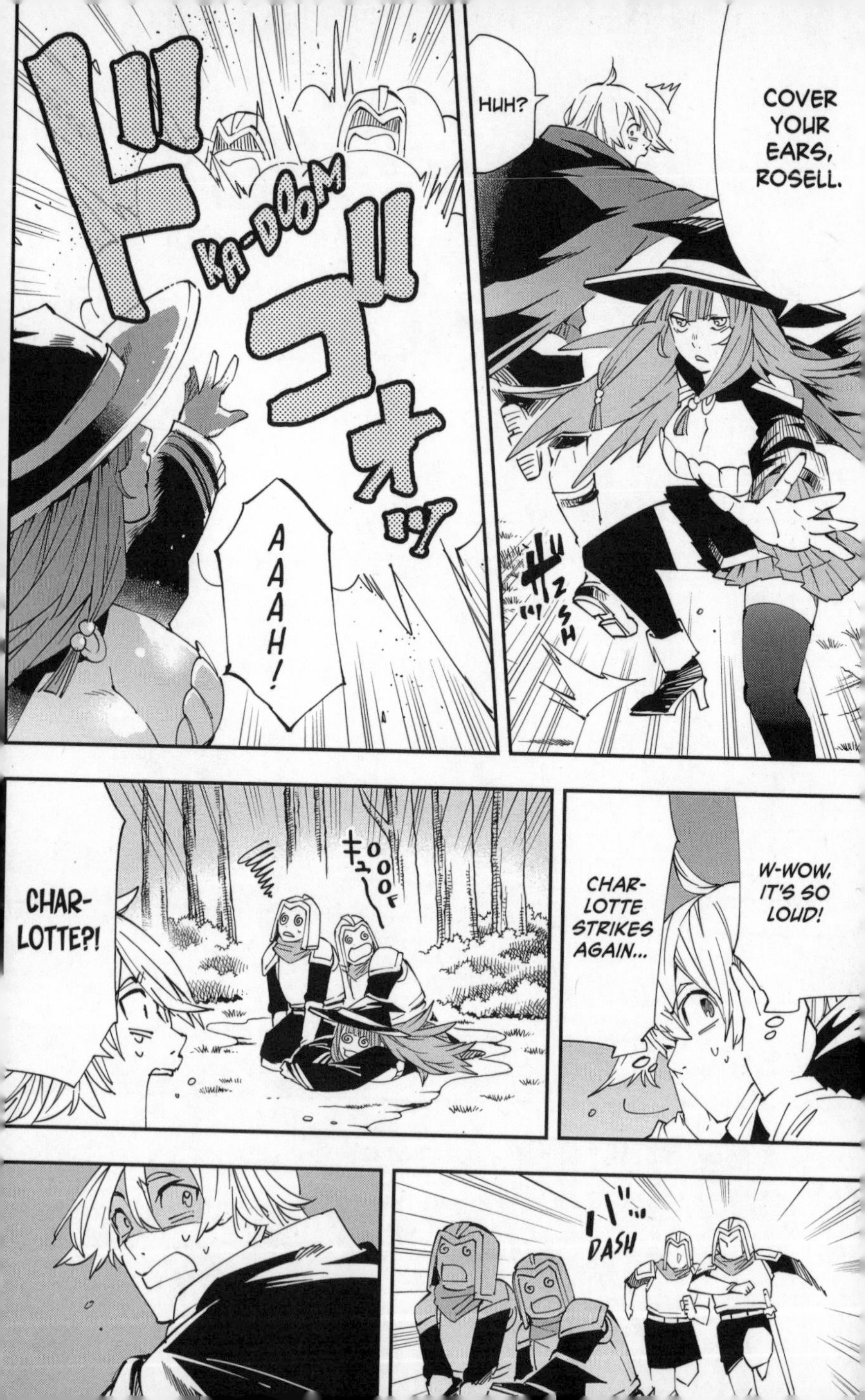
COVER YOUR EARS, ROSELL.
HUH?
ZSH
KA-DOOM
AAAAH!
OOOF
CHAR-LOTTE?!
W-WOW, IT'S SO LOUD!
CHAR-LOTTE STRIKES AGAIN...
DASH

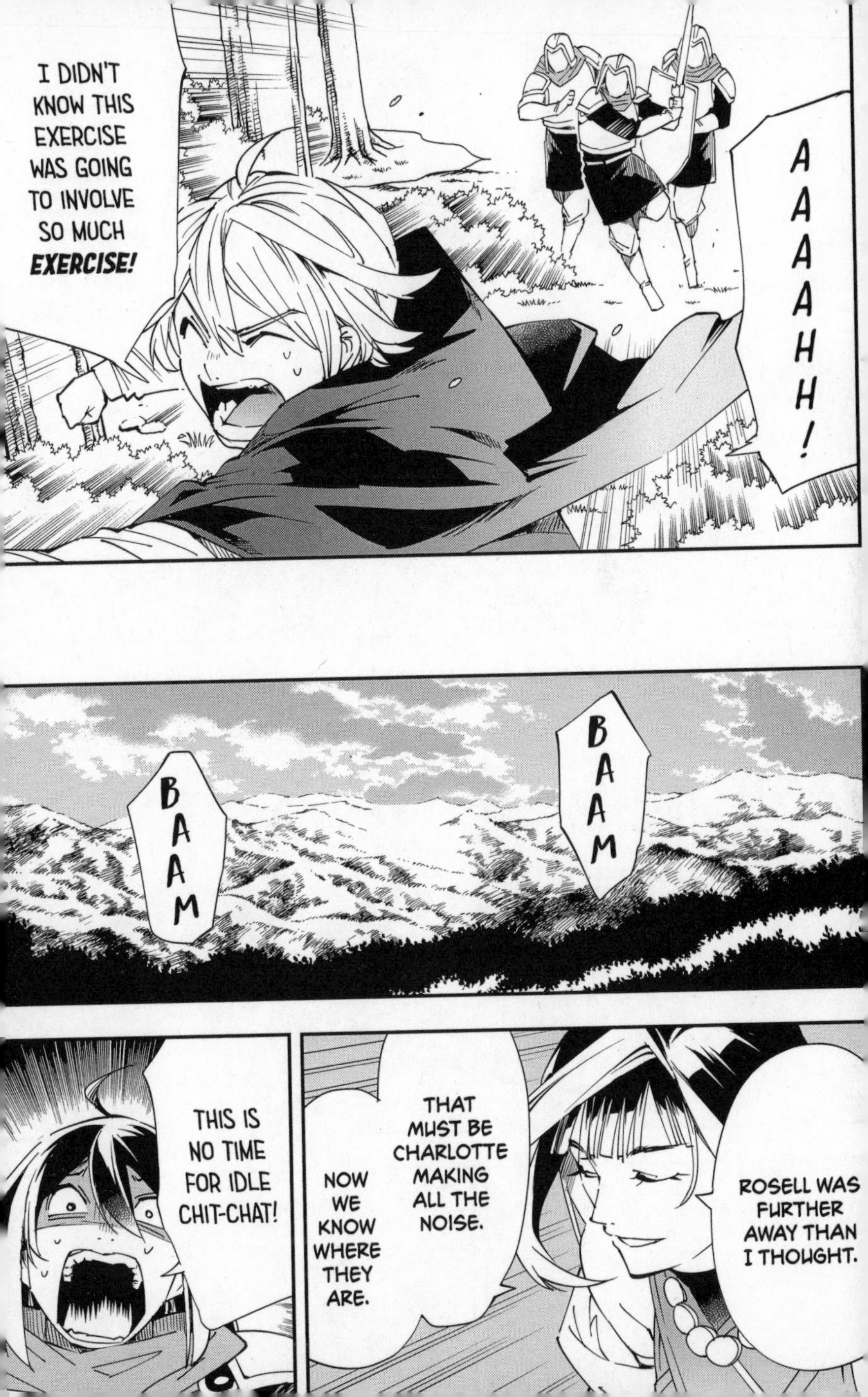
AAAAAHH!
I DIDN'T KNOW THIS EXERCISE WAS GOING TO INVOLVE SO MUCH **EXERCISE!**
BAAM
BAAM
ROSELL WAS FURTHER AWAY THAN I THOUGHT.
THAT MUST BE CHARLOTTE MAKING ALL THE NOISE.
NOW WE KNOW WHERE THEY ARE.
THIS IS NO TIME FOR IDLE CHIT-CHAT!

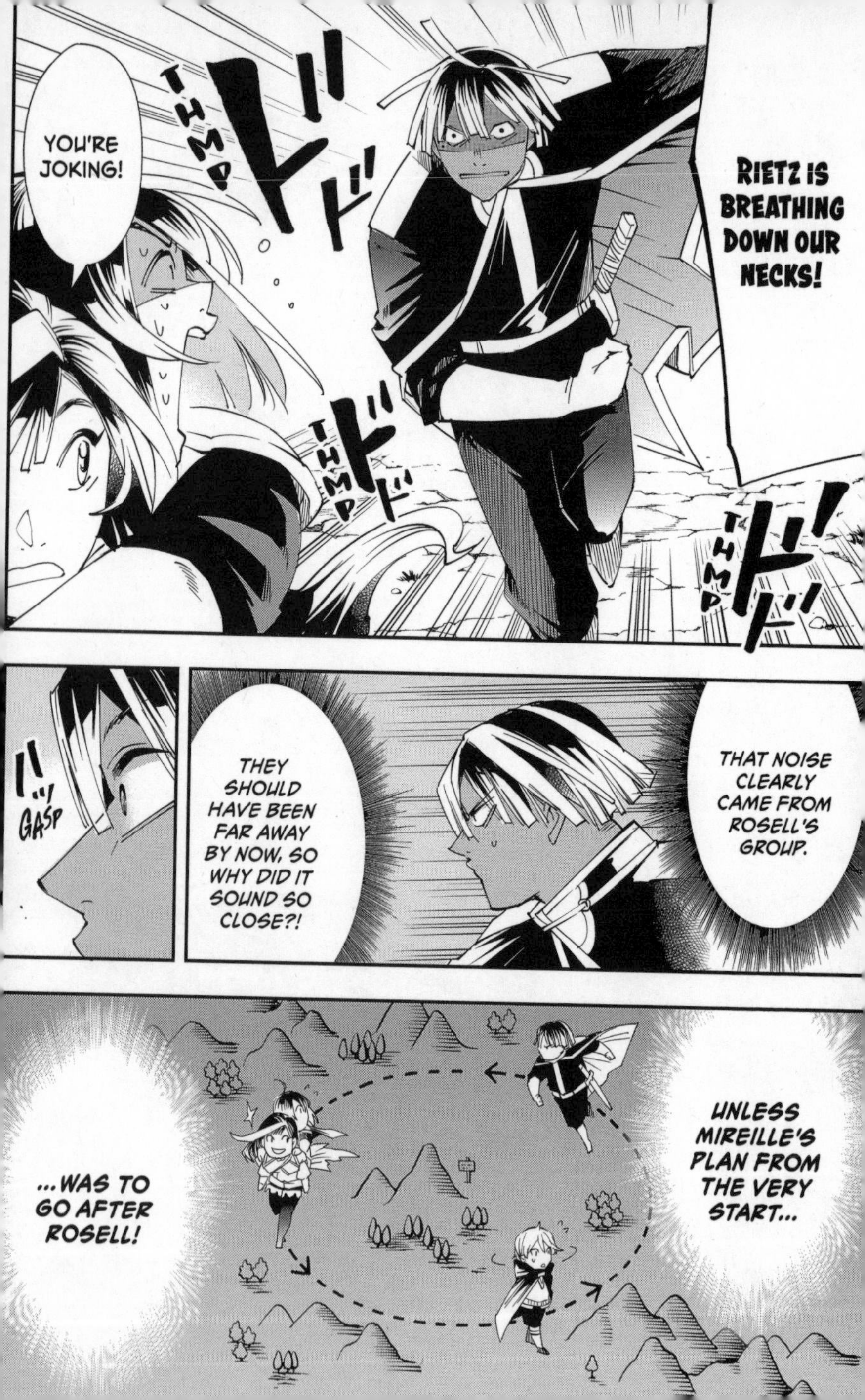
RIETZ IS BREATHING DOWN OUR NECKS!
THMP
THMP
YOU'RE JOKING!
THMP
THAT NOISE CLEARLY CAME FROM ROSELL'S GROUP.
THEY SHOULD HAVE BEEN FAR AWAY BY NOW, SO WHY DID IT SOUND SO CLOSE?!
GASP
UNLESS MIREILLE'S PLAN FROM THE VERY START...
...WAS TO GO AFTER ROSELL!

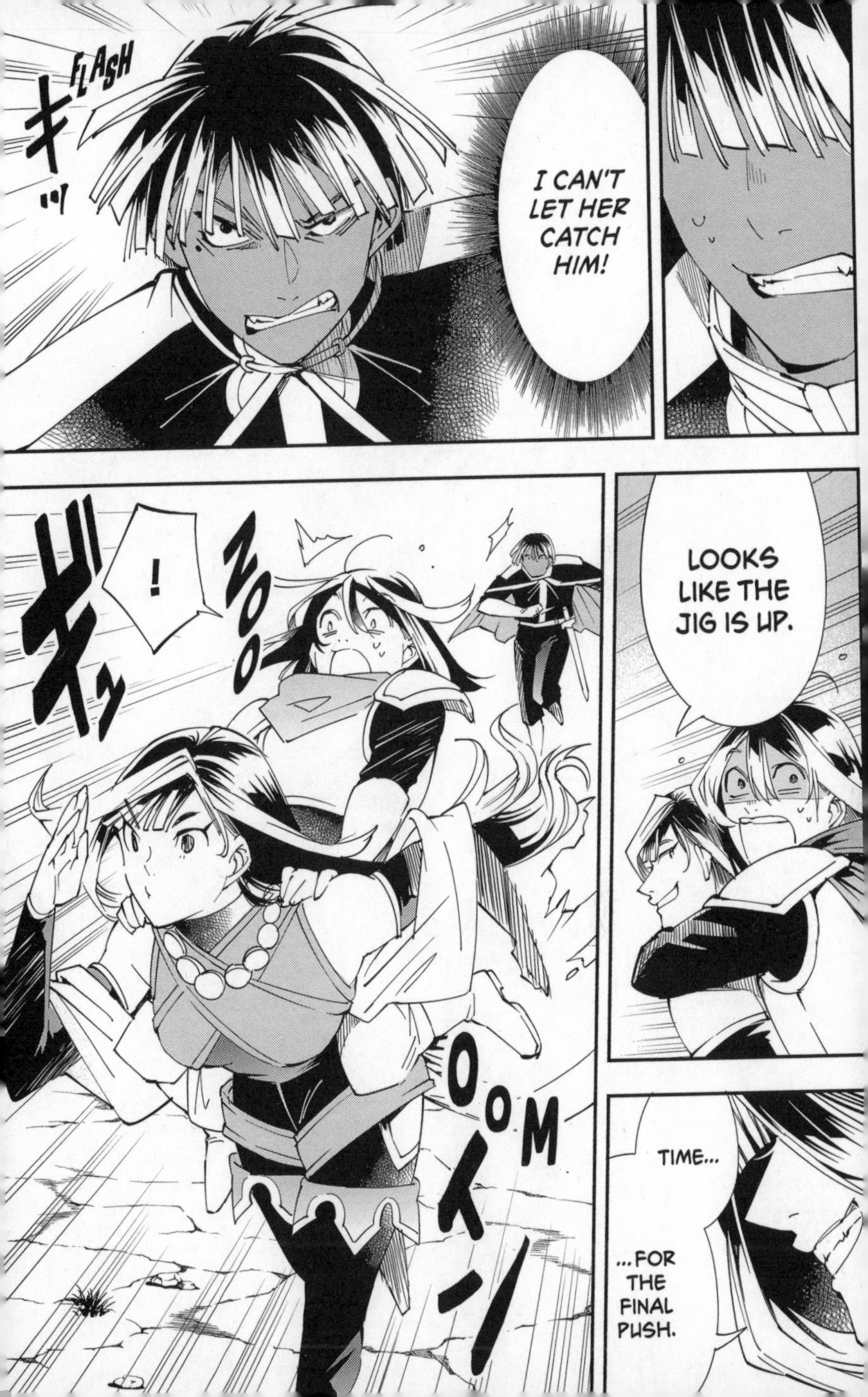
I CAN'T LET HER CATCH HIM!
FLASH
LOOKS LIKE THE JIG IS UP.
TIME...
...FOR THE FINAL PUSH.
NOO
!
OOM

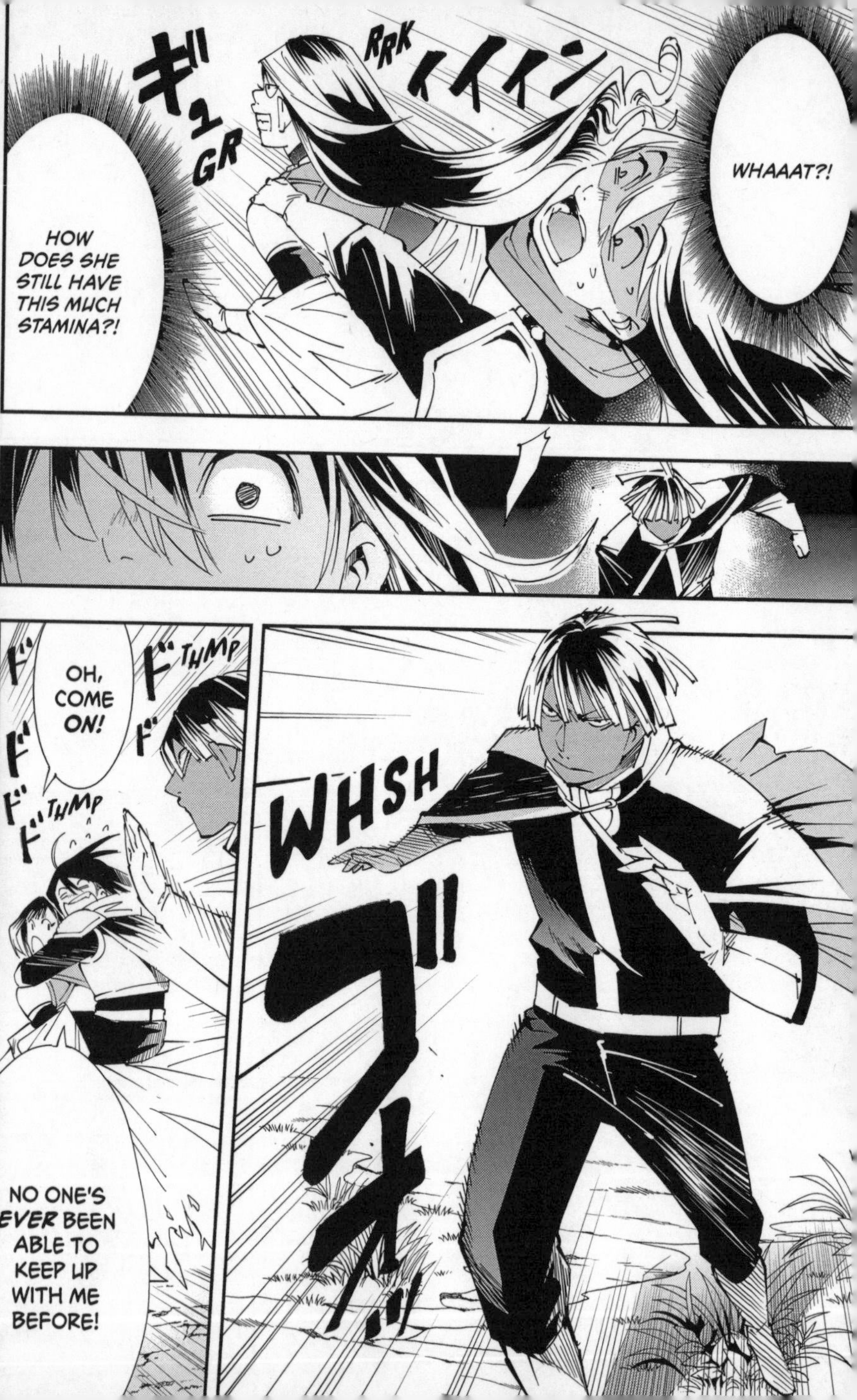
WHAAAT?!
RRK
GR
HOW DOES SHE STILL HAVE THIS MUCH STAMINA?!
WHSH
THMP
OH, COME ON!
THMP
NO ONE'S **EVER** BEEN ABLE TO KEEP UP WITH ME BEFORE!

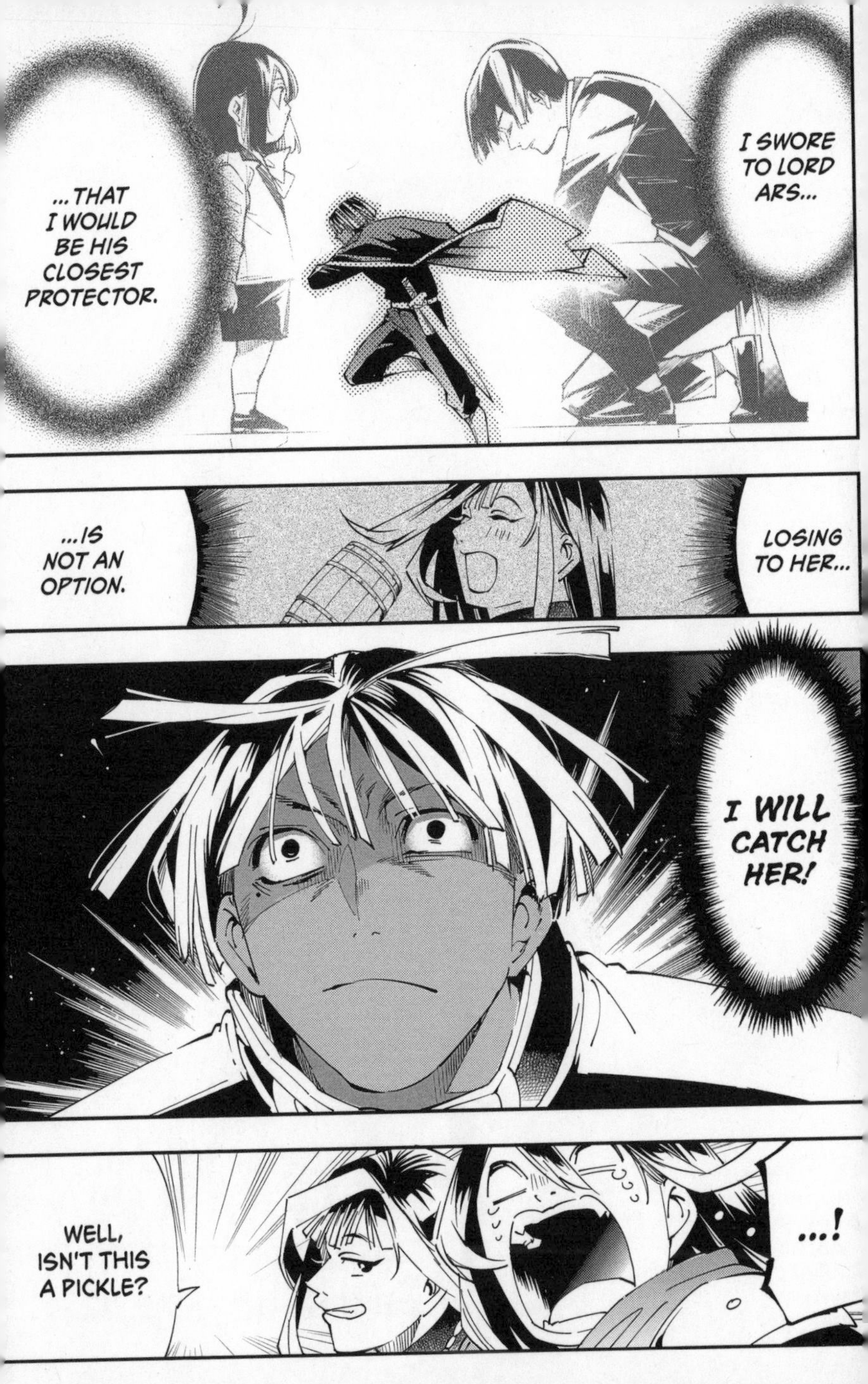
I SWORE TO LORD ARS...
...THAT I WOULD BE HIS CLOSEST PROTECTOR.
LOSING TO HER...
...IS NOT AN OPTION.
I WILL CATCH HER!
...!
WELL, ISN'T THIS A PICKLE?

As a Reincarnated
ARISTOCRAT,
I'll Use My Appraisal Skill to
Rise in the World

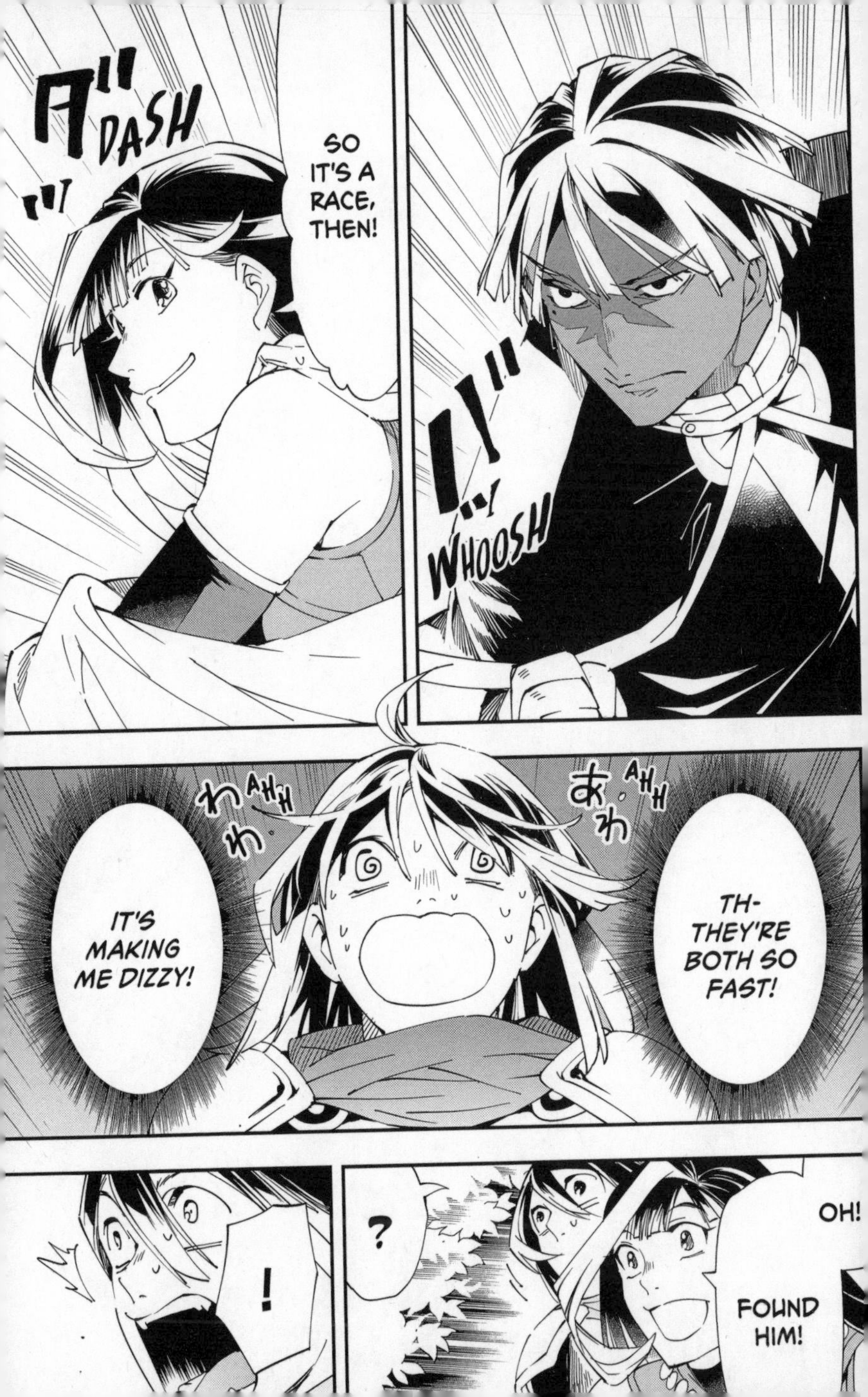

WHOOSH
DASH
SO IT'S A RACE, THEN!
あわ AHH
わわ AHH
TH- THEY'RE BOTH SO FAST!
IT'S MAKING ME DIZZY!
OH!
FOUND HIM!
?
!

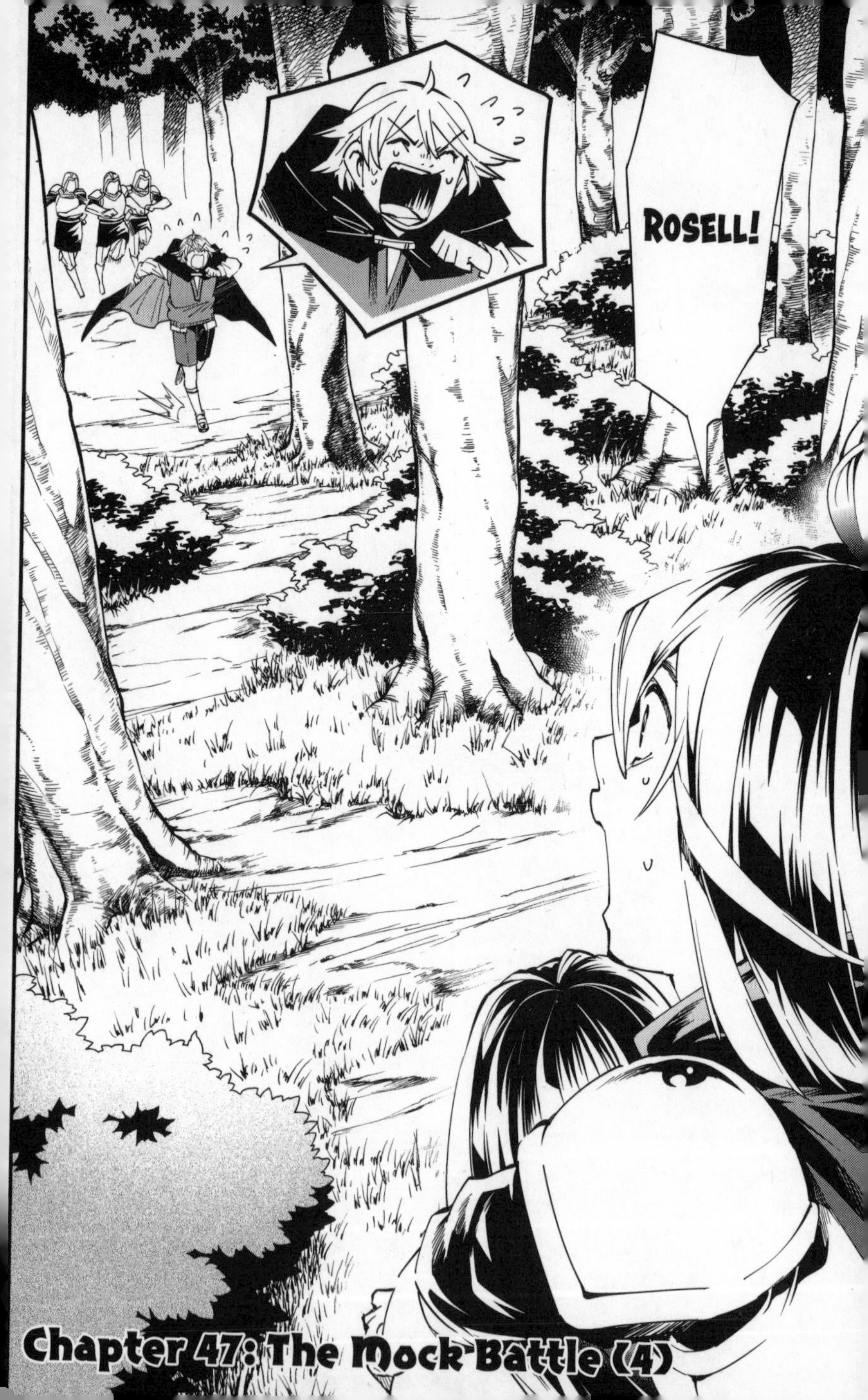
ROSELL!
Chapter 47: The Mock Battle (4)

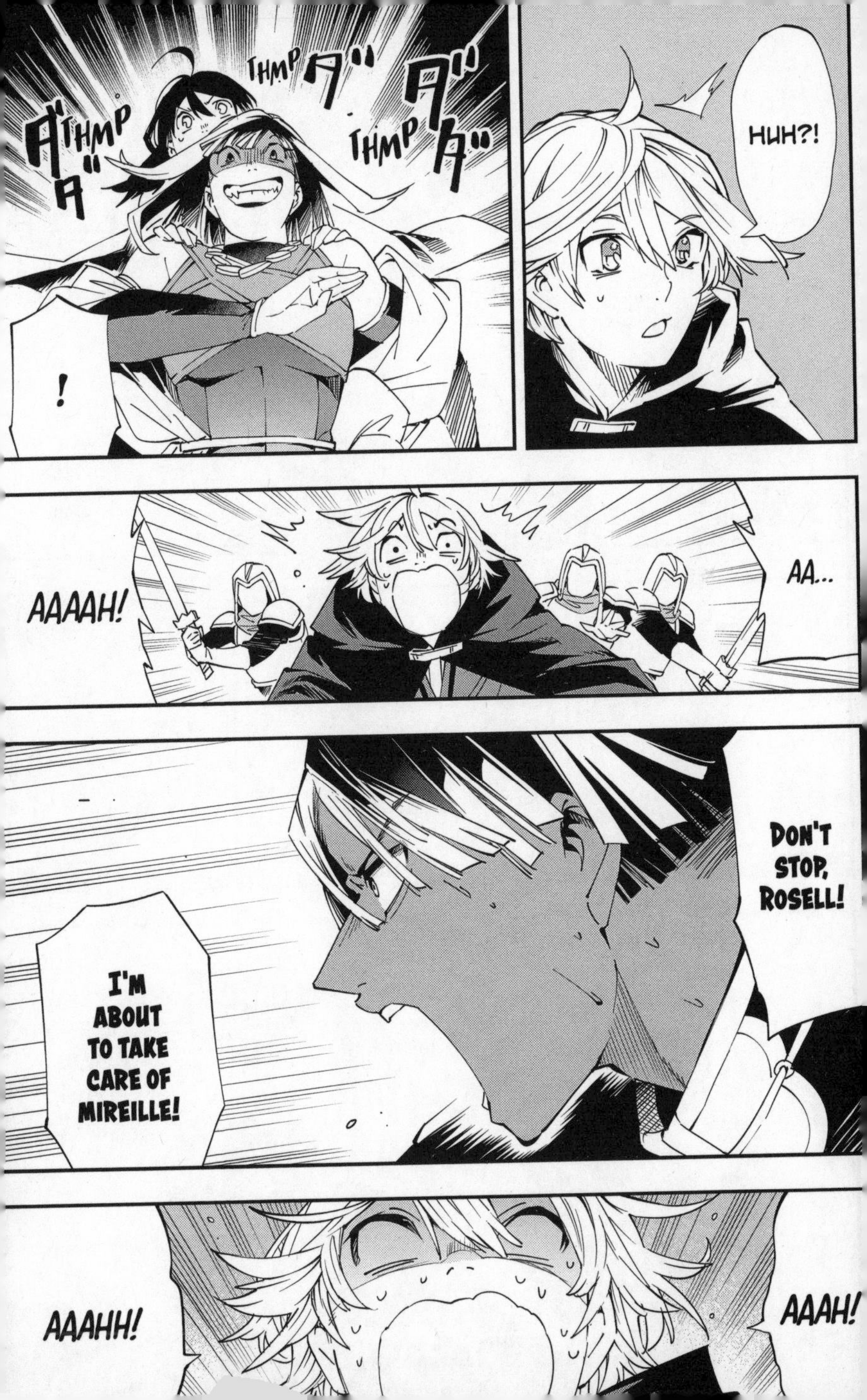
HUH?!
THMP
THMP
THMP
!
AA...
AAAAH!
DON'T STOP, ROSELL!
I'M ABOUT TO TAKE CARE OF MIREILLE!
AAAH!
AAAHH!

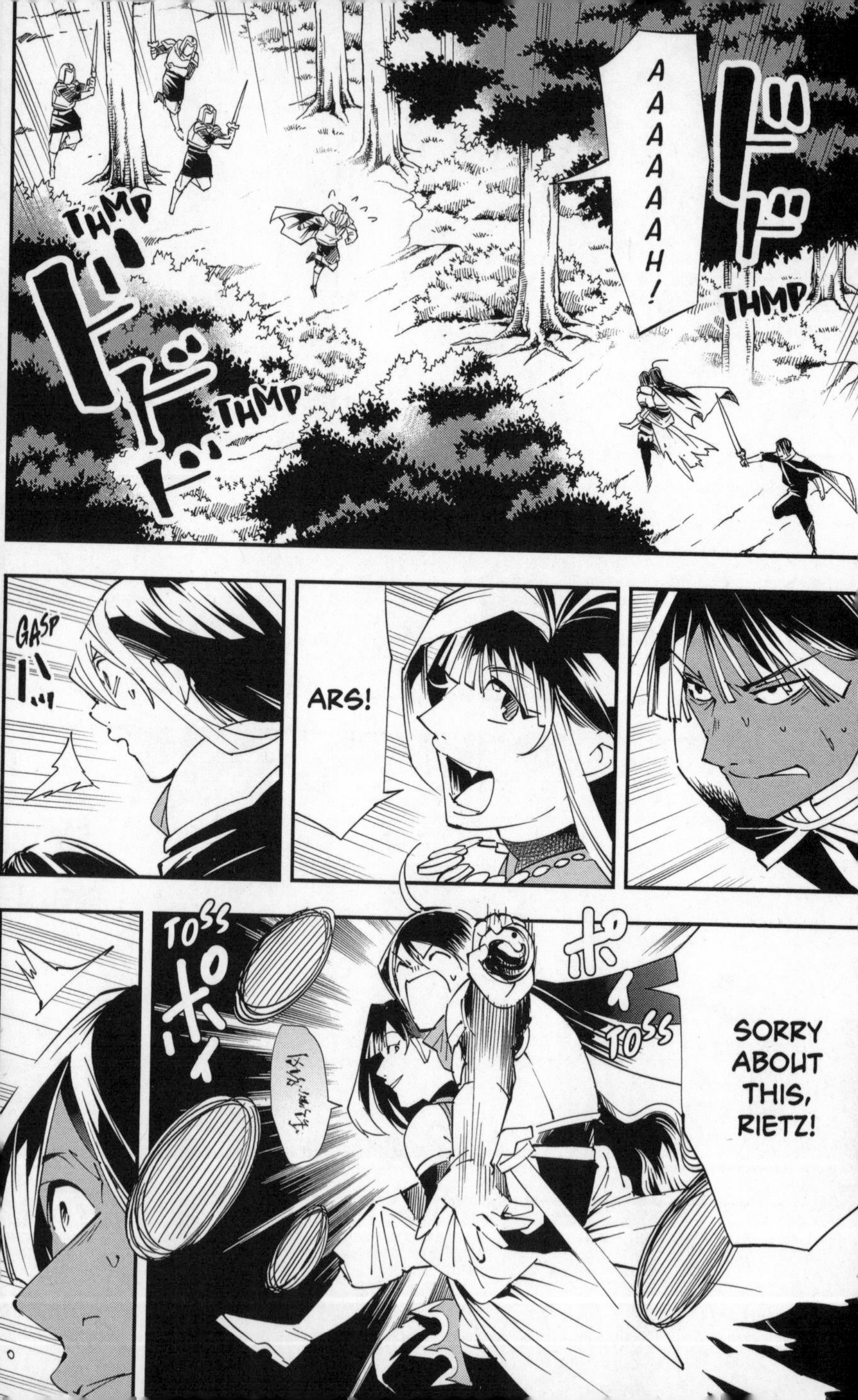

AAAAAAAH!
THMP
THMP
THMP
ARS!
GASP
SORRY ABOUT THIS, RIETZ!
TOSS
TOSS

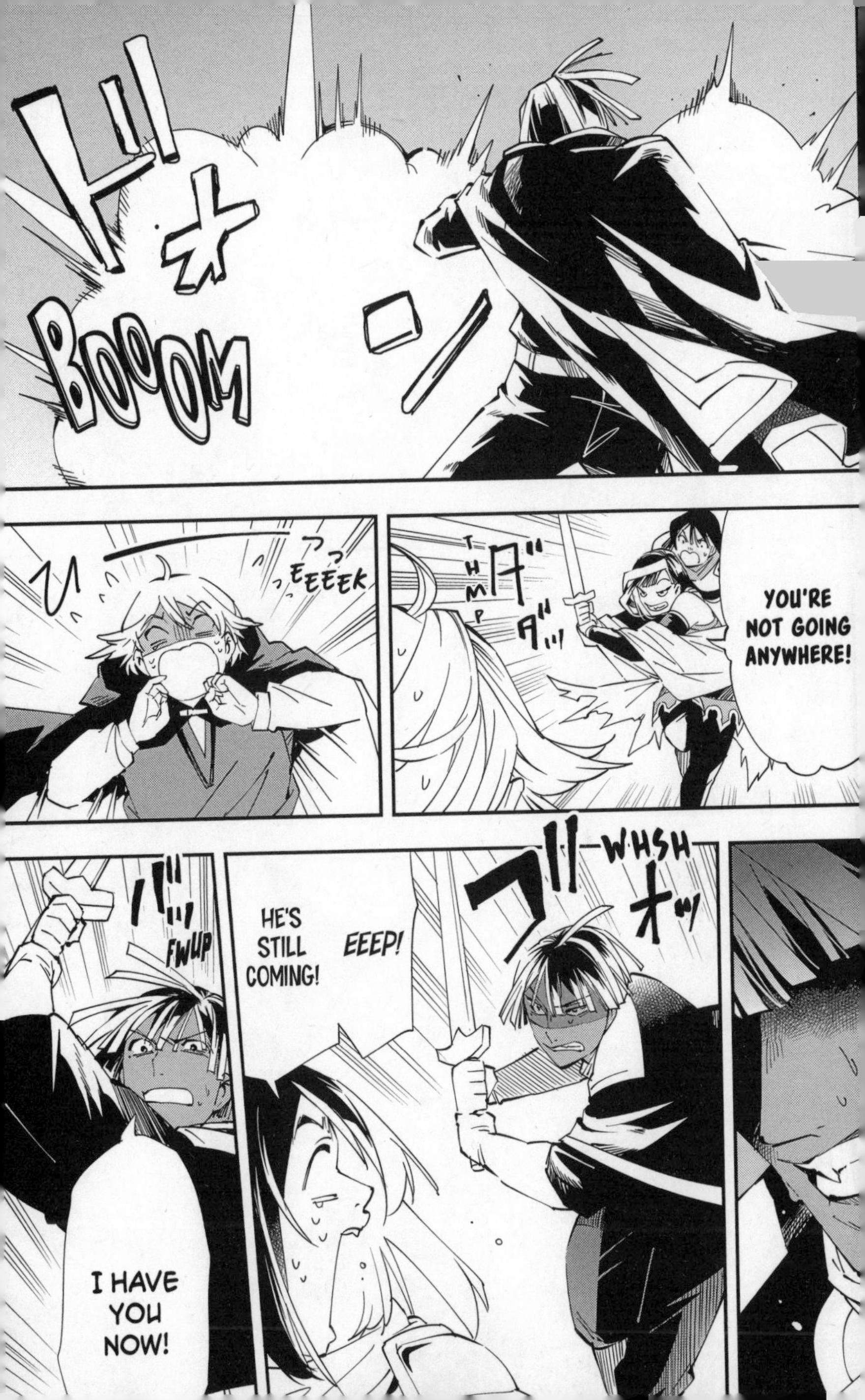
BOOOM
YOU'RE NOT GOING ANYWHERE!
THMP
EEEEK
WHSH
EEEP!
HE'S STILL COMING!
FWUP
I HAVE YOU NOW!

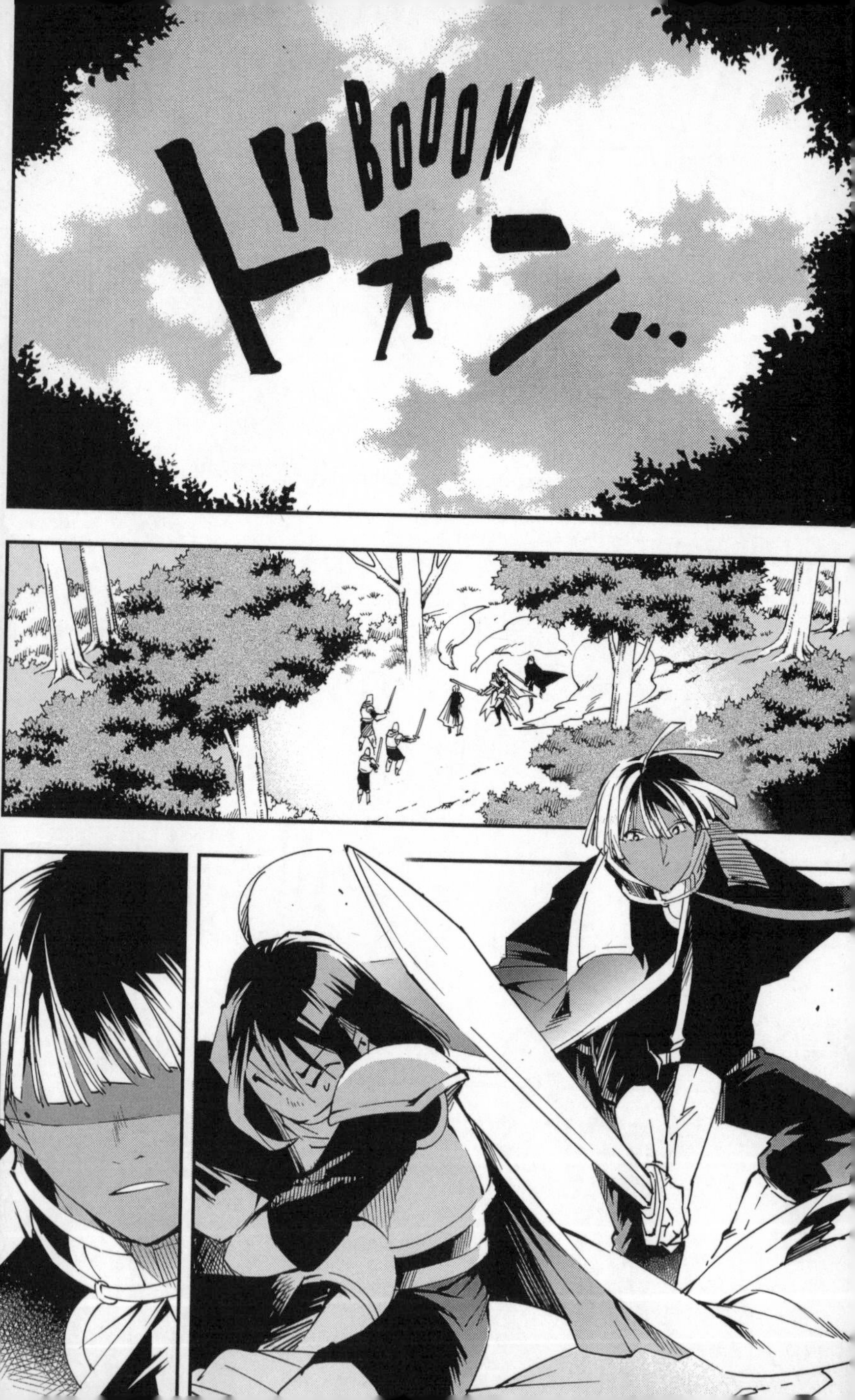
ドォン…
BOOOM

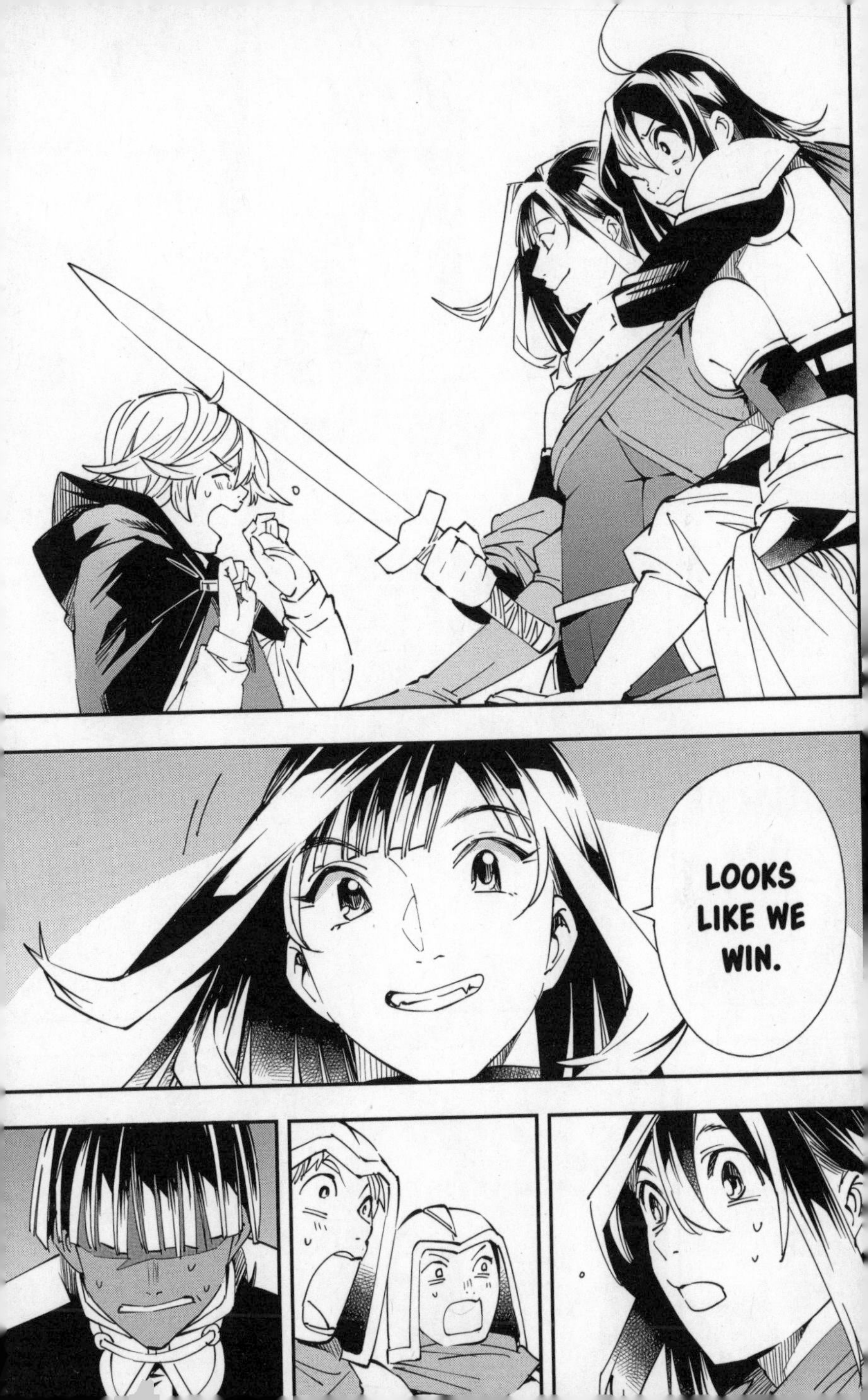
LOOKS LIKE WE WIN.

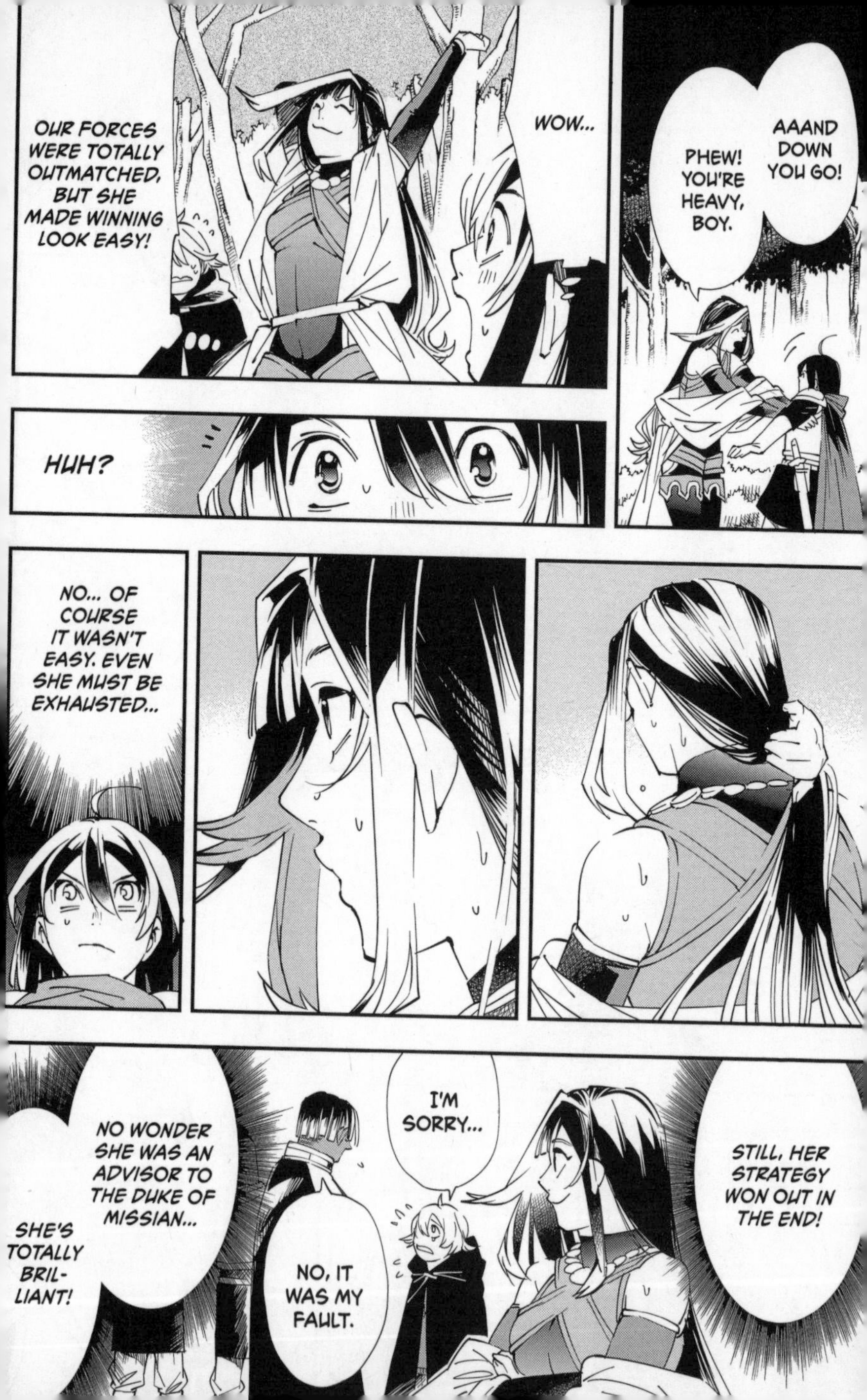
AAAND DOWN YOU GO!
PHEW! YOU'RE HEAVY, BOY.
WOW...
OUR FORCES WERE TOTALLY OUTMATCHED, BUT SHE MADE WINNING LOOK EASY!
HUH?
NO... OF COURSE IT WASN'T EASY. EVEN SHE MUST BE EXHAUSTED...
STILL, HER STRATEGY WON OUT IN THE END!
I'M SORRY...
NO, IT WAS MY FAULT.
NO WONDER SHE WAS AN ADVISOR TO THE DUKE OF MISSIAN...
SHE'S TOTALLY BRIL-LIANT!

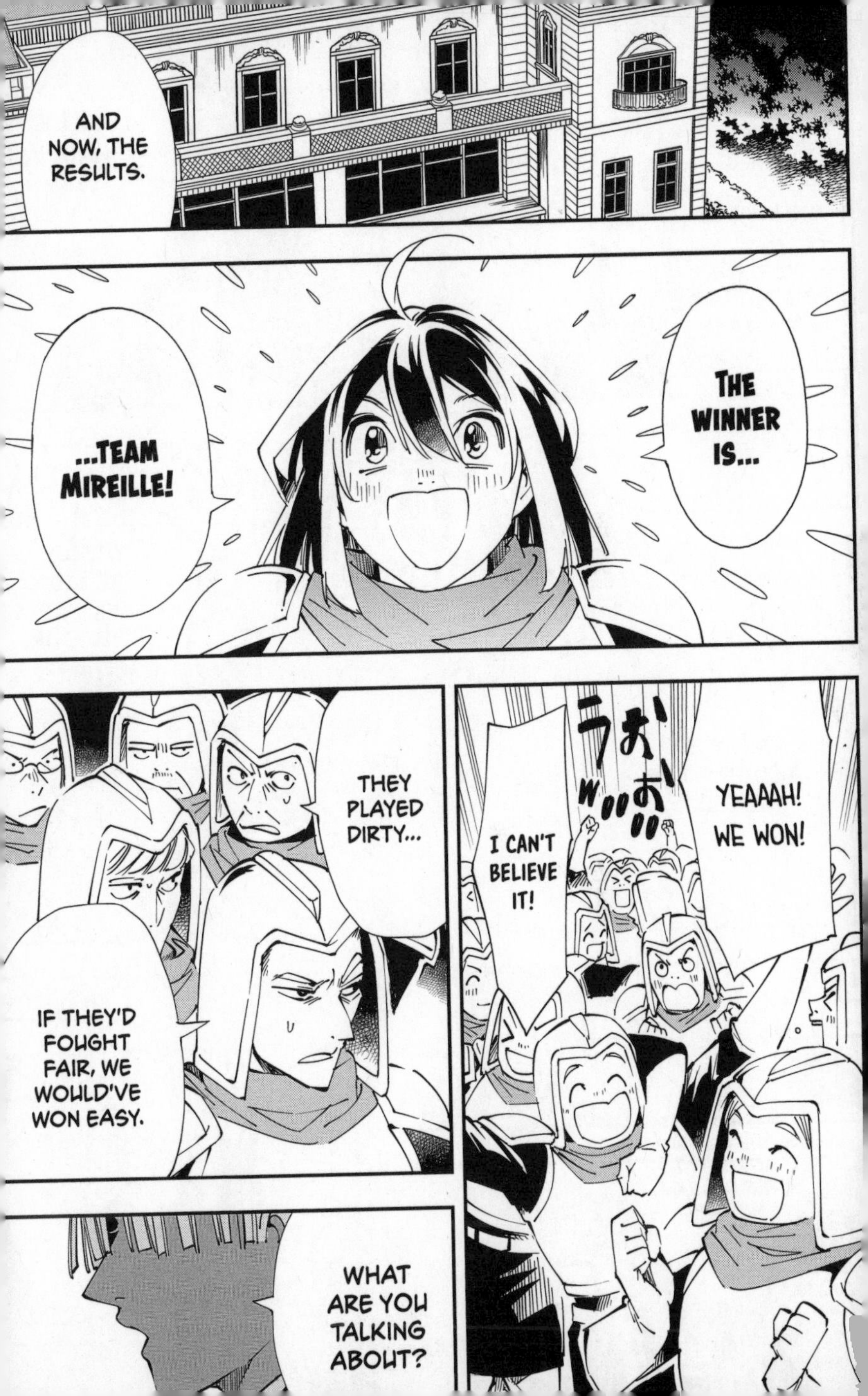
AND NOW, THE RESULTS.
THE WINNER IS...
...TEAM MIREILLE!
YEAAAH! WE WON!
I CAN'T BELIEVE IT!
WOOOOO
THEY PLAYED DIRTY...
IF THEY'D FOUGHT FAIR, WE WOULD'VE WON EASY.
WHAT ARE YOU TALKING ABOUT?

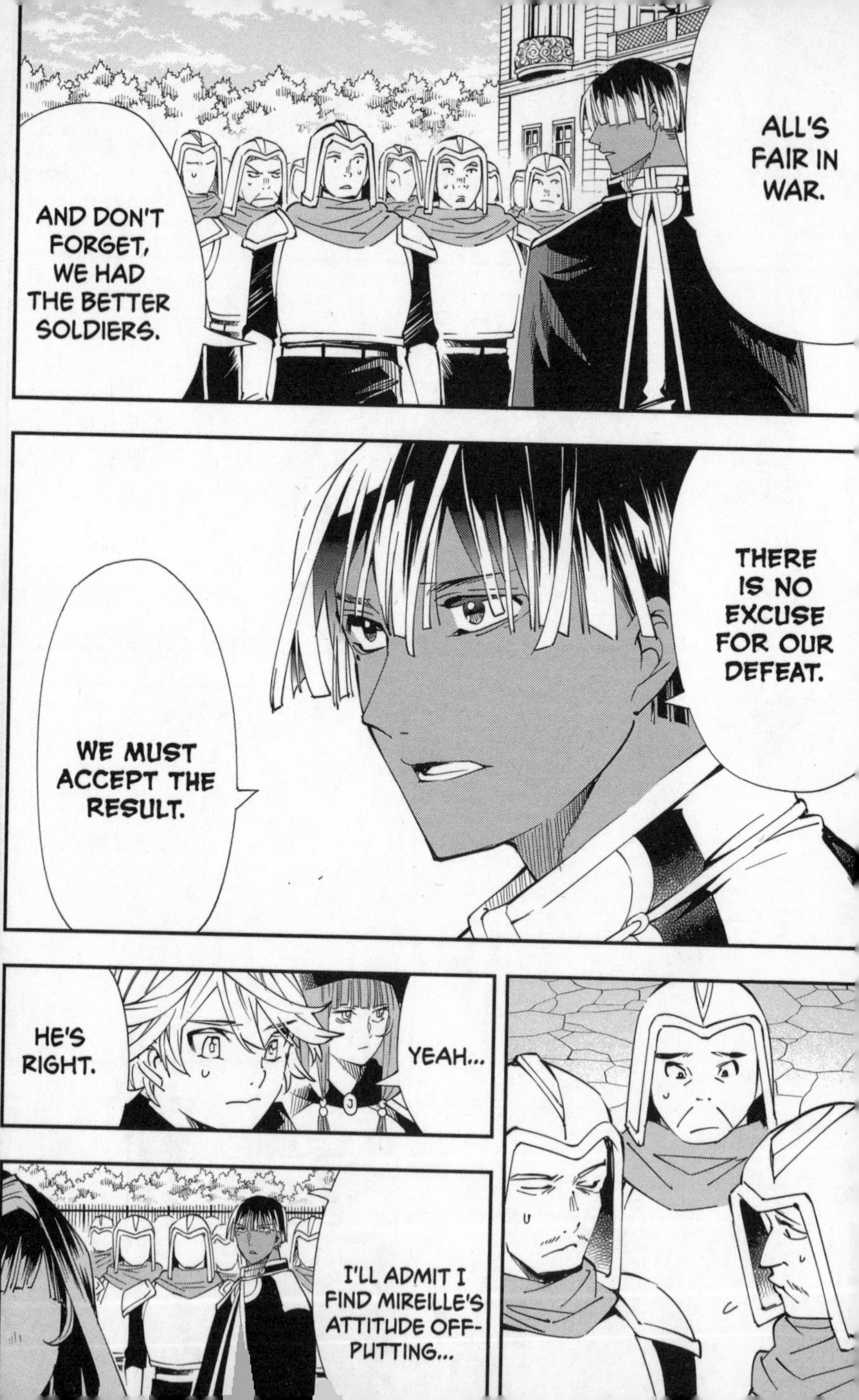
ALL'S FAIR IN WAR.
AND DON'T FORGET, WE HAD THE BETTER SOLDIERS.
THERE IS NO EXCUSE FOR OUR DEFEAT.
WE MUST ACCEPT THE RESULT.
YEAH...
HE'S RIGHT.
I'LL ADMIT I FIND MIREILLE'S ATTITUDE OFF-PUTTING...

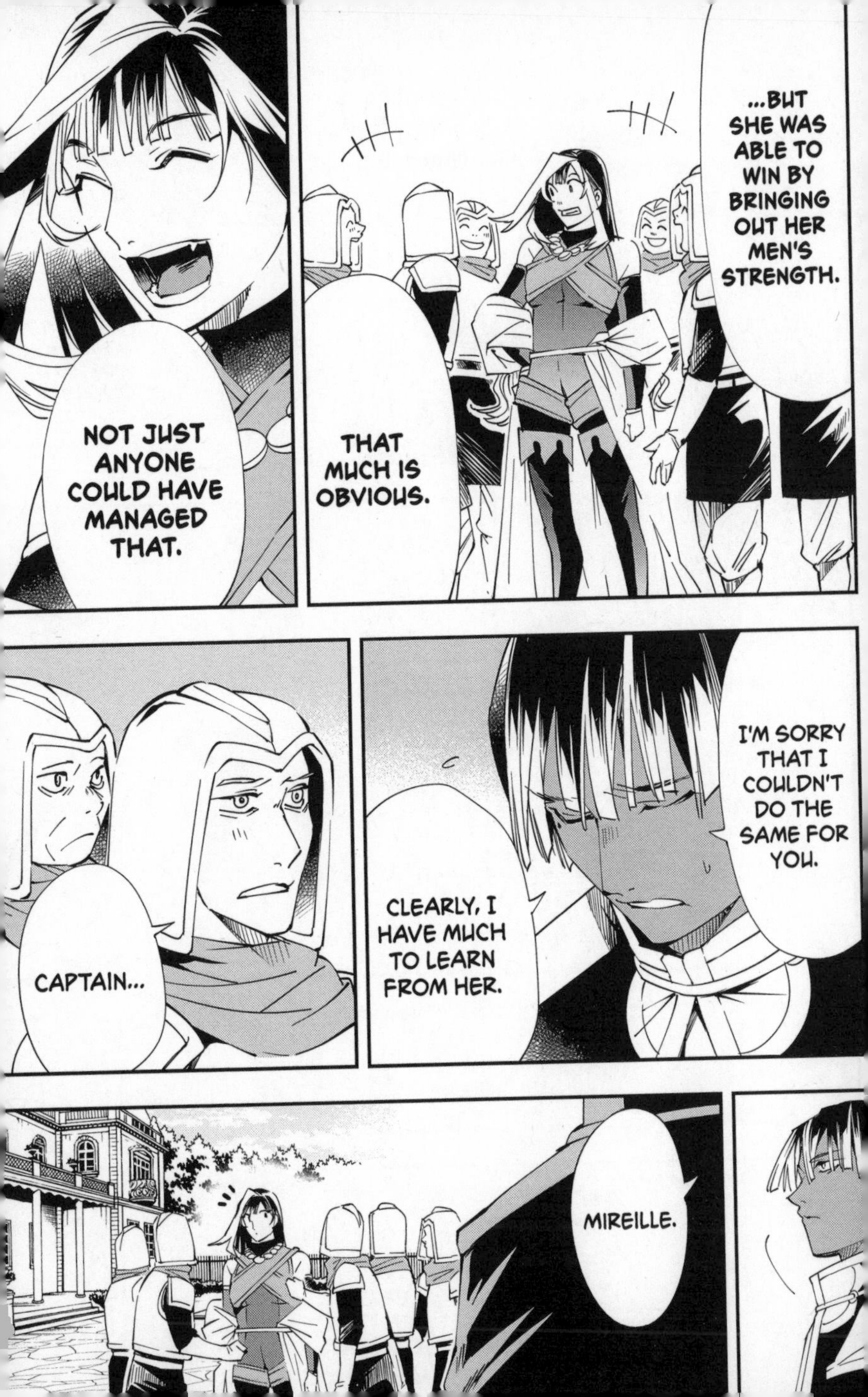
...BUT SHE WAS ABLE TO WIN BY BRINGING OUT HER MEN'S STRENGTH.
THAT MUCH IS OBVIOUS.
NOT JUST ANYONE COULD HAVE MANAGED THAT.
I'M SORRY THAT I COULDN'T DO THE SAME FOR YOU.
CLEARLY, I HAVE MUCH TO LEARN FROM HER.
CAPTAIN...
MIREILLE.

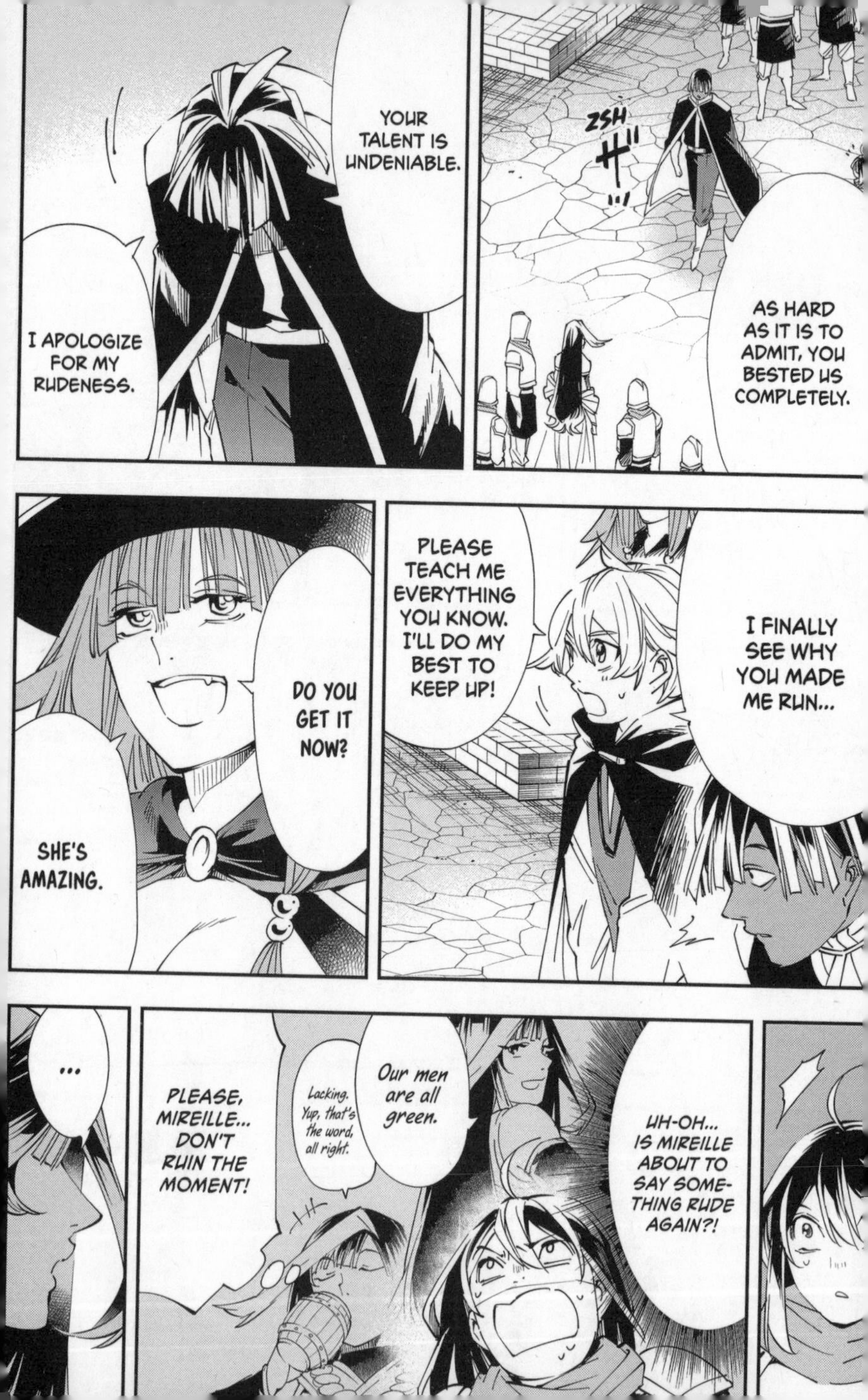
ZSH
AS HARD AS IT IS TO ADMIT, YOU BESTED US COMPLETELY.
YOUR TALENT IS UNDENIABLE.
I APOLOGIZE FOR MY RUDENESS.
I FINALLY SEE WHY YOU MADE ME RUN...
PLEASE TEACH ME EVERYTHING YOU KNOW. I'LL DO MY BEST TO KEEP UP!
DO YOU GET IT NOW?
SHE'S AMAZING.
UH-OH... IS MIREILLE ABOUT TO SAY SOME-THING RUDE AGAIN?!
Our men are all green.
Lacking. Yup, that's the word, all right.
PLEASE, MIREILLE... DON'T RUIN THE MOMENT!
...

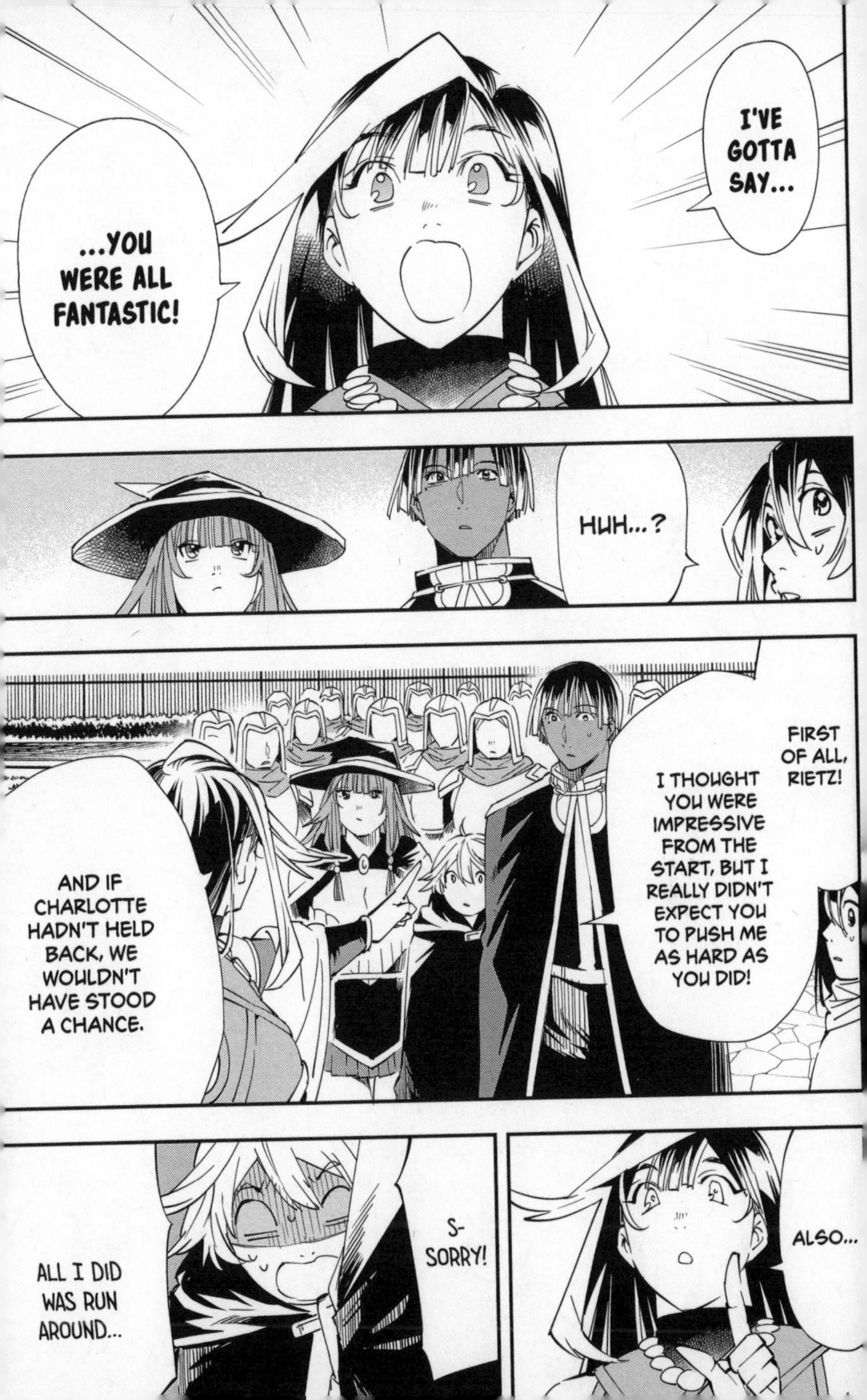
I'VE GOTTA SAY...
...YOU WERE ALL FANTASTIC!
HUH...?
FIRST OF ALL, RIETZ!
I THOUGHT YOU WERE IMPRESSIVE FROM THE START, BUT I REALLY DIDN'T EXPECT YOU TO PUSH ME AS HARD AS YOU DID!
AND IF CHARLOTTE HADN'T HELD BACK, WE WOULDN'T HAVE STOOD A CHANCE.
ALSO...
S-SORRY!
ALL I DID WAS RUN AROUND...

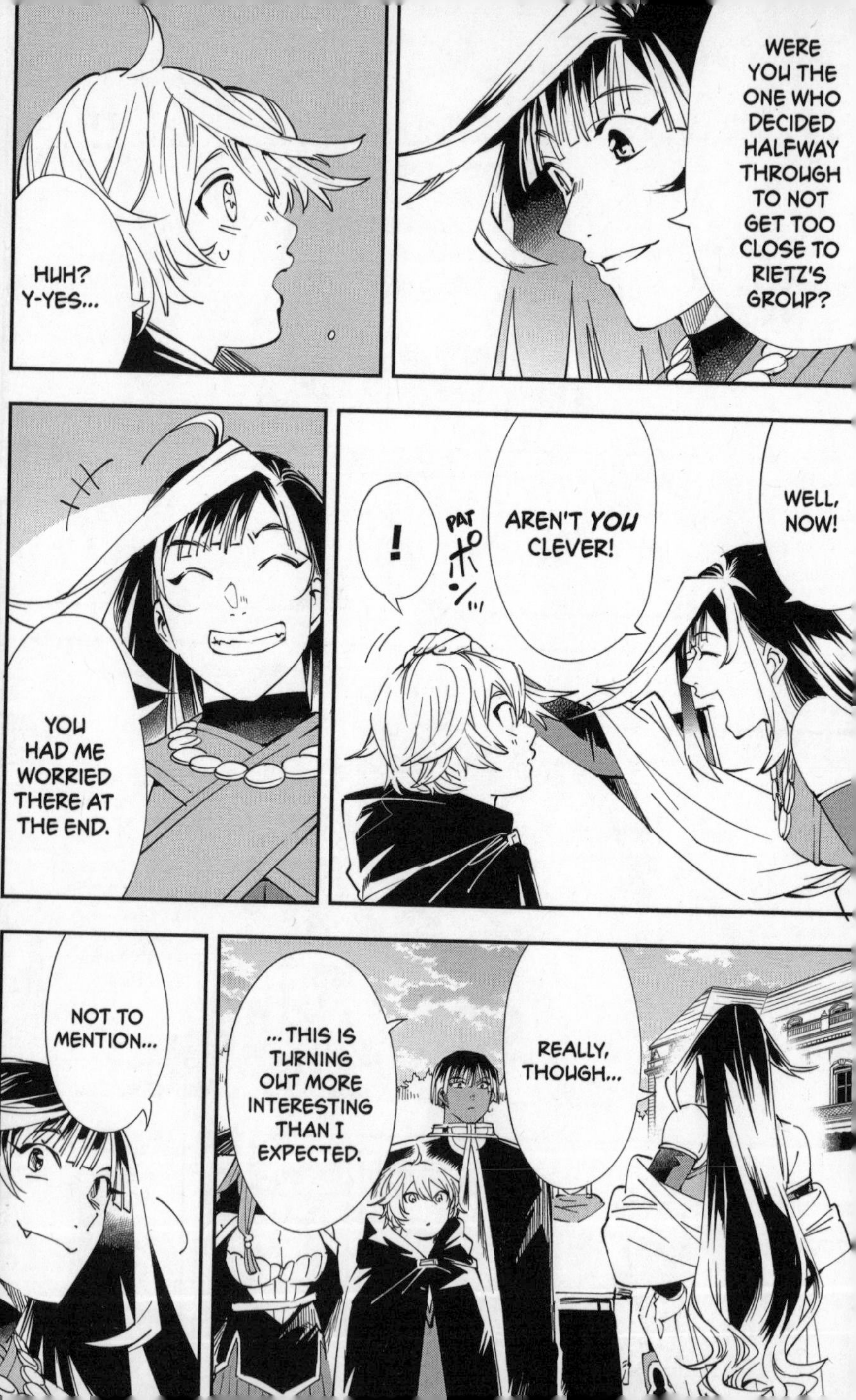
WERE YOU THE ONE WHO DECIDED HALFWAY THROUGH TO NOT GET TOO CLOSE TO RIETZ'S GROUP?
HUH? Y-YES...
WELL, NOW!
AREN'T *YOU* CLEVER!
PAT
!
YOU HAD ME WORRIED THERE AT THE END.
REALLY, THOUGH...
...THIS IS TURNING OUT MORE INTERESTING THAN I EXPECTED.
NOT TO MENTION...

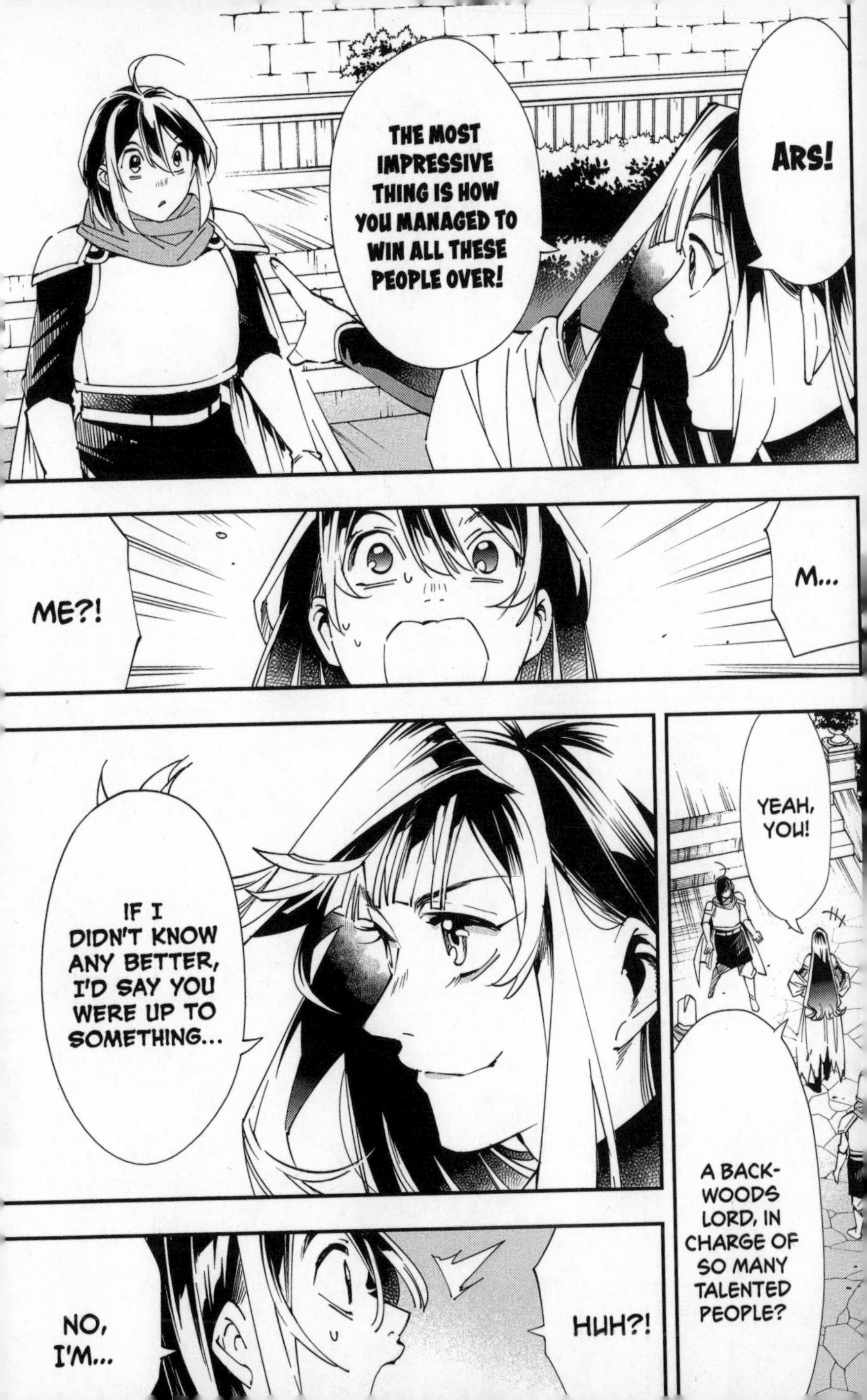
ARS!
THE MOST IMPRESSIVE THING IS HOW YOU MANAGED TO WIN ALL THESE PEOPLE OVER!
M...
ME?!
YEAH, YOU!
A BACK-WOODS LORD, IN CHARGE OF SO MANY TALENTED PEOPLE?
IF I DIDN'T KNOW ANY BETTER, I'D SAY YOU WERE UP TO SOMETHING...
HUH?!
NO, I'M...

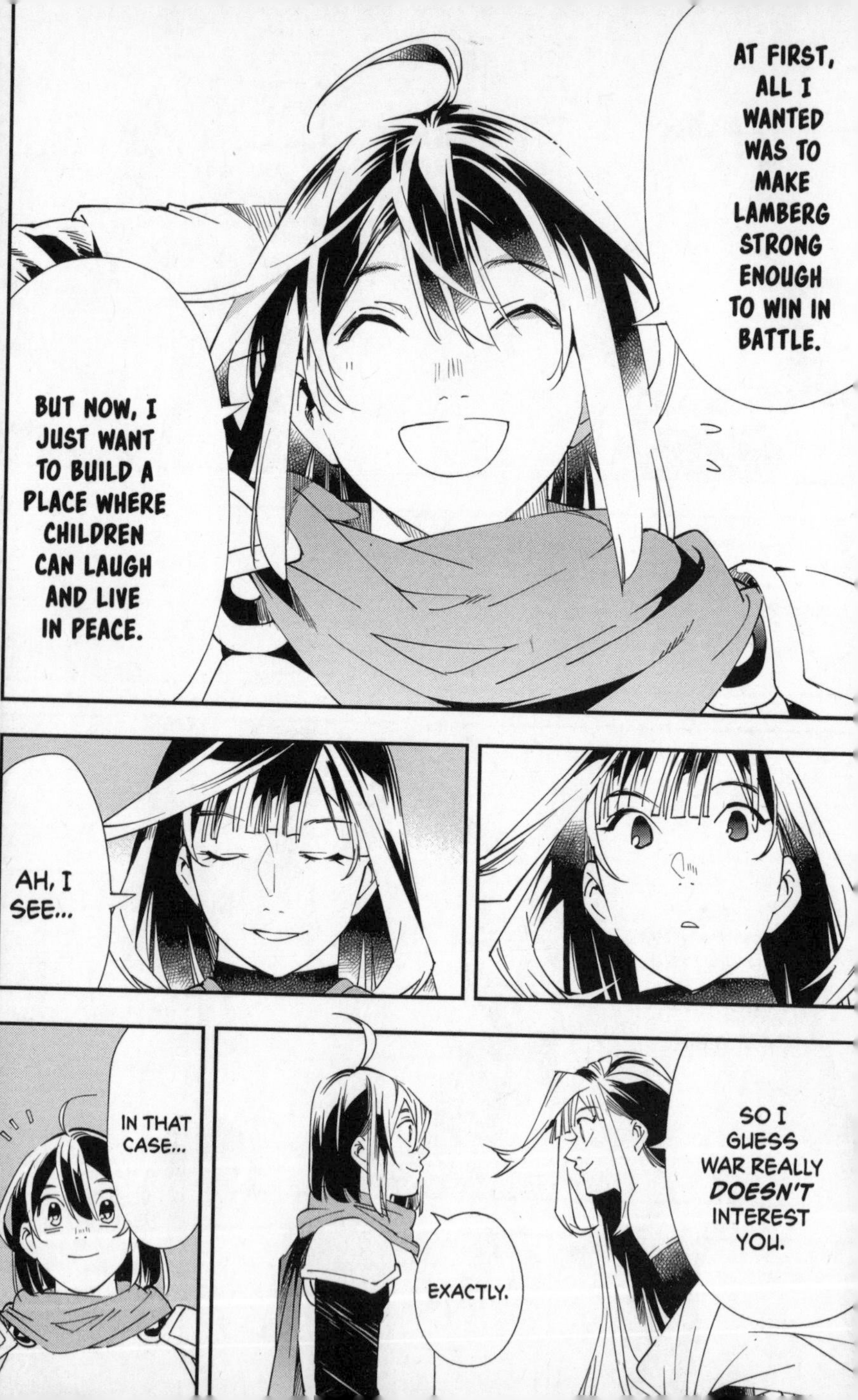
AT FIRST, ALL I WANTED WAS TO MAKE LAMBERG STRONG ENOUGH TO WIN IN BATTLE.
BUT NOW, I JUST WANT TO BUILD A PLACE WHERE CHILDREN CAN LAUGH AND LIVE IN PEACE.
AH, I SEE...
SO I GUESS WAR REALLY *DOESN'T* INTEREST YOU.
EXACTLY.
IN THAT CASE...

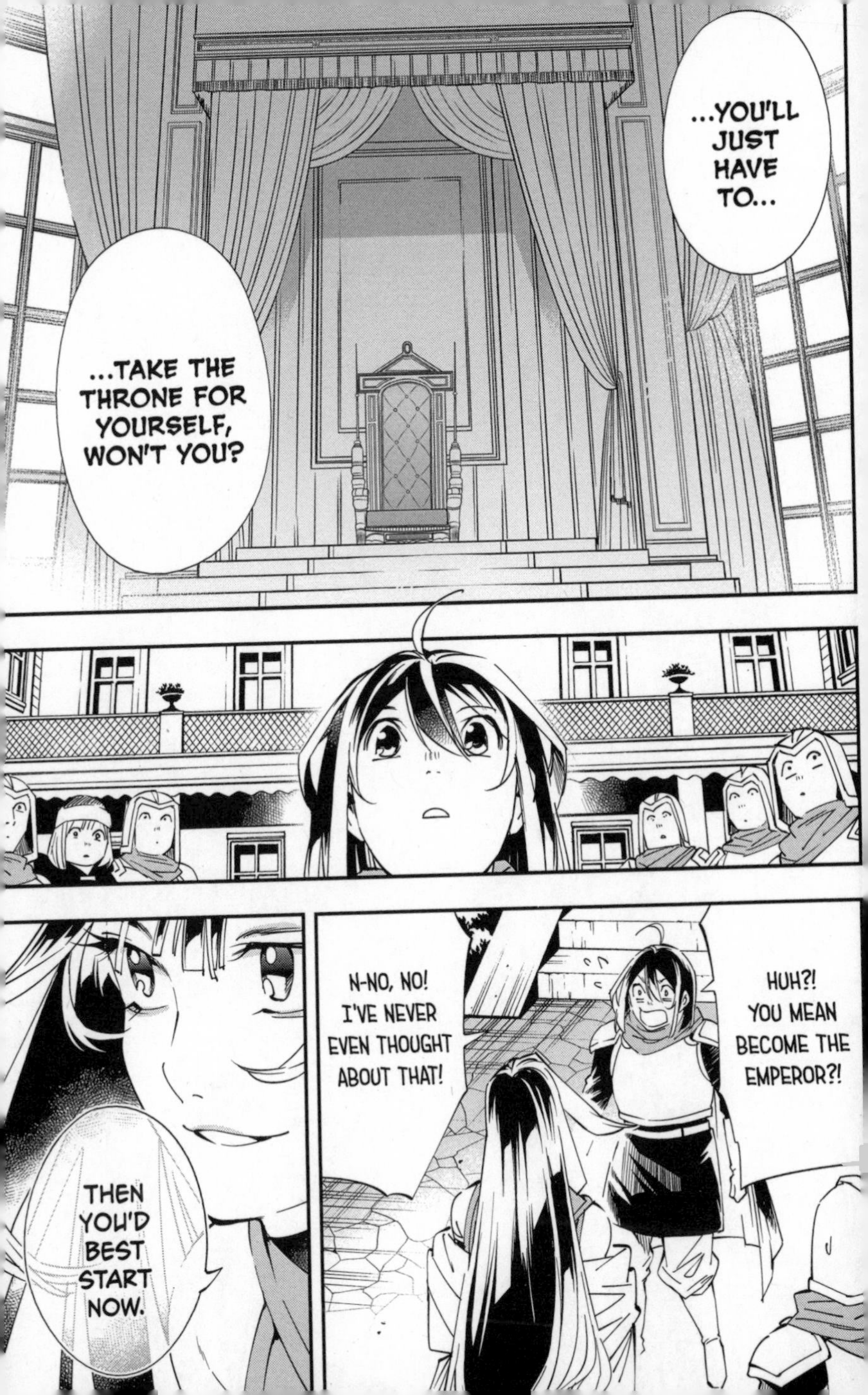
...YOU'LL JUST HAVE TO...
...TAKE THE THRONE FOR YOURSELF, WON'T YOU?
HUH?! YOU MEAN BECOME THE EMPEROR?!
N-NO, NO! I'VE NEVER EVEN THOUGHT ABOUT THAT!
THEN YOU'D BEST START NOW.

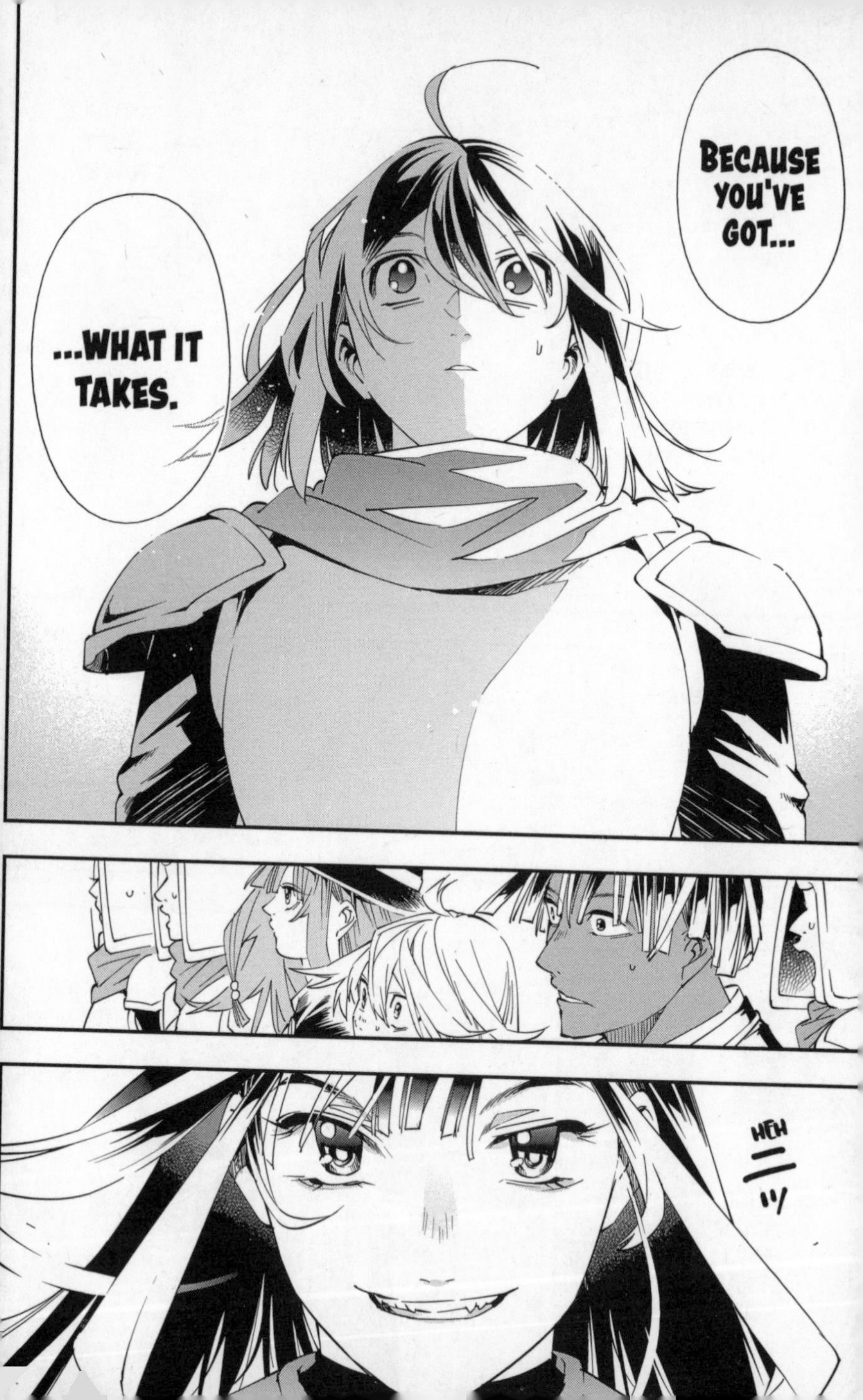
BECAUSE YOU'VE GOT...
...WHAT IT TAKES.
HEH
ニッ

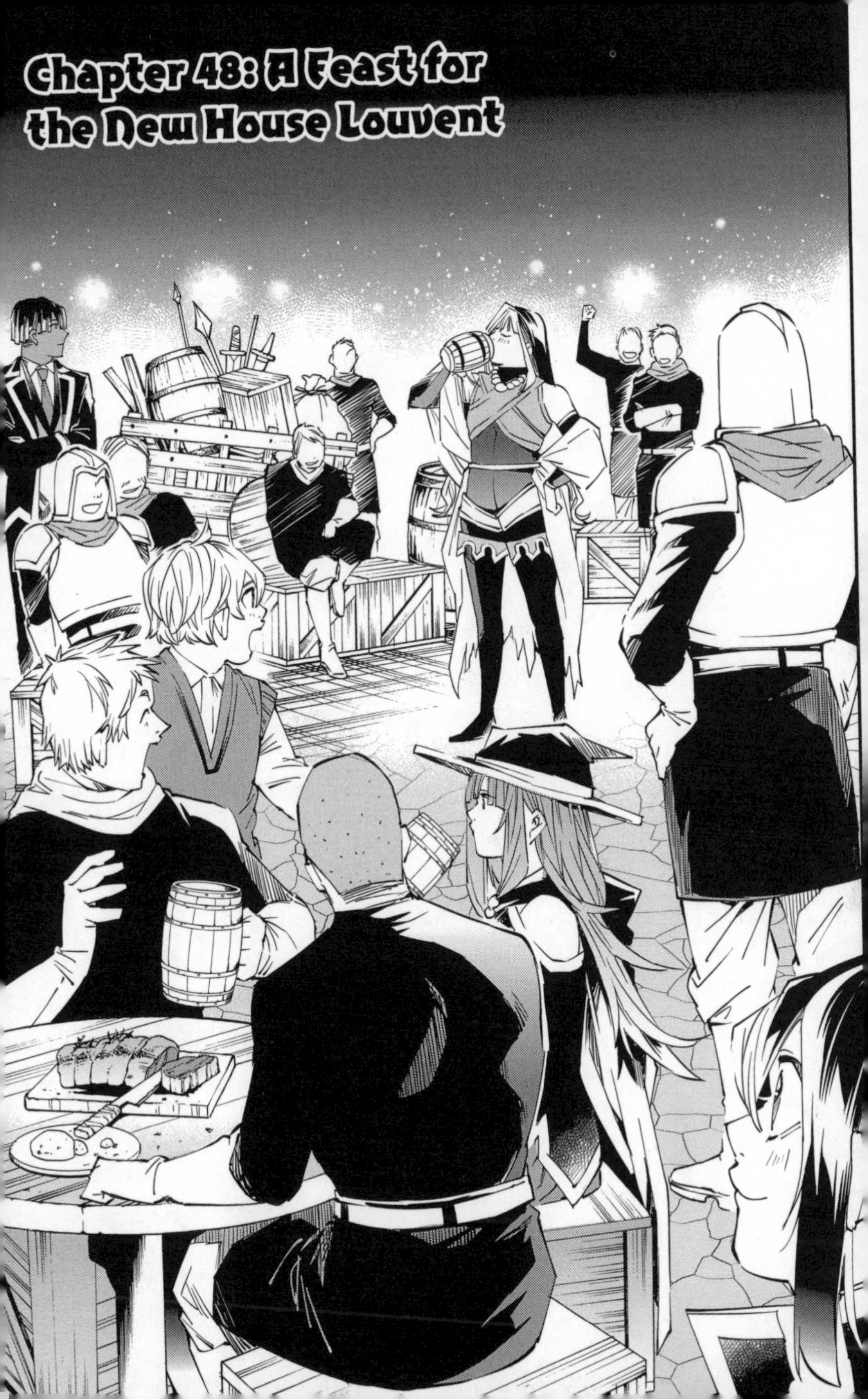
Chapter 48: A Feast for the New House Louvent

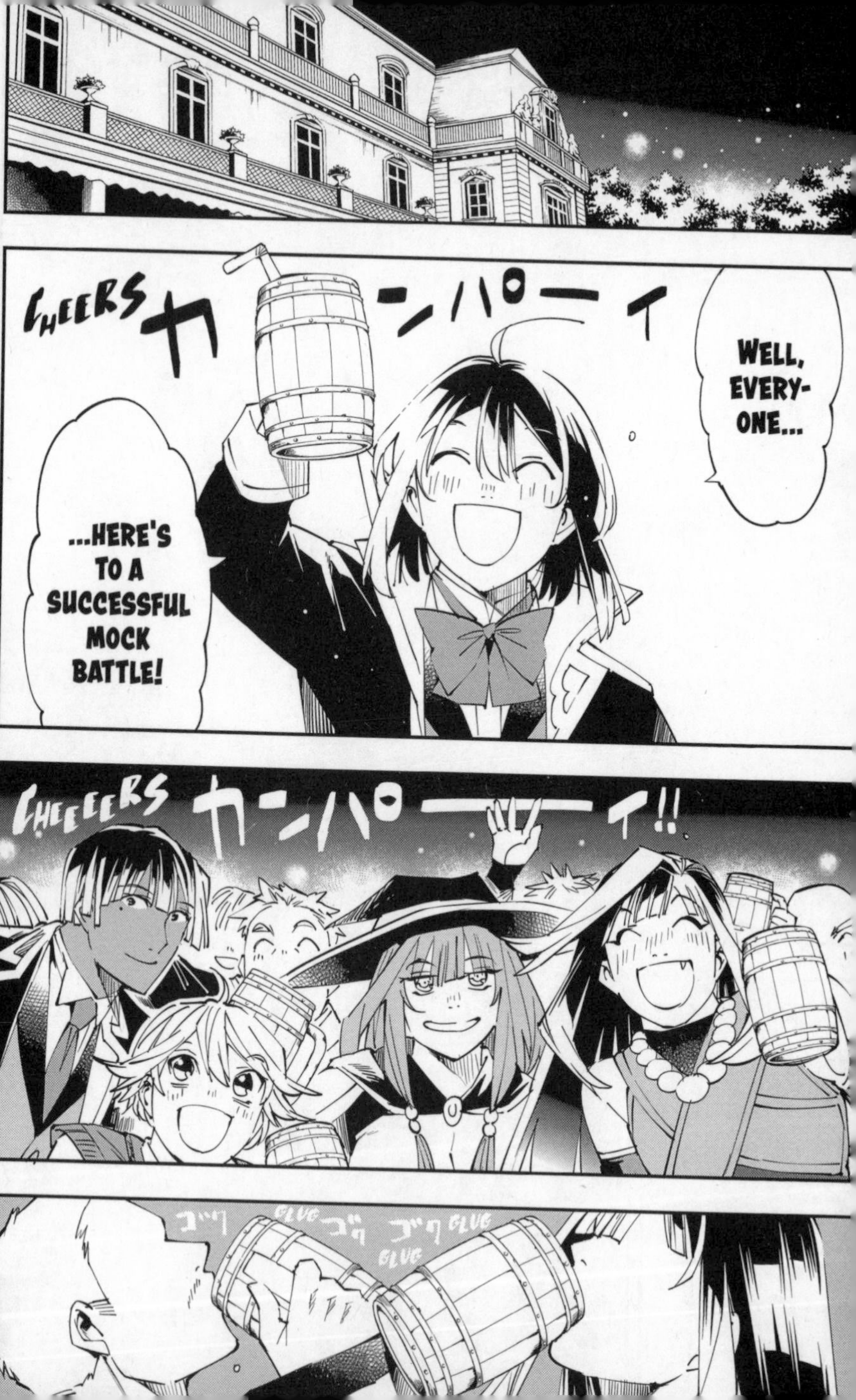
WELL, EVERY-ONE...
CHEERS カンパーイ
...HERE'S TO A SUCCESSFUL MOCK BATTLE!
CHEEEERS カンパーーーイ!!
ゴク GLUG ゴク GLUG ゴク GLUG

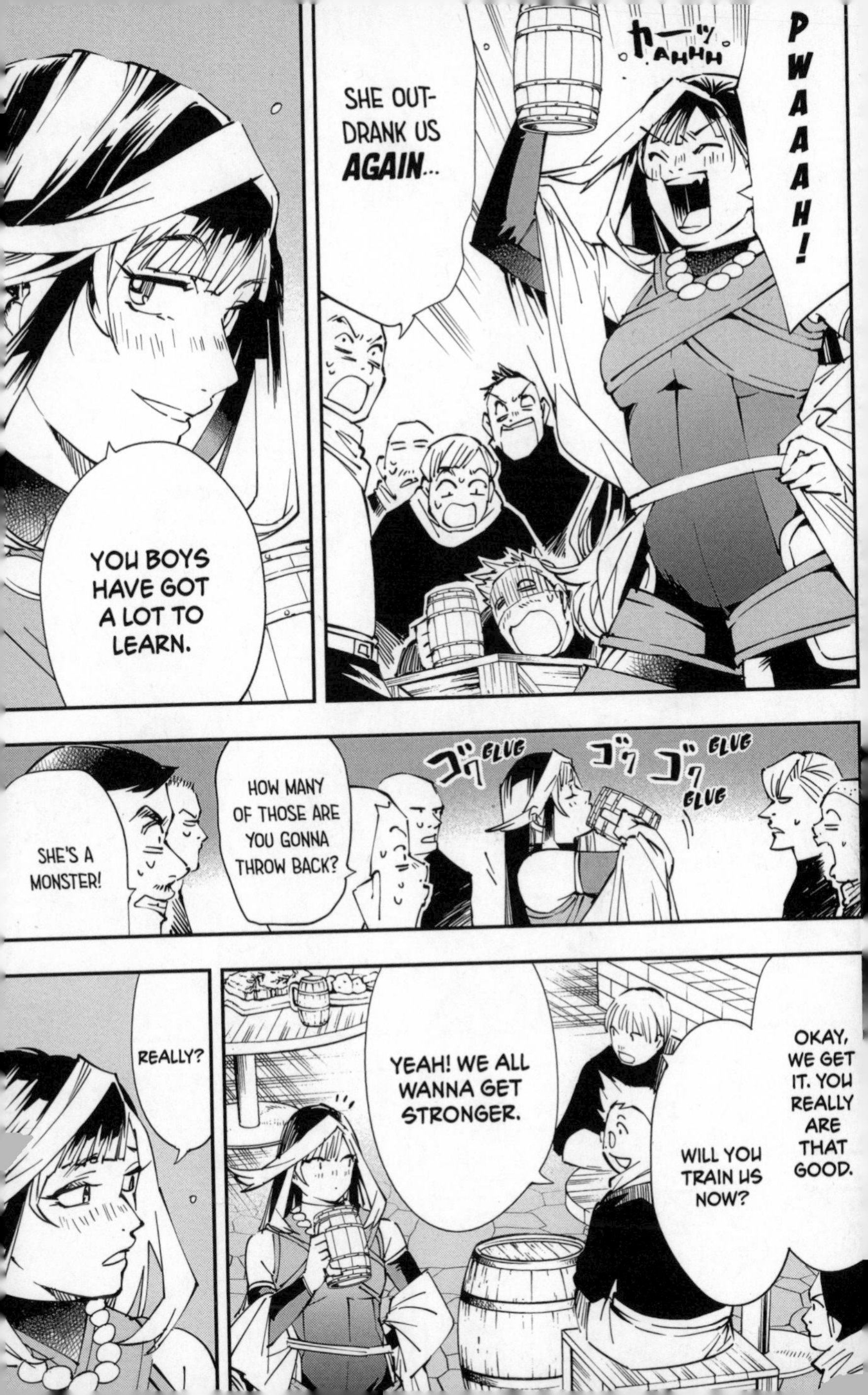
PWAAAAH!
カーッ AHHH
SHE OUT-DRANK US AGAIN...
YOU BOYS HAVE GOT A LOT TO LEARN.
ゴク GLUG
ゴク GLUG
ゴク GLUG
HOW MANY OF THOSE ARE YOU GONNA THROW BACK?
SHE'S A MONSTER!
OKAY, WE GET IT. YOU REALLY ARE THAT GOOD.
WILL YOU TRAIN US NOW?
YEAH! WE ALL WANNA GET STRONGER.
REALLY?

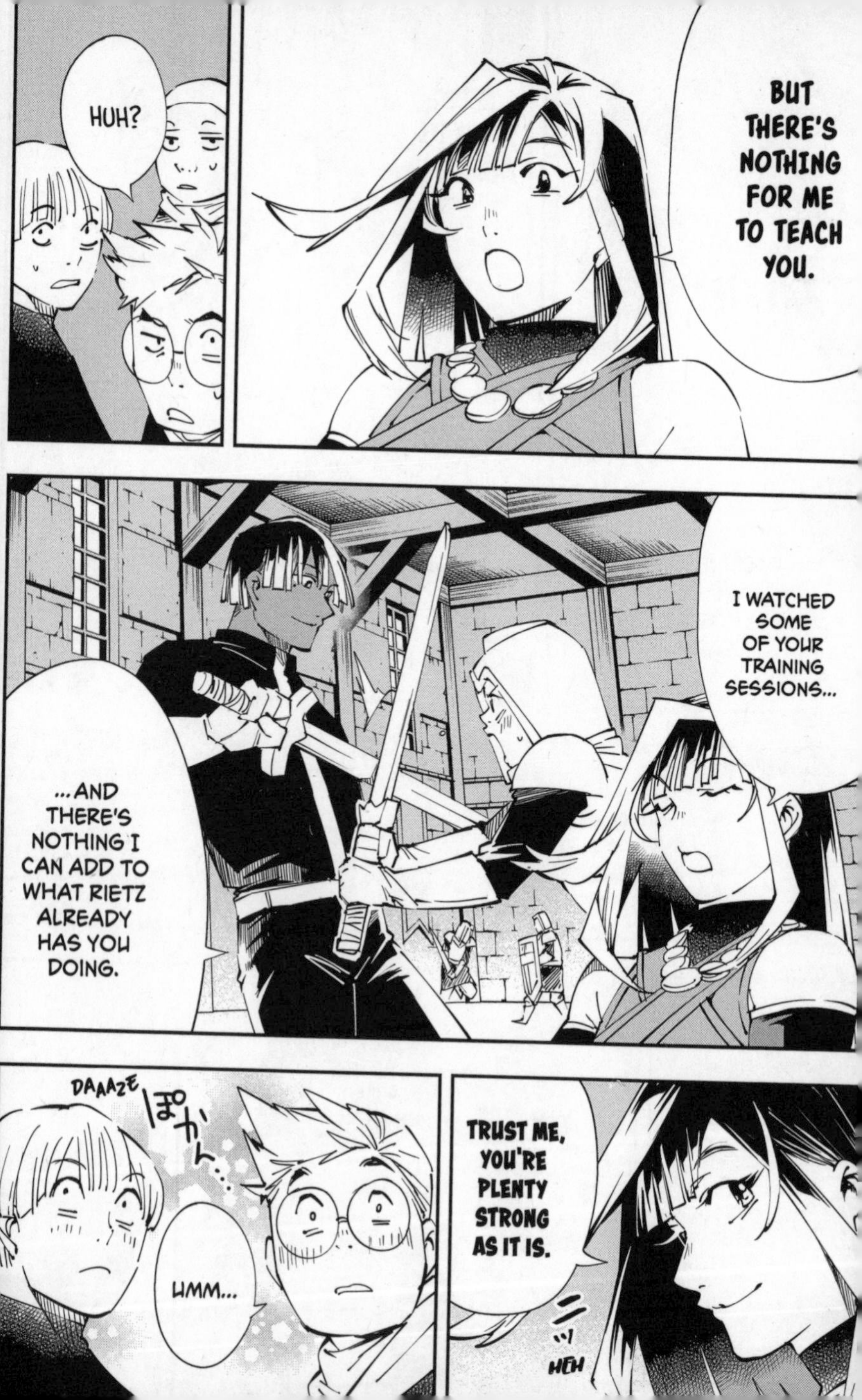
BUT THERE'S NOTHING FOR ME TO TEACH YOU.
HUH?
I WATCHED SOME OF YOUR TRAINING SESSIONS...
...AND THERE'S NOTHING I CAN ADD TO WHAT RIETZ ALREADY HAS YOU DOING.
TRUST ME, YOU'RE PLENTY STRONG AS IT IS.
HEH
DAAAZE
ぽかん…
UMM...

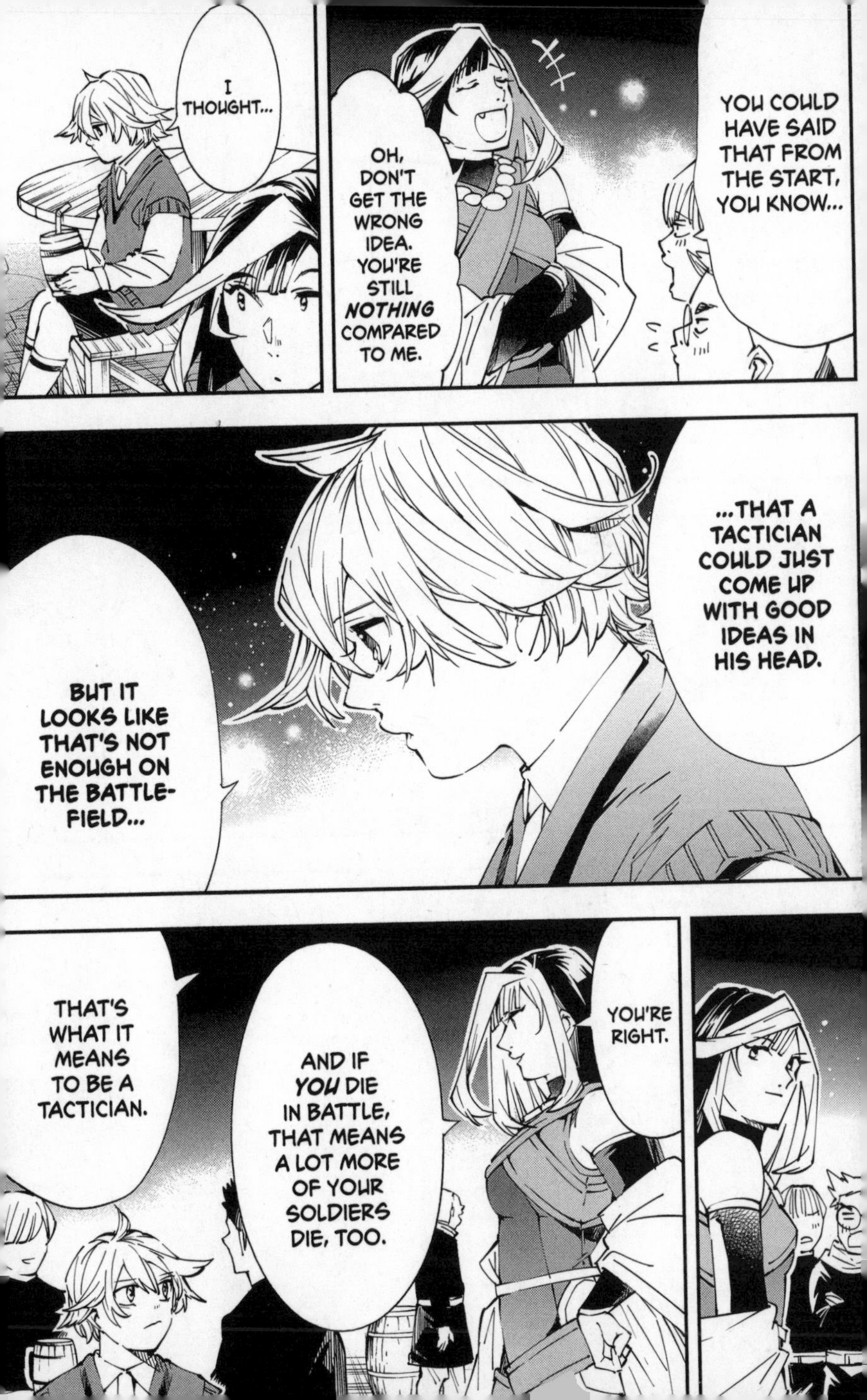
YOU COULD HAVE SAID THAT FROM THE START, YOU KNOW...
OH, DON'T GET THE WRONG IDEA. YOU'RE STILL *NOTHING* COMPARED TO ME.
I THOUGHT...
...THAT A TACTICIAN COULD JUST COME UP WITH GOOD IDEAS IN HIS HEAD.
BUT IT LOOKS LIKE THAT'S NOT ENOUGH ON THE BATTLE-FIELD...
YOU'RE RIGHT.
AND IF *YOU* DIE IN BATTLE, THAT MEANS A LOT MORE OF YOUR SOLDIERS DIE, TOO.
THAT'S WHAT IT MEANS TO BE A TACTICIAN.

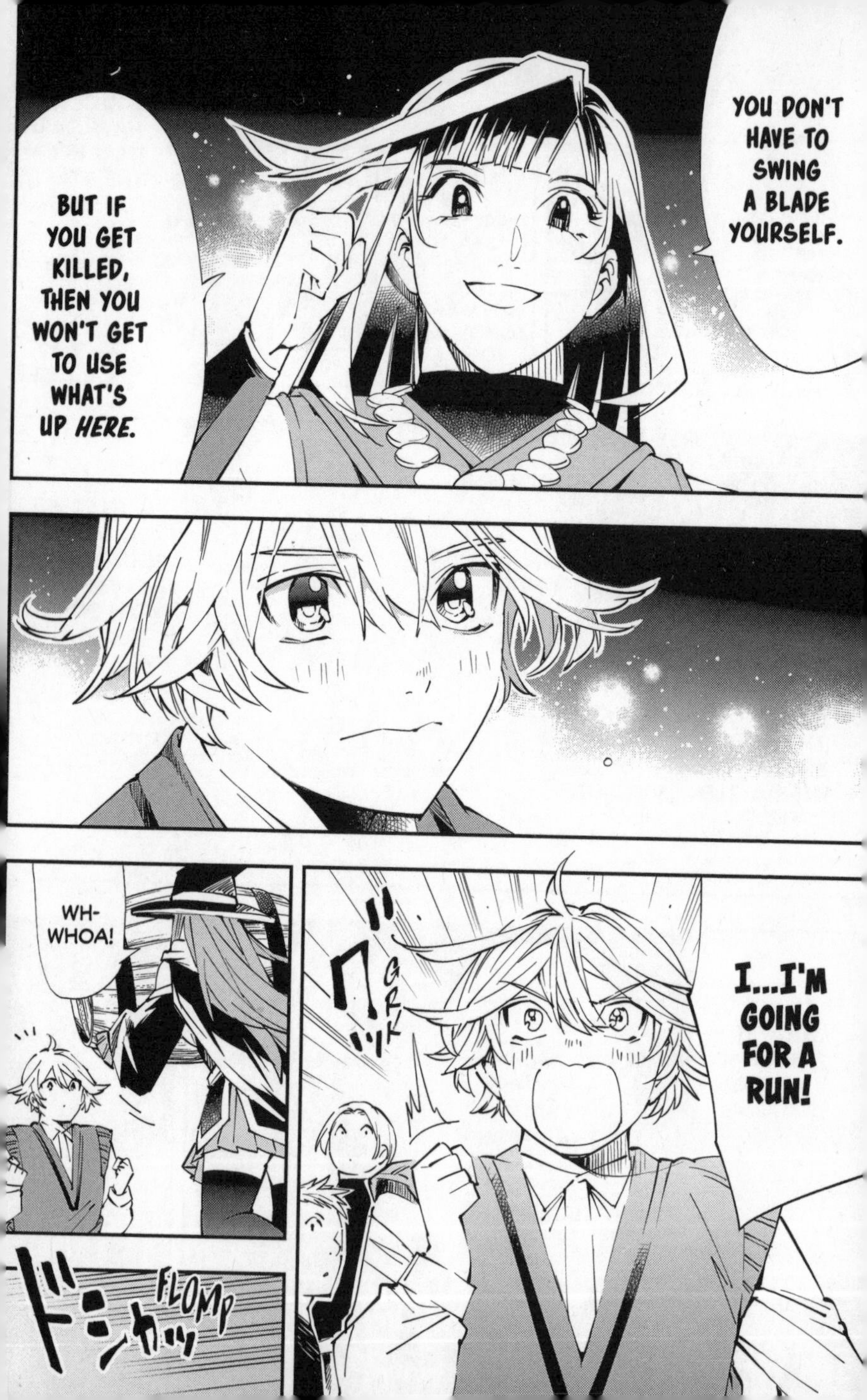
YOU DON'T HAVE TO SWING A BLADE YOURSELF.
BUT IF YOU GET KILLED, THEN YOU WON'T GET TO USE WHAT'S UP *HERE.*
GRK
I...I'M GOING FOR A RUN!
WH- WHOA!
FLOMP

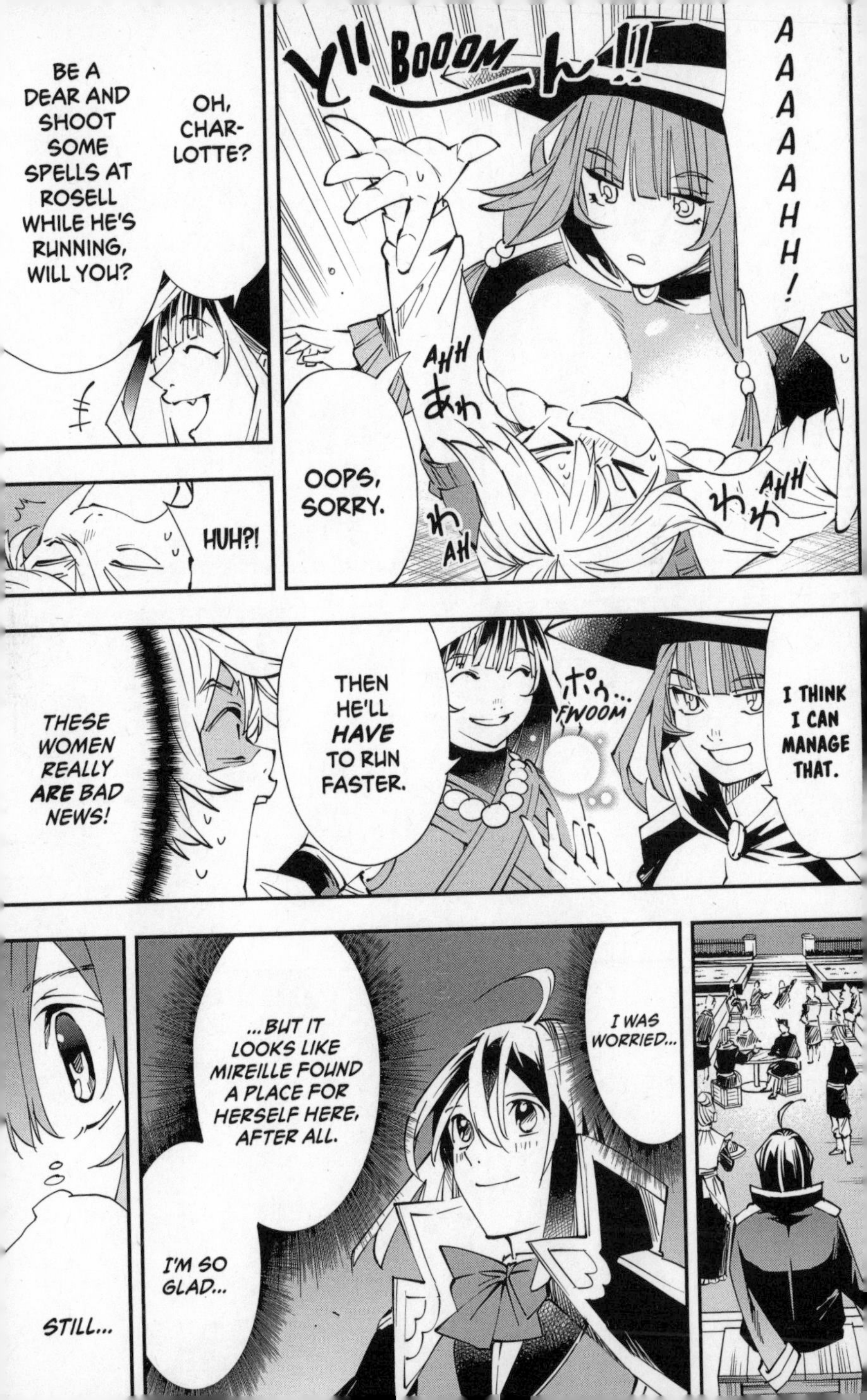
BOOOM
AAAAAAHH!
AHH あわ
OOPS, SORRY.
AHH
AH
OH, CHAR-LOTTE?
BE A DEAR AND SHOOT SOME SPELLS AT ROSELL WHILE HE'S RUNNING, WILL YOU?
HUH?!
I THINK I CAN MANAGE THAT.
ポゥ... FWOOM
THEN HE'LL *HAVE* TO RUN FASTER.
THESE WOMEN REALLY *ARE* BAD NEWS!
I WAS WORRIED...
...BUT IT LOOKS LIKE MIREILLE FOUND A PLACE FOR HERSELF HERE, AFTER ALL.
I'M SO GLAD...
STILL...

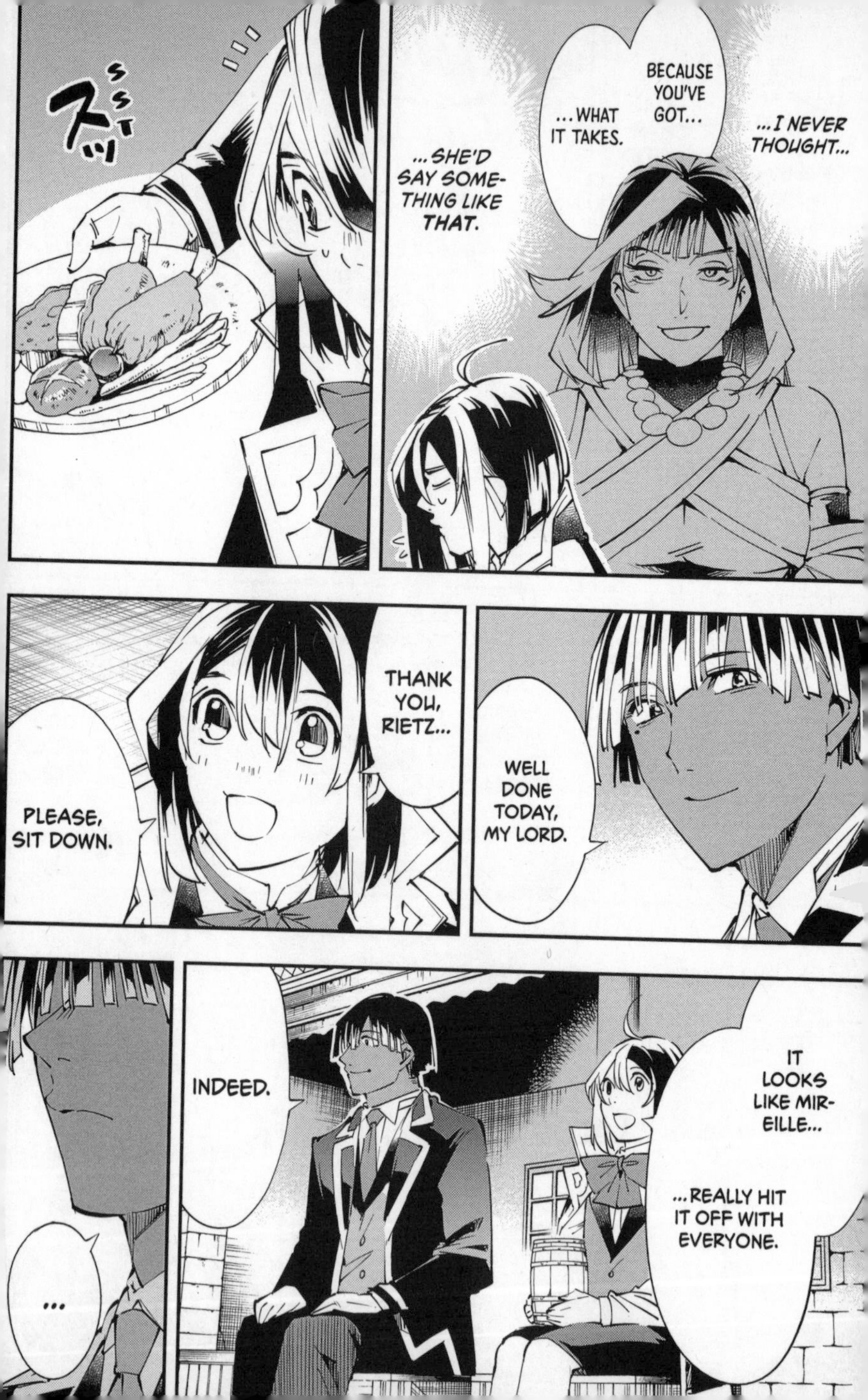
BECAUSE YOU'VE GOT... ...WHAT IT TAKES.
...I NEVER THOUGHT...
...SHE'D SAY SOME-THING LIKE THAT.
スッ
SST
WELL DONE TODAY, MY LORD.
THANK YOU, RIETZ...
PLEASE, SIT DOWN.
IT LOOKS LIKE MIR-EILLE...
...REALLY HIT IT OFF WITH EVERYONE.
INDEED.
...

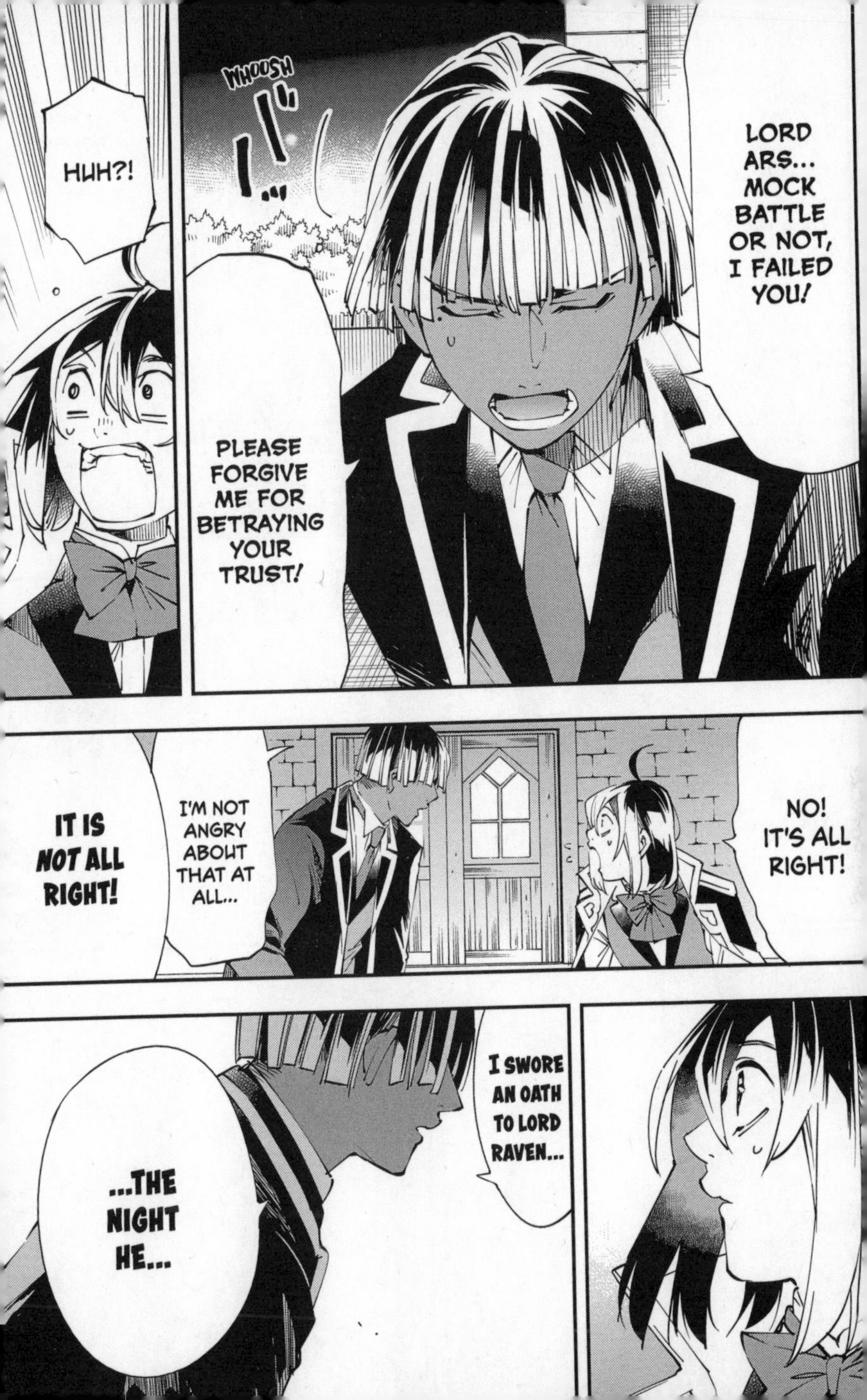
LORD ARS... MOCK BATTLE OR NOT, I FAILED YOU!
WHOOSH
PLEASE FORGIVE ME FOR BETRAYING YOUR TRUST!
HUH?!
NO! IT'S ALL RIGHT!
I'M NOT ANGRY ABOUT THAT AT ALL...
IT IS NOT ALL RIGHT!
I SWORE AN OATH TO LORD RAVEN...
...THE NIGHT HE...

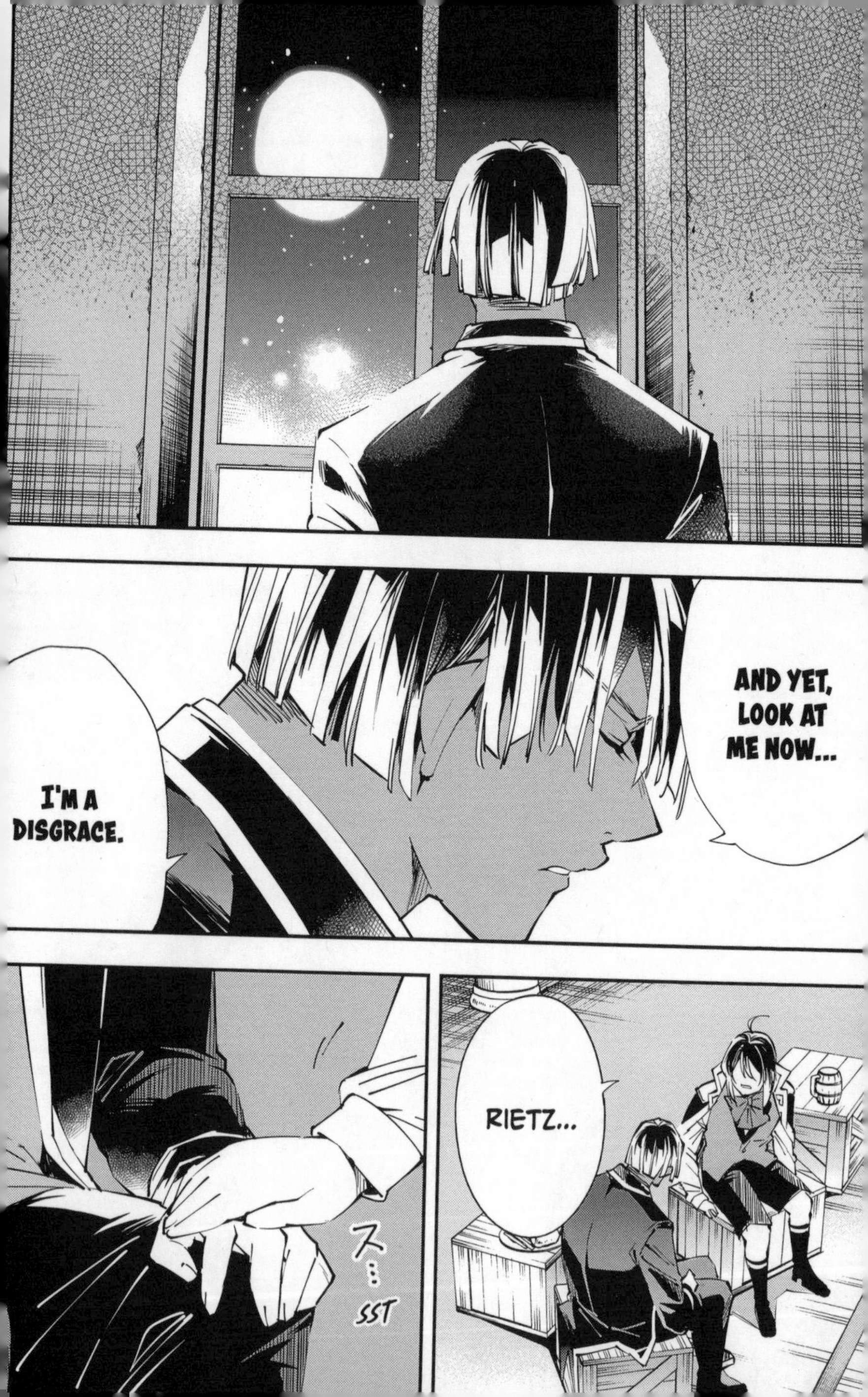
AND YET, LOOK AT ME NOW...
I'M A DISGRACE.
RIETZ...
SST

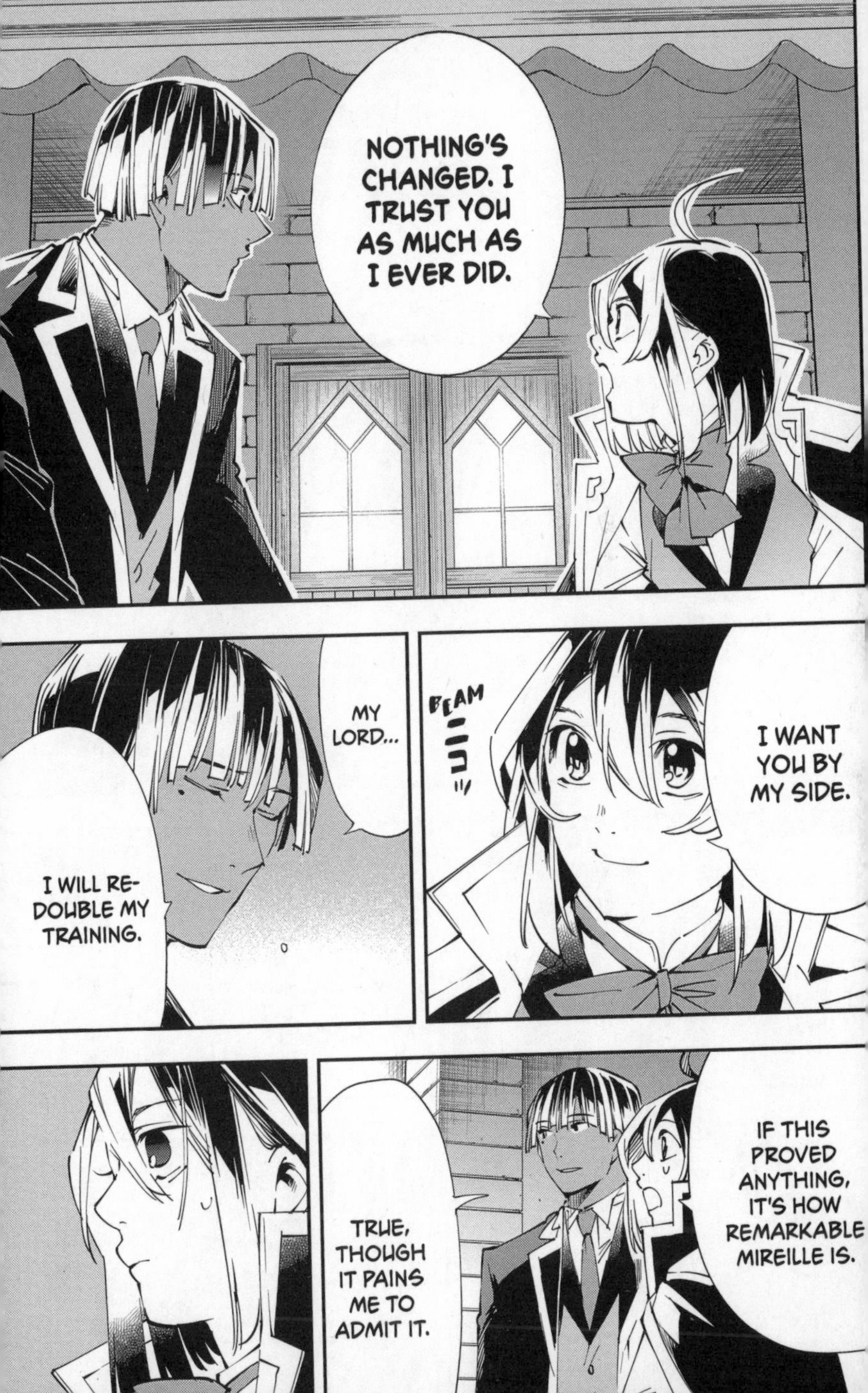
NOTHING'S CHANGED. I TRUST YOU AS MUCH AS I EVER DID.
I WANT YOU BY MY SIDE.
BEAM
MY LORD...
I WILL RE-DOUBLE MY TRAINING.
IF THIS PROVED ANYTHING, IT'S HOW REMARKABLE MIREILLE IS.
TRUE, THOUGH IT PAINS ME TO ADMIT IT.

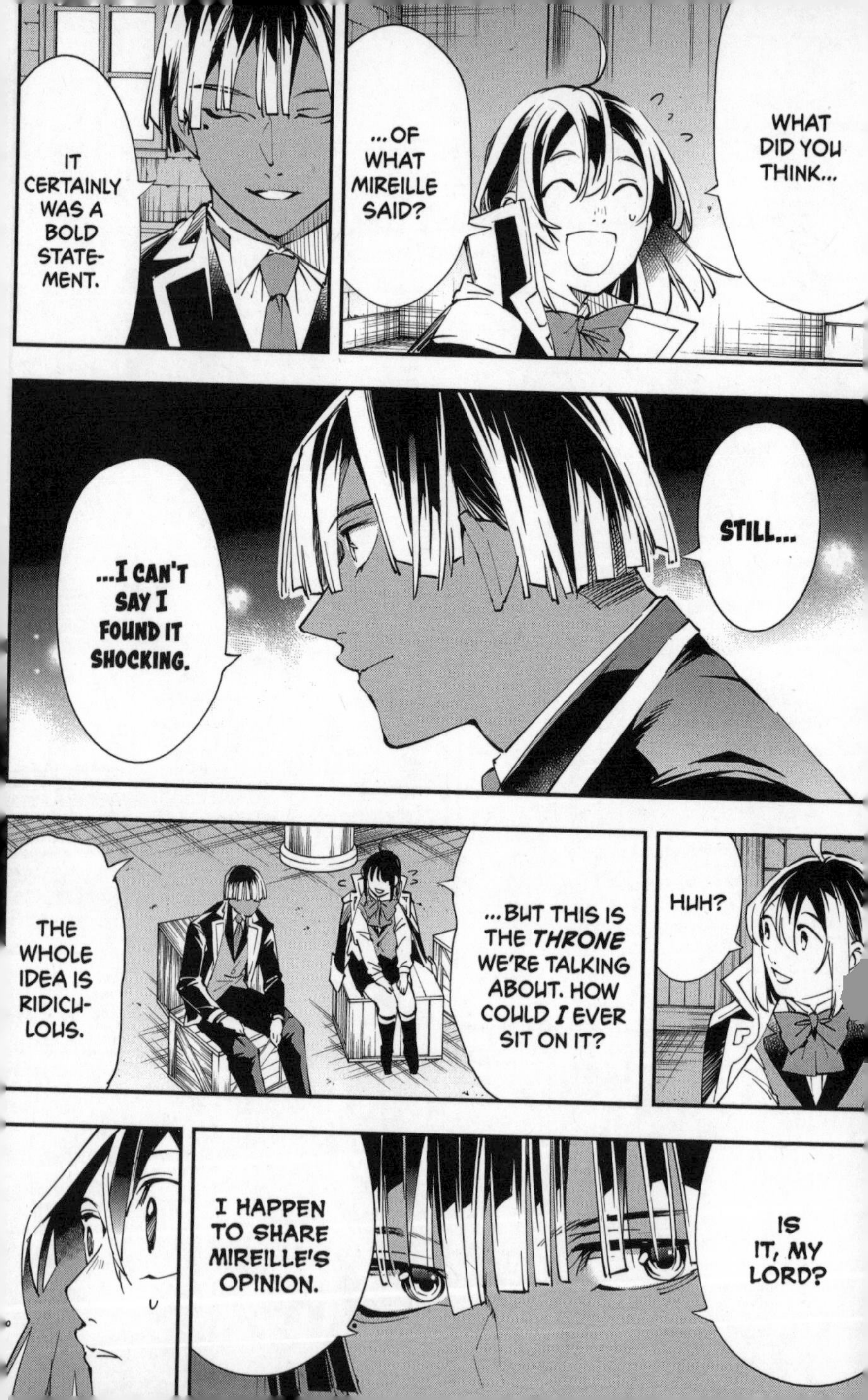
WHAT DID YOU THINK...
...OF WHAT MIREILLE SAID?
IT CERTAINLY WAS A BOLD STATEMENT.
STILL...
...I CAN'T SAY I FOUND IT SHOCKING.
HUH?
...BUT THIS IS THE *THRONE* WE'RE TALKING ABOUT. HOW COULD *I* EVER SIT ON IT?
THE WHOLE IDEA IS RIDICULOUS.
IS IT, MY LORD?
I HAPPEN TO SHARE MIREILLE'S OPINION.

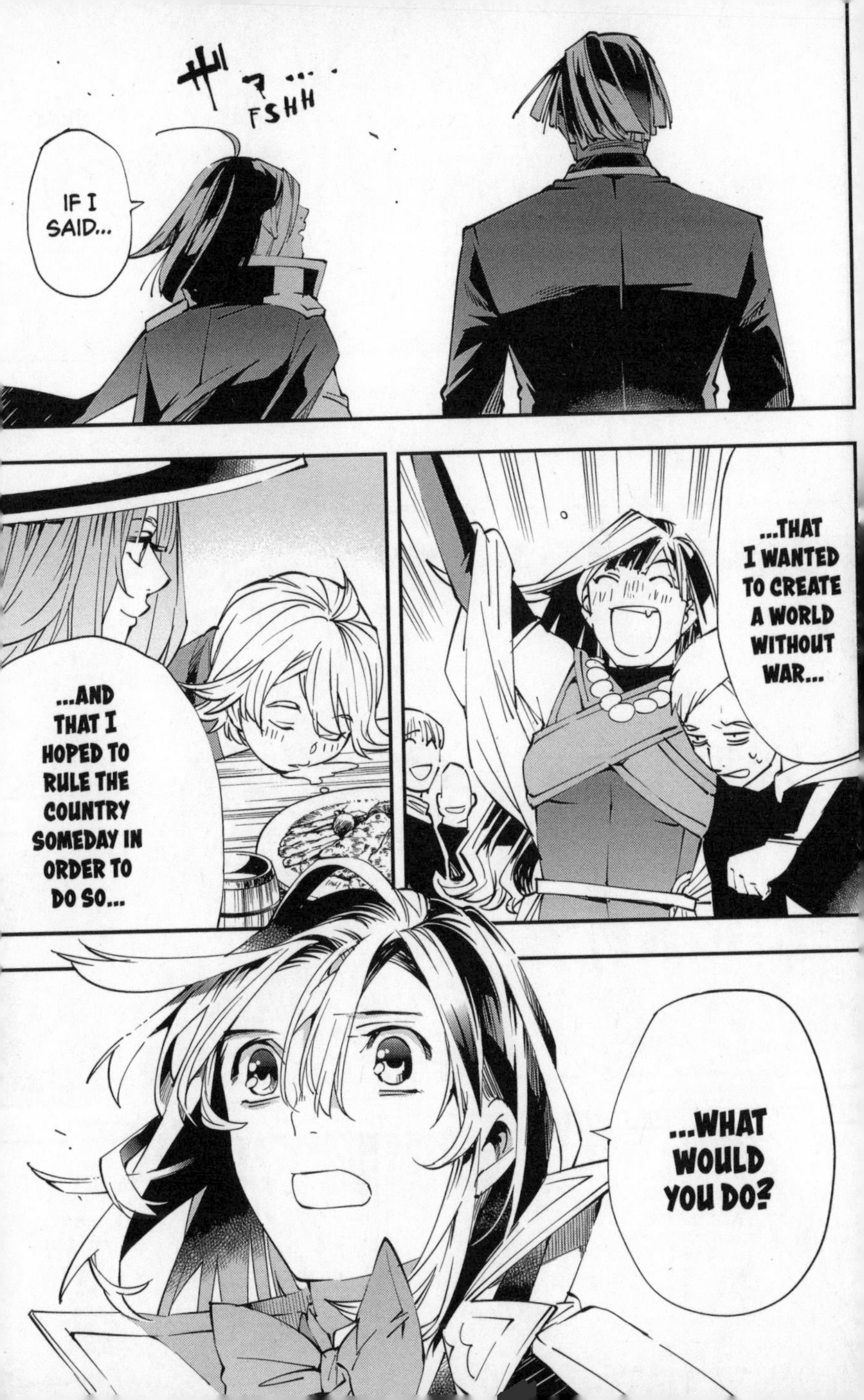
FSHH
IF I SAID...
...THAT I WANTED TO CREATE A WORLD WITHOUT WAR...
...AND THAT I HOPED TO RULE THE COUNTRY SOMEDAY IN ORDER TO DO SO...
...WHAT WOULD YOU DO?

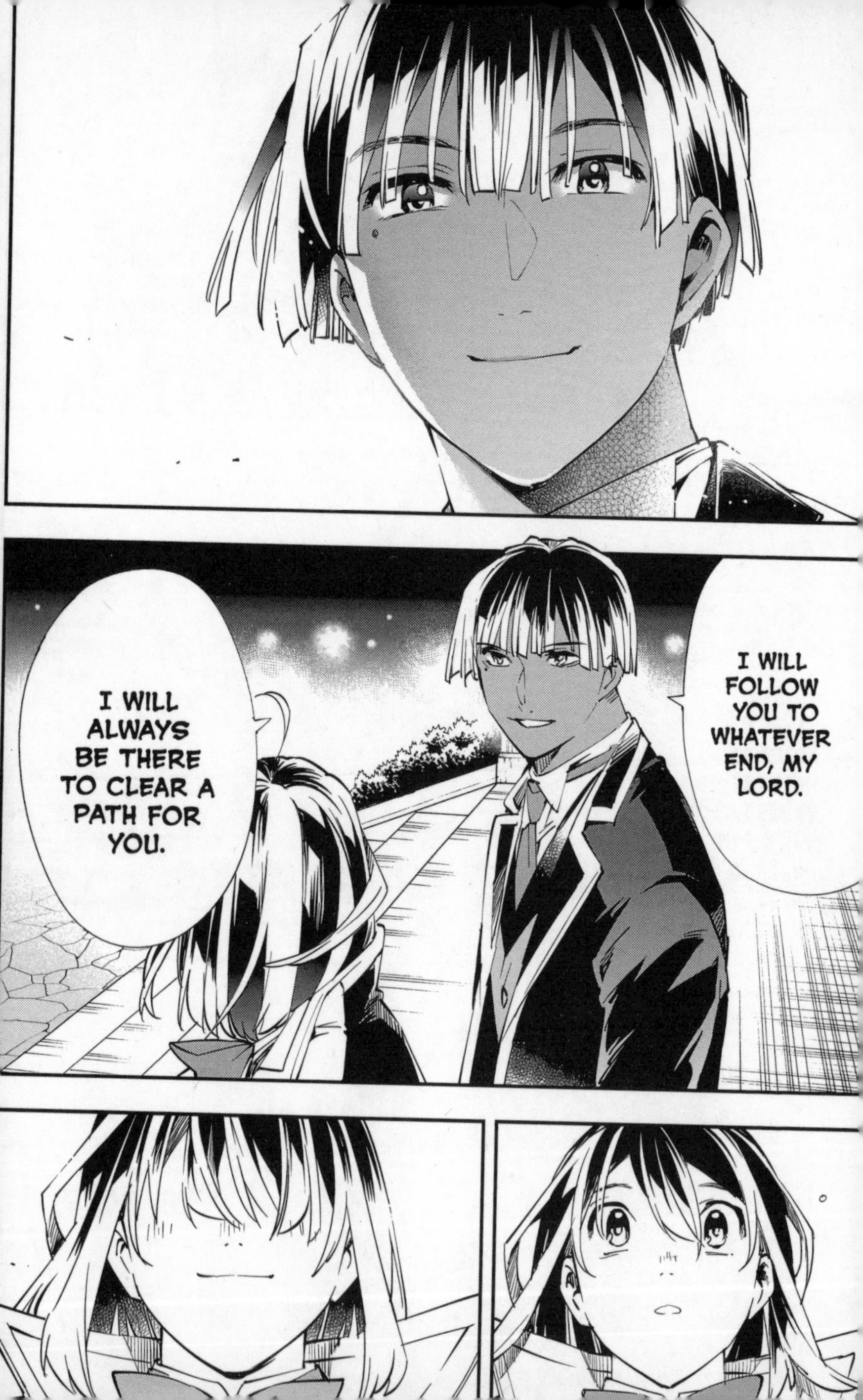
I WILL FOLLOW YOU TO WHATEVER END, MY LORD.
I WILL ALWAYS BE THERE TO CLEAR A PATH FOR YOU.

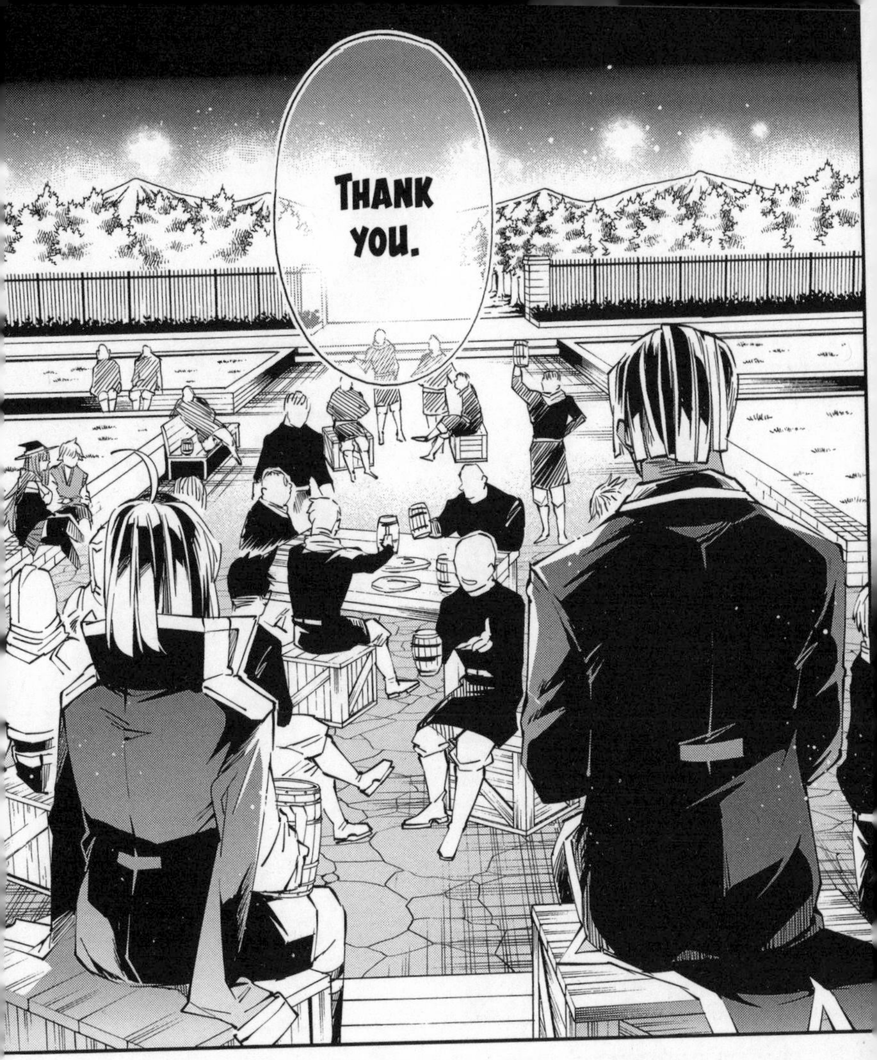
THANK YOU.

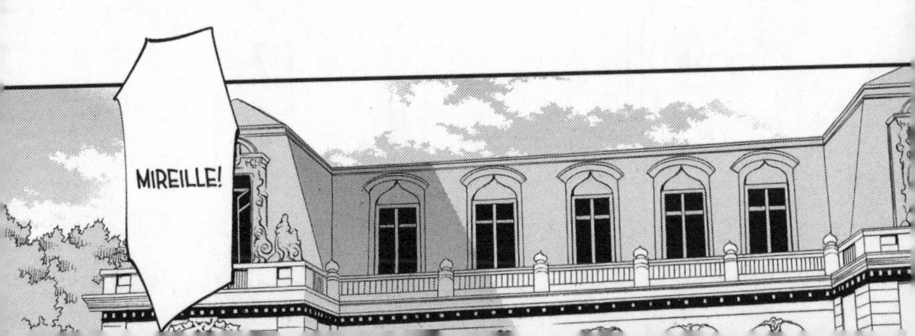
MIREILLE!

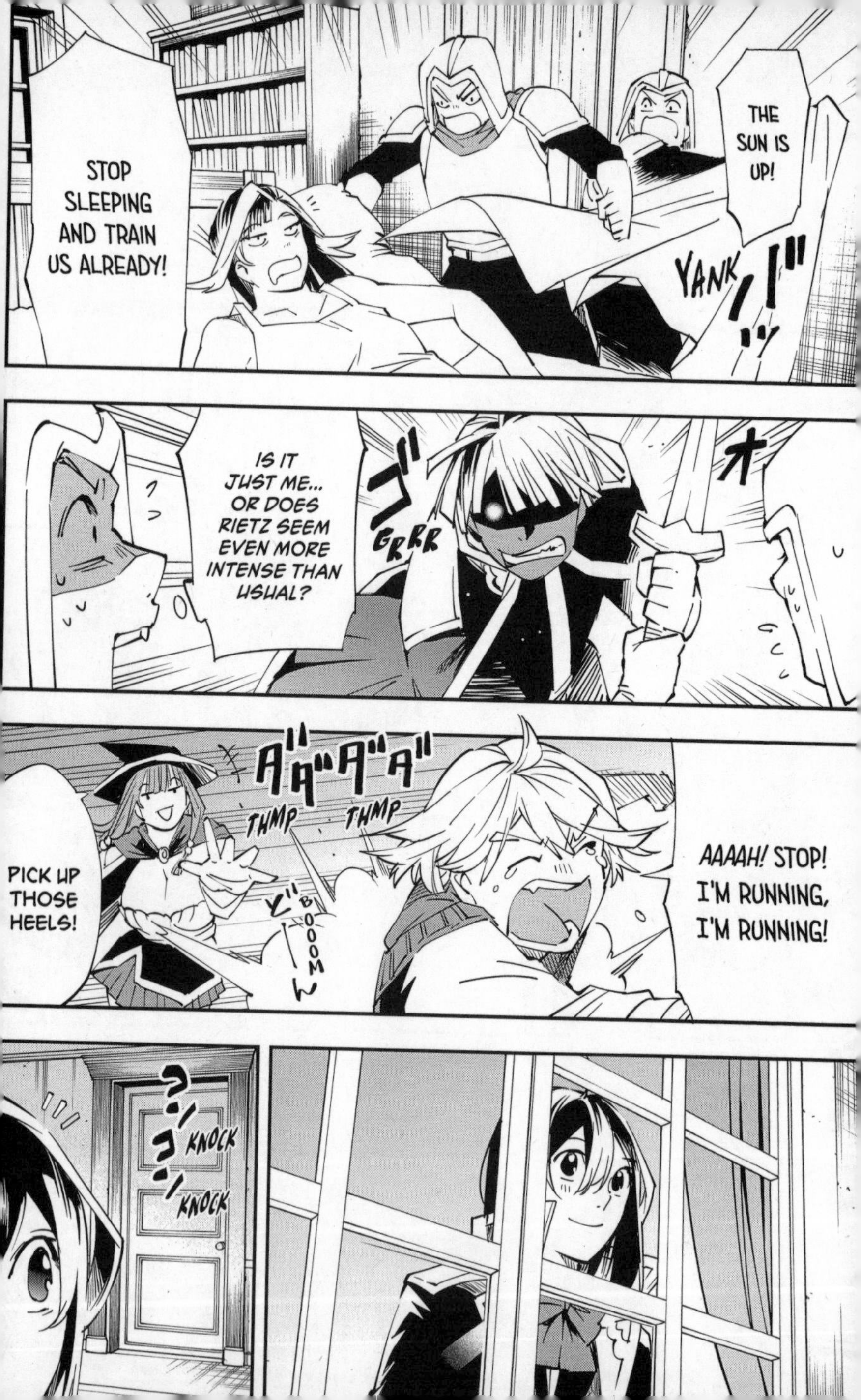
THE SUN IS UP!
YANK
STOP SLEEPING AND TRAIN US ALREADY!
GRRR
IS IT JUST ME... OR DOES RIETZ SEEM EVEN MORE INTENSE THAN USUAL?
AAAAH! STOP! I'M RUNNING, I'M RUNNING!
THMP THMP
BOOOOM
PICK UP THOSE HEELS!
KNOCK
KNOCK

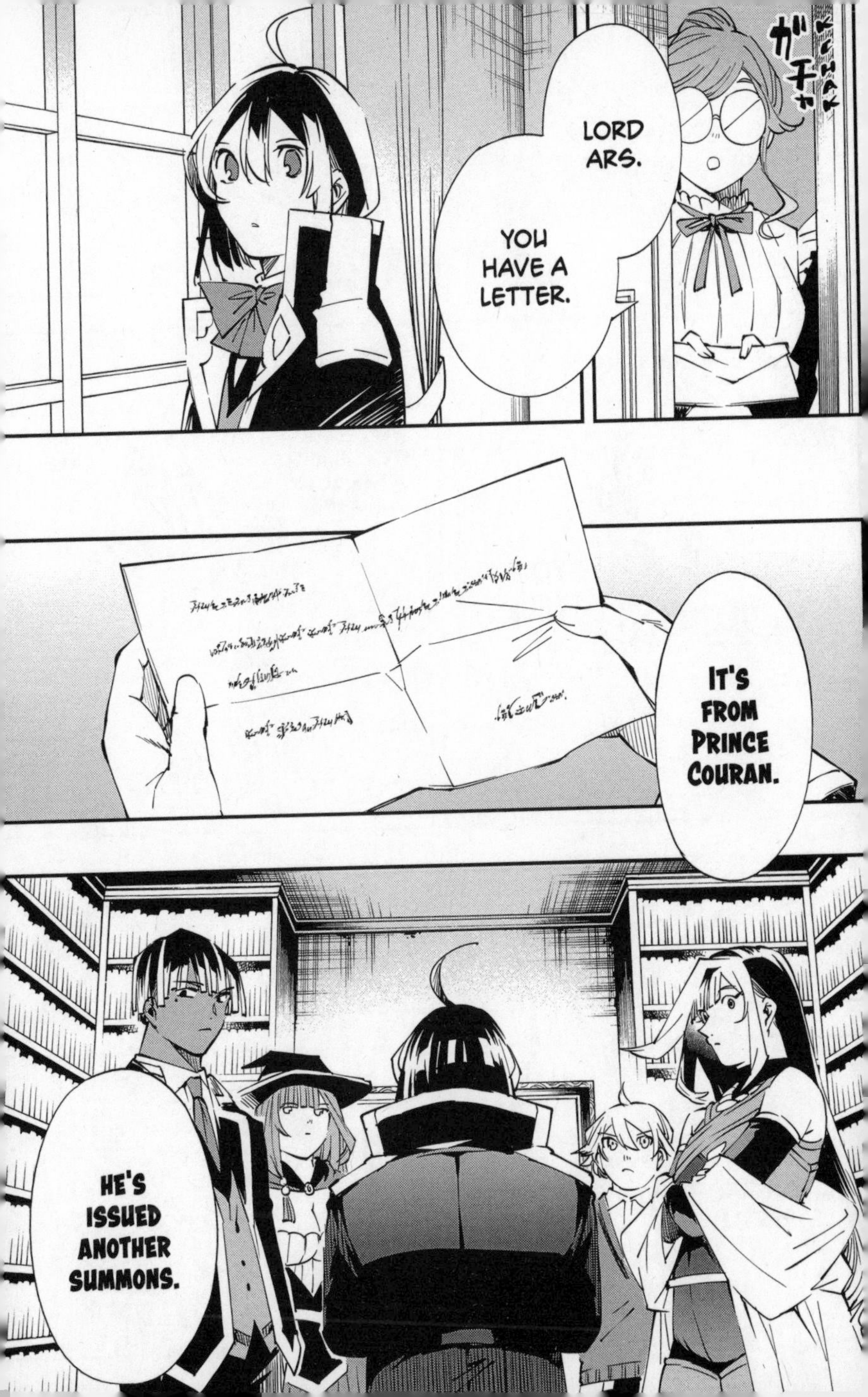
ガチャ KACHAK
LORD ARS.
YOU HAVE A LETTER.
IT'S FROM PRINCE COURAN.
HE'S ISSUED ANOTHER SUMMONS.

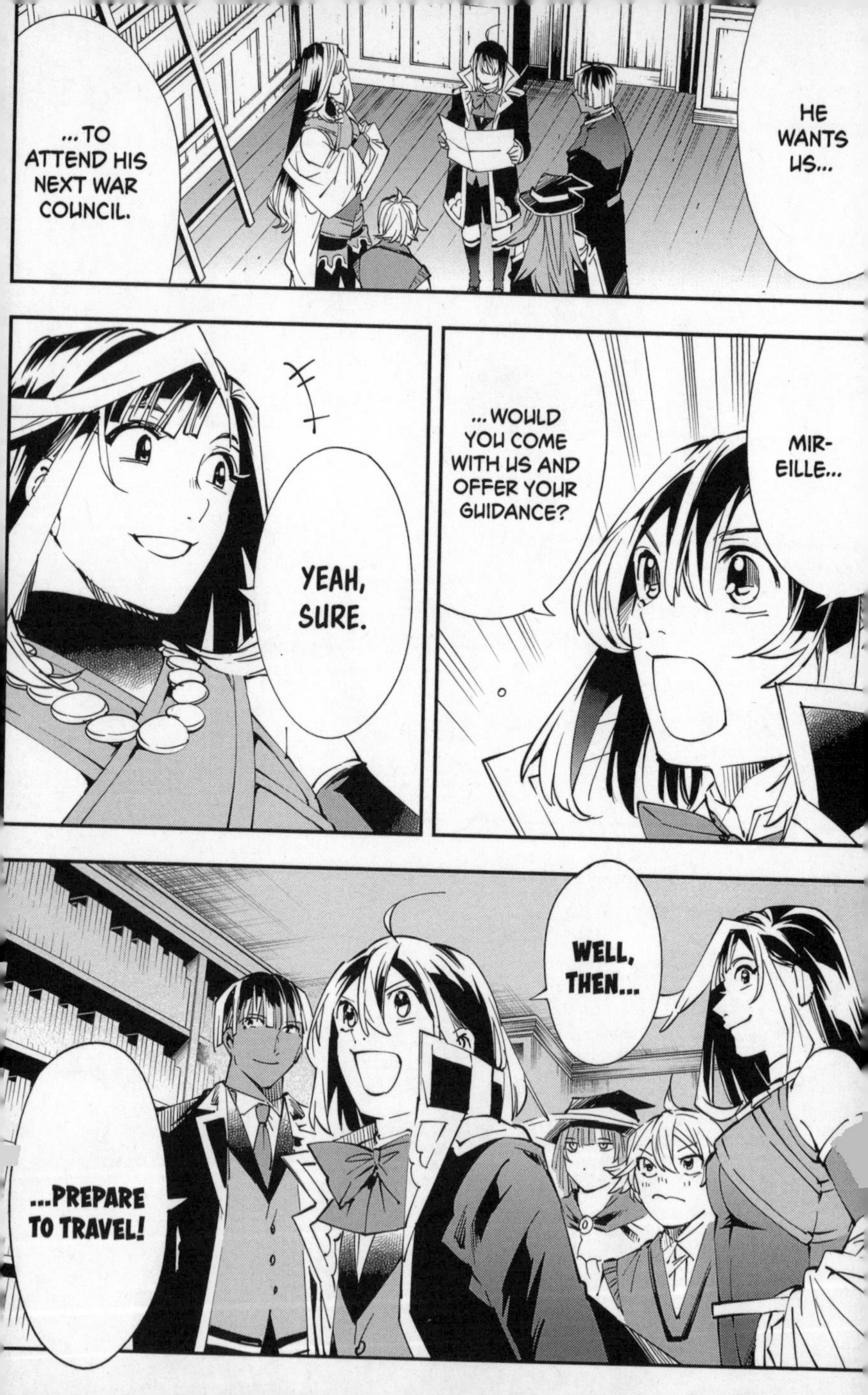
HE WANTS US...
...TO ATTEND HIS NEXT WAR COUNCIL.
MIR-EILLE...
...WOULD YOU COME WITH US AND OFFER YOUR GUIDANCE?
YEAH, SURE.
WELL, THEN...
...PREPARE TO TRAVEL!

As a Reincarnated
ARISTOCRAT,
I'll Use My Appraisal Skill to
Rise in the World

As a Reincarnated
ARISTOCRAT,
I'll Use My Appraisal Skill to
Rise in the World

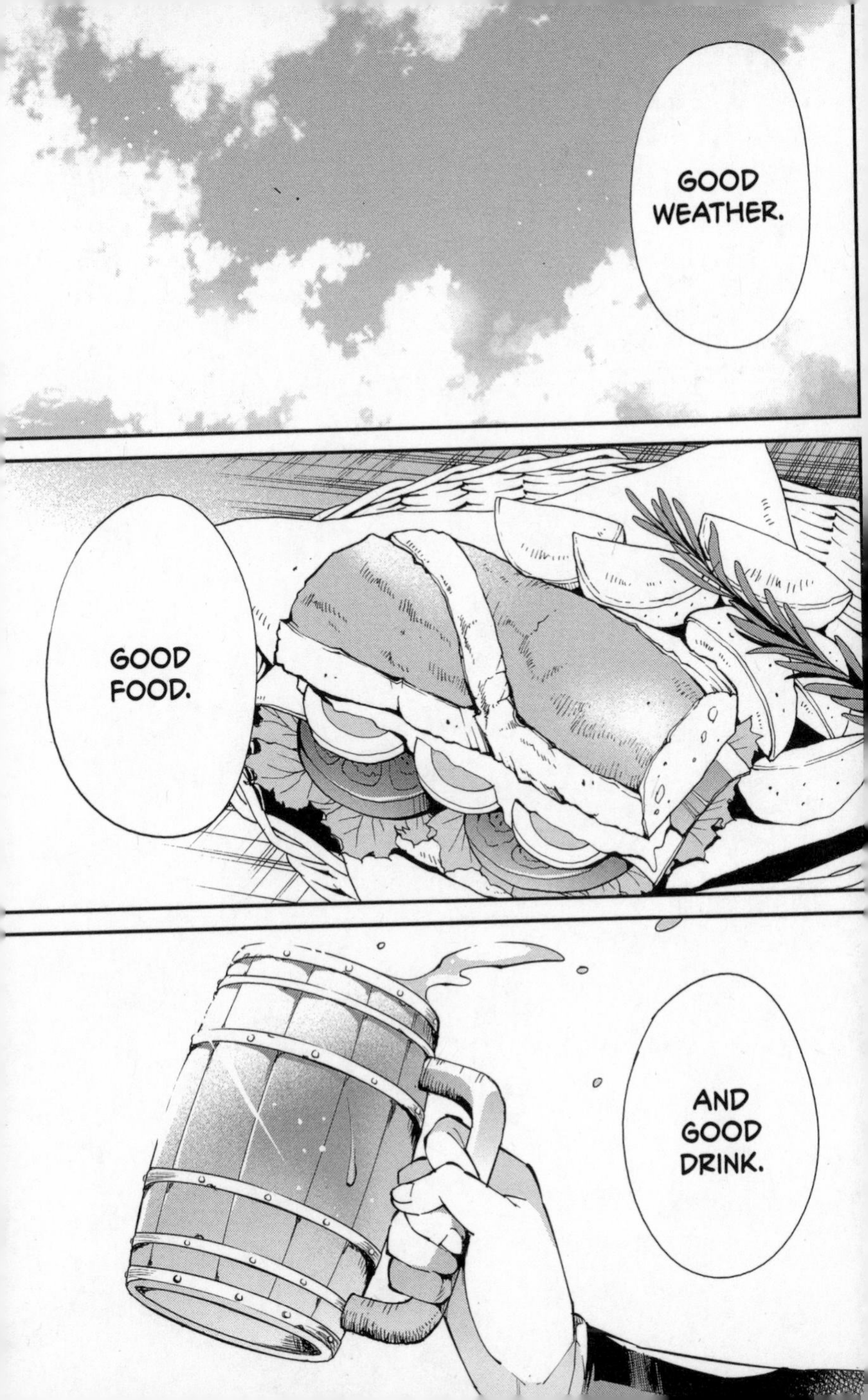
GOOD WEATHER.
GOOD FOOD.
AND GOOD DRINK.

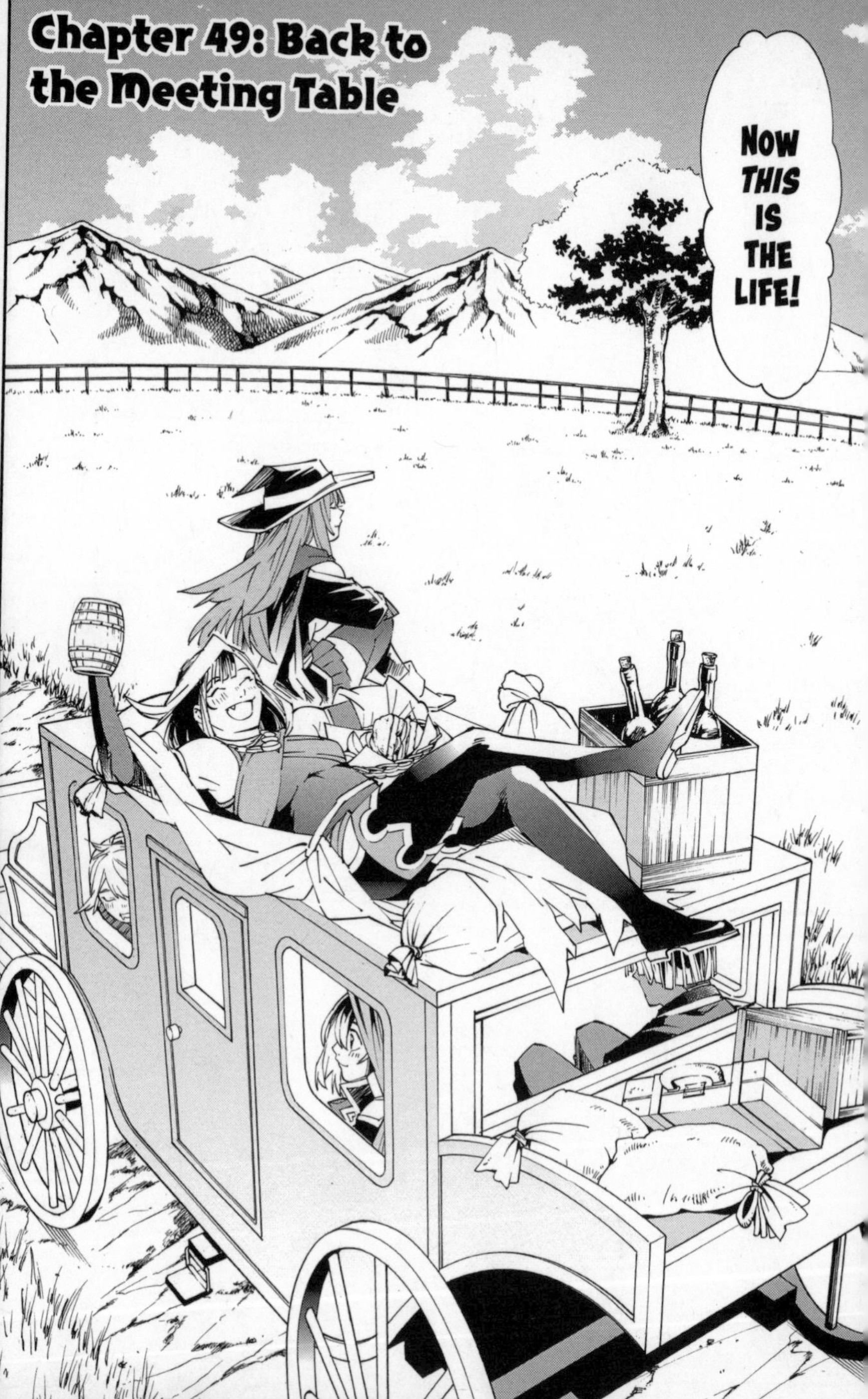
Chapter 49: Back to the Meeting Table
NOW THIS IS THE LIFE!

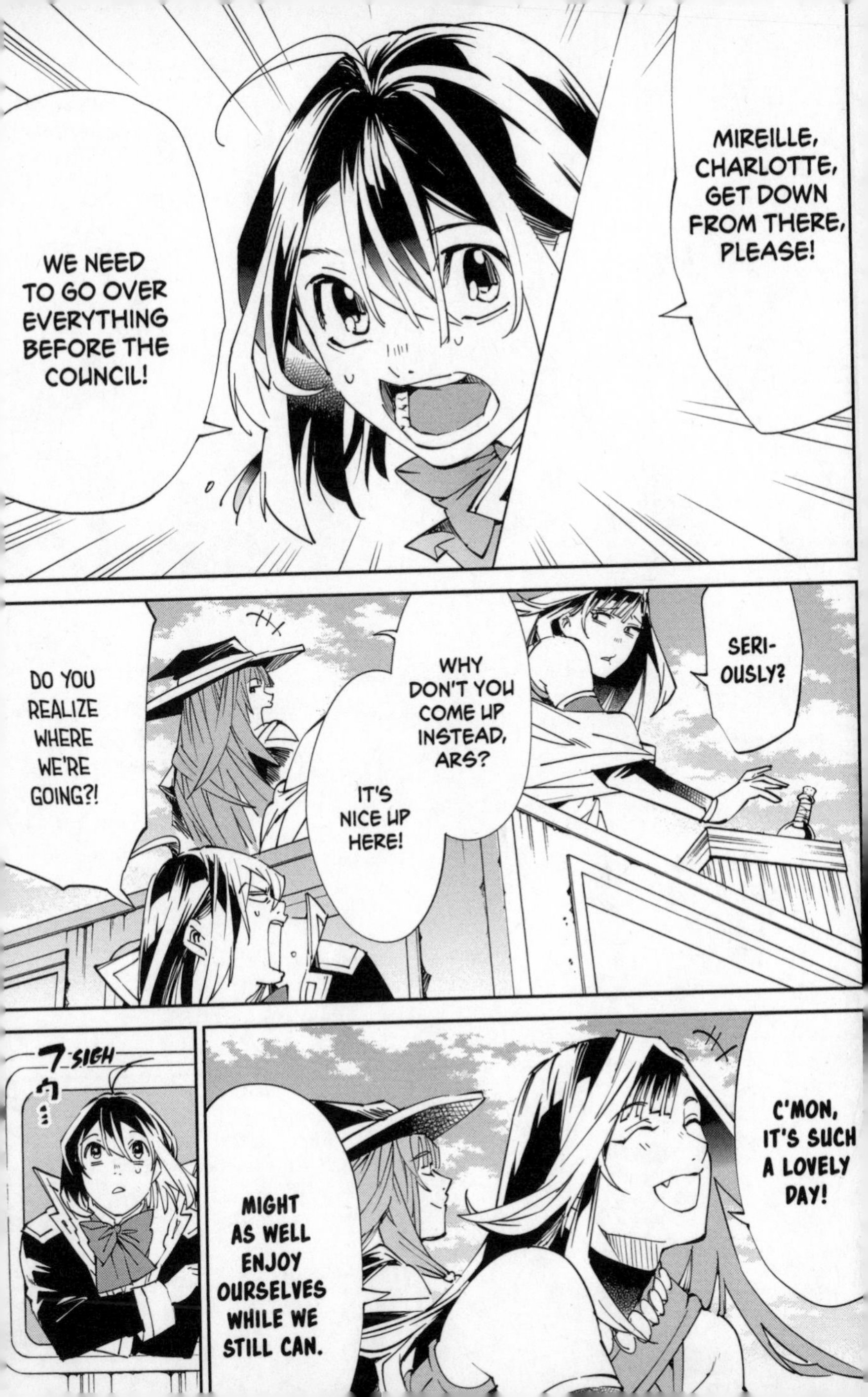
MIREILLE, CHARLOTTE, GET DOWN FROM THERE, PLEASE!
WE NEED TO GO OVER EVERYTHING BEFORE THE COUNCIL!
SERI-OUSLY?
WHY DON'T YOU COME UP INSTEAD, ARS?
IT'S NICE UP HERE!
DO YOU REALIZE WHERE WE'RE GOING?!
C'MON, IT'S SUCH A LOVELY DAY!
MIGHT AS WELL ENJOY OURSELVES WHILE WE STILL CAN.
SIGH

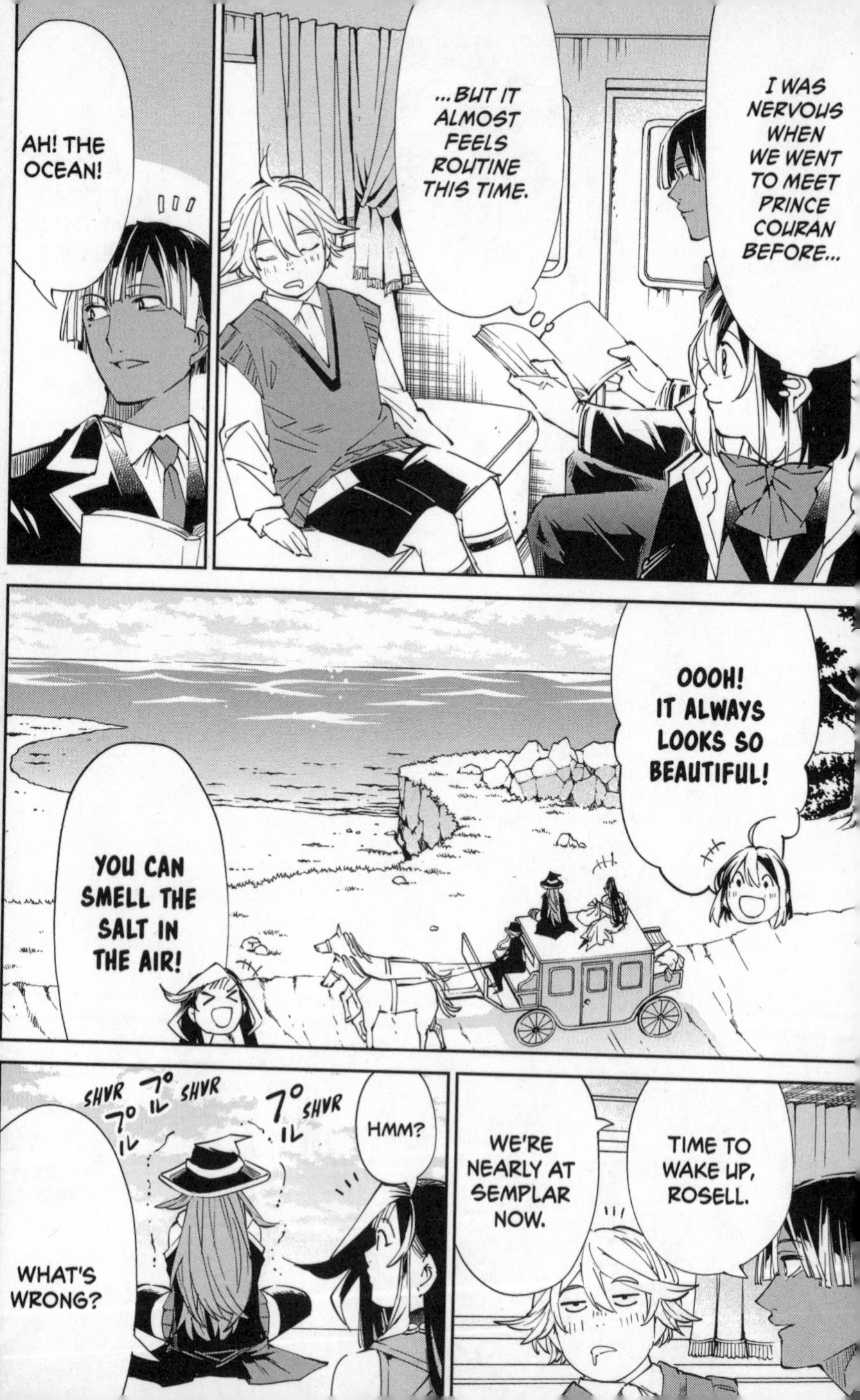
I WAS NERVOUS WHEN WE WENT TO MEET PRINCE COURAN BEFORE...
...BUT IT ALMOST FEELS ROUTINE THIS TIME.
AH! THE OCEAN!
OOOH! IT ALWAYS LOOKS SO BEAUTIFUL!
YOU CAN SMELL THE SALT IN THE AIR!
TIME TO WAKE UP, ROSELL.
WE'RE NEARLY AT SEMPLAR NOW.
HMM?
SHVR
プル
SHVR
プル
SHVR
プル
WHAT'S WRONG?

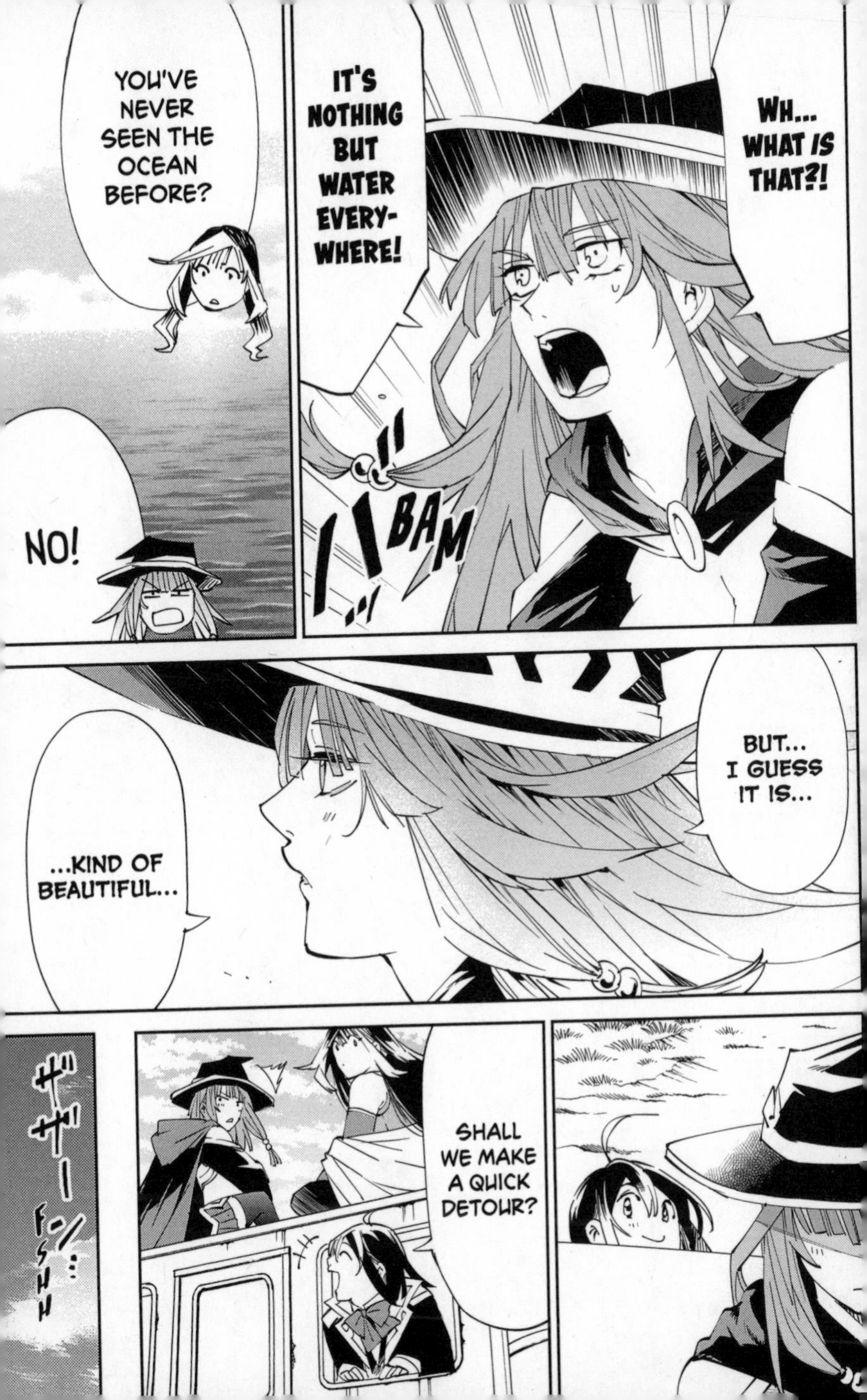
WH... WHAT IS THAT?!
IT'S NOTHING BUT WATER EVERYWHERE!
!!
BAM
YOU'VE NEVER SEEN THE OCEAN BEFORE?
NO!
BUT... I GUESS IT IS...
...KIND OF BEAUTIFUL...
SHALL WE MAKE A QUICK DETOUR?
FSHH

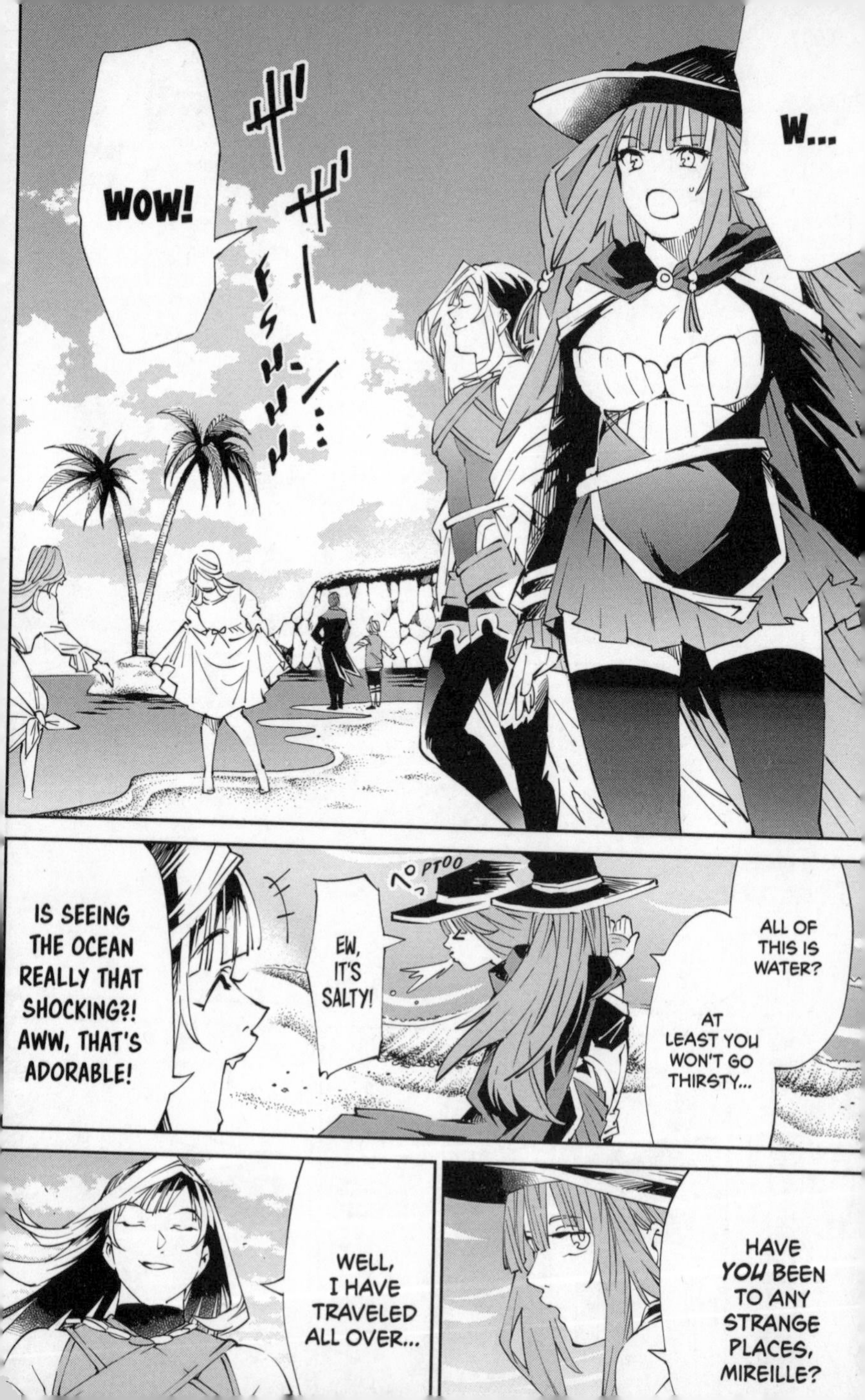
W...
FSHHHH
WOW!
ALL OF THIS IS WATER?
AT LEAST YOU WON'T GO THIRSTY...
PTOO
EW, IT'S SALTY!
IS SEEING THE OCEAN REALLY THAT SHOCKING?! AWW, THAT'S ADORABLE!
HAVE *YOU* BEEN TO ANY STRANGE PLACES, MIREILLE?
WELL, I HAVE TRAVELED ALL OVER...

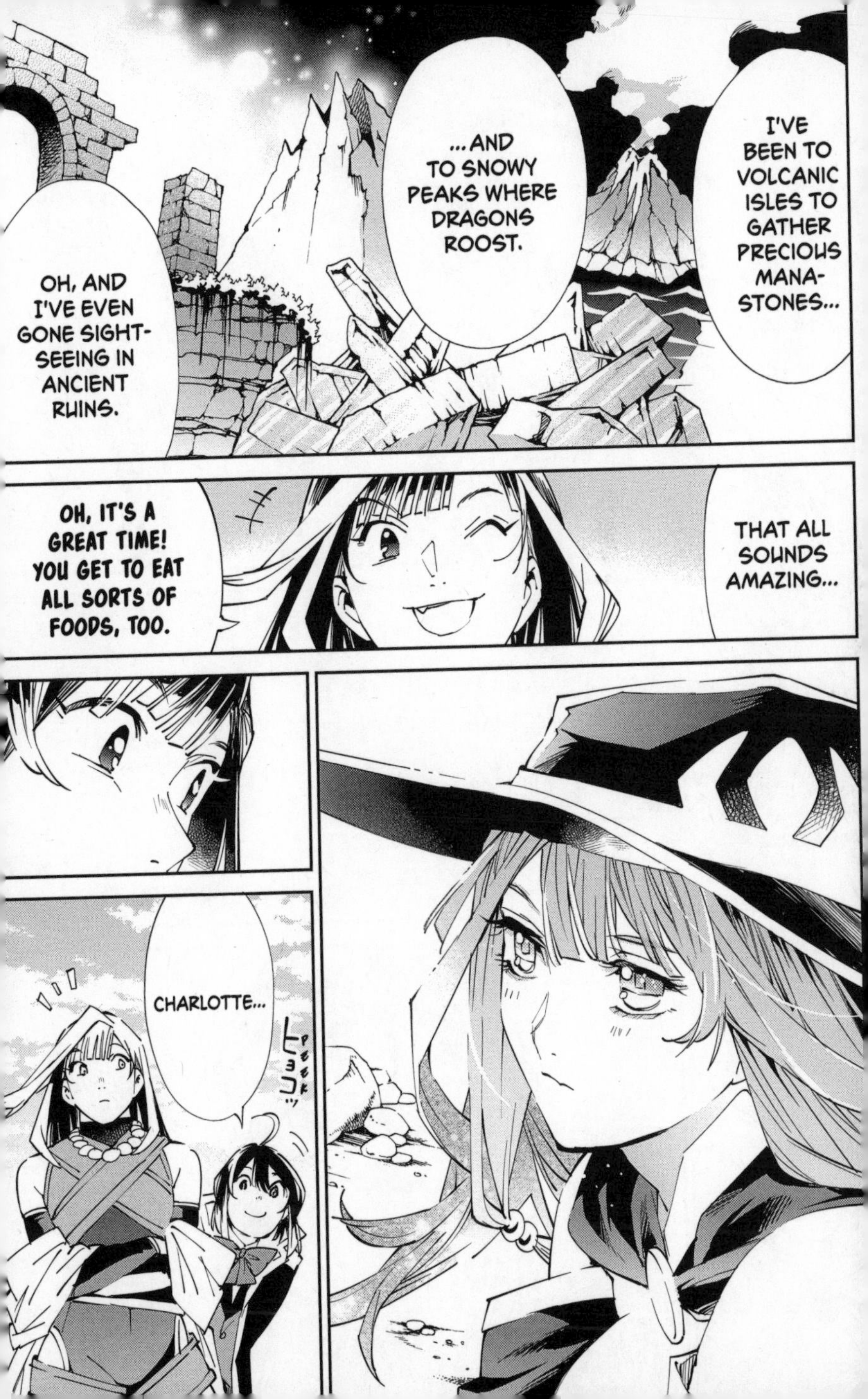
I'VE BEEN TO VOLCANIC ISLES TO GATHER PRECIOUS MANA-STONES...
...AND TO SNOWY PEAKS WHERE DRAGONS ROOST.
OH, AND I'VE EVEN GONE SIGHT-SEEING IN ANCIENT RUINS.
THAT ALL SOUNDS AMAZING...
OH, IT'S A GREAT TIME! YOU GET TO EAT ALL SORTS OF FOODS, TOO.
CHARLOTTE...
PEEK

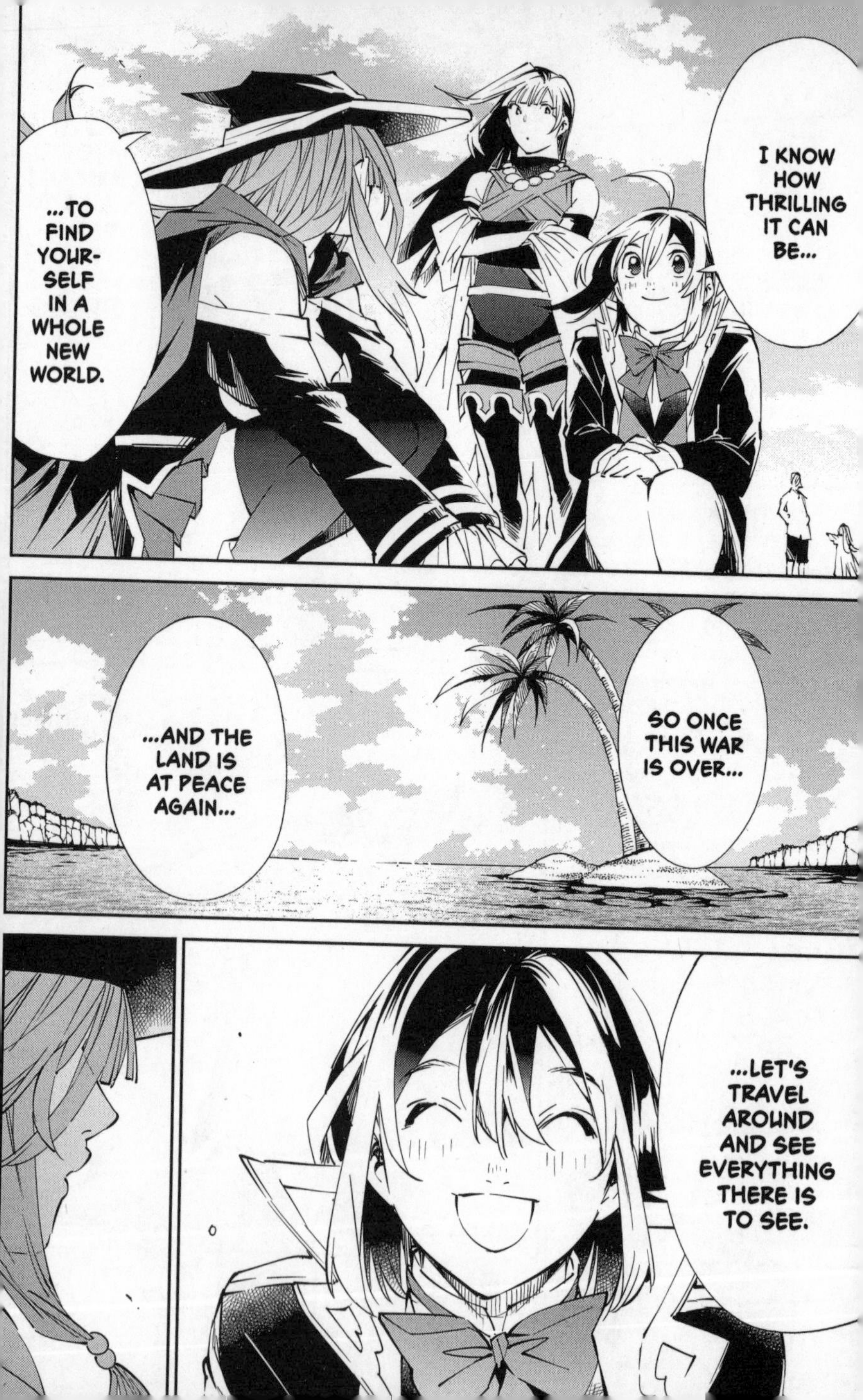
I KNOW HOW THRILLING IT CAN BE...
...TO FIND YOURSELF IN A WHOLE NEW WORLD.
SO ONCE THIS WAR IS OVER...
...AND THE LAND IS AT PEACE AGAIN...
...LET'S TRAVEL AROUND AND SEE EVERYTHING THERE IS TO SEE.

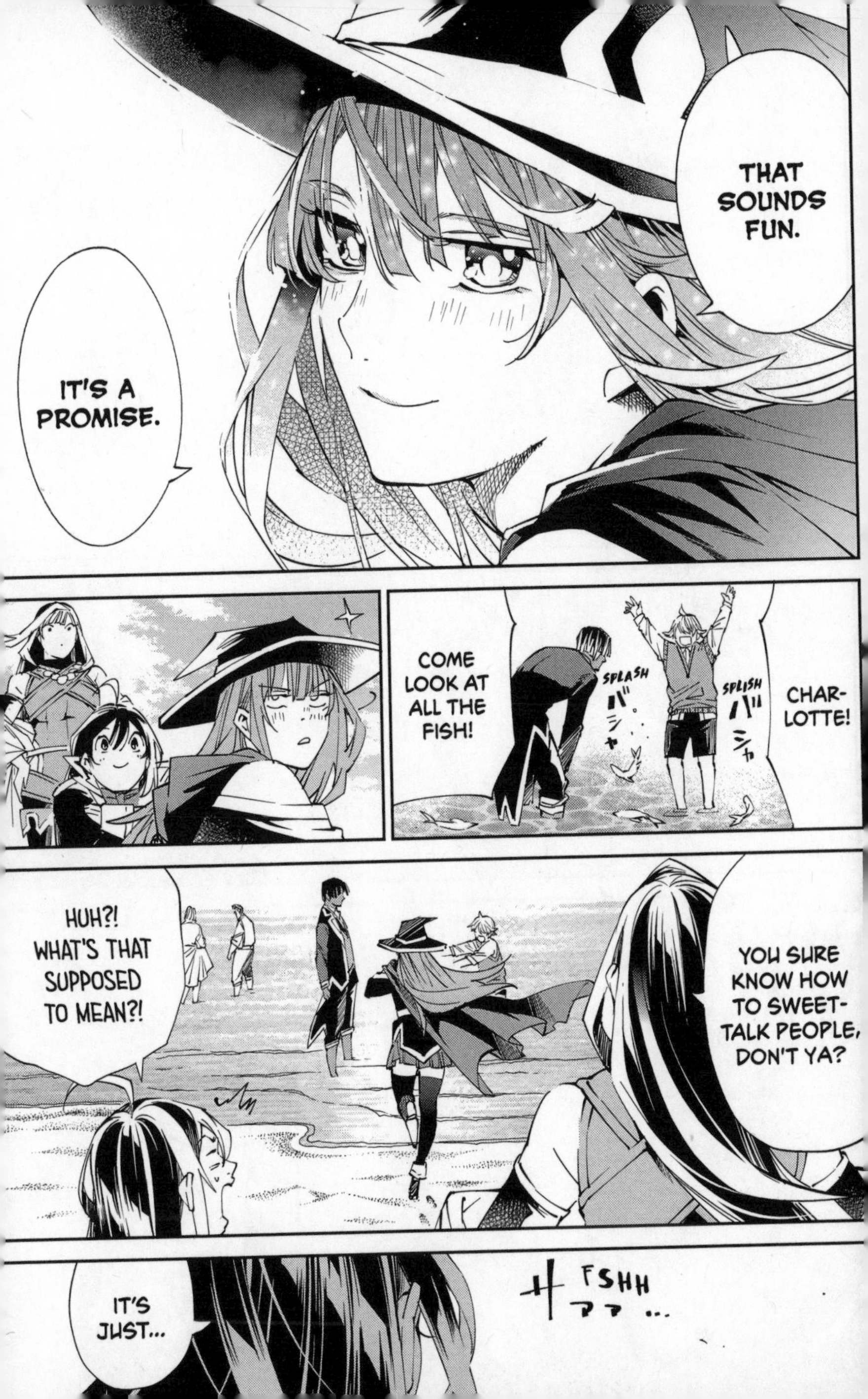
THAT SOUNDS FUN.
IT'S A PROMISE.
CHAR-LOTTE!
SPLISH
バシャ
SPLASH
バシャ
COME LOOK AT ALL THE FISH!
YOU SURE KNOW HOW TO SWEET-TALK PEOPLE, DON'T YA?
HUH?! WHAT'S THAT SUPPOSED TO MEAN?!
FSHH
IT'S JUST...

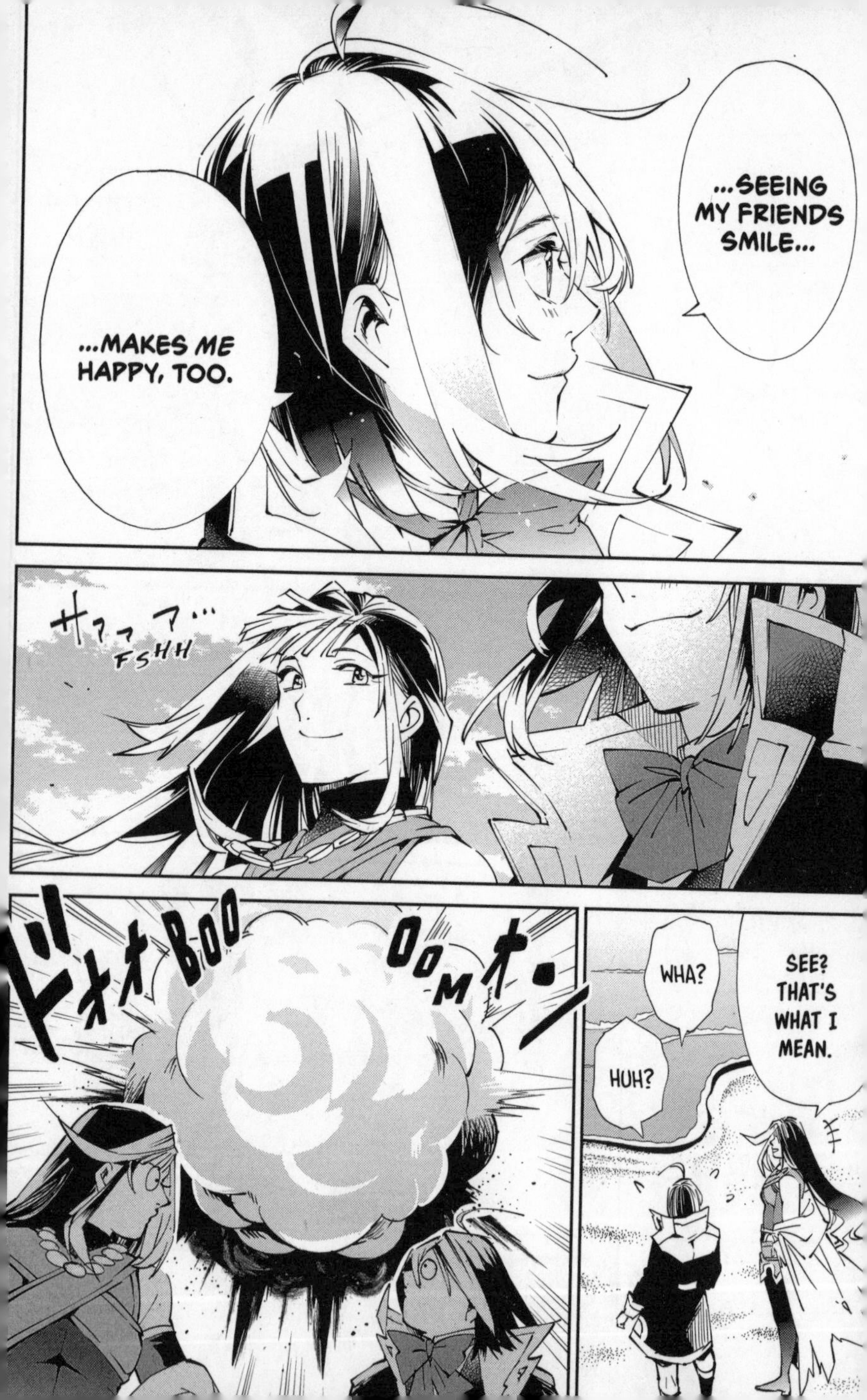
...SEEING MY FRIENDS SMILE...
...MAKES ME HAPPY, TOO.
サァァァ…
FSHH
SEE? THAT'S WHAT I MEAN.
WHA?
HUH?
ドオオオ・
BOOOOM

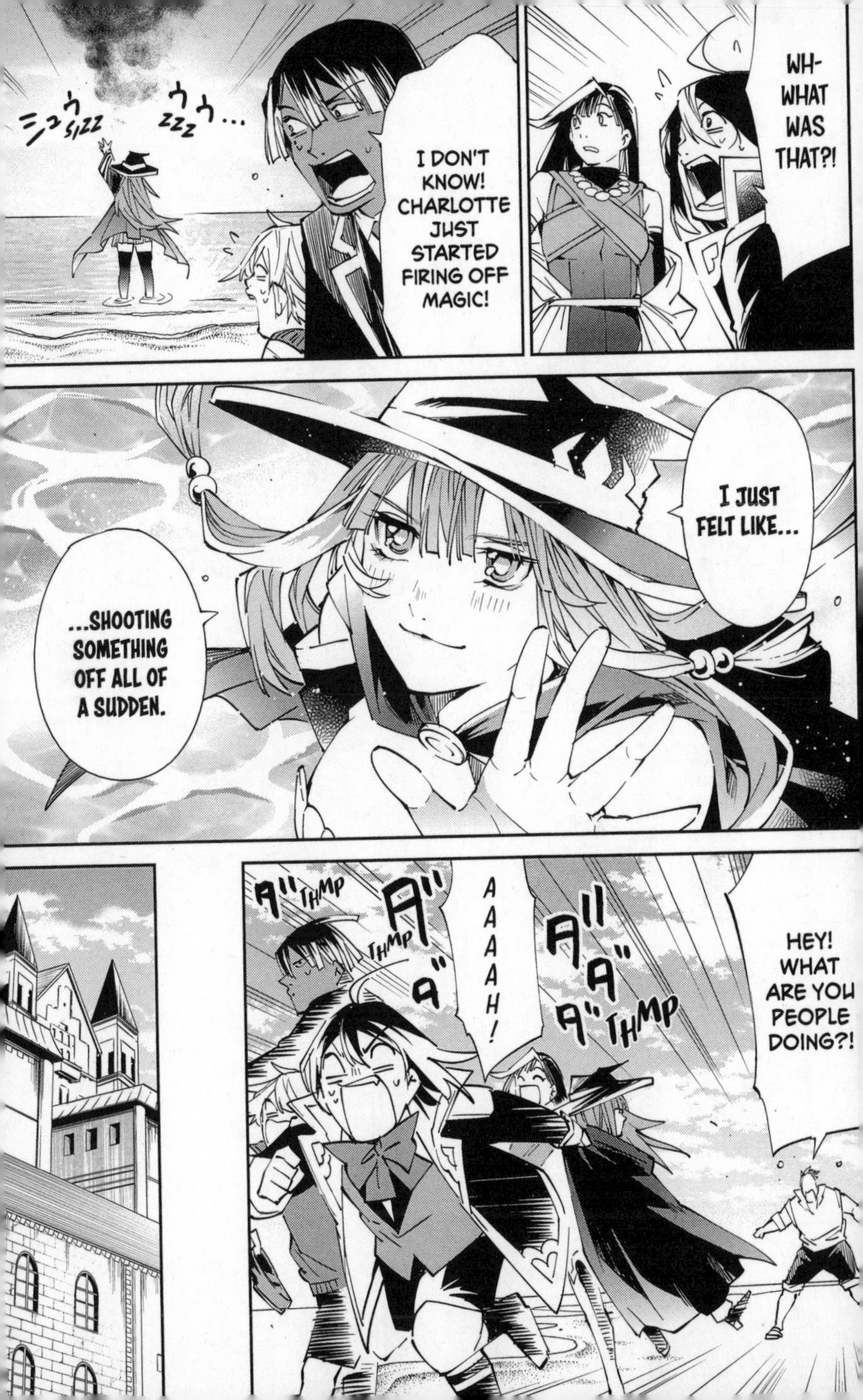
WH- WHAT WAS THAT?!
I DON'T KNOW! CHARLOTTE JUST STARTED FIRING OFF MAGIC!
SIZZ
ZZZ...
I JUST FELT LIKE...
...SHOOTING SOMETHING OFF ALL OF A SUDDEN.
HEY! WHAT ARE YOU PEOPLE DOING?!
THMP
AAAAAH!
THMP
THMP

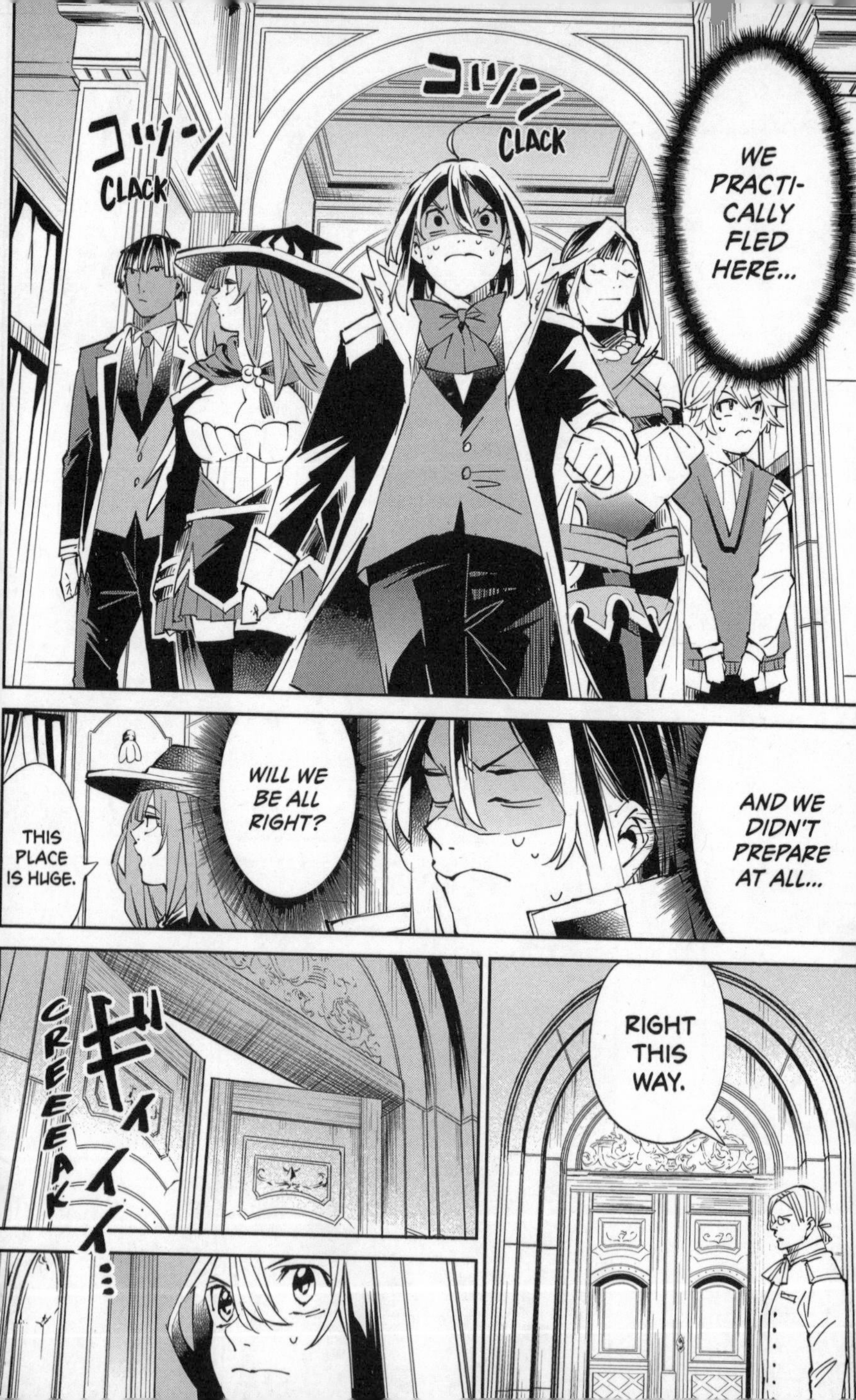

WE PRACTI-CALLY FLED HERE...
CLACK
CLACK
AND WE DIDN'T PREPARE AT ALL...
WILL WE BE ALL RIGHT?
THIS PLACE IS HUGE.
RIGHT THIS WAY.
CREEEAK

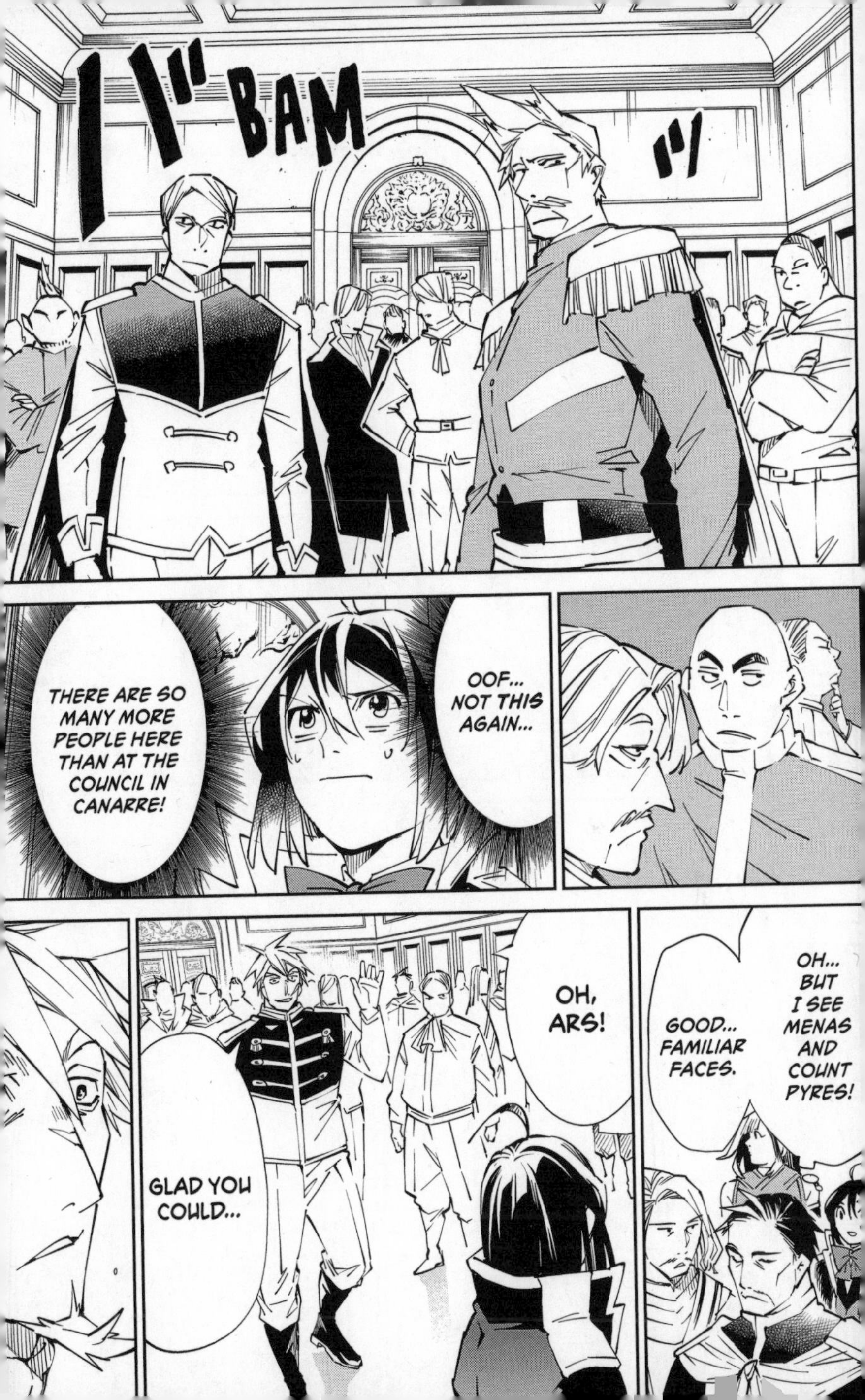
BAM
OOF... NOT THIS AGAIN...
THERE ARE SO MANY MORE PEOPLE HERE THAN AT THE COUNCIL IN CANARRE!
OH... BUT I SEE MENAS AND COUNT PYRES!
GOOD... FAMILIAR FACES.
OH, ARS!
GLAD YOU COULD...

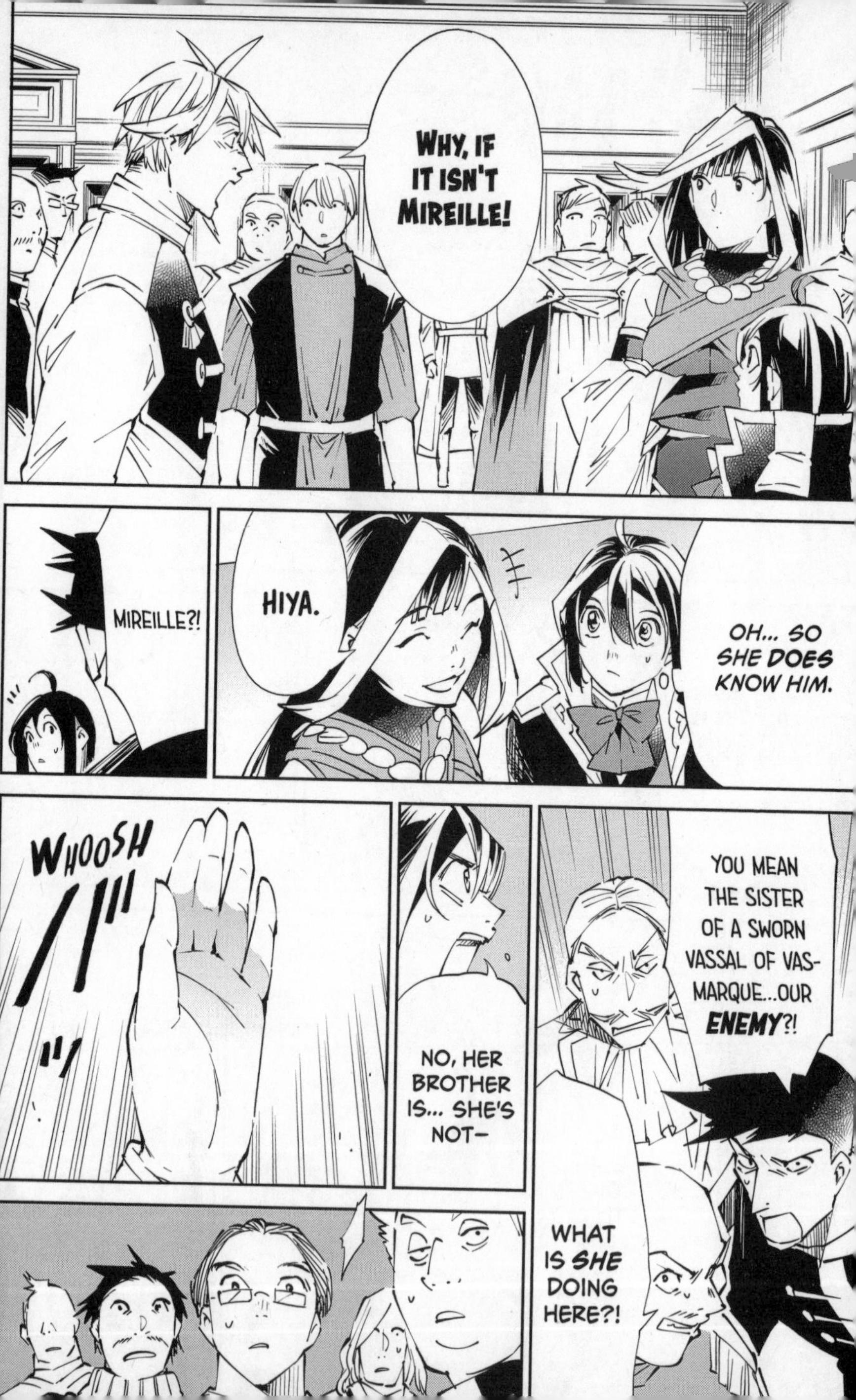
WHY, IF IT ISN'T MIREILLE!
HIYA.
OH... SO SHE DOES KNOW HIM.
MIREILLE?!
YOU MEAN THE SISTER OF A SWORN VASSAL OF VAS-MARQUE...OUR ENEMY?!
WHAT IS SHE DOING HERE?!
NO, HER BROTHER IS... SHE'S NOT–
WHOOSH

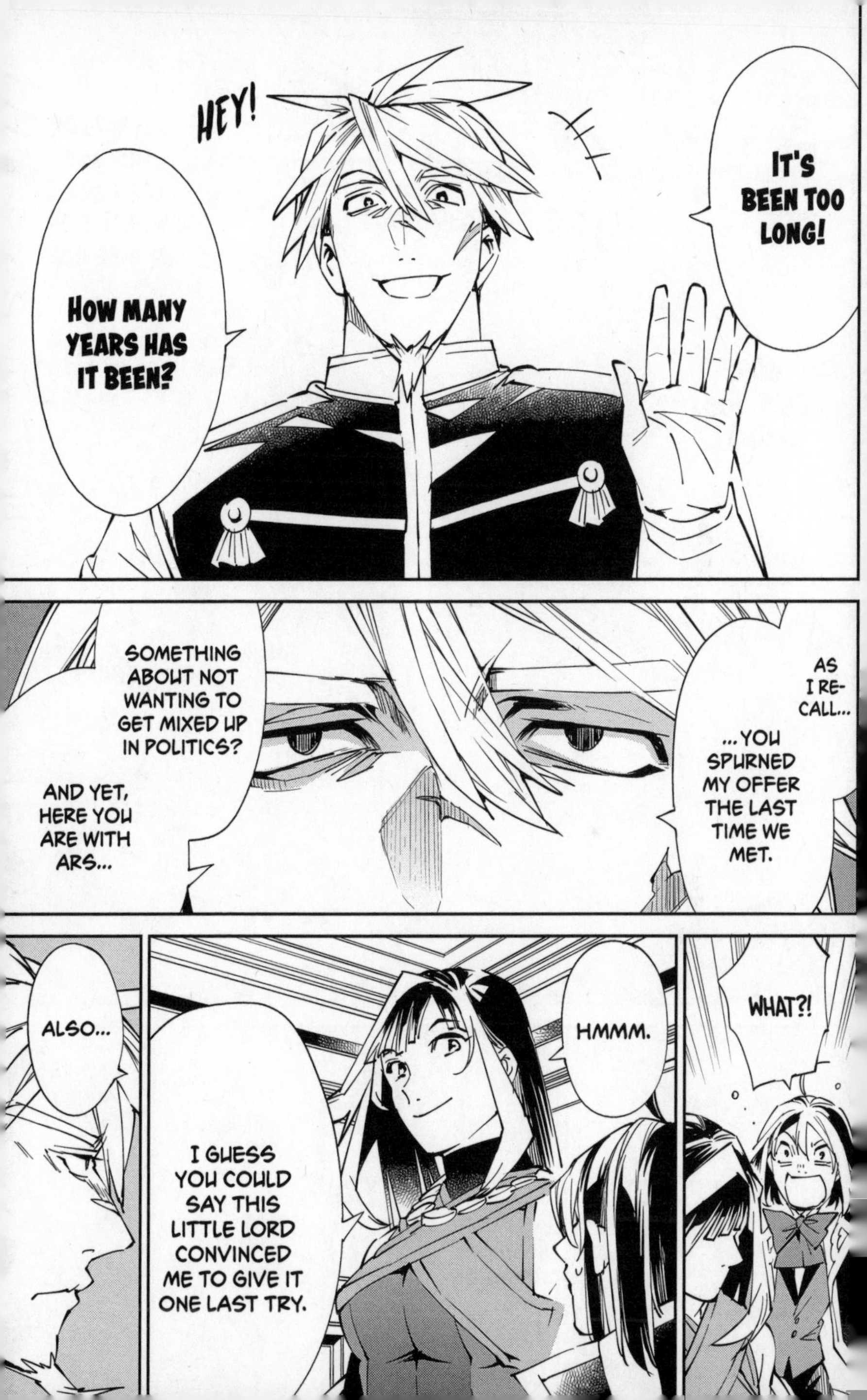
IT'S BEEN TOO LONG!
HEY!
HOW MANY YEARS HAS IT BEEN?
AS I RE-CALL...
...YOU SPURNED MY OFFER THE LAST TIME WE MET.
SOMETHING ABOUT NOT WANTING TO GET MIXED UP IN POLITICS?
AND YET, HERE YOU ARE WITH ARS...
WHAT?!
HMMM.
I GUESS YOU COULD SAY THIS LITTLE LORD CONVINCED ME TO GIVE IT ONE LAST TRY.
ALSO...

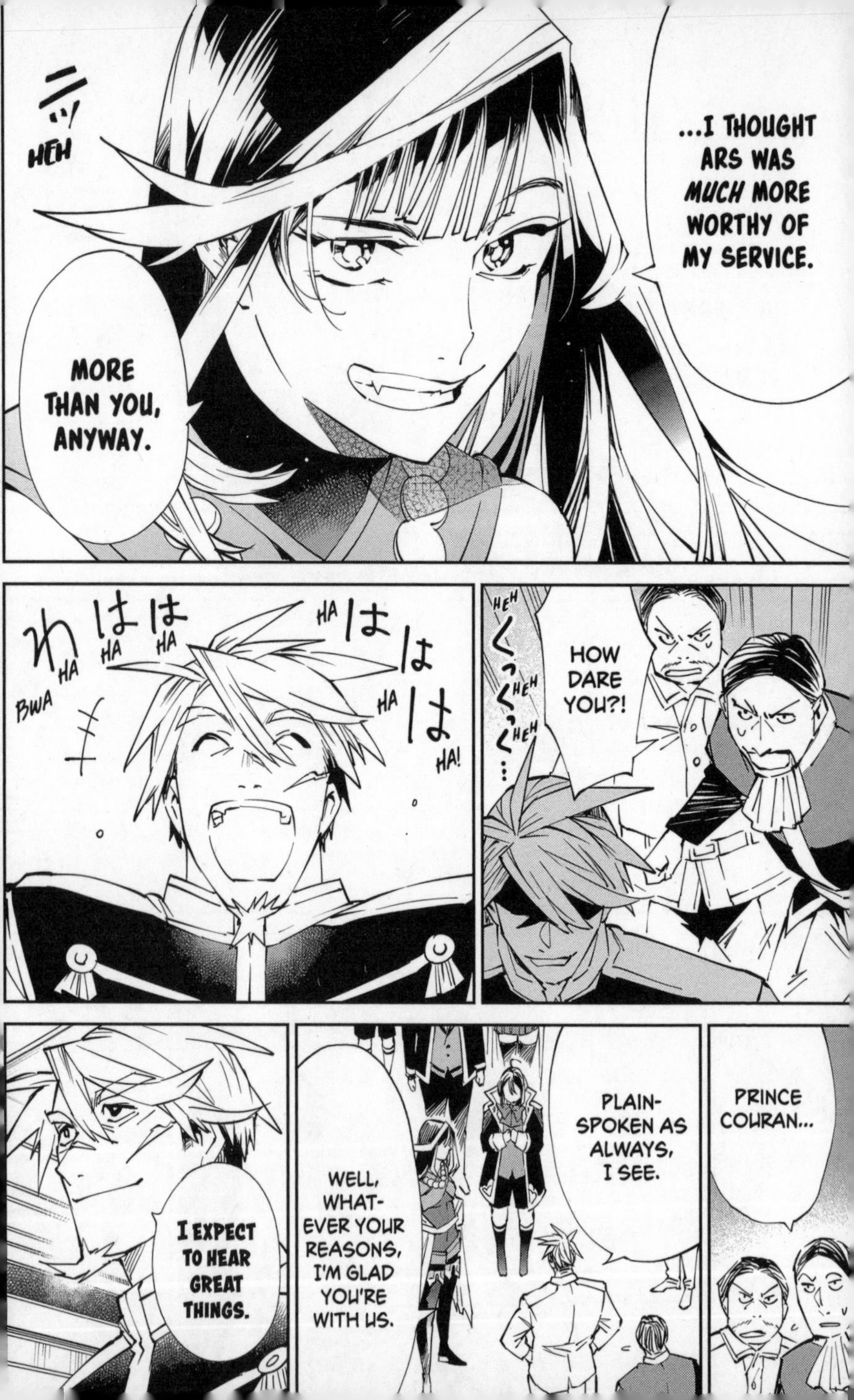
...I THOUGHT ARS WAS *MUCH* MORE WORTHY OF MY SERVICE.
ニッ HEH
MORE THAN YOU, ANYWAY.
HOW DARE YOU?!
くっくっく... HEH HEH HEH
わははははは BWA HA HA HA HA HA HA!
PRINCE COURAN...
PLAIN-SPOKEN AS ALWAYS, I SEE.
WELL, WHAT-EVER YOUR REASONS, I'M GLAD YOU'RE WITH US.
I EXPECT TO HEAR GREAT THINGS.

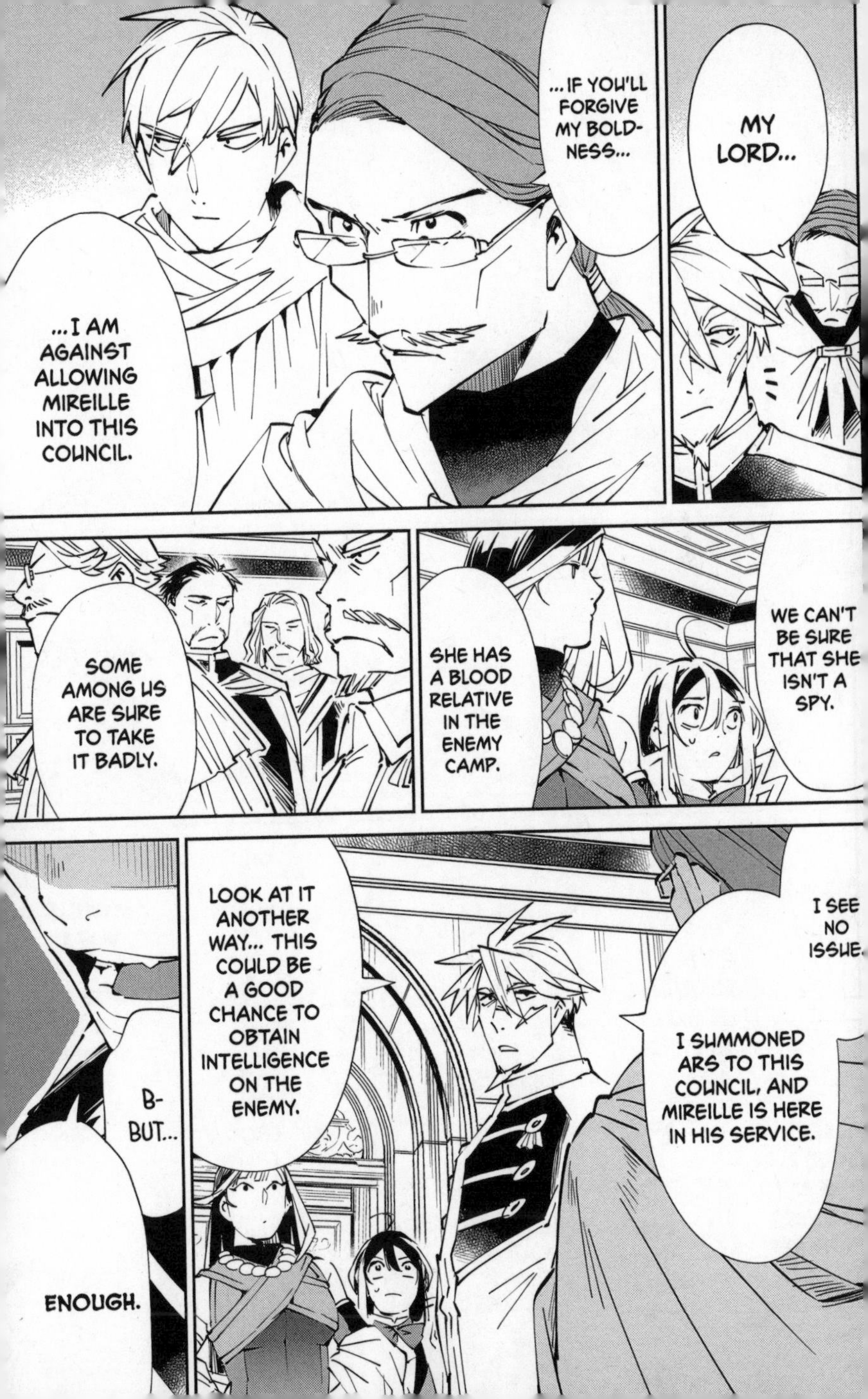
MY LORD...
...IF YOU'LL FORGIVE MY BOLDNESS...
...I AM AGAINST ALLOWING MIREILLE INTO THIS COUNCIL.
WE CAN'T BE SURE THAT SHE ISN'T A SPY.
SHE HAS A BLOOD RELATIVE IN THE ENEMY CAMP.
SOME AMONG US ARE SURE TO TAKE IT BADLY.
I SEE NO ISSUE.
I SUMMONED ARS TO THIS COUNCIL, AND MIREILLE IS HERE IN HIS SERVICE.
LOOK AT IT ANOTHER WAY... THIS COULD BE A GOOD CHANCE TO OBTAIN INTELLIGENCE ON THE ENEMY.
B-BUT...
ENOUGH.

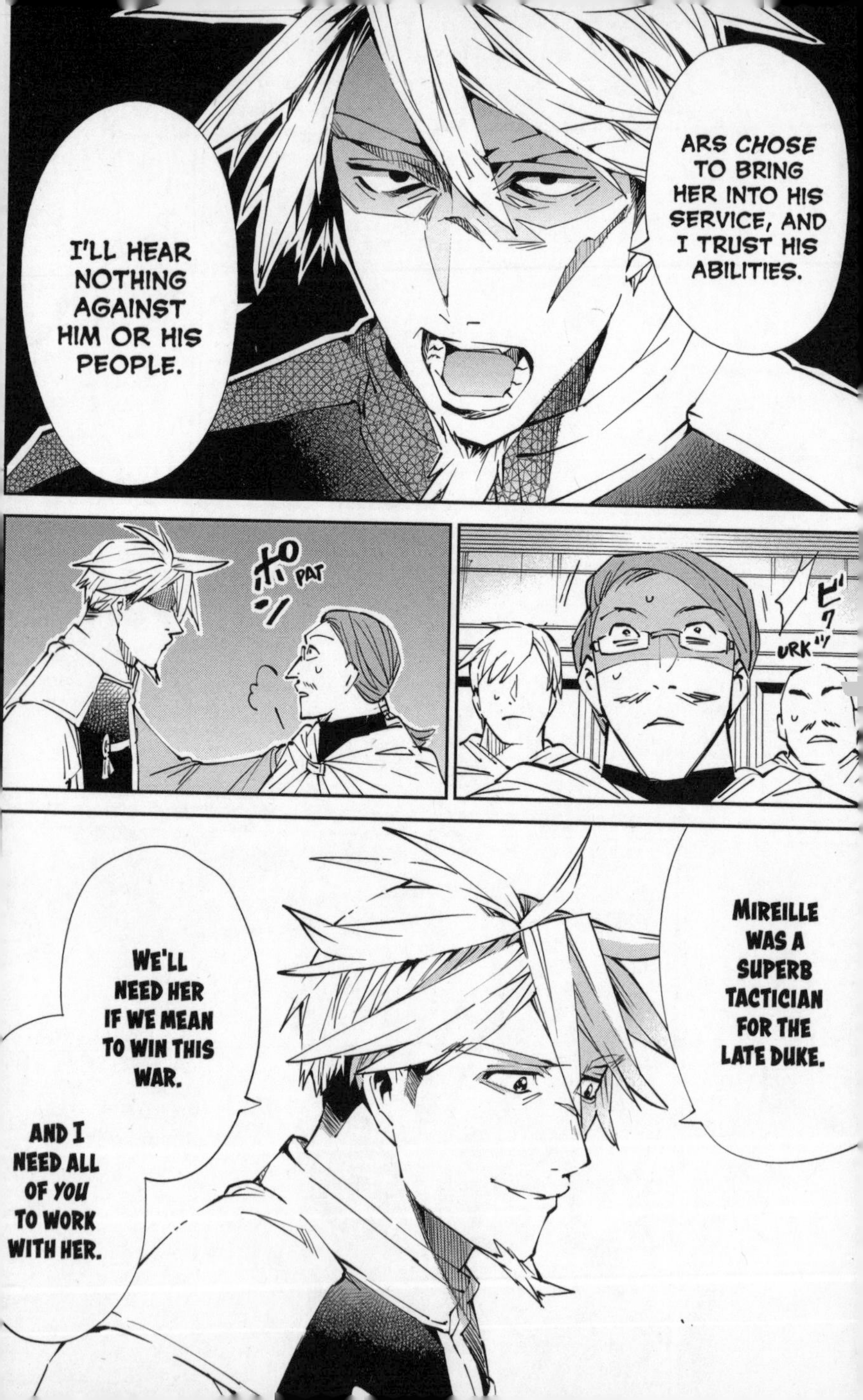
ARS CHOSE TO BRING HER INTO HIS SERVICE, AND I TRUST HIS ABILITIES.
I'LL HEAR NOTHING AGAINST HIM OR HIS PEOPLE.
URK
PAT
MIREILLE WAS A SUPERB TACTICIAN FOR THE LATE DUKE.
WE'LL NEED HER IF WE MEAN TO WIN THIS WAR.
AND I NEED ALL OF YOU TO WORK WITH HER.

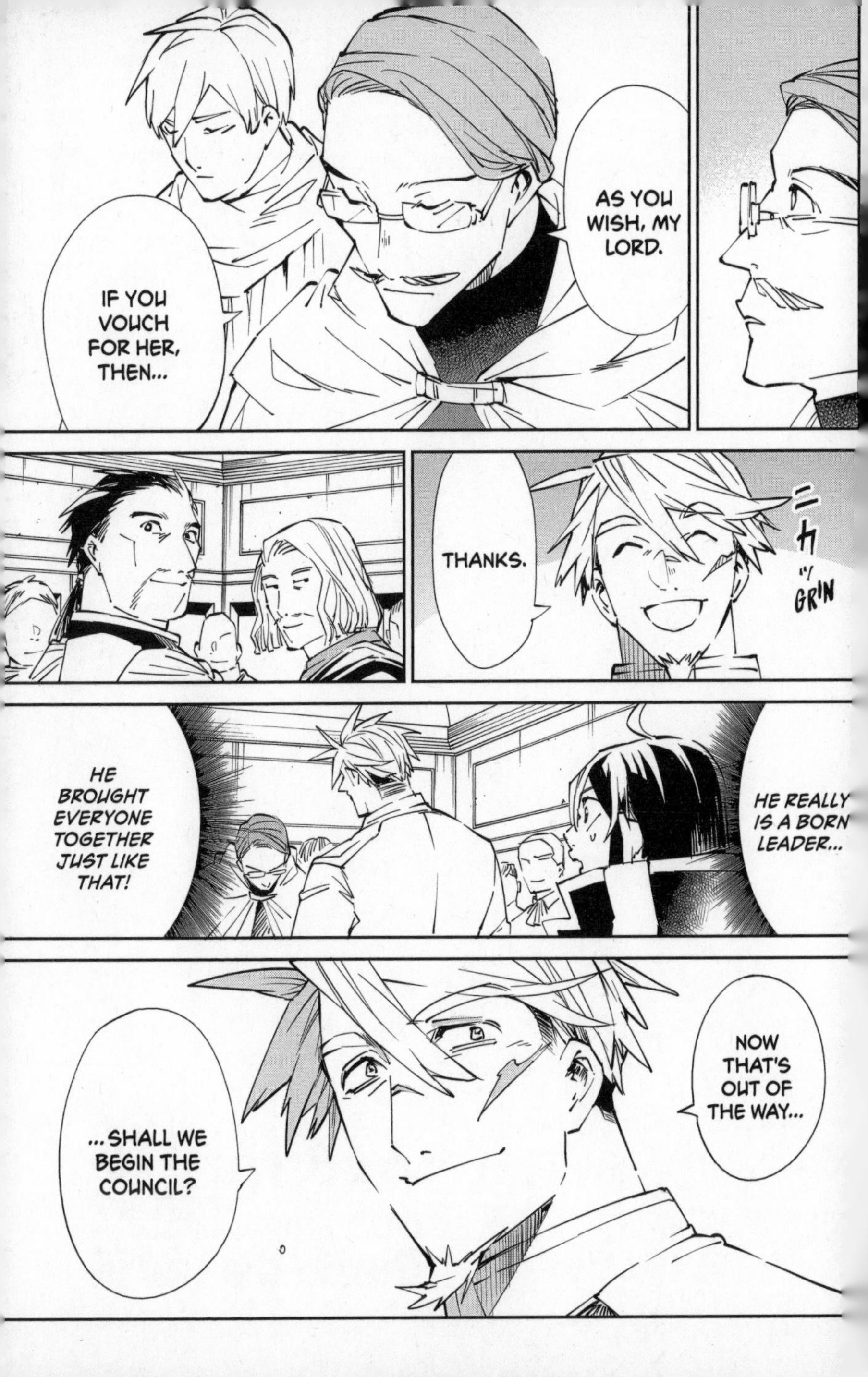
AS YOU WISH, MY LORD.
IF YOU VOUCH FOR HER, THEN...
GRIN
THANKS.
HE REALLY IS A BORN LEADER...
HE BROUGHT EVERYONE TOGETHER JUST LIKE THAT!
NOW THAT'S OUT OF THE WAY...
...SHALL WE BEGIN THE COUNCIL?

As a Reincarnated
ARISTOCRAT,
I'll Use My Appraisal Skill to
Rise in the World

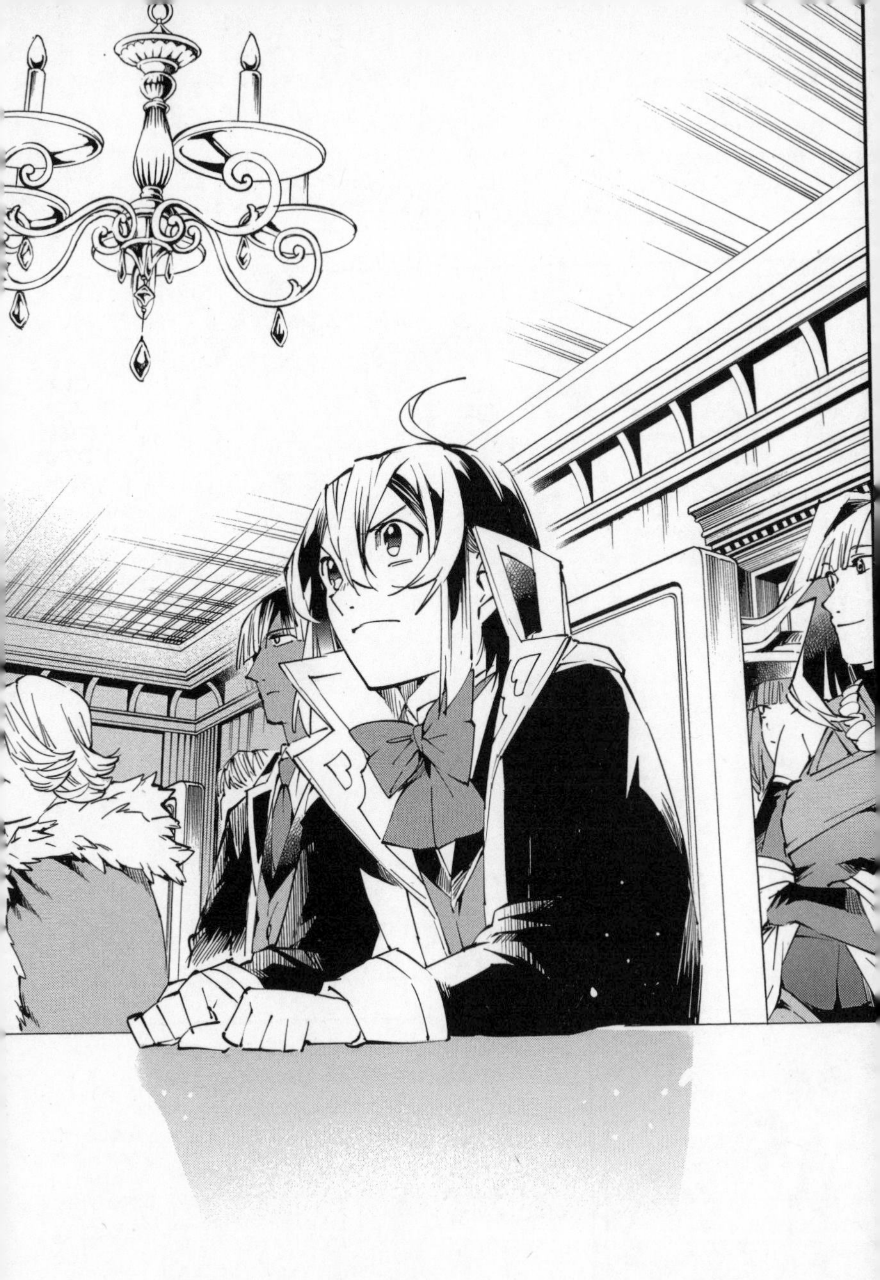

Chapter 50: Intellect

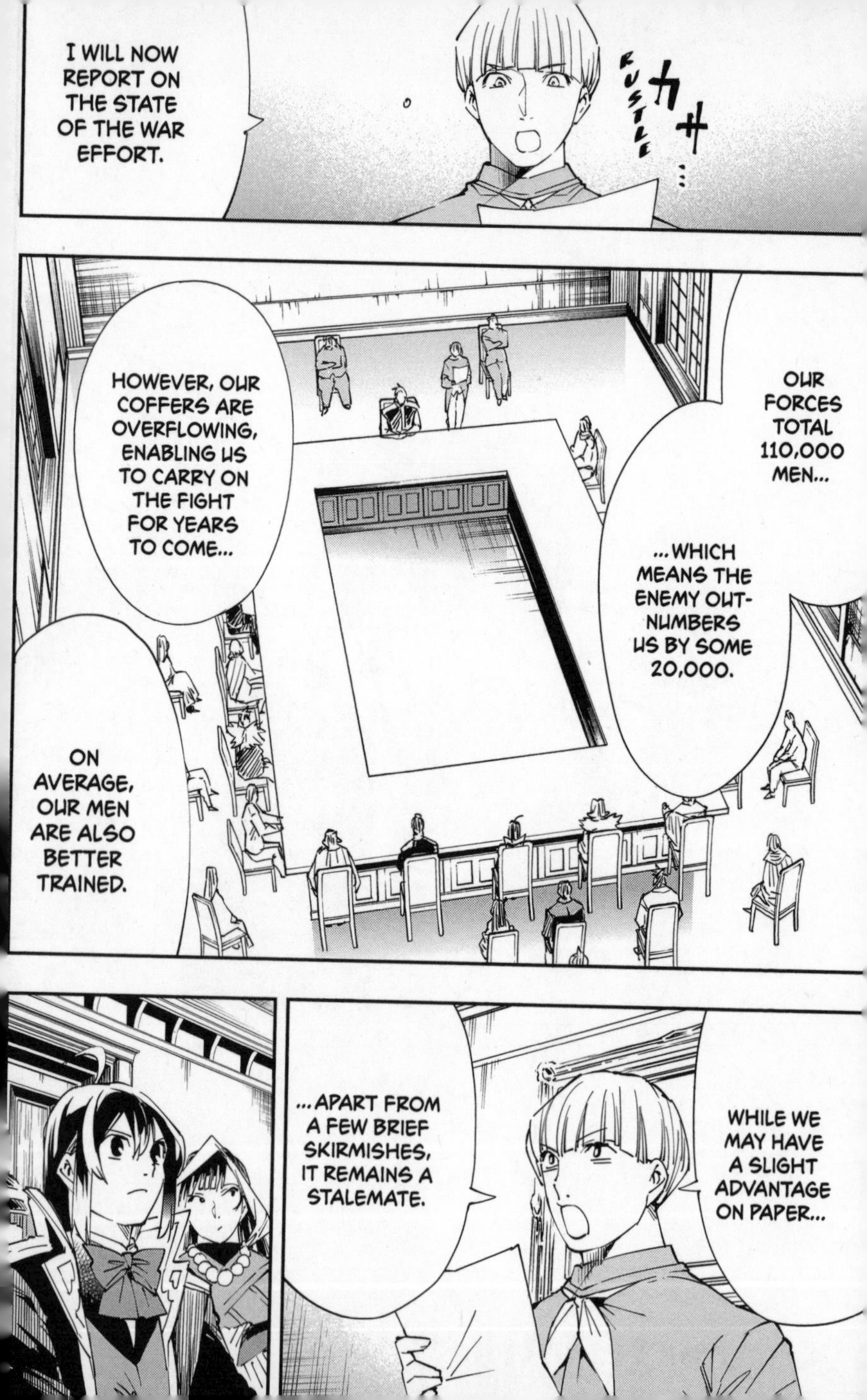
RUSTLE
I WILL NOW REPORT ON THE STATE OF THE WAR EFFORT.
OUR FORCES TOTAL 110,000 MEN...
...WHICH MEANS THE ENEMY OUT-NUMBERS US BY SOME 20,000.
HOWEVER, OUR COFFERS ARE OVERFLOWING, ENABLING US TO CARRY ON THE FIGHT FOR YEARS TO COME...
ON AVERAGE, OUR MEN ARE ALSO BETTER TRAINED.
WHILE WE MAY HAVE A SLIGHT ADVANTAGE ON PAPER...
...APART FROM A FEW BRIEF SKIRMISHES, IT REMAINS A STALEMATE.

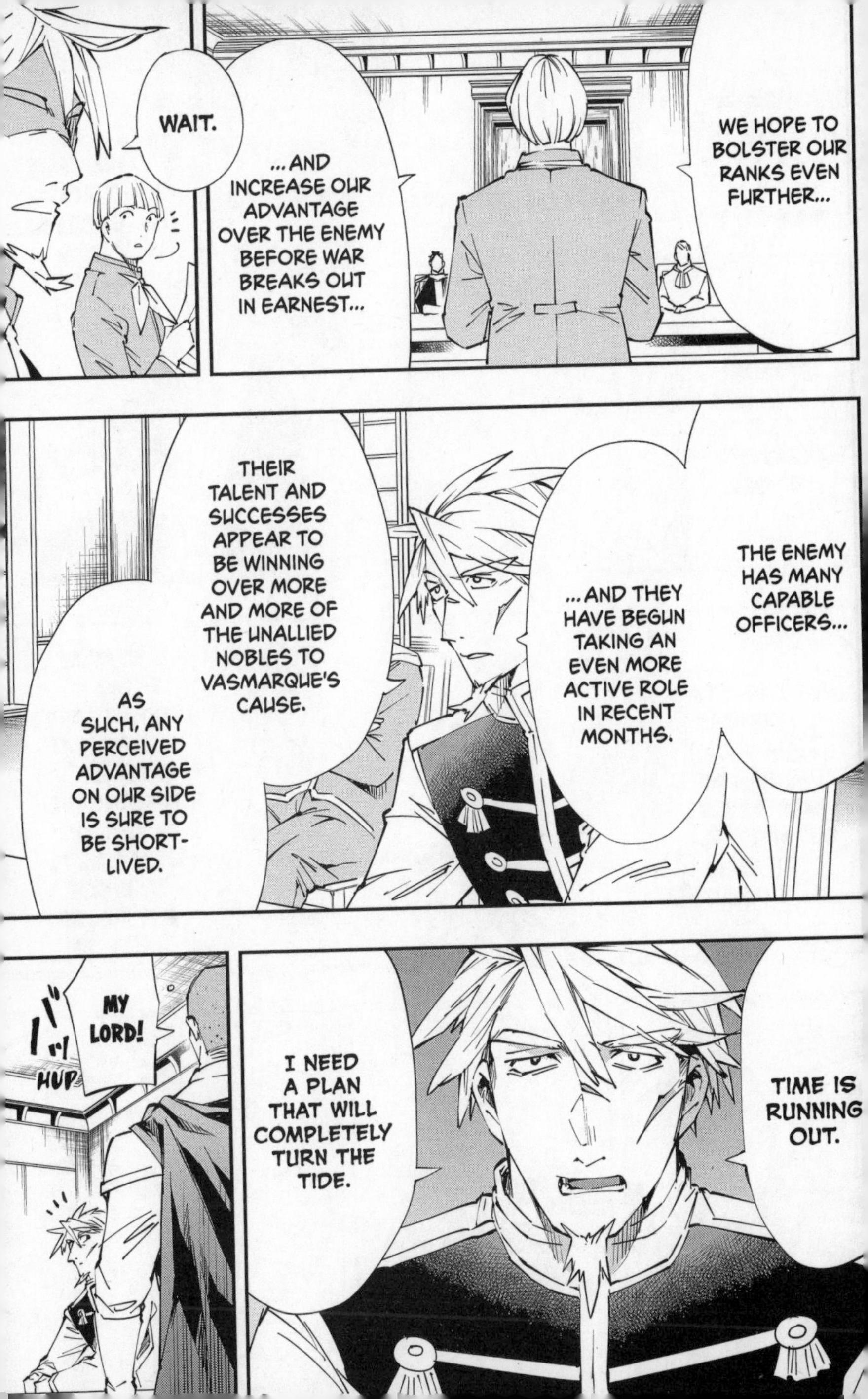
WE HOPE TO BOLSTER OUR RANKS EVEN FURTHER...
...AND INCREASE OUR ADVANTAGE OVER THE ENEMY BEFORE WAR BREAKS OUT IN EARNEST...
WAIT.
THE ENEMY HAS MANY CAPABLE OFFICERS...
...AND THEY HAVE BEGUN TAKING AN EVEN MORE ACTIVE ROLE IN RECENT MONTHS.
THEIR TALENT AND SUCCESSES APPEAR TO BE WINNING OVER MORE AND MORE OF THE UNALLIED NOBLES TO VASMARQUE'S CAUSE.
AS SUCH, ANY PERCEIVED ADVANTAGE ON OUR SIDE IS SURE TO BE SHORT-LIVED.
TIME IS RUNNING OUT.
I NEED A PLAN THAT WILL COMPLETELY TURN THE TIDE.
MY LORD!
HUP

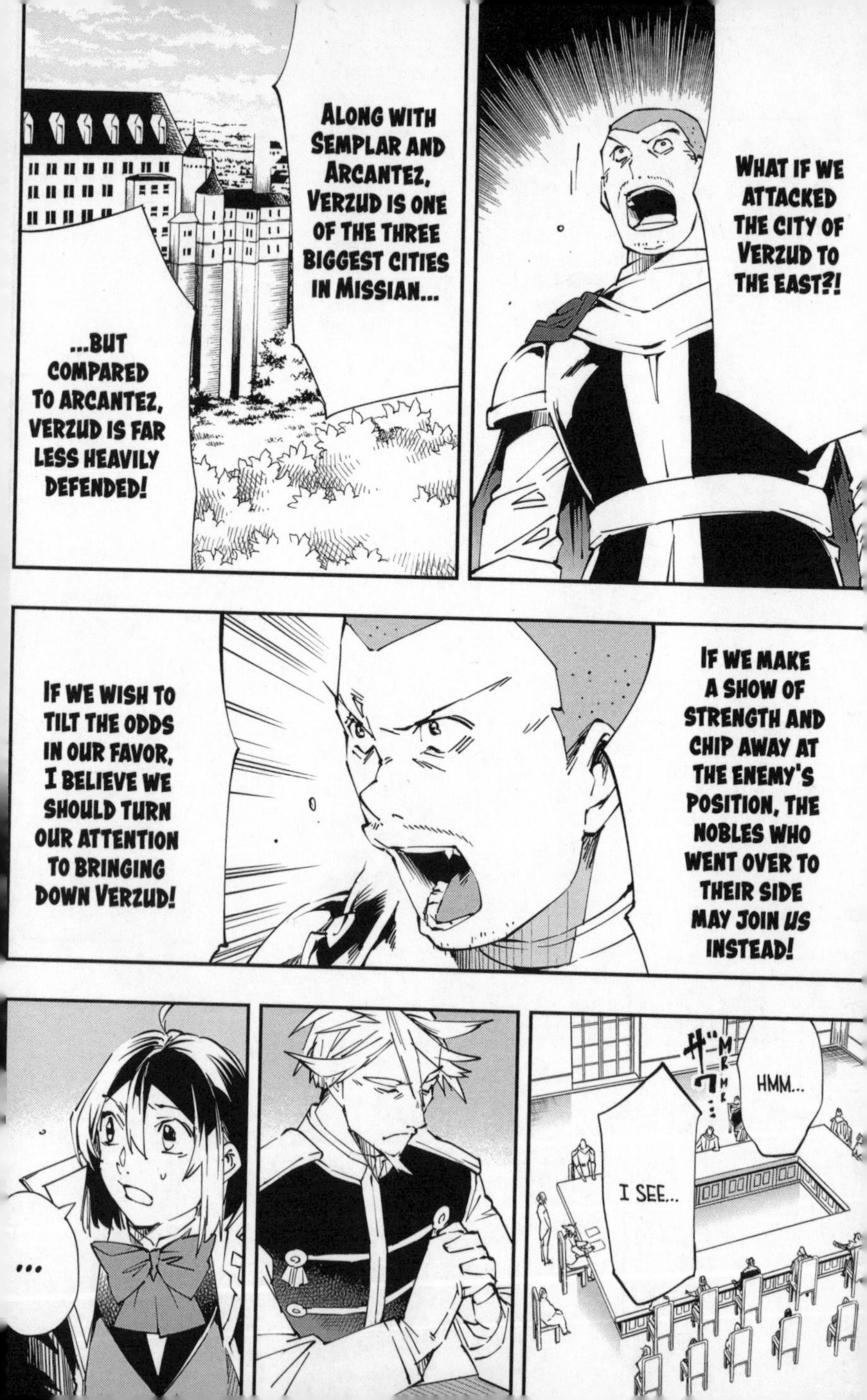
WHAT IF WE ATTACKED THE CITY OF VERZUD TO THE EAST?!
ALONG WITH SEMPLAR AND ARCANTEZ, VERZUD IS ONE OF THE THREE BIGGEST CITIES IN MISSIAN...
...BUT COMPARED TO ARCANTEZ, VERZUD IS FAR LESS HEAVILY DEFENDED!
IF WE MAKE A SHOW OF STRENGTH AND CHIP AWAY AT THE ENEMY'S POSITION, THE NOBLES WHO WENT OVER TO THEIR SIDE MAY JOIN *US* INSTEAD!
IF WE WISH TO TILT THE ODDS IN OUR FAVOR, I BELIEVE WE SHOULD TURN OUR ATTENTION TO BRINGING DOWN VERZUD!
ザワ
MRMR...
HMM...
I SEE...
...

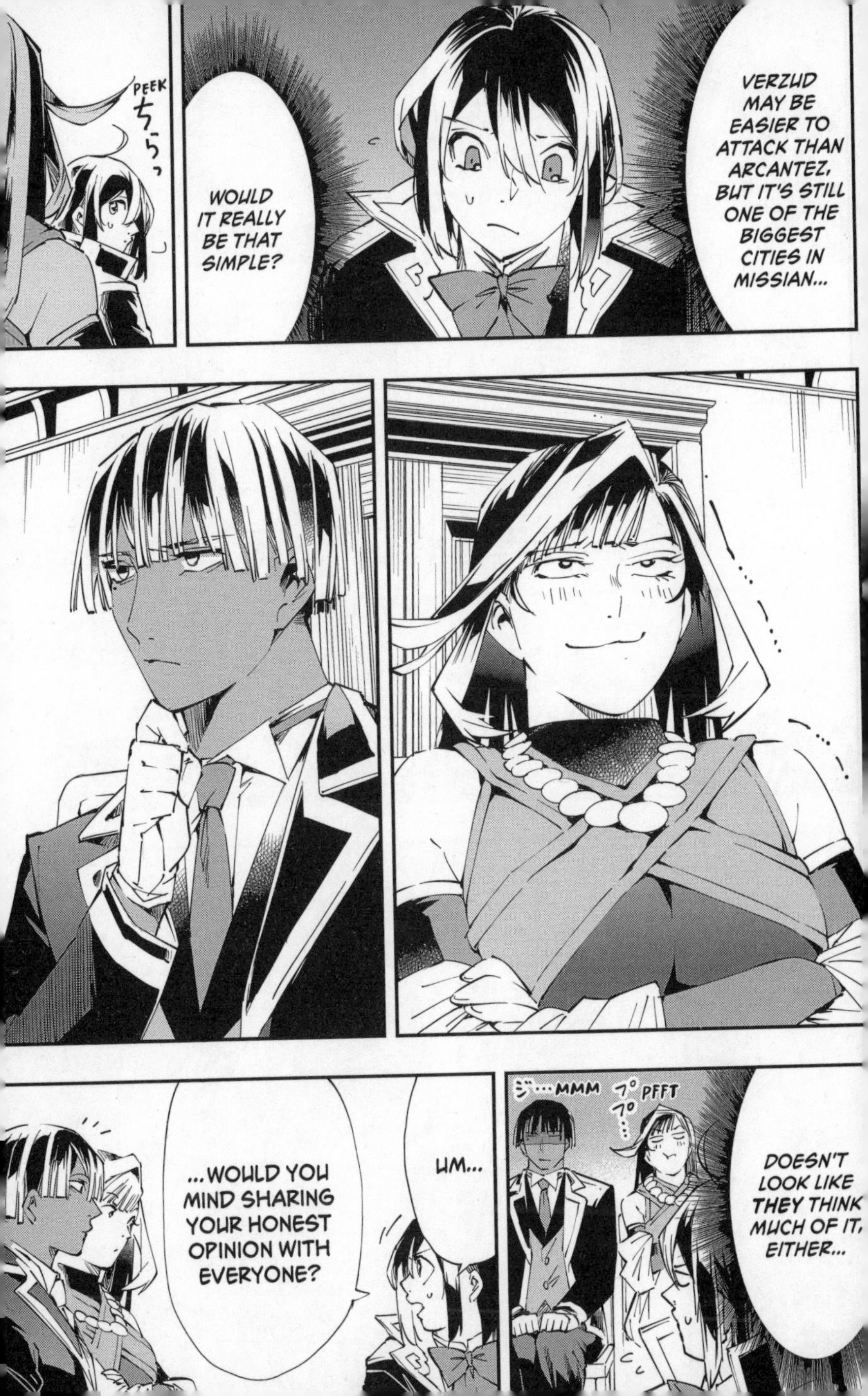
VERZUD MAY BE EASIER TO ATTACK THAN ARCANTEZ, BUT IT'S STILL ONE OF THE BIGGEST CITIES IN MISSIAN...
WOULD IT REALLY BE THAT SIMPLE?
PEEK
ちらっ
DOESN'T LOOK LIKE THEY THINK MUCH OF IT, EITHER...
プププ PFFT
ジー… MMM
UM...
...WOULD YOU MIND SHARING YOUR HONEST OPINION WITH EVERYONE?

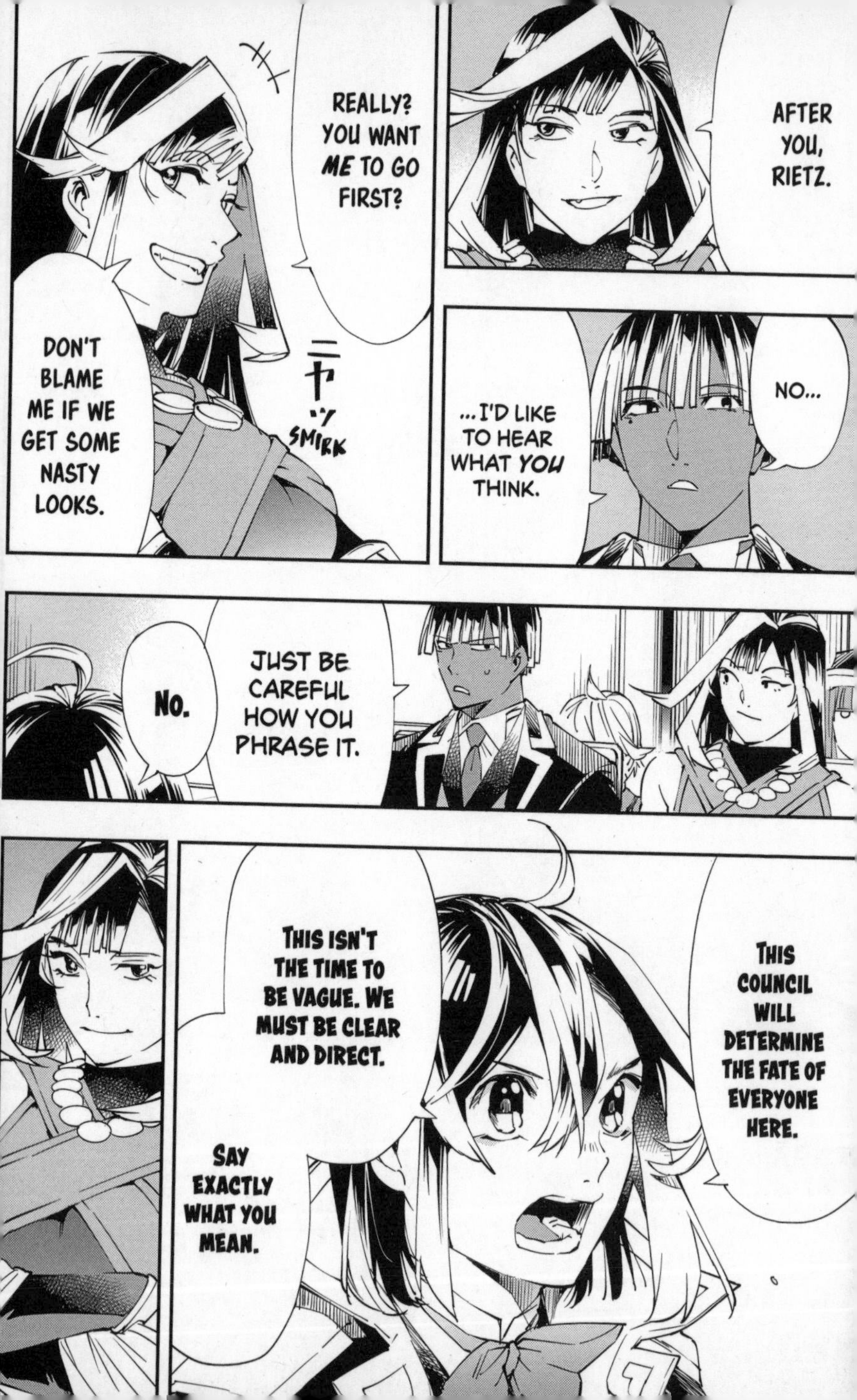
AFTER YOU, RIETZ.
NO...
...I'D LIKE TO HEAR WHAT *YOU* THINK.
REALLY? YOU WANT *ME* TO GO FIRST?
ニヤッ SMIRK
DON'T BLAME ME IF WE GET SOME NASTY LOOKS.
JUST BE CAREFUL HOW YOU PHRASE IT.
No.
THIS COUNCIL WILL DETERMINE THE FATE OF EVERYONE HERE.
THIS ISN'T THE TIME TO BE VAGUE. WE MUST BE CLEAR AND DIRECT.
SAY EXACTLY WHAT YOU MEAN.

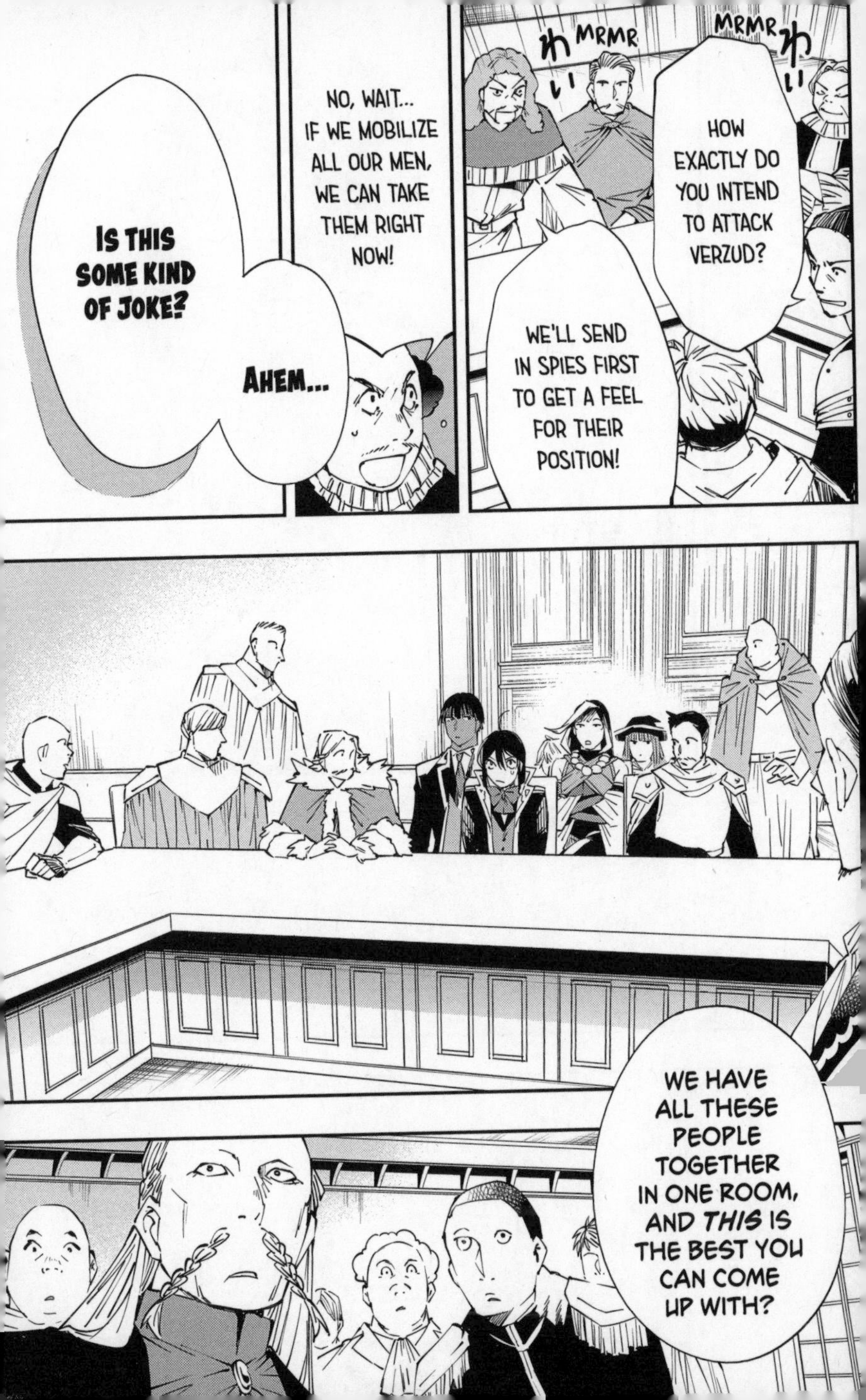

MRMR
わい
MRMR
わい
HOW EXACTLY DO YOU INTEND TO ATTACK VERZUD?
WE'LL SEND IN SPIES FIRST TO GET A FEEL FOR THEIR POSITION!
NO, WAIT... IF WE MOBILIZE ALL OUR MEN, WE CAN TAKE THEM RIGHT NOW!
AHEM...
IS THIS SOME KIND OF JOKE?
WE HAVE ALL THESE PEOPLE TOGETHER IN ONE ROOM, AND *THIS* IS THE BEST YOU CAN COME UP WITH?

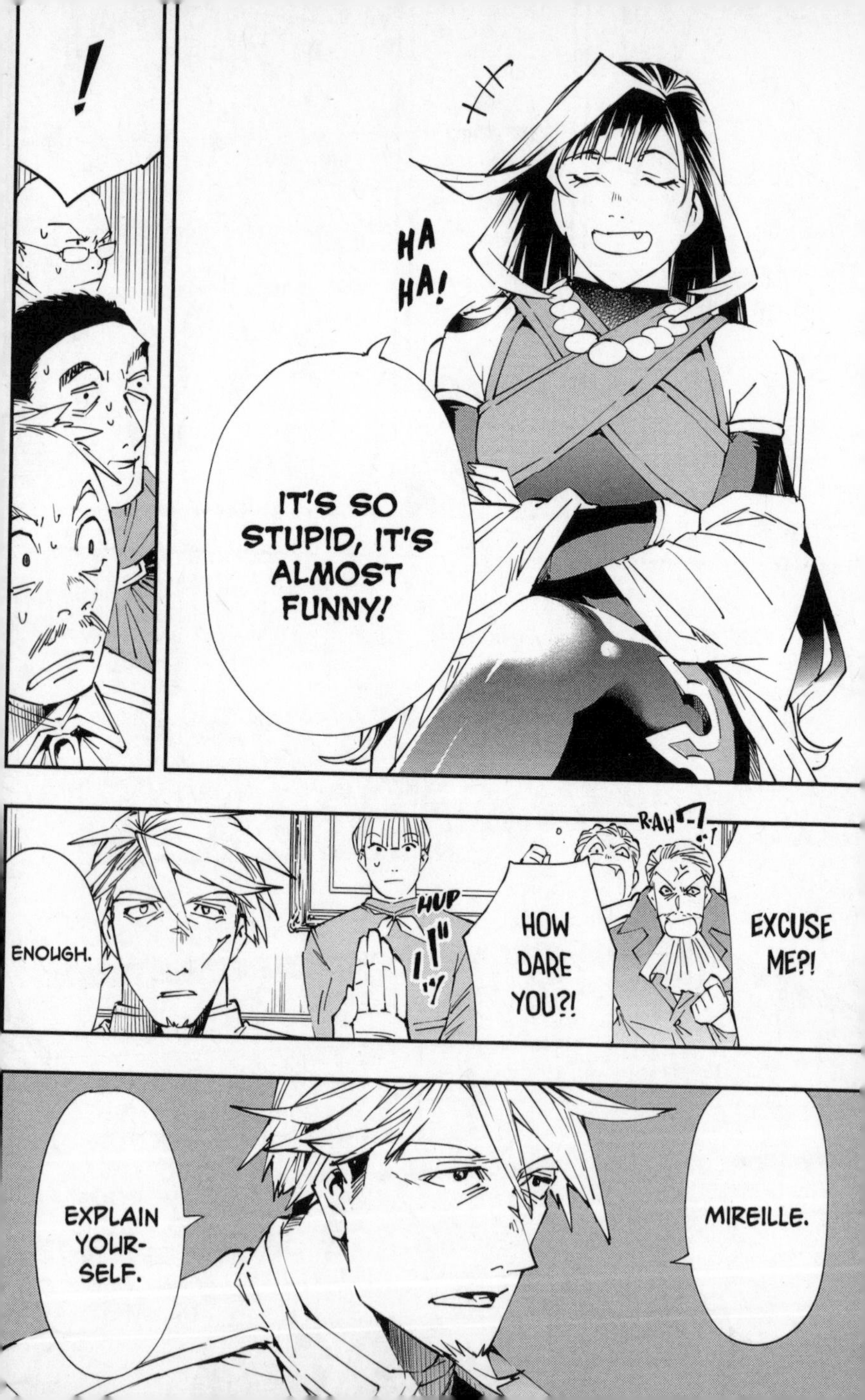
HA HA!
IT'S SO STUPID, IT'S ALMOST FUNNY!
!
EXCUSE ME?!
RAH
HOW DARE YOU?!
HUP
ENOUGH.
MIREILLE.
EXPLAIN YOUR-SELF.

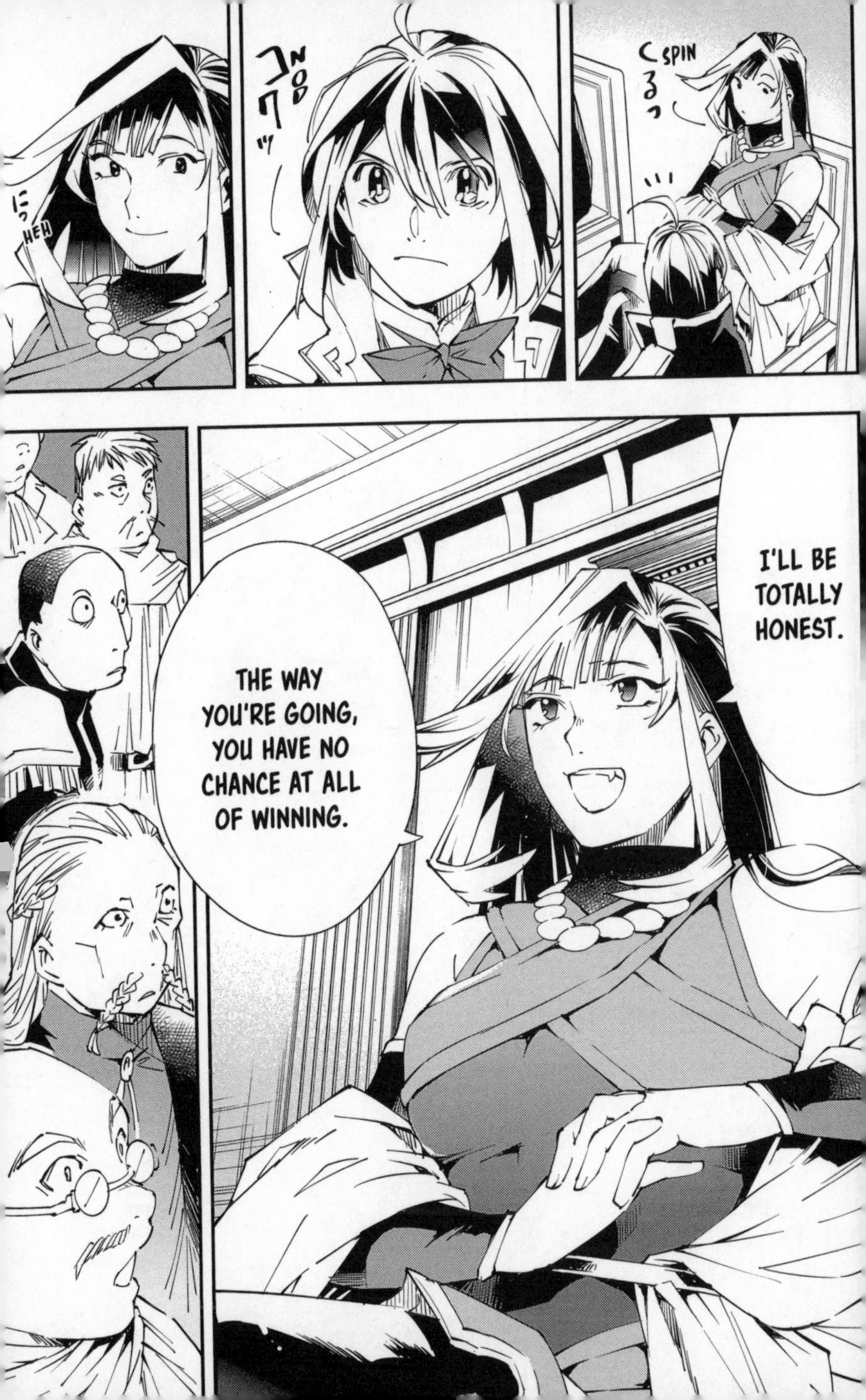
SPIN
NOD
HEH
I'LL BE TOTALLY HONEST.
THE WAY YOU'RE GOING, YOU HAVE NO CHANCE AT ALL OF WINNING.

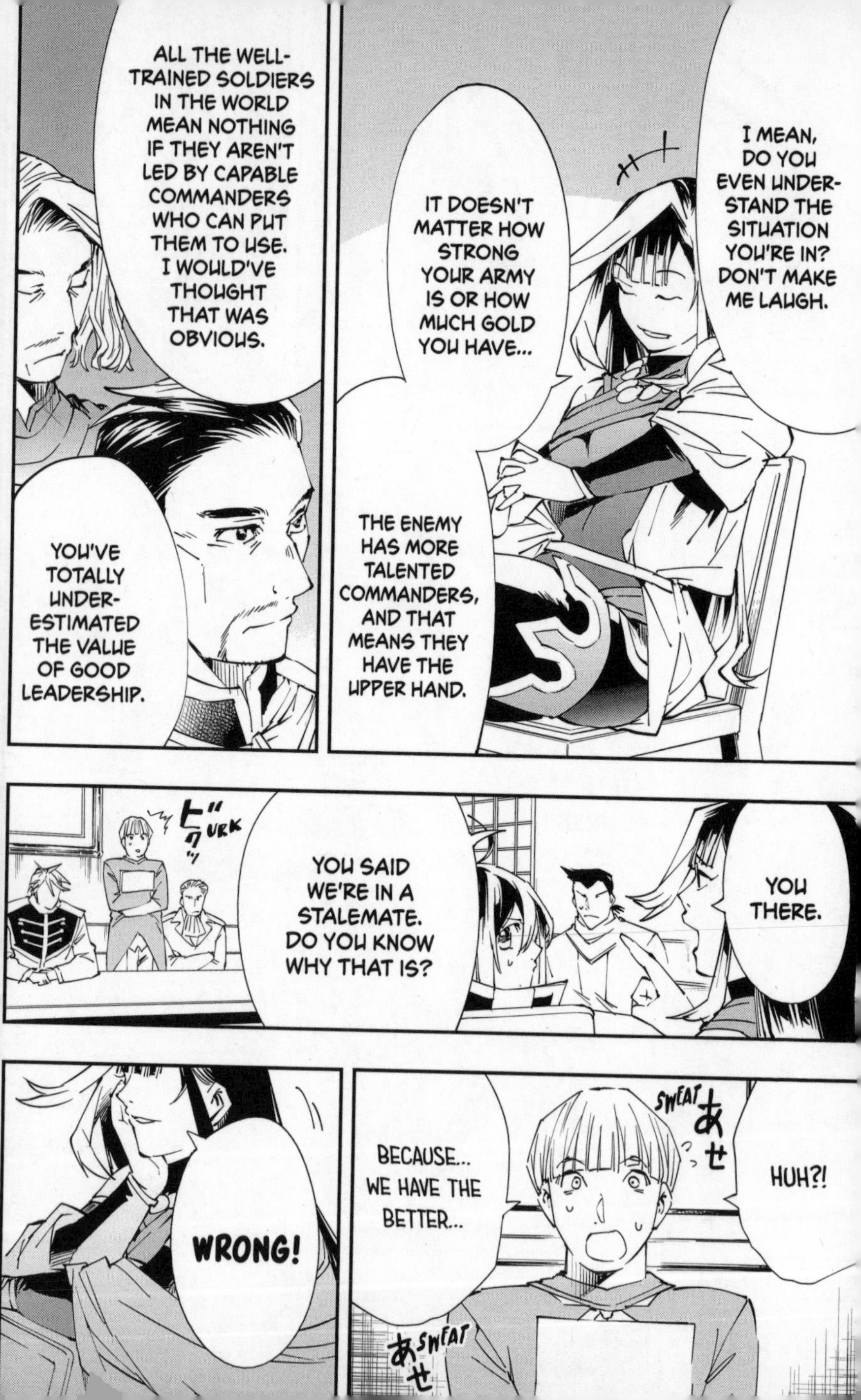
I MEAN, DO YOU EVEN UNDER-STAND THE SITUATION YOU'RE IN? DON'T MAKE ME LAUGH.
IT DOESN'T MATTER HOW STRONG YOUR ARMY IS OR HOW MUCH GOLD YOU HAVE...
THE ENEMY HAS MORE TALENTED COMMANDERS, AND THAT MEANS THEY HAVE THE UPPER HAND.
ALL THE WELL-TRAINED SOLDIERS IN THE WORLD MEAN NOTHING IF THEY AREN'T LED BY CAPABLE COMMANDERS WHO CAN PUT THEM TO USE. I WOULD'VE THOUGHT THAT WAS OBVIOUS.
YOU'VE TOTALLY UNDER-ESTIMATED THE VALUE OF GOOD LEADERSHIP.
YOU THERE.
YOU SAID WE'RE IN A STALEMATE. DO YOU KNOW WHY THAT IS?
URK
HUH?!
あせ SWEAT
BECAUSE... WE HAVE THE BETTER...
あせ SWEAT
WRONG!

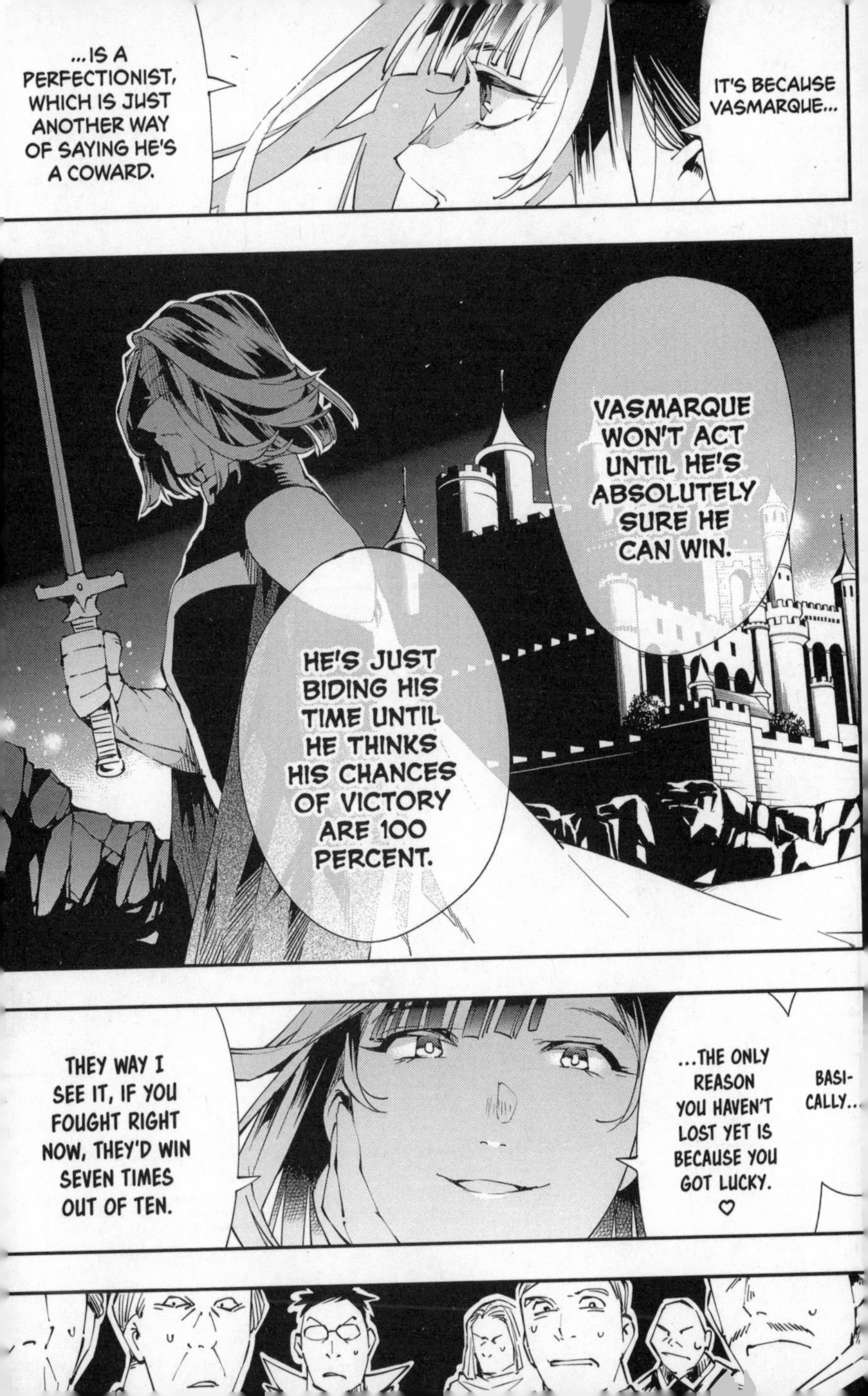
IT'S BECAUSE VASMARQUE...
...IS A PERFECTIONIST, WHICH IS JUST ANOTHER WAY OF SAYING HE'S A COWARD.
VASMARQUE WON'T ACT UNTIL HE'S ABSOLUTELY SURE HE CAN WIN.
HE'S JUST BIDING HIS TIME UNTIL HE THINKS HIS CHANCES OF VICTORY ARE 100 PERCENT.
BASI-CALLY...
...THE ONLY REASON YOU HAVEN'T LOST YET IS BECAUSE YOU GOT LUCKY. ♡
THEY WAY I SEE IT, IF YOU FOUGHT RIGHT NOW, THEY'D WIN SEVEN TIMES OUT OF TEN.

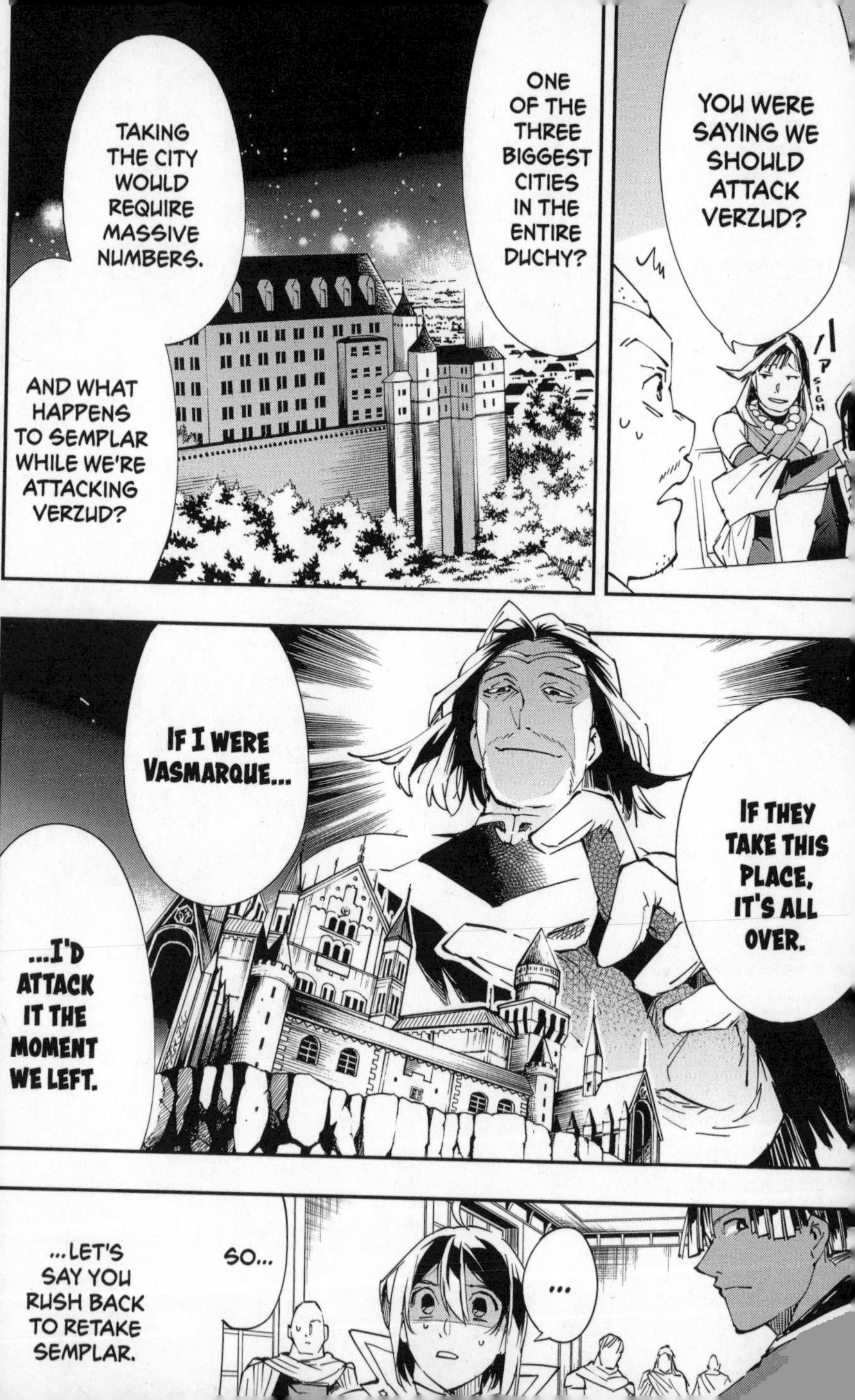
YOU WERE SAYING WE SHOULD ATTACK VERZUD?
SIGH
ONE OF THE THREE BIGGEST CITIES IN THE ENTIRE DUCHY?
TAKING THE CITY WOULD REQUIRE MASSIVE NUMBERS.
AND WHAT HAPPENS TO SEMPLAR WHILE WE'RE ATTACKING VERZUD?
IF THEY TAKE THIS PLACE, IT'S ALL OVER.
IF I WERE VASMARQUE...
...I'D ATTACK IT THE MOMENT WE LEFT.
...
SO...
...LET'S SAY YOU RUSH BACK TO RETAKE SEMPLAR.

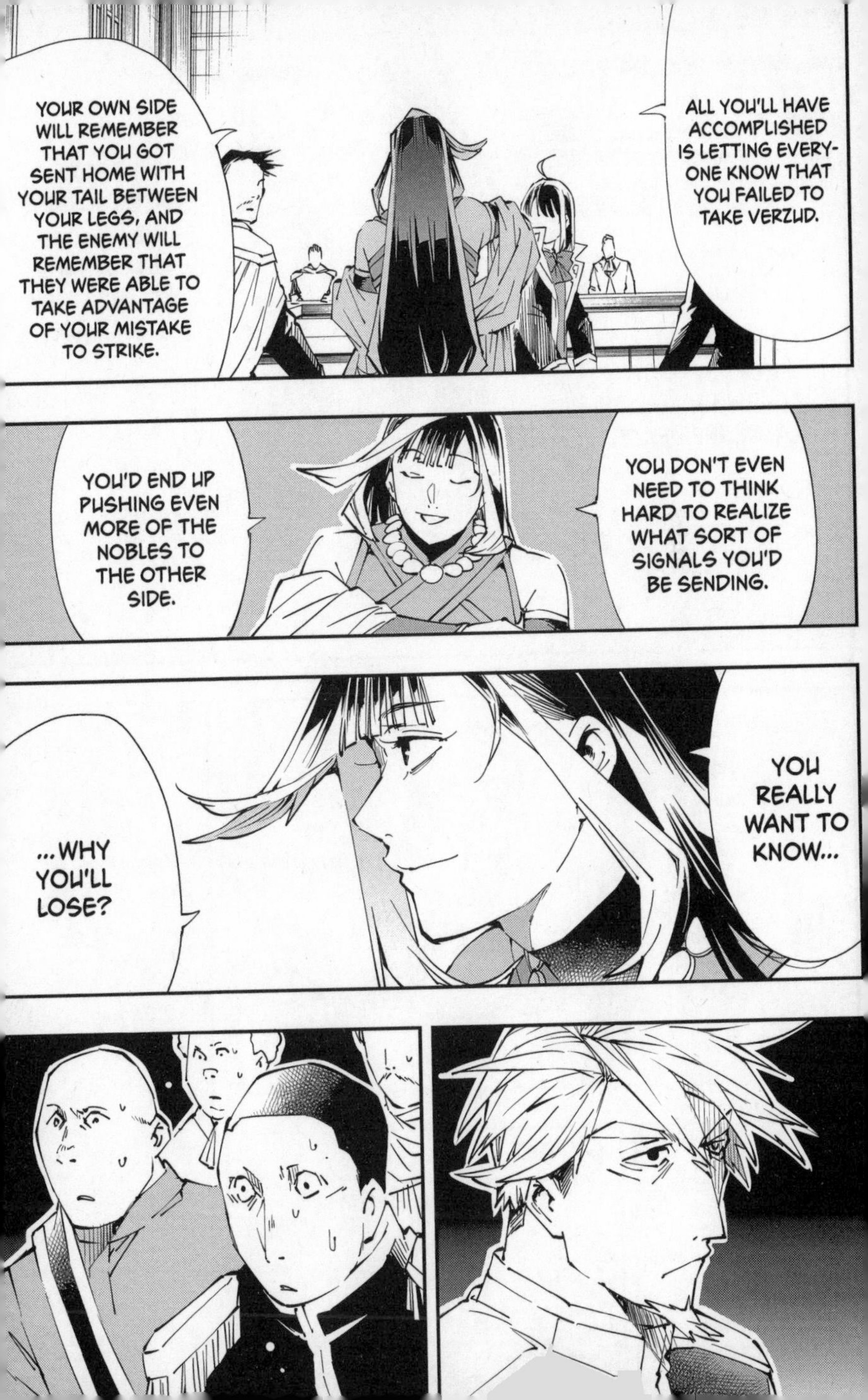
ALL YOU'LL HAVE ACCOMPLISHED IS LETTING EVERY-ONE KNOW THAT YOU FAILED TO TAKE VERZUD.
YOUR OWN SIDE WILL REMEMBER THAT YOU GOT SENT HOME WITH YOUR TAIL BETWEEN YOUR LEGS, AND THE ENEMY WILL REMEMBER THAT THEY WERE ABLE TO TAKE ADVANTAGE OF YOUR MISTAKE TO STRIKE.
YOU DON'T EVEN NEED TO THINK HARD TO REALIZE WHAT SORT OF SIGNALS YOU'D BE SENDING.
YOU'D END UP PUSHING EVEN MORE OF THE NOBLES TO THE OTHER SIDE.
YOU REALLY WANT TO KNOW...
...WHY YOU'LL LOSE?

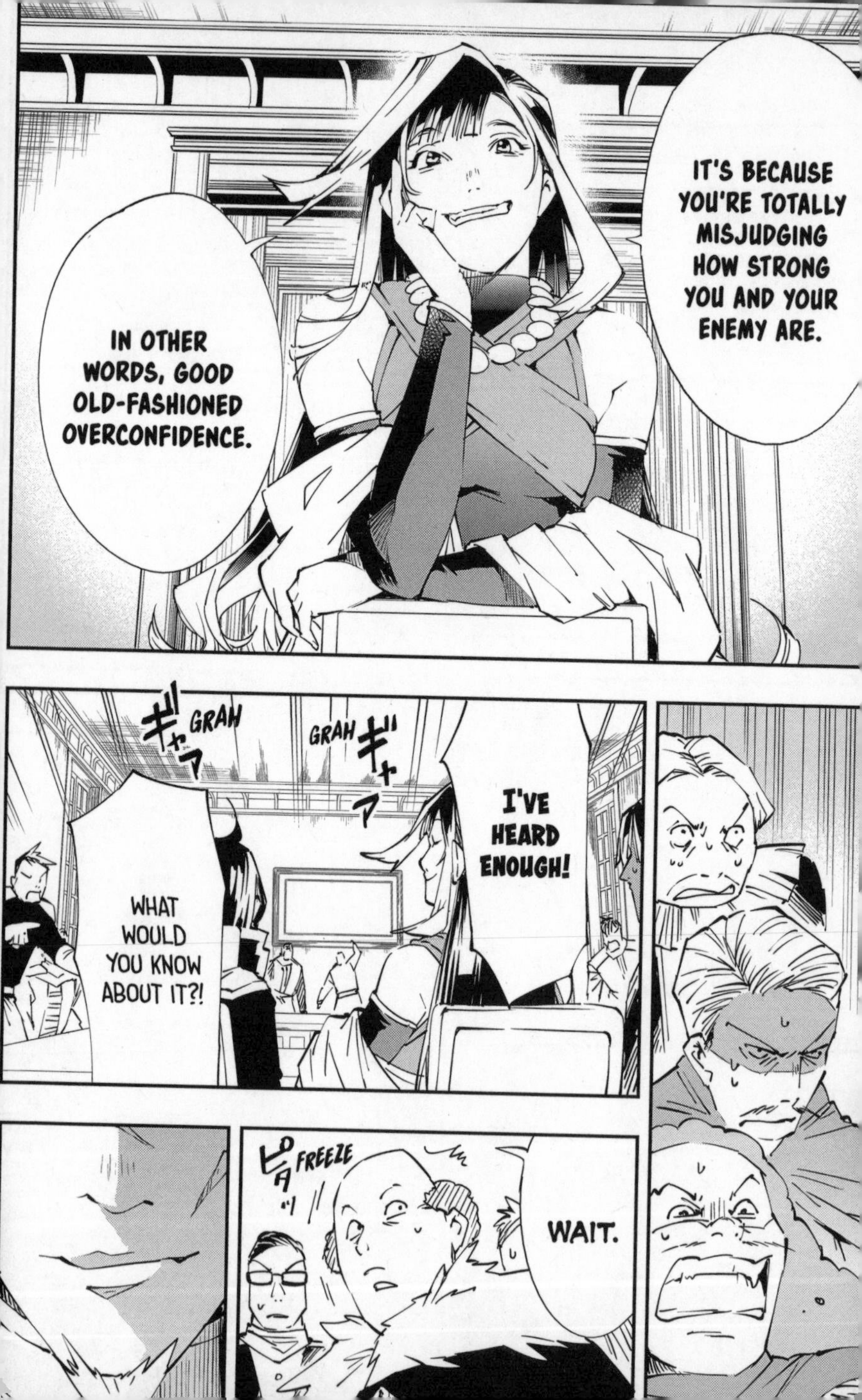
IT'S BECAUSE YOU'RE TOTALLY MISJUDGING HOW STRONG YOU AND YOUR ENEMY ARE.
IN OTHER WORDS, GOOD OLD-FASHIONED OVERCONFIDENCE.
ギャア GRAH
I'VE HEARD ENOUGH!
ギャア GRAH
WHAT WOULD YOU KNOW ABOUT IT?!
WAIT.
ピタッ FREEZE

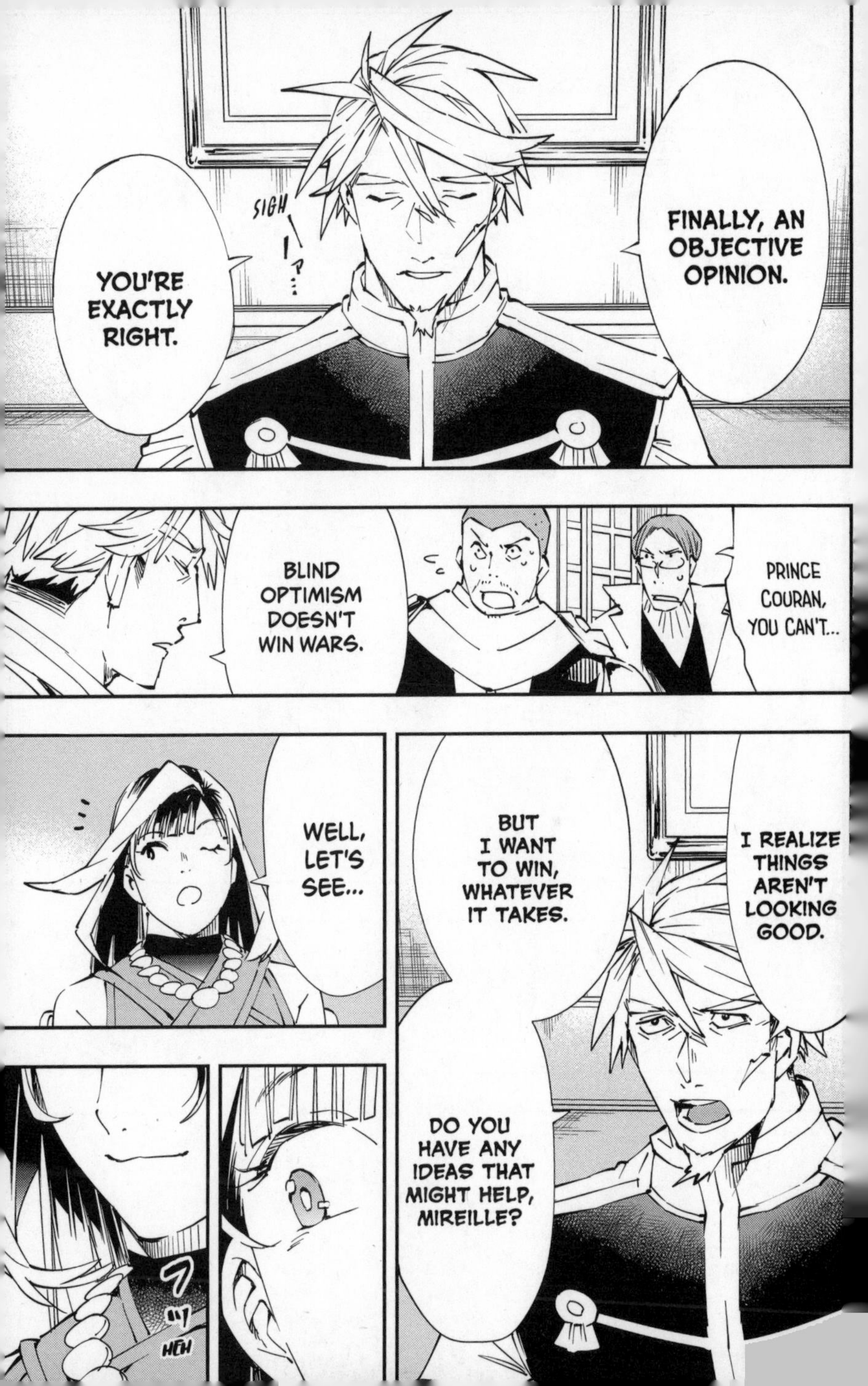
FINALLY, AN OBJECTIVE OPINION.
SIGH
YOU'RE EXACTLY RIGHT.
PRINCE COURAN, YOU CAN'T...
BLIND OPTIMISM DOESN'T WIN WARS.
I REALIZE THINGS AREN'T LOOKING GOOD.
BUT I WANT TO WIN, WHATEVER IT TAKES.
DO YOU HAVE ANY IDEAS THAT MIGHT HELP, MIREILLE?
WELL, LET'S SEE...
HEH

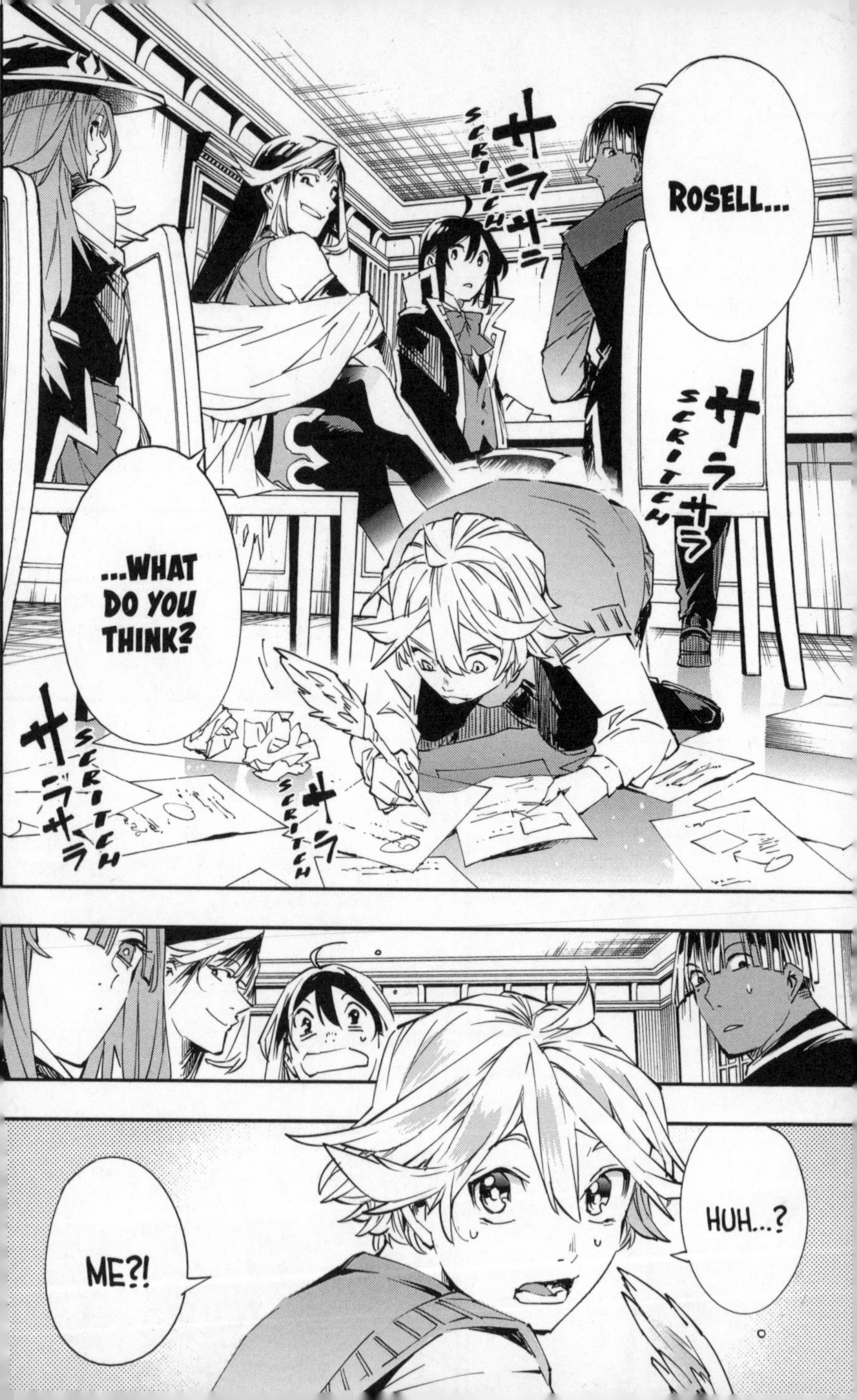
SCRITCH
ROSELL...
SCRITCH
...WHAT DO YOU THINK?
SCRITCH
SCRITCH
HUH...?
ME?!

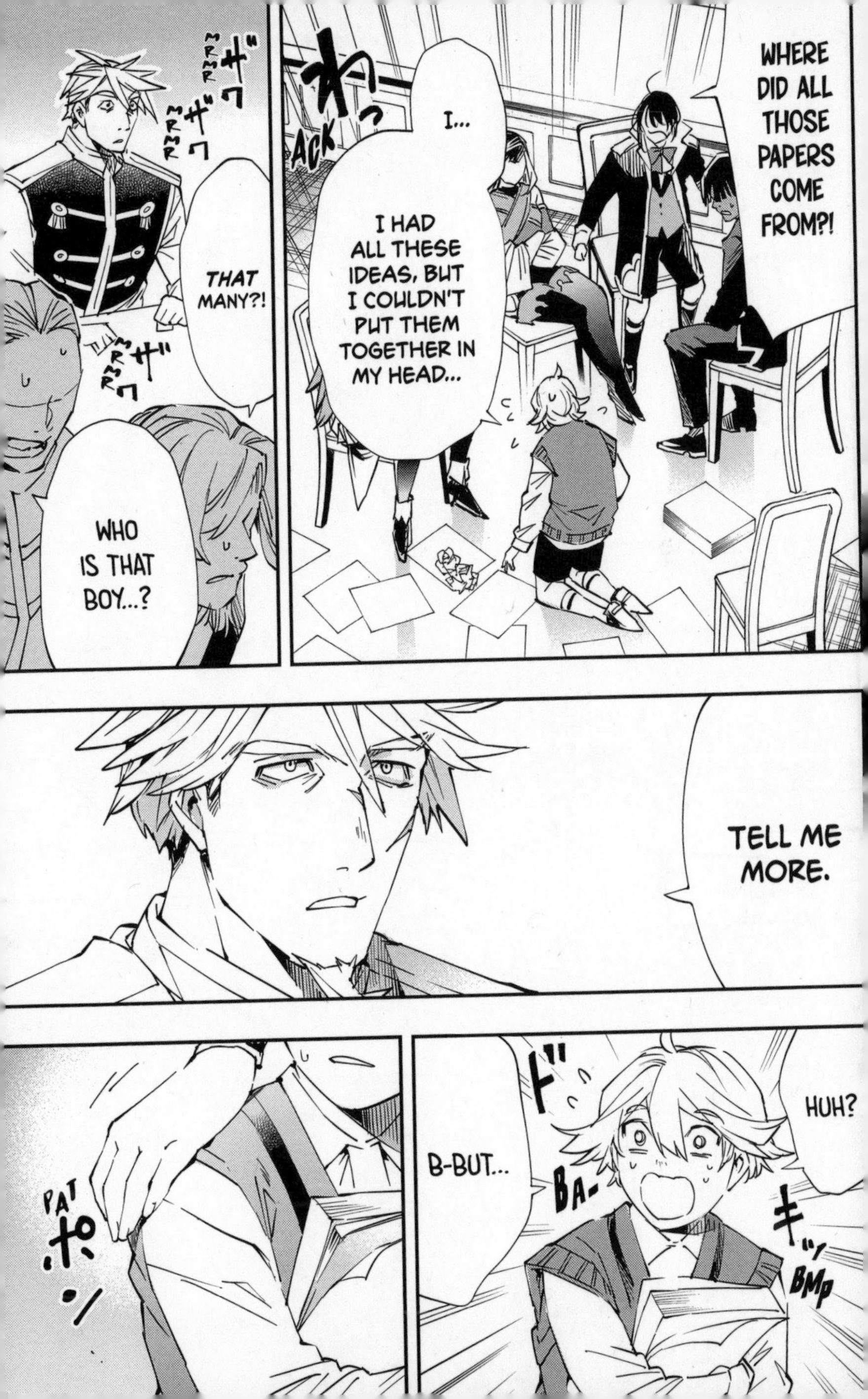
WHERE DID ALL THOSE PAPERS COME FROM?!
ACK
I...
I HAD ALL THESE IDEAS, BUT I COULDN'T PUT THEM TOGETHER IN MY HEAD...
MRMR
MRMR
THAT MANY?!
MRMR
WHO IS THAT BOY...?
TELL ME MORE.
HUH?
BA-
B-BUT...
BMP
PAT

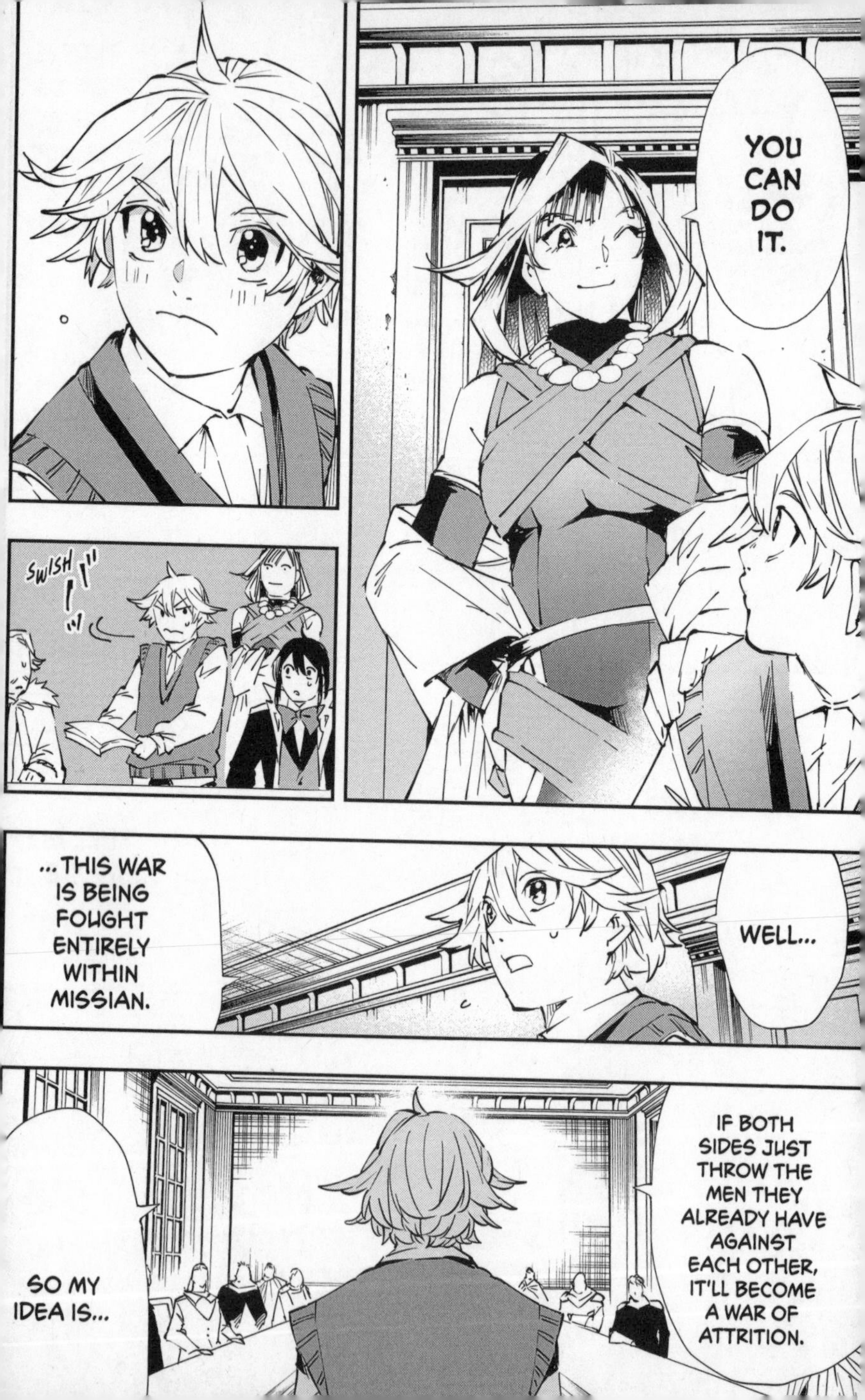
YOU CAN DO IT.
SWISH
WELL...
...THIS WAR IS BEING FOUGHT ENTIRELY WITHIN MISSIAN.
IF BOTH SIDES JUST THROW THE MEN THEY ALREADY HAVE AGAINST EACH OTHER, IT'LL BECOME A WAR OF ATTRITION.
SO MY IDEA IS...

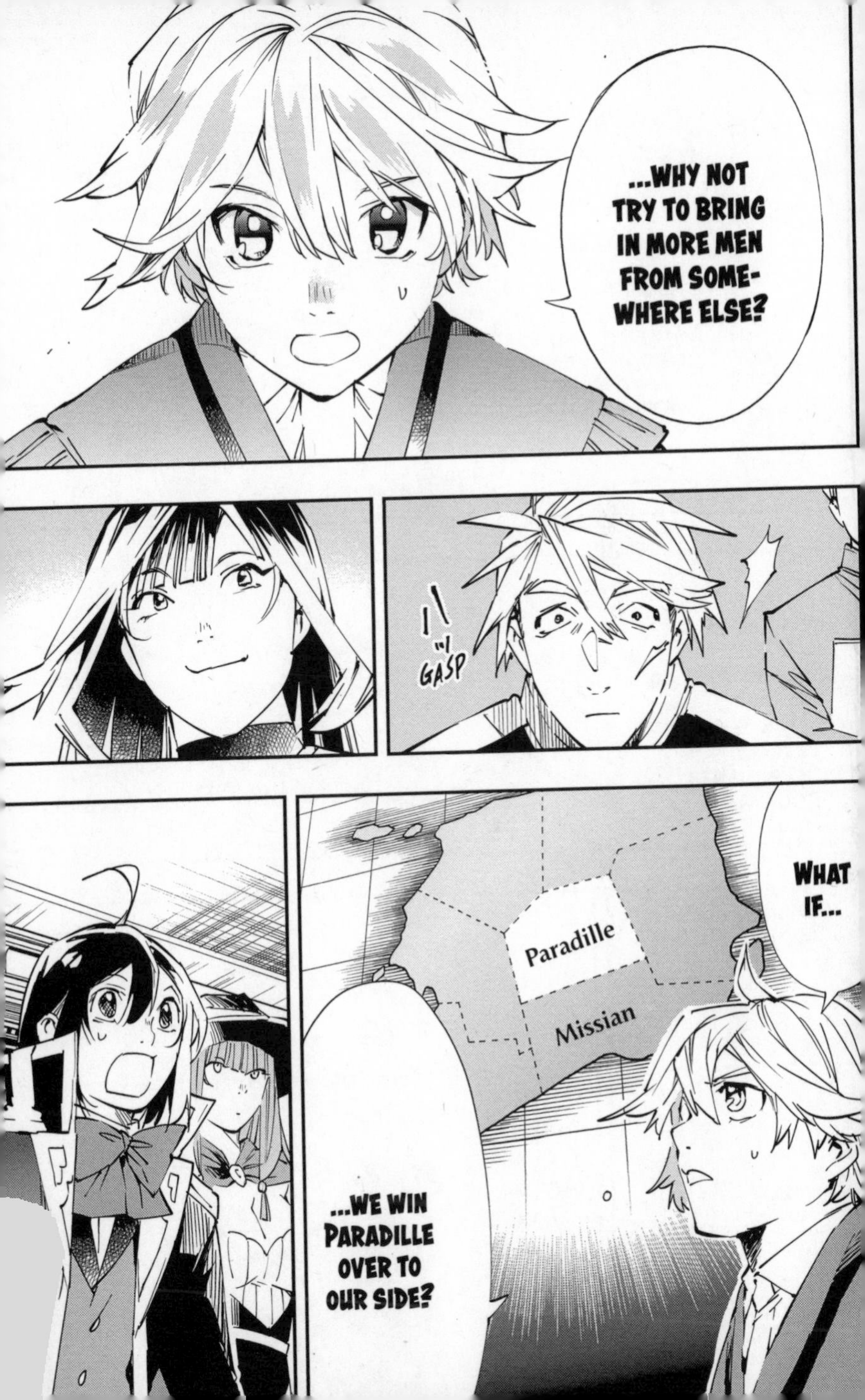
...WHY NOT TRY TO BRING IN MORE MEN FROM SOME-WHERE ELSE?
GASP
WHAT IF...
Paradille
Missian
...WE WIN PARADILLE OVER TO OUR SIDE?

THAT'S PREPOSTEROUS!

THE WHOLE EMPIRE IS TEARING ITSELF APART. THE OTHER DUCHIES HAVE THEIR OWN SURVIVAL TO WORRY ABOUT.

ずⅡ MRR 7 MR …

THEY WON'T HELP US... NOT WHEN *WE'RE* TRYING TO ESTABLISH OUR OWN INDEPENDENT COUNTRY.

PARADILLE IS ONE OF THE FEW THAT'S STILL LOYAL TO THE THRONE.

WHAT?!

BUT WHO...

WHICH IS WHY WE'LL SEEK OUT AN INTERMEDIARY.

RIGHT.

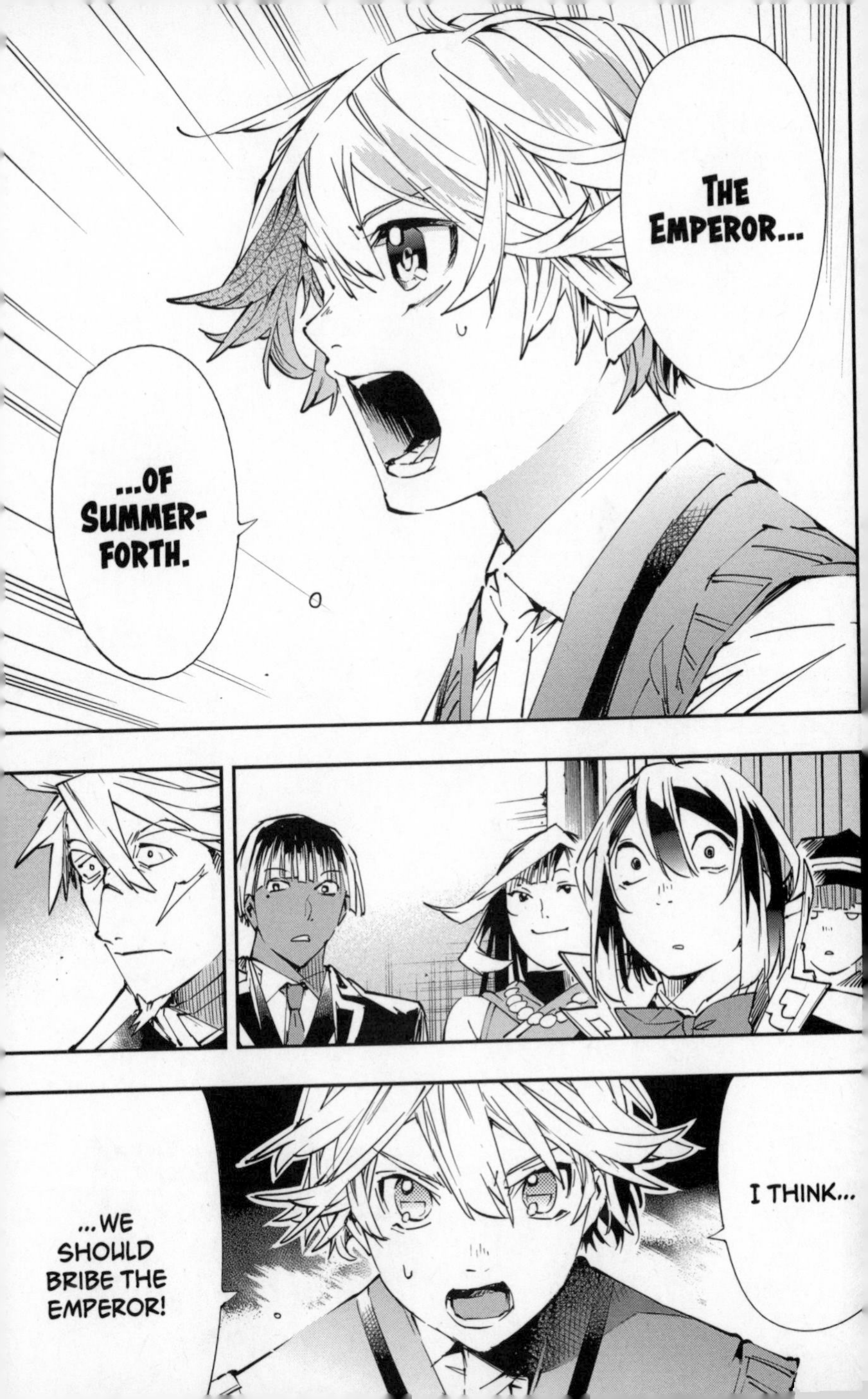
THE EMPEROR...
...OF SUMMER-FORTH.
I THINK...
...WE SHOULD BRIBE THE EMPEROR!

As a Reincarnated ARISTOCRAT, I'll Use My Appraisal Skill to Rise in the World

Chapter 51: A Weighty Task

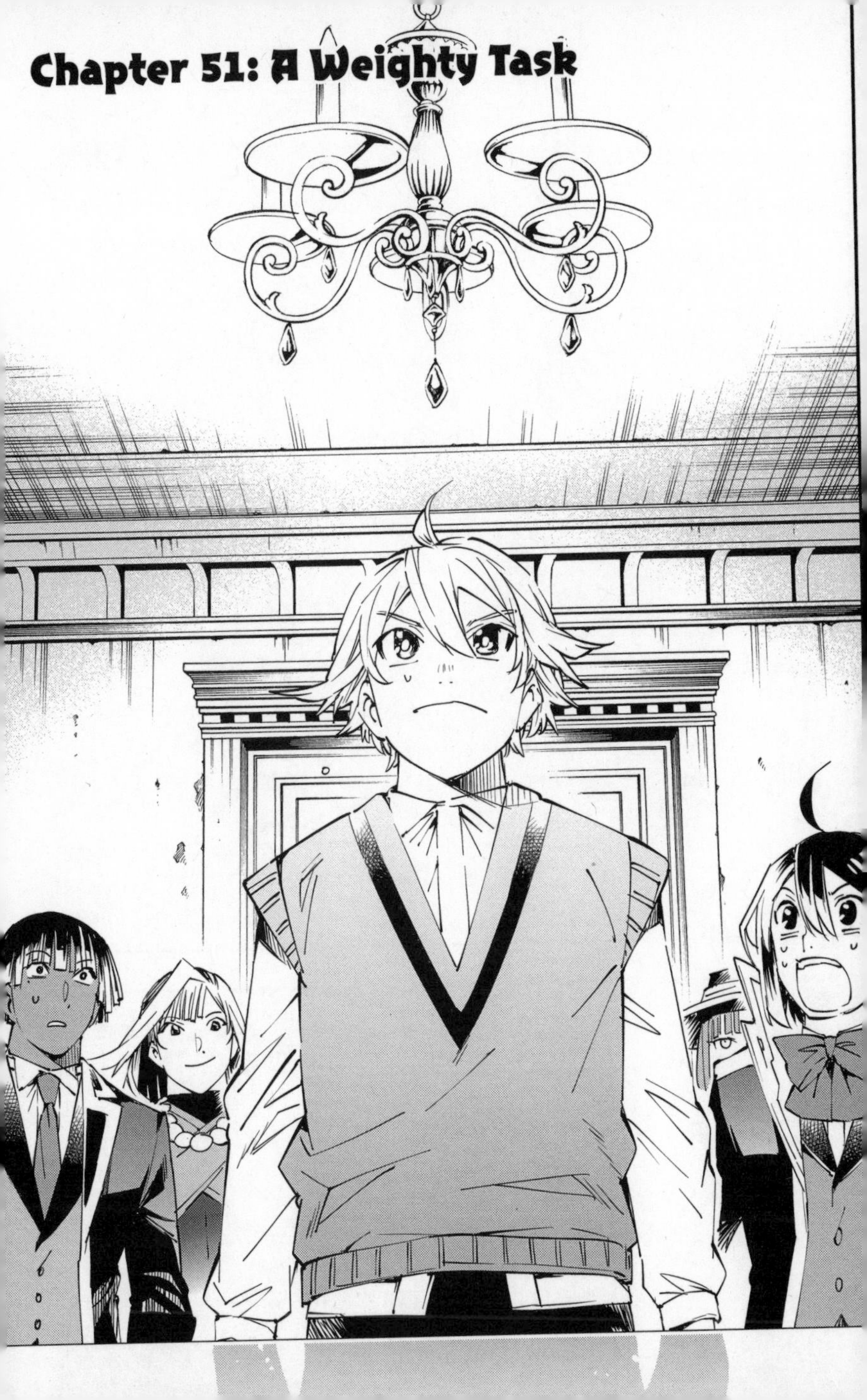

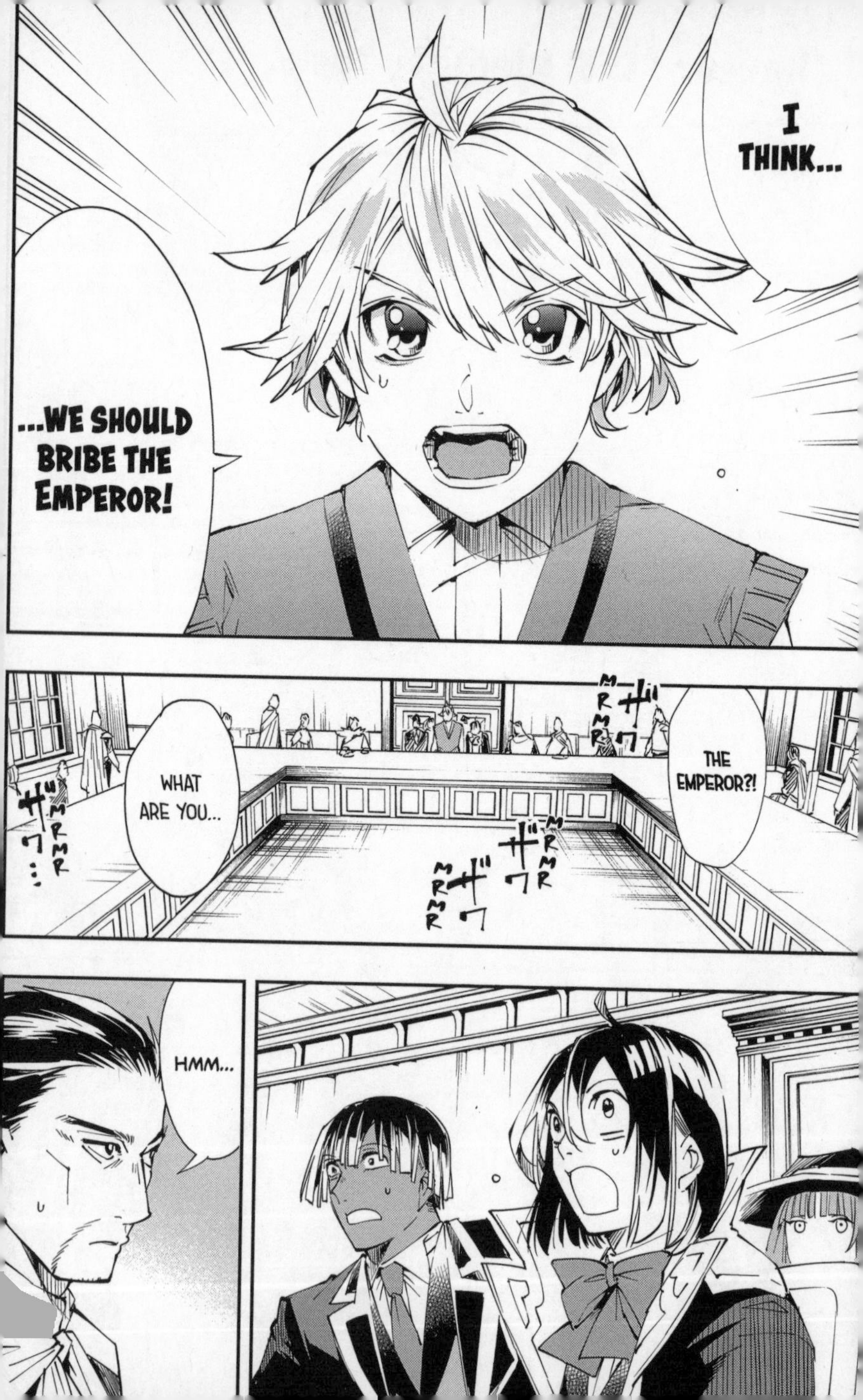
I THINK...
...WE SHOULD BRIBE THE EMPEROR!
MRMR
THE EMPEROR?!
MRMR
MRMR
WHAT ARE YOU...
MRMR...
HMM...

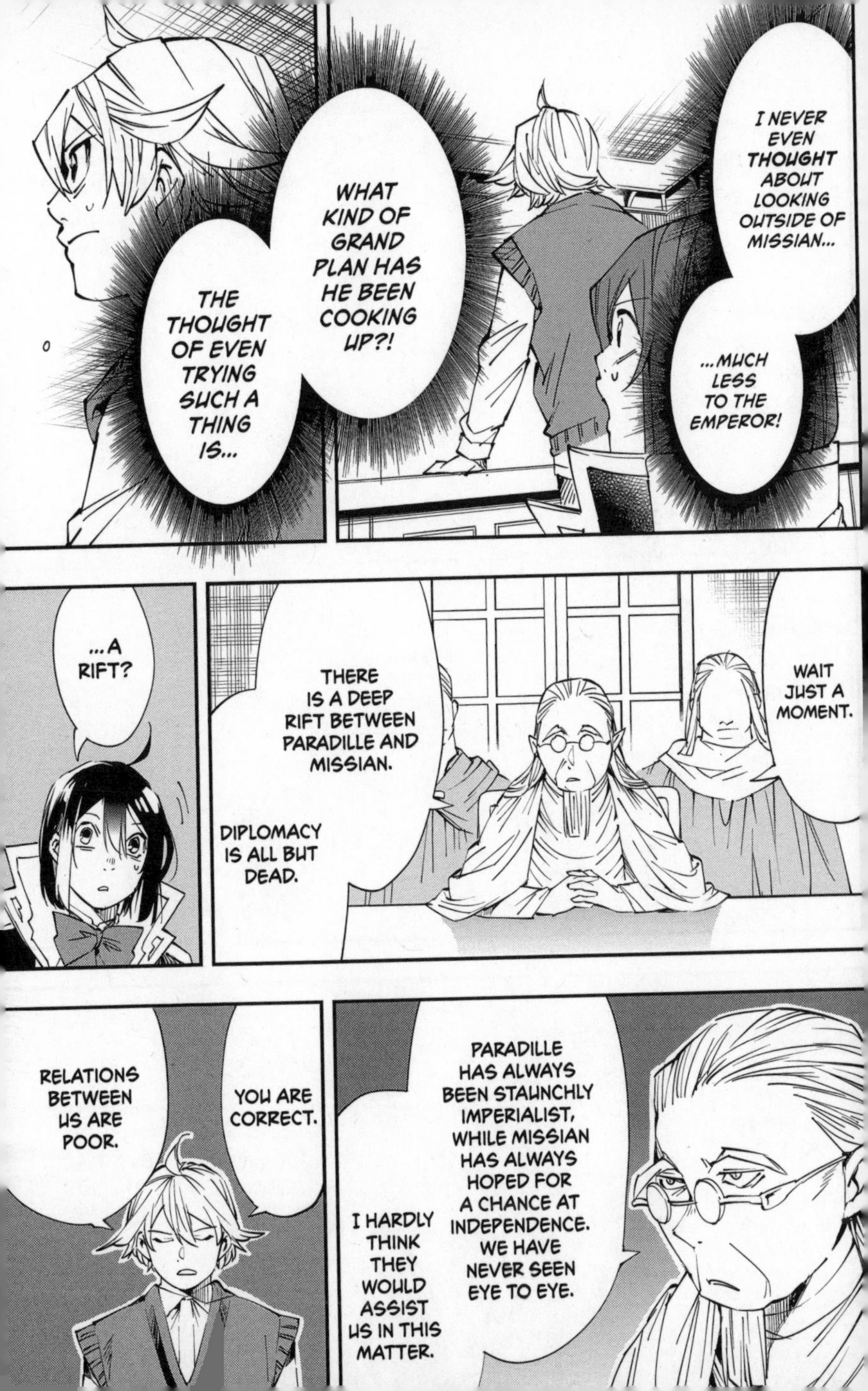
I NEVER EVEN THOUGHT ABOUT LOOKING OUTSIDE OF MISSIAN...
...MUCH LESS TO THE EMPEROR!
WHAT KIND OF GRAND PLAN HAS HE BEEN COOKING UP?!
THE THOUGHT OF EVEN TRYING SUCH A THING IS...
WAIT JUST A MOMENT.
THERE IS A DEEP RIFT BETWEEN PARADILLE AND MISSIAN.
DIPLOMACY IS ALL BUT DEAD.
...A RIFT?
PARADILLE HAS ALWAYS BEEN STAUNCHLY IMPERIALIST, WHILE MISSIAN HAS ALWAYS HOPED FOR A CHANCE AT INDEPENDENCE. WE HAVE NEVER SEEN EYE TO EYE.
I HARDLY THINK THEY WOULD ASSIST US IN THIS MATTER.
YOU ARE CORRECT.
RELATIONS BETWEEN US ARE POOR.

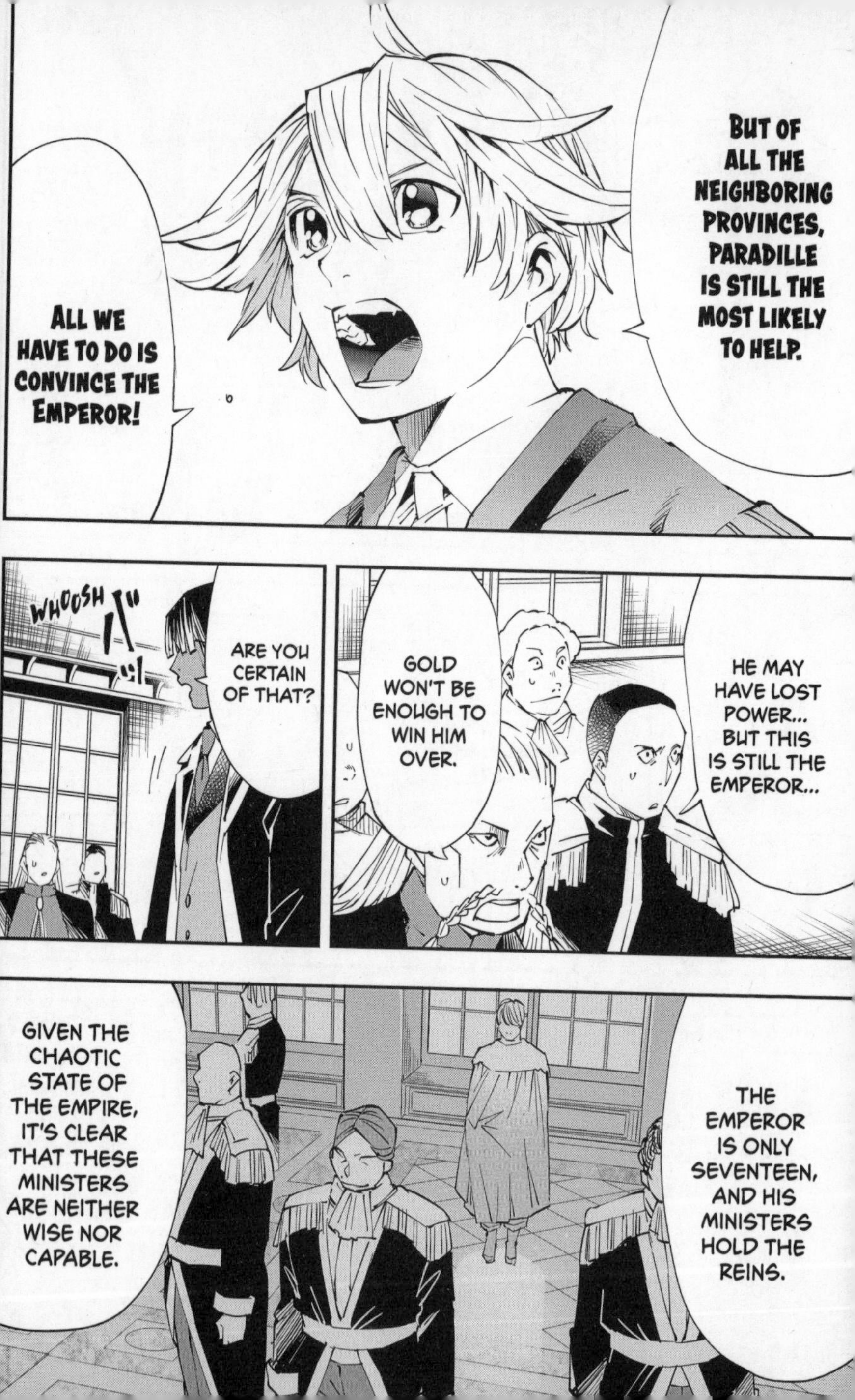
BUT OF ALL THE NEIGHBORING PROVINCES, PARADILLE IS STILL THE MOST LIKELY TO HELP.
ALL WE HAVE TO DO IS CONVINCE THE EMPEROR!
HE MAY HAVE LOST POWER... BUT THIS IS STILL THE EMPEROR...
GOLD WON'T BE ENOUGH TO WIN HIM OVER.
WHOOSH
ARE YOU CERTAIN OF THAT?
THE EMPEROR IS ONLY SEVENTEEN, AND HIS MINISTERS HOLD THE REINS.
GIVEN THE CHAOTIC STATE OF THE EMPIRE, IT'S CLEAR THAT THESE MINISTERS ARE NEITHER WISE NOR CAPABLE.

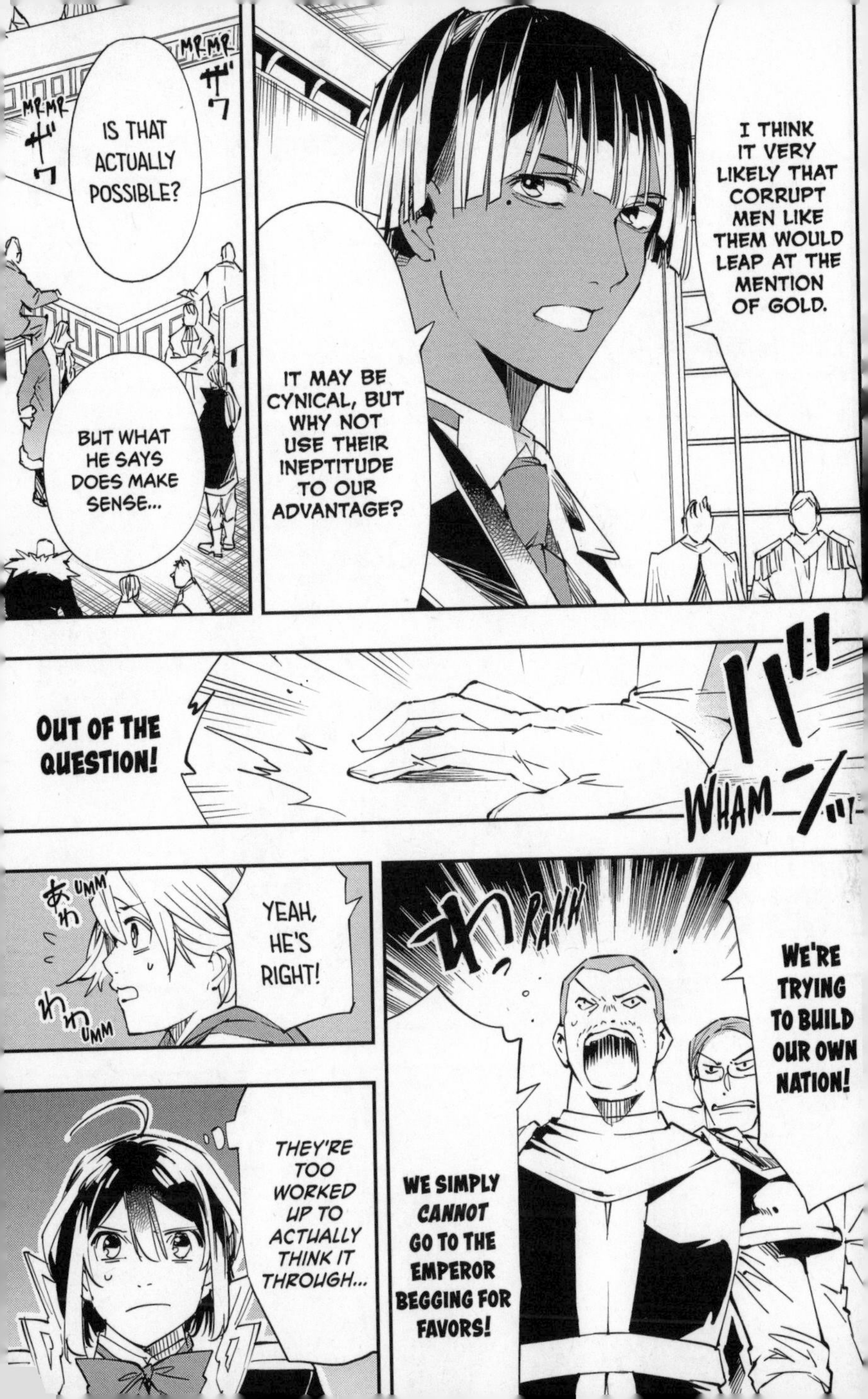
I THINK IT VERY LIKELY THAT CORRUPT MEN LIKE THEM WOULD LEAP AT THE MENTION OF GOLD.
IT MAY BE CYNICAL, BUT WHY NOT USE THEIR INEPTITUDE TO OUR ADVANTAGE?
MR MR
MR MR
IS THAT ACTUALLY POSSIBLE?
BUT WHAT HE SAYS DOES MAKE SENSE...
WHAM
OUT OF THE QUESTION!
RAHH
WE'RE TRYING TO BUILD OUR OWN NATION!
WE SIMPLY CANNOT GO TO THE EMPEROR BEGGING FOR FAVORS!
UMM
YEAH, HE'S RIGHT!
UMM
THEY'RE TOO WORKED UP TO ACTUALLY THINK IT THROUGH...

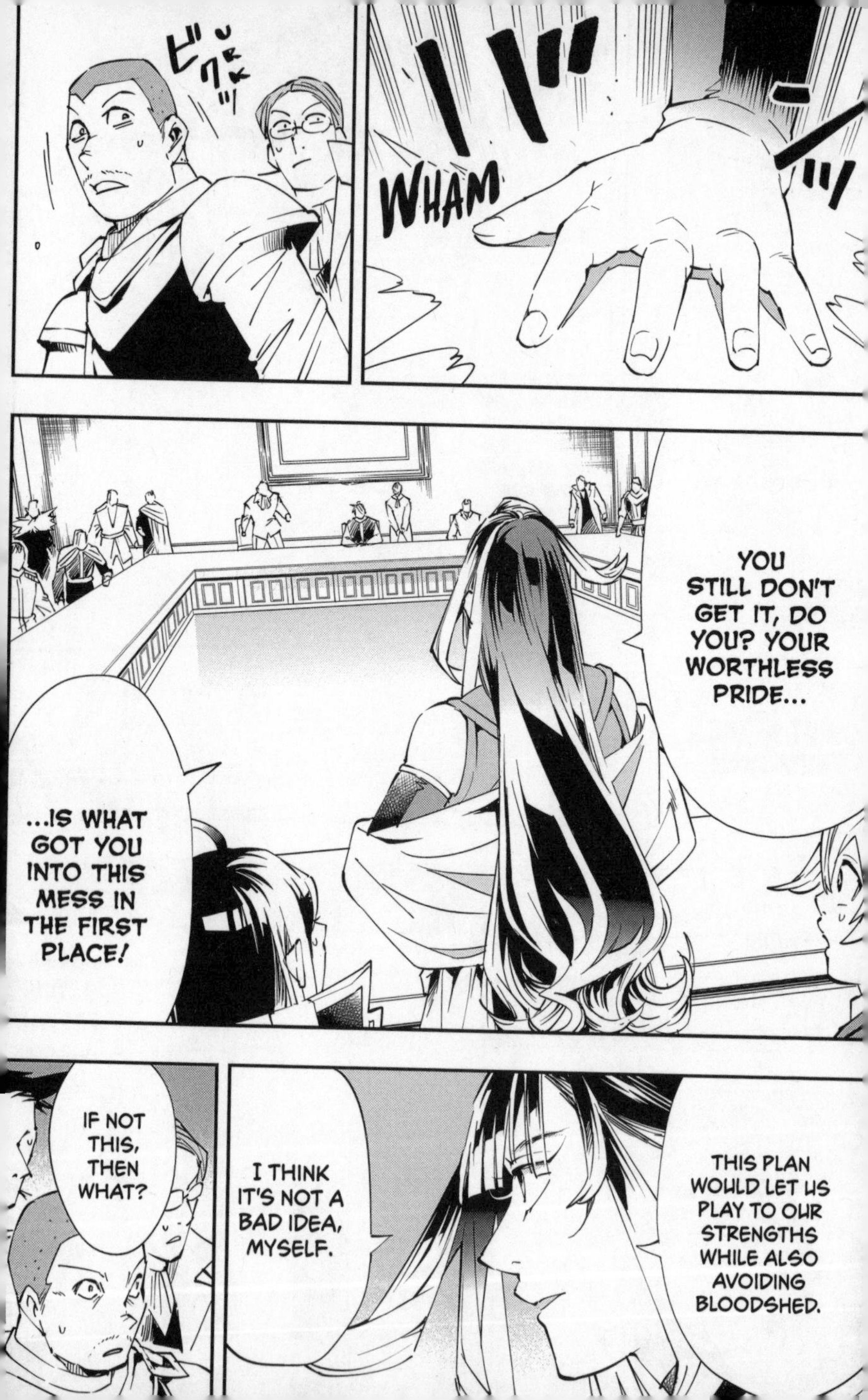
WHAM
ビクッ
YOU STILL DON'T GET IT, DO YOU? YOUR WORTHLESS PRIDE...
...IS WHAT GOT YOU INTO THIS MESS IN THE FIRST PLACE!
THIS PLAN WOULD LET US PLAY TO OUR STRENGTHS WHILE ALSO AVOIDING BLOODSHED.
I THINK IT'S NOT A BAD IDEA, MYSELF.
IF NOT THIS, THEN WHAT?

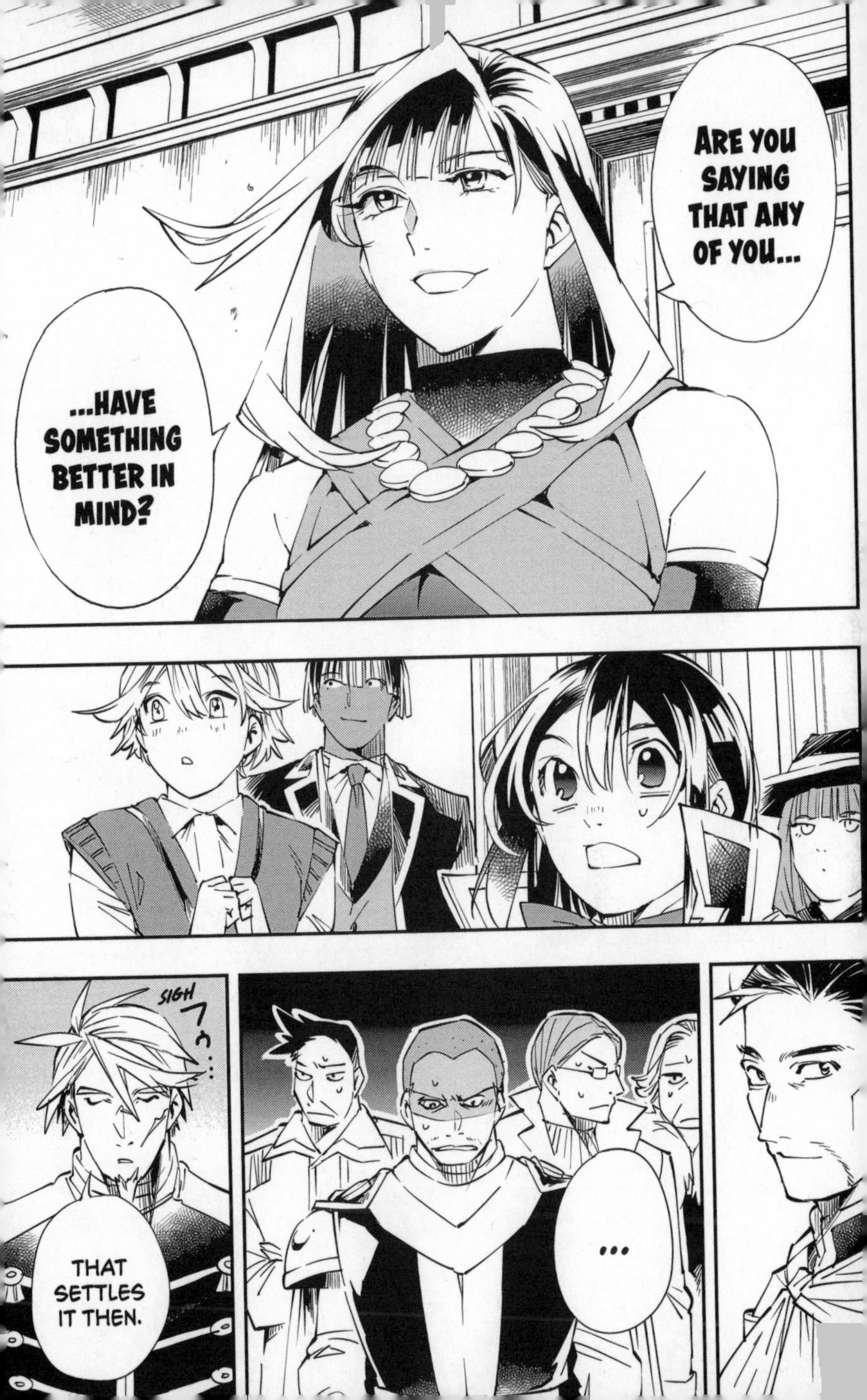
ARE YOU SAYING THAT ANY OF YOU...
...HAVE SOMETHING BETTER IN MIND?
...
SIGH
THAT SETTLES IT THEN.

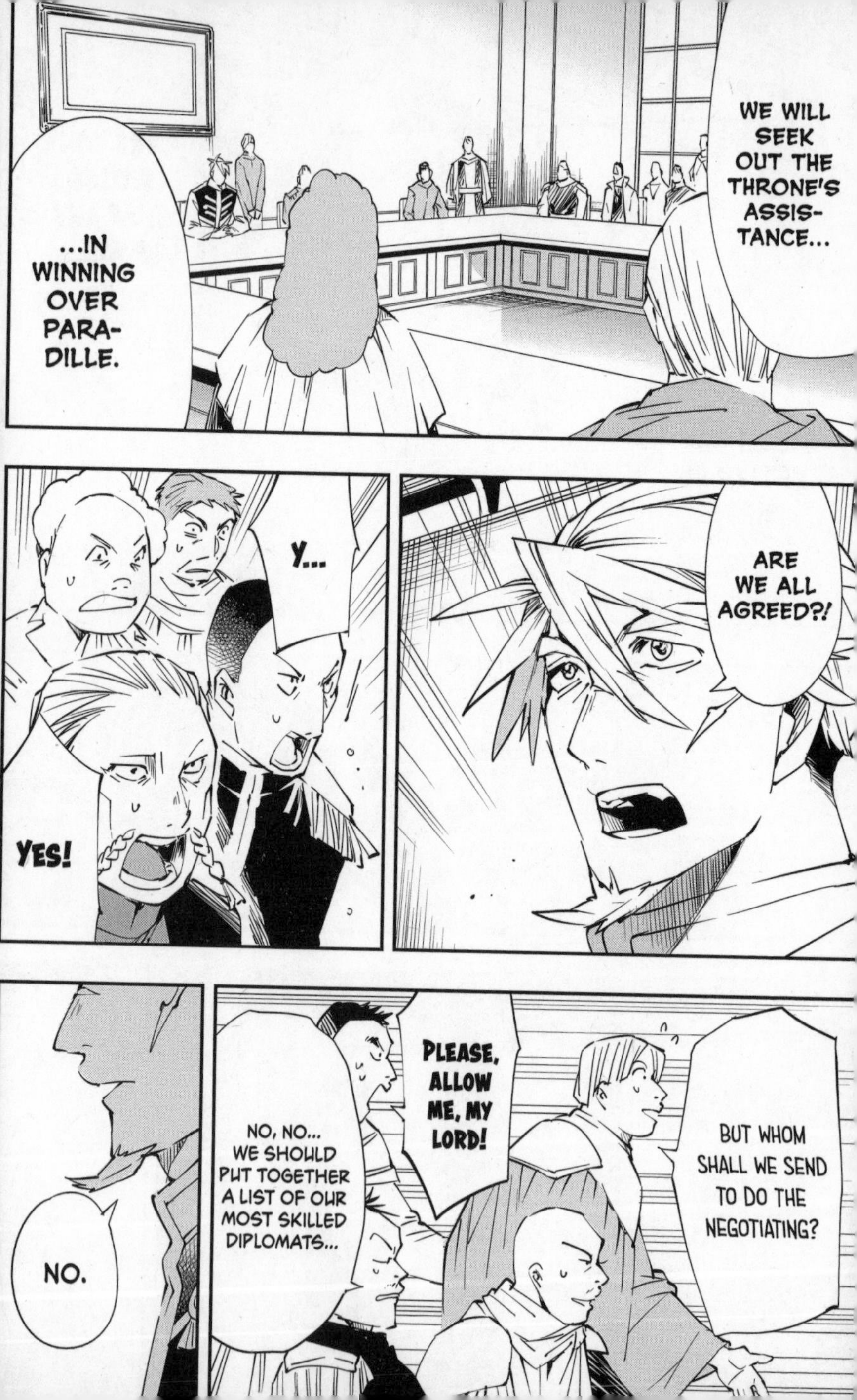
WE WILL SEEK OUT THE THRONE'S ASSISTANCE...
...IN WINNING OVER PARA-DILLE.
ARE WE ALL AGREED?!
Y...
YES!
BUT WHOM SHALL WE SEND TO DO THE NEGOTIATING?
PLEASE, ALLOW ME, MY LORD!
NO, NO... WE SHOULD PUT TOGETHER A LIST OF OUR MOST SKILLED DIPLOMATS...
NO.

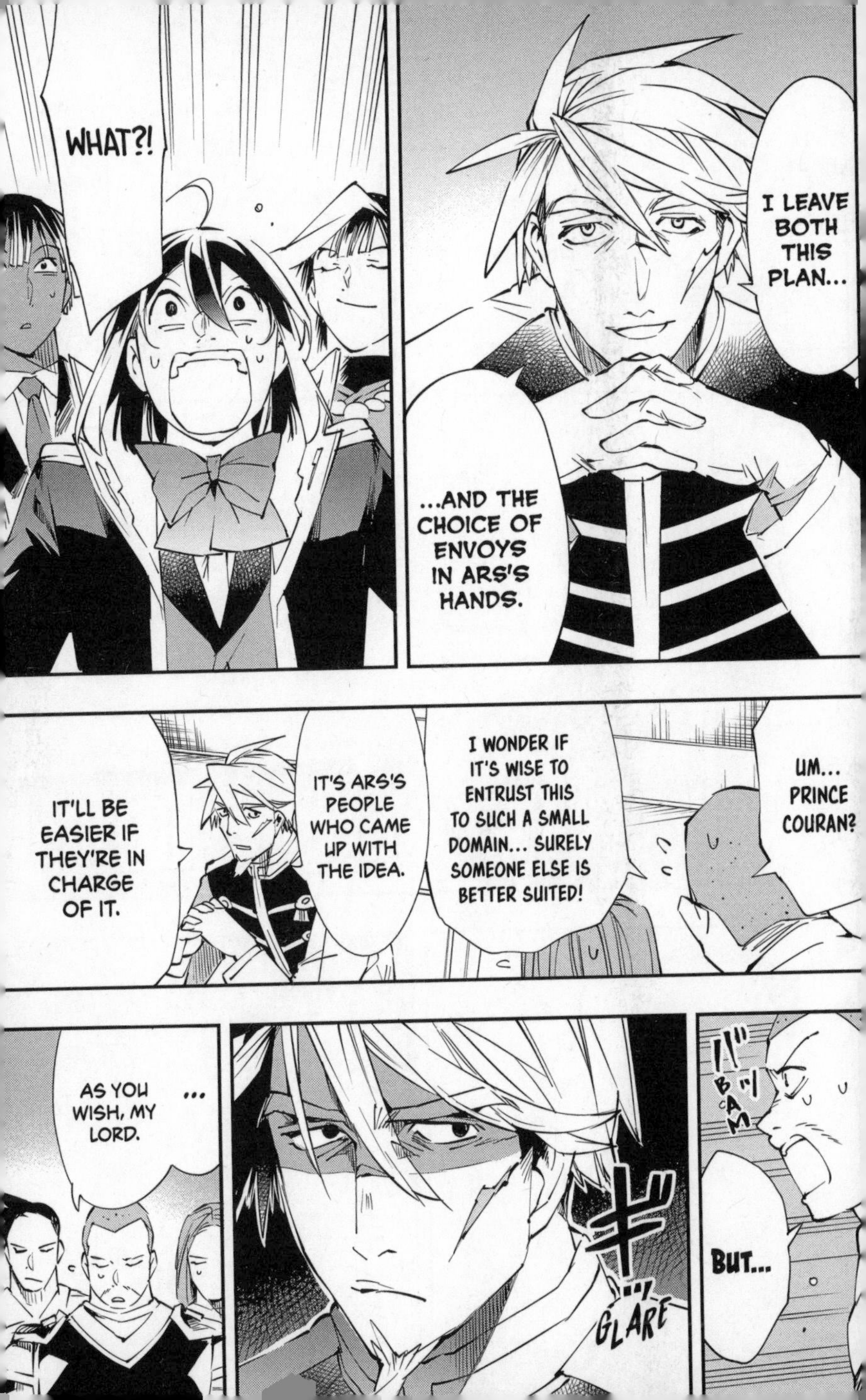

I LEAVE BOTH THIS PLAN...
...AND THE CHOICE OF ENVOYS IN ARS'S HANDS.
WHAT?!
UM... PRINCE COURAN?
I WONDER IF IT'S WISE TO ENTRUST THIS TO SUCH A SMALL DOMAIN... SURELY SOMEONE ELSE IS BETTER SUITED!
IT'S ARS'S PEOPLE WHO CAME UP WITH THE IDEA.
IT'LL BE EASIER IF THEY'RE IN CHARGE OF IT.
BAM
BUT...
GLARE
...
AS YOU WISH, MY LORD.

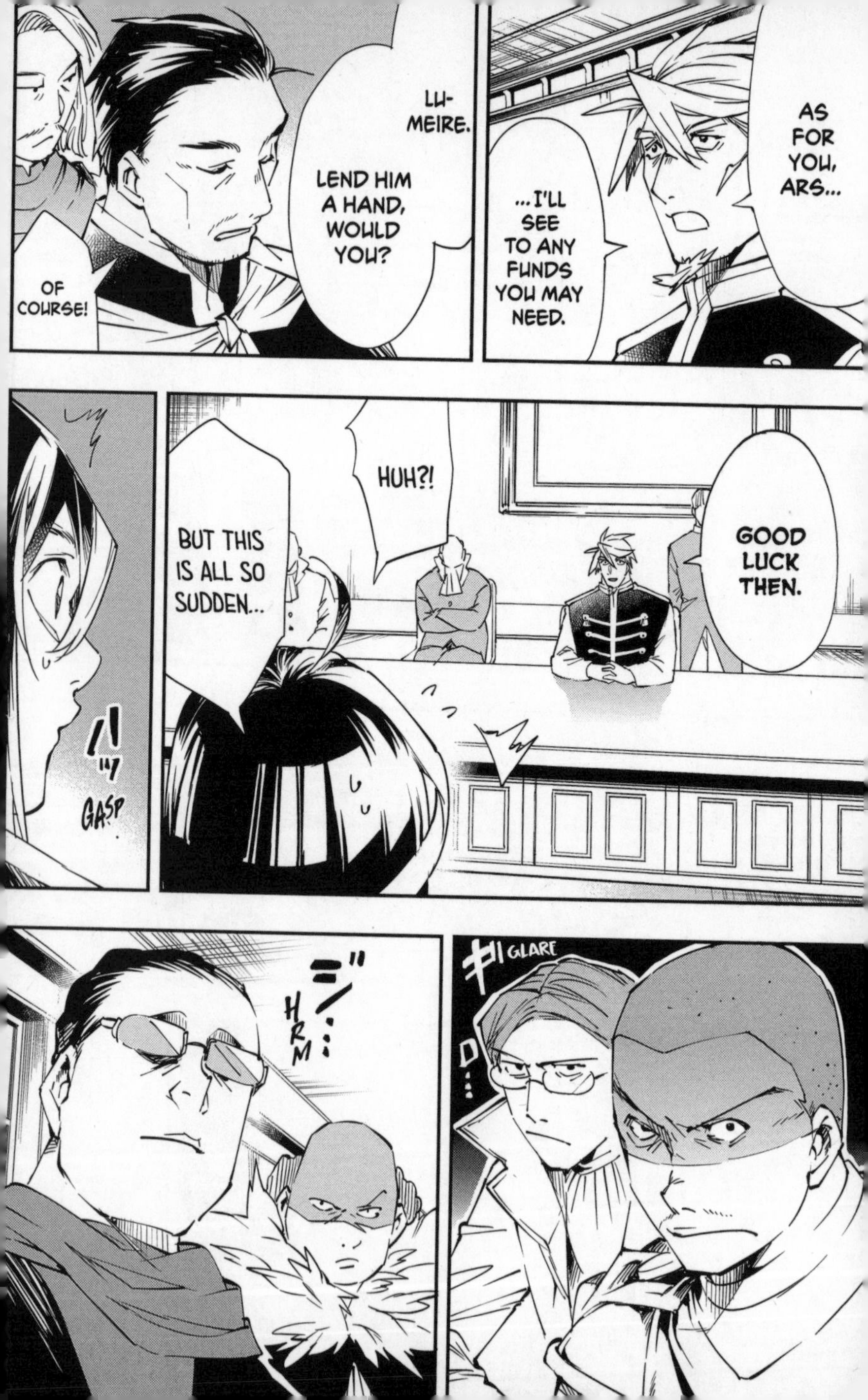
AS FOR YOU, ARS...
...I'LL SEE TO ANY FUNDS YOU MAY NEED.
LU-MEIRE.
LEND HIM A HAND, WOULD YOU?
OF COURSE!
GOOD LUCK THEN.
HUH?!
BUT THIS IS ALL SO SUDDEN...
GASP
GLARE
D...
HRM

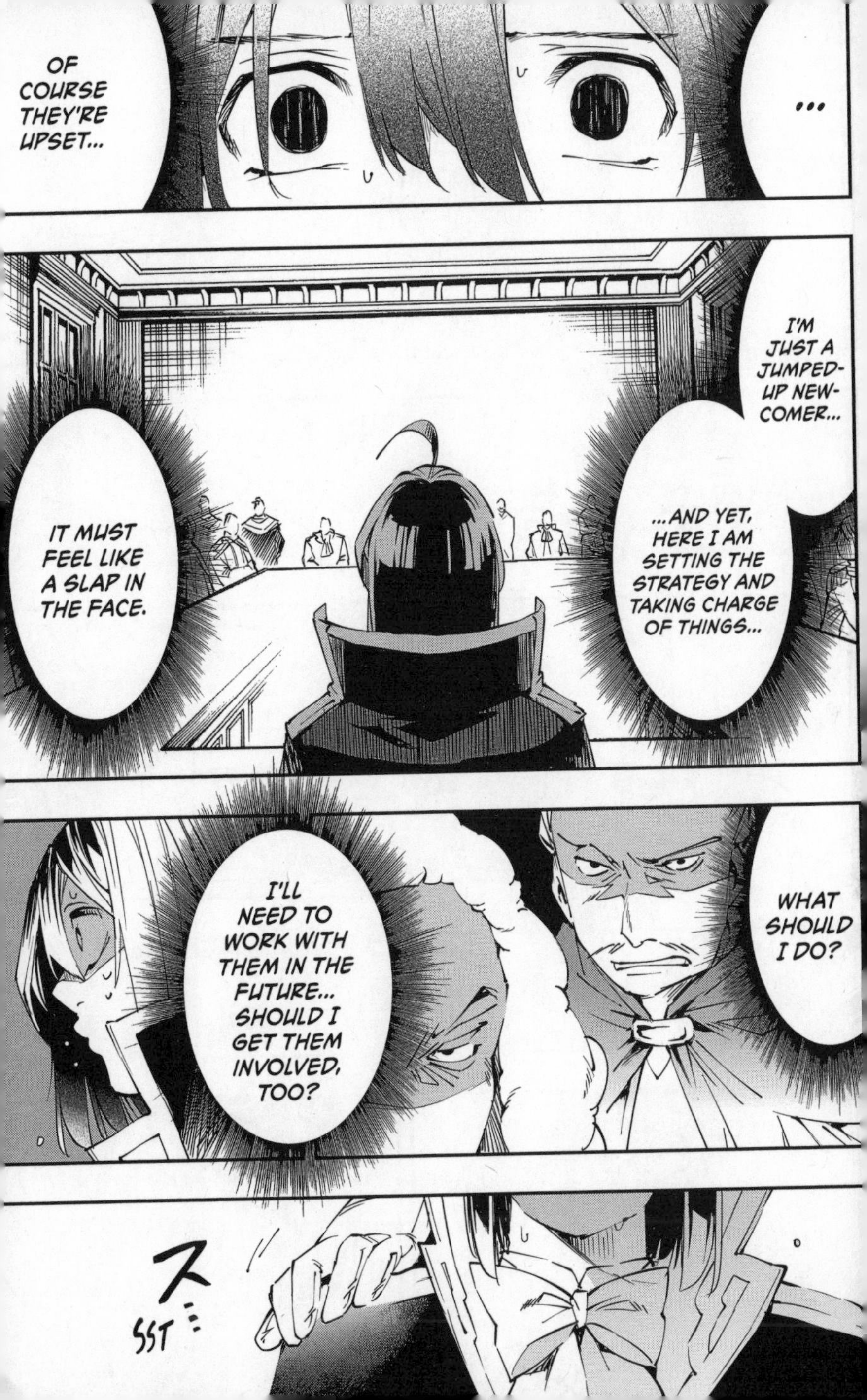
...
OF COURSE THEY'RE UPSET...
I'M JUST A JUMPED-UP NEW-COMER...
...AND YET, HERE I AM SETTING THE STRATEGY AND TAKING CHARGE OF THINGS...
IT MUST FEEL LIKE A SLAP IN THE FACE.
WHAT SHOULD I DO?
I'LL NEED TO WORK WITH THEM IN THE FUTURE... SHOULD I GET THEM INVOLVED, TOO?
ス
SST

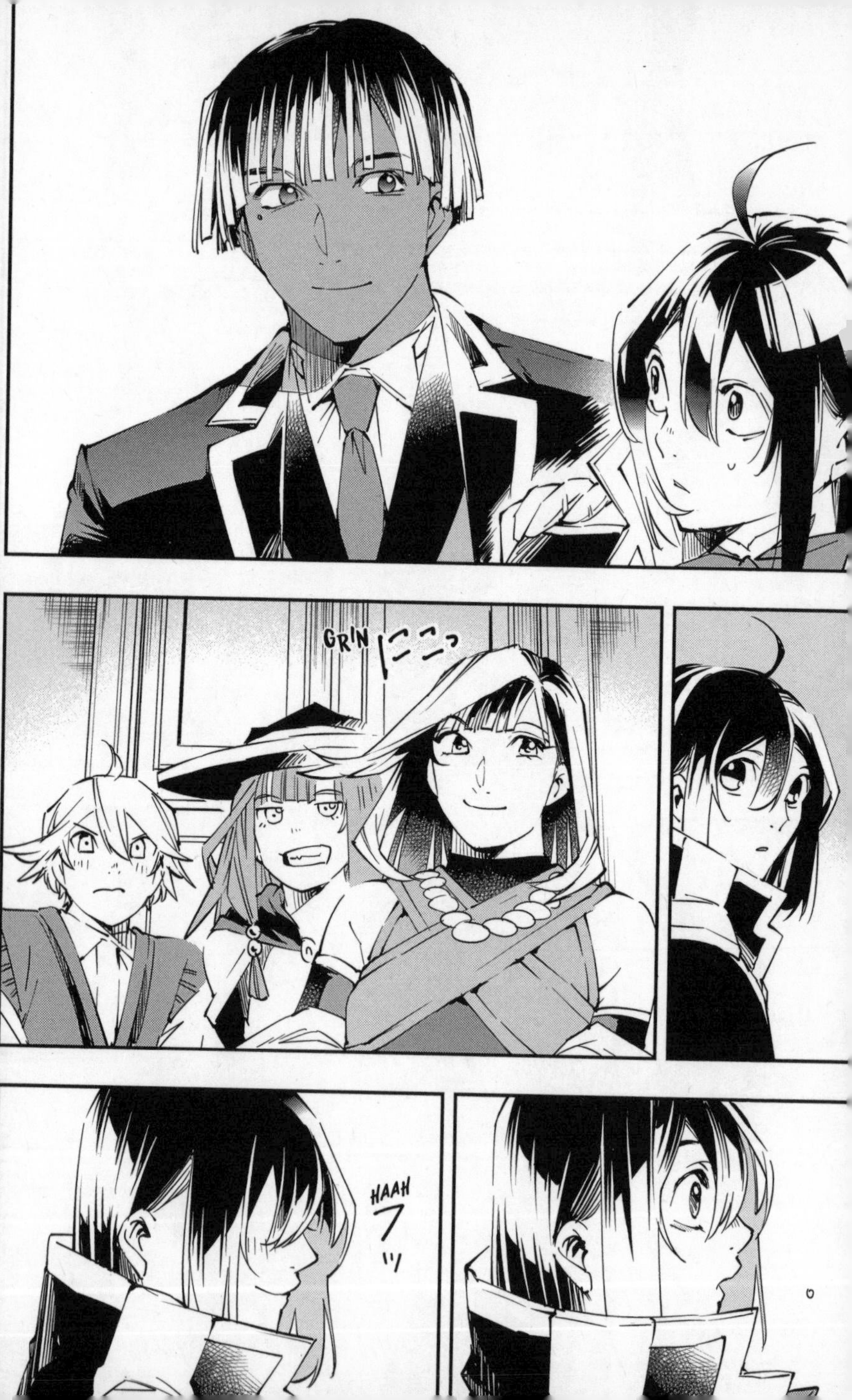
GRIN にこっ
HAAH フッ

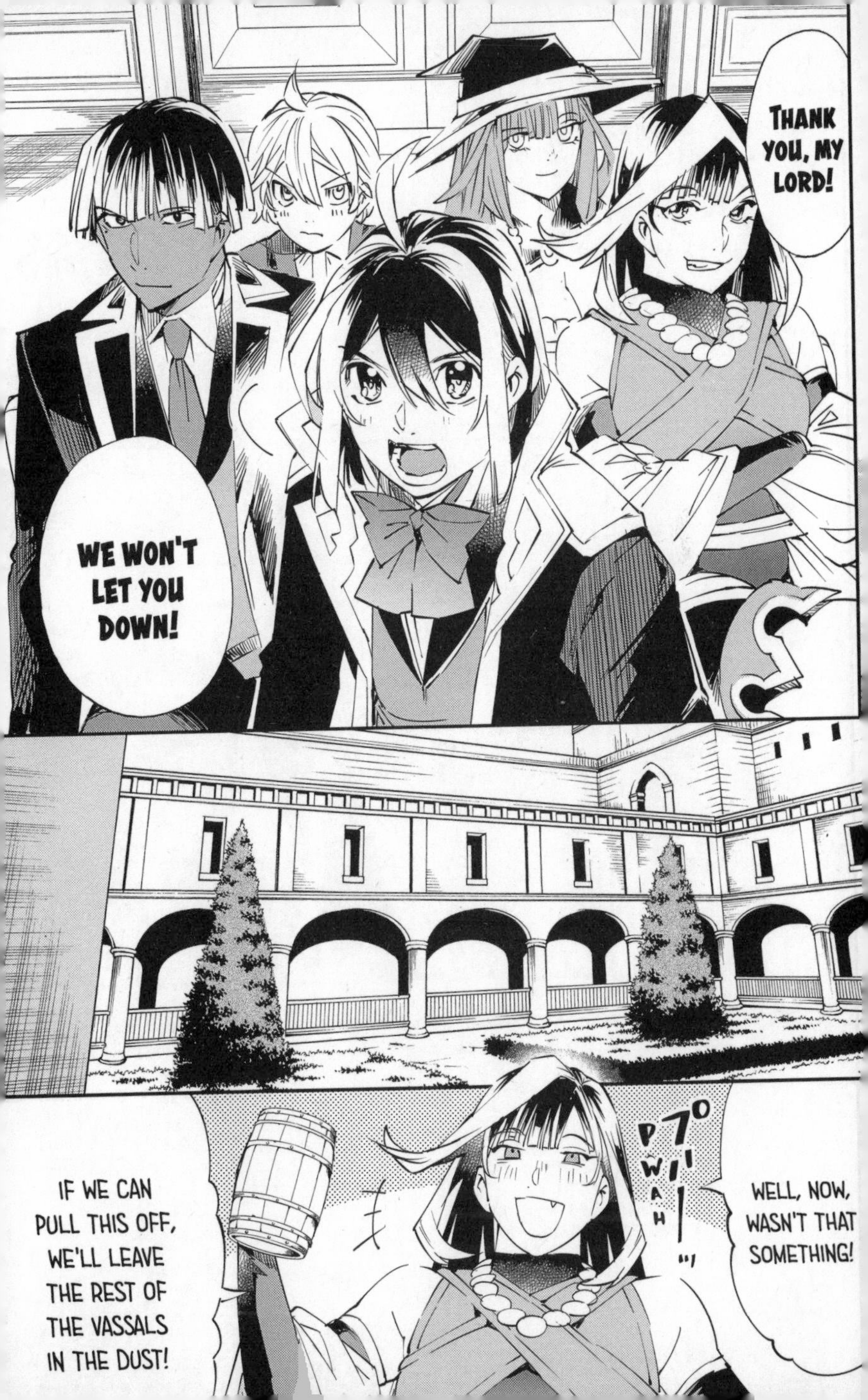
THANK YOU, MY LORD!
WE WON'T LET YOU DOWN!
WELL, NOW, WASN'T THAT SOMETHING!
PWAH
IF WE CAN PULL THIS OFF, WE'LL LEAVE THE REST OF THE VASSALS IN THE DUST!

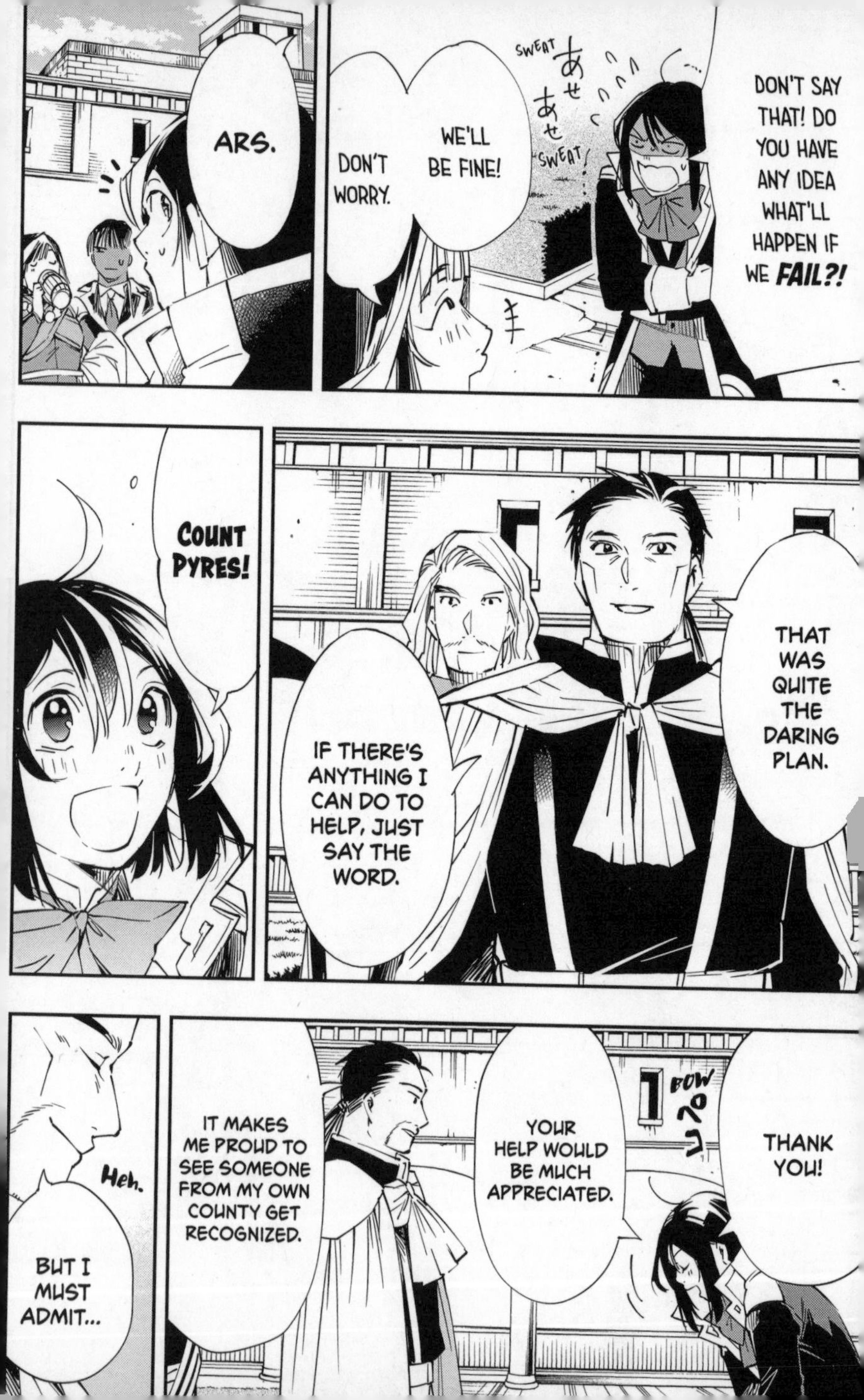

DON'T SAY THAT! DO YOU HAVE ANY IDEA WHAT'LL HAPPEN IF WE **FAIL?!**
SWEAT
あせ あせ
SWEAT
WE'LL BE FINE!
DON'T WORRY.
ARS.
THAT WAS QUITE THE DARING PLAN.
IF THERE'S ANYTHING I CAN DO TO HELP, JUST SAY THE WORD.
COUNT PYRES!
THANK YOU!
BOW
ペコ
YOUR HELP WOULD BE MUCH APPRECIATED.
IT MAKES ME PROUD TO SEE SOMEONE FROM MY OWN COUNTY GET RECOGNIZED.
Heh.
BUT I MUST ADMIT...

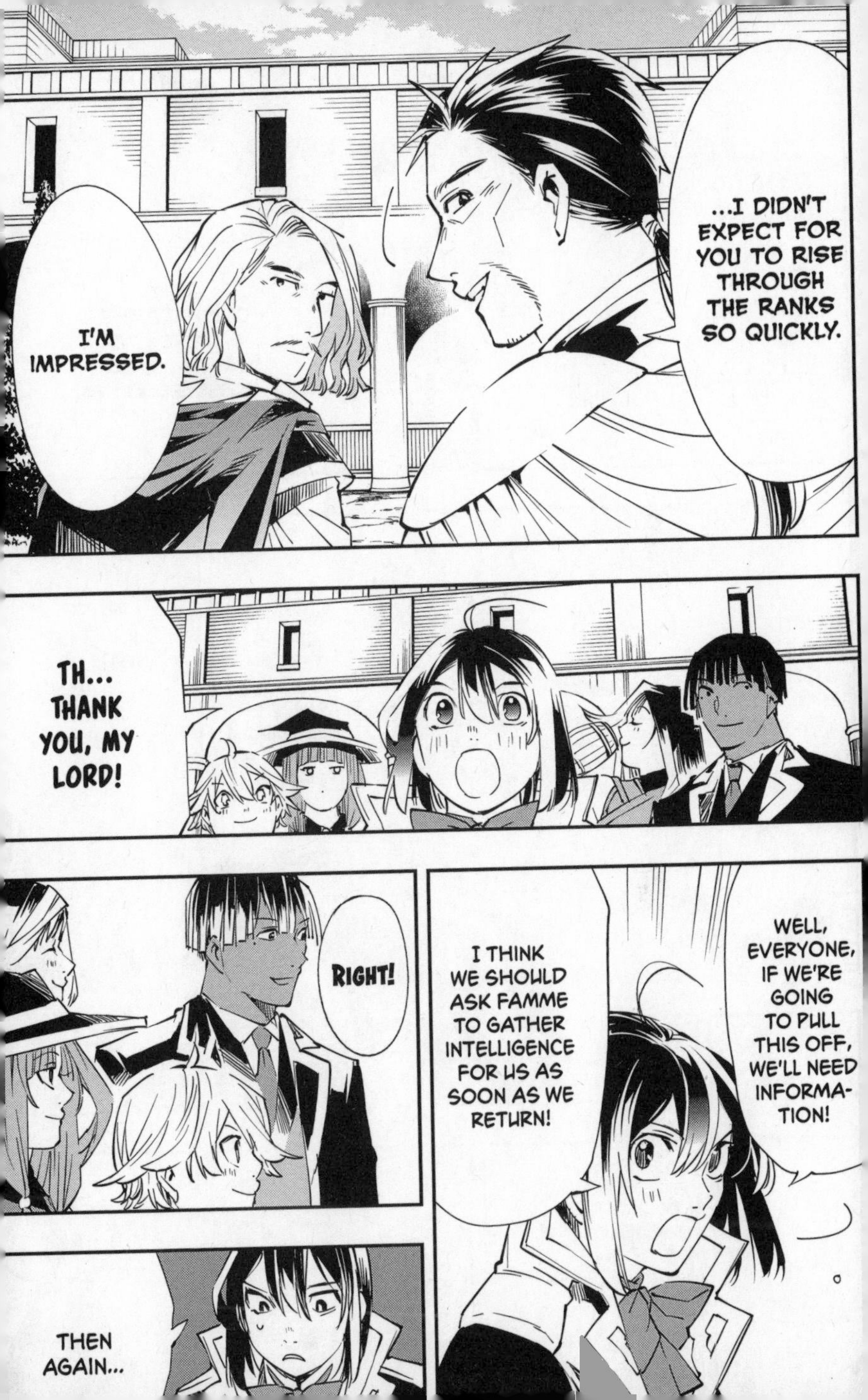
...I DIDN'T EXPECT FOR YOU TO RISE THROUGH THE RANKS SO QUICKLY.
I'M IMPRESSED.
TH... THANK YOU, MY LORD!
WELL, EVERYONE, IF WE'RE GOING TO PULL THIS OFF, WE'LL NEED INFORMATION!
I THINK WE SHOULD ASK FAMME TO GATHER INTELLIGENCE FOR US AS SOON AS WE RETURN!
RIGHT!
THEN AGAIN...

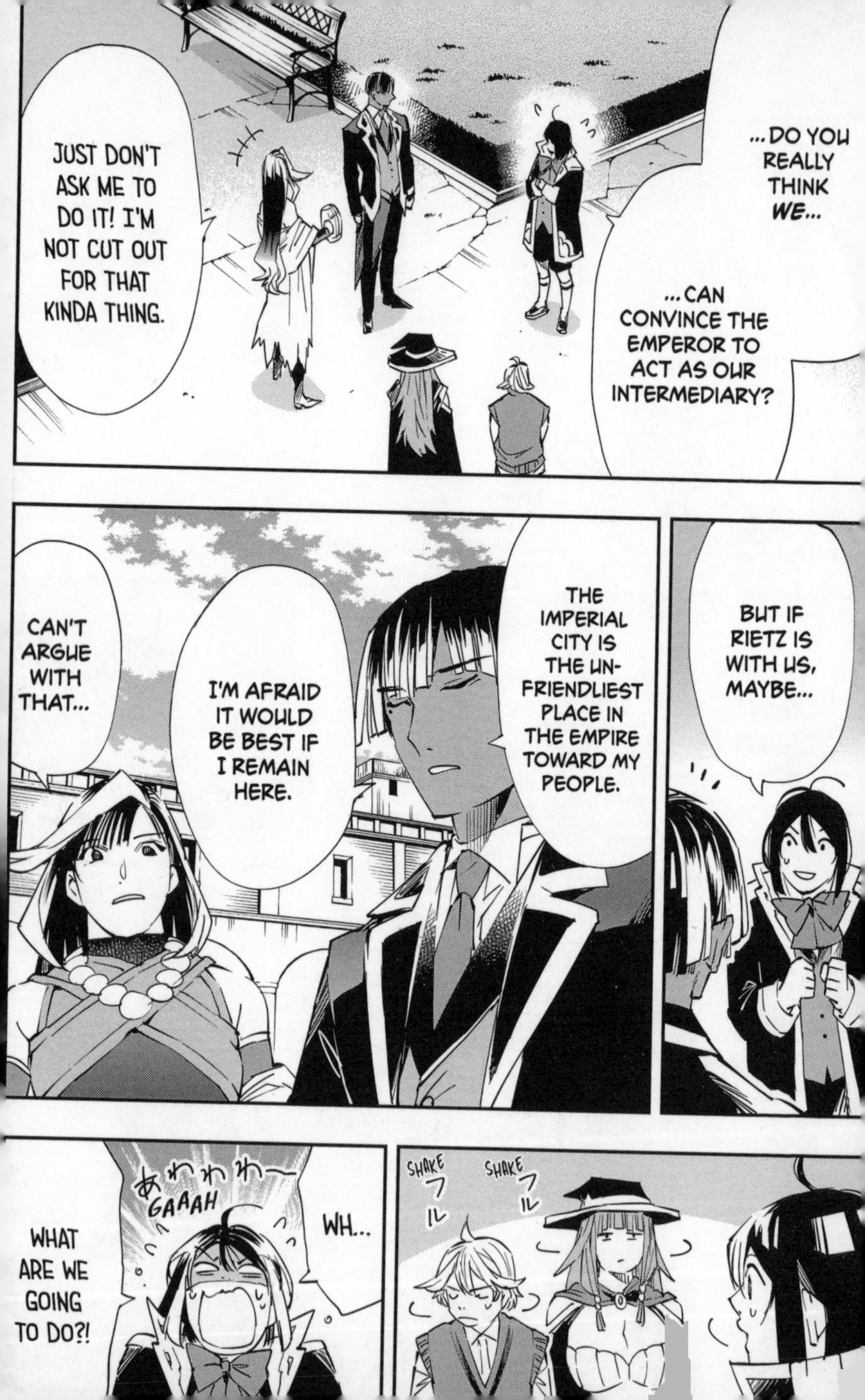
...DO YOU REALLY THINK WE...
...CAN CONVINCE THE EMPEROR TO ACT AS OUR INTERMEDIARY?
JUST DON'T ASK ME TO DO IT! I'M NOT CUT OUT FOR THAT KINDA THING.
BUT IF RIETZ IS WITH US, MAYBE...
THE IMPERIAL CITY IS THE UN-FRIENDLIEST PLACE IN THE EMPIRE TOWARD MY PEOPLE.
I'M AFRAID IT WOULD BE BEST IF I REMAIN HERE.
CAN'T ARGUE WITH THAT...
SHAKE フル
SHAKE フル
WH...
あわわわー GAAAH
WHAT ARE WE GOING TO DO?!

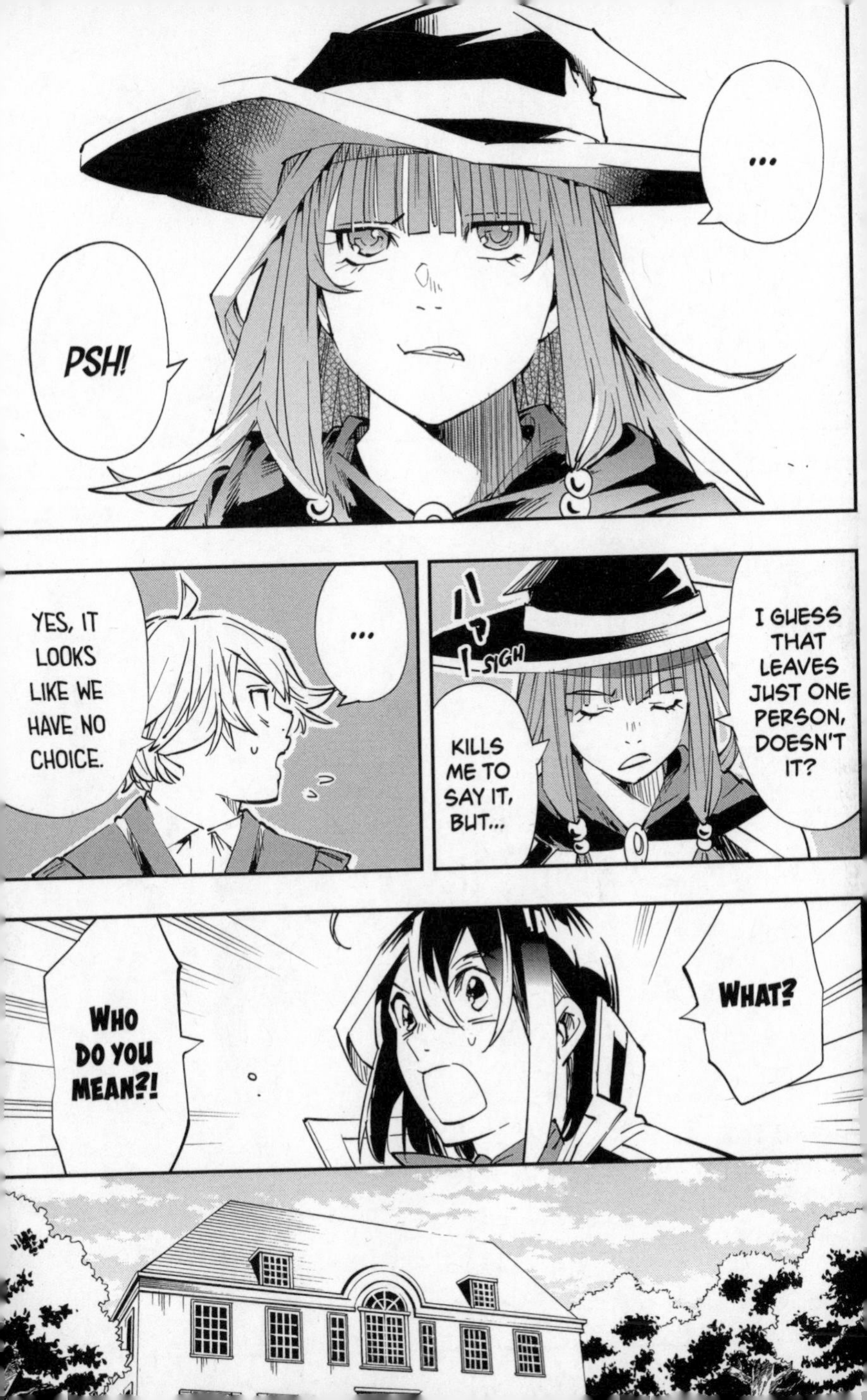
...
PSH!
SIGH
KILLS ME TO SAY IT, BUT...
I GUESS THAT LEAVES JUST ONE PERSON, DOESN'T IT?
...
YES, IT LOOKS LIKE WE HAVE NO CHOICE.
WHAT?
WHO DO YOU MEAN?!

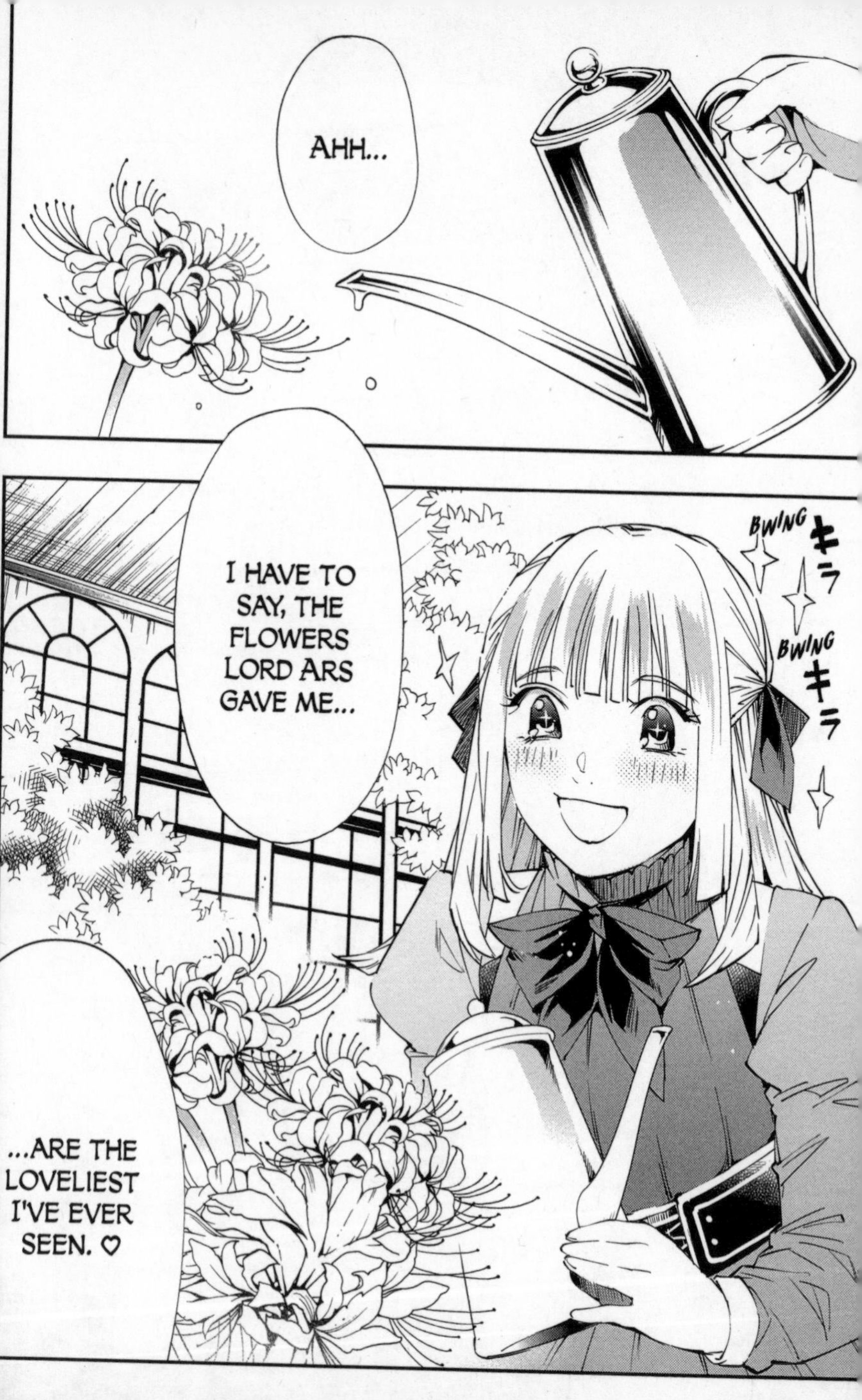
AHH...
BWING キラ
I HAVE TO SAY, THE FLOWERS LORD ARS GAVE ME...
BWING キラ
...ARE THE LOVELIEST I'VE EVER SEEN. ♡

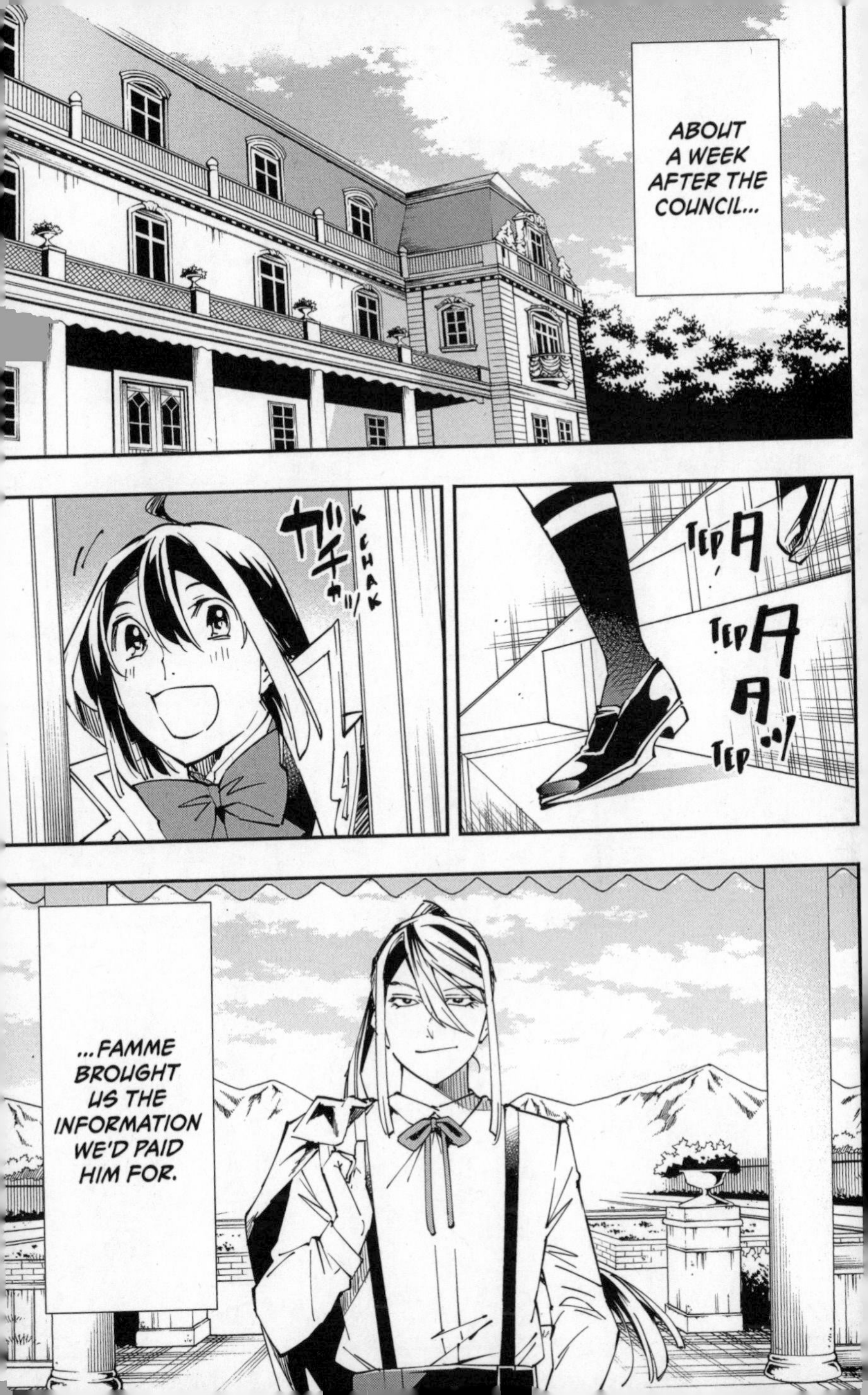
ABOUT A WEEK AFTER THE COUNCIL...
TEP
TEP
TEP
KCHAK
...FAMME BROUGHT US THE INFORMATION WE'D PAID HIM FOR.

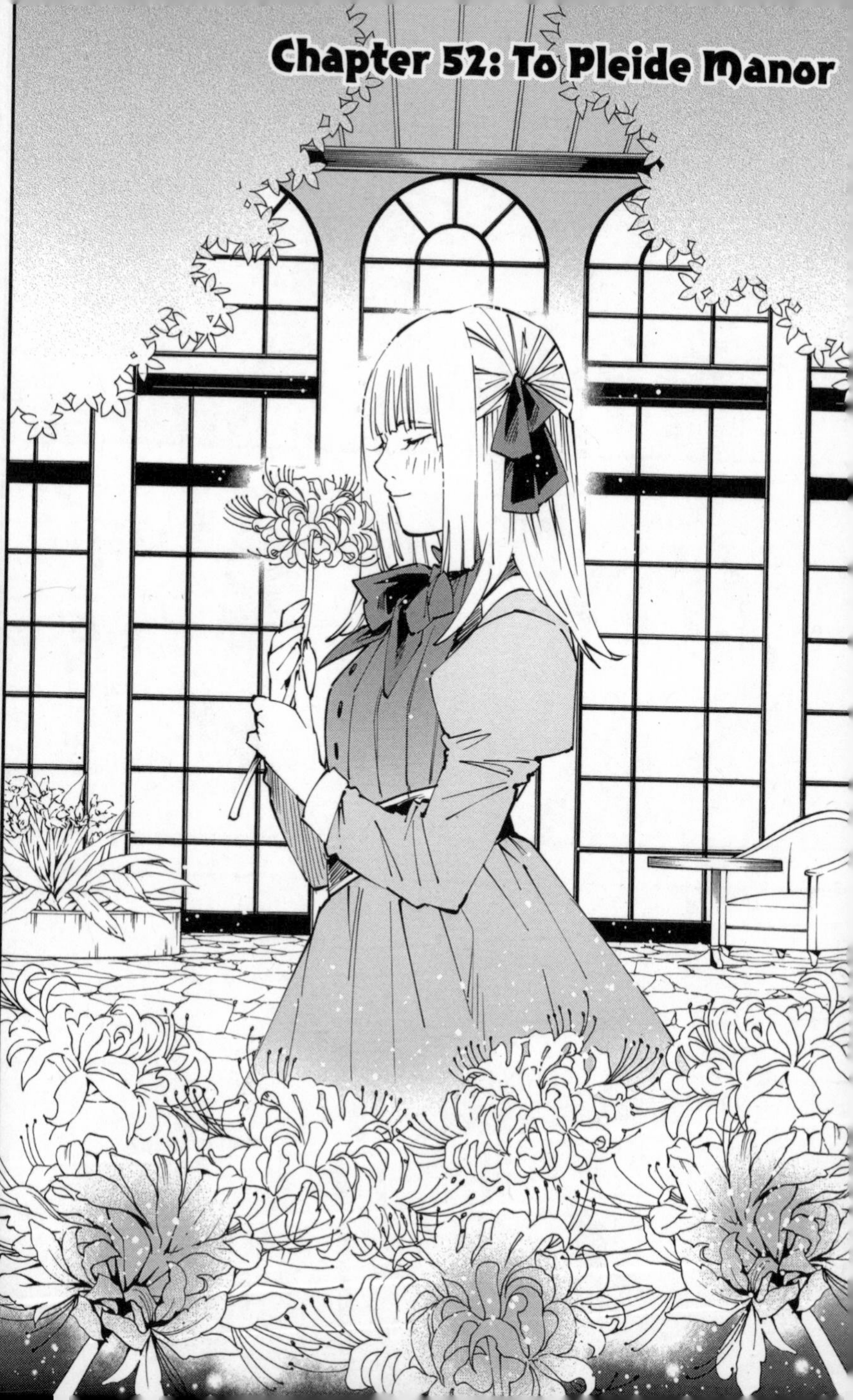
Chapter 52: To Pleide Manor

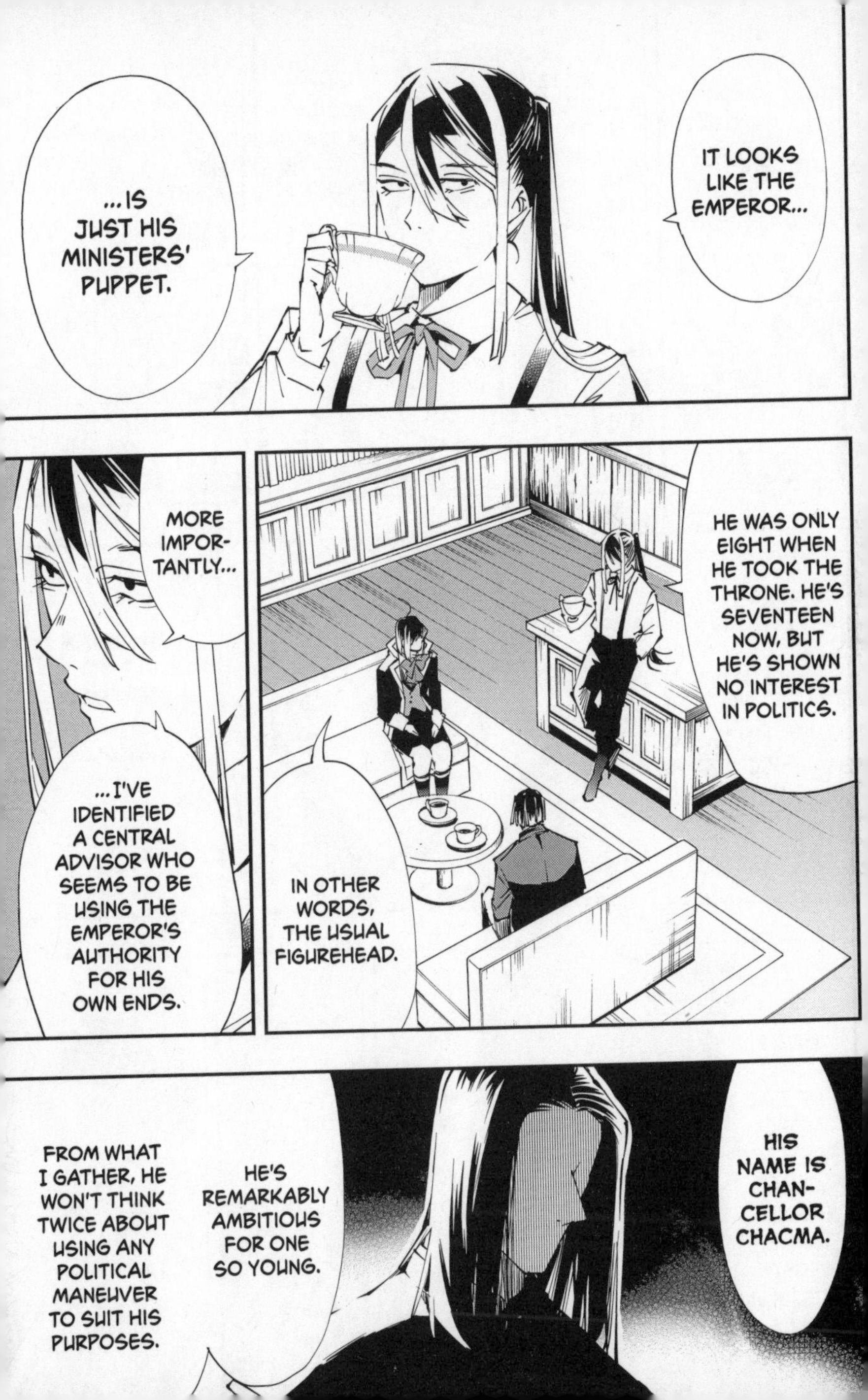
IT LOOKS LIKE THE EMPEROR...
...IS JUST HIS MINISTERS' PUPPET.
HE WAS ONLY EIGHT WHEN HE TOOK THE THRONE. HE'S SEVENTEEN NOW, BUT HE'S SHOWN NO INTEREST IN POLITICS.
IN OTHER WORDS, THE USUAL FIGUREHEAD.
MORE IMPOR-TANTLY...
...I'VE IDENTIFIED A CENTRAL ADVISOR WHO SEEMS TO BE USING THE EMPEROR'S AUTHORITY FOR HIS OWN ENDS.
HIS NAME IS CHAN-CELLOR CHACMA.
HE'S REMARKABLY AMBITIOUS FOR ONE SO YOUNG.
FROM WHAT I GATHER, HE WON'T THINK TWICE ABOUT USING ANY POLITICAL MANEUVER TO SUIT HIS PURPOSES.

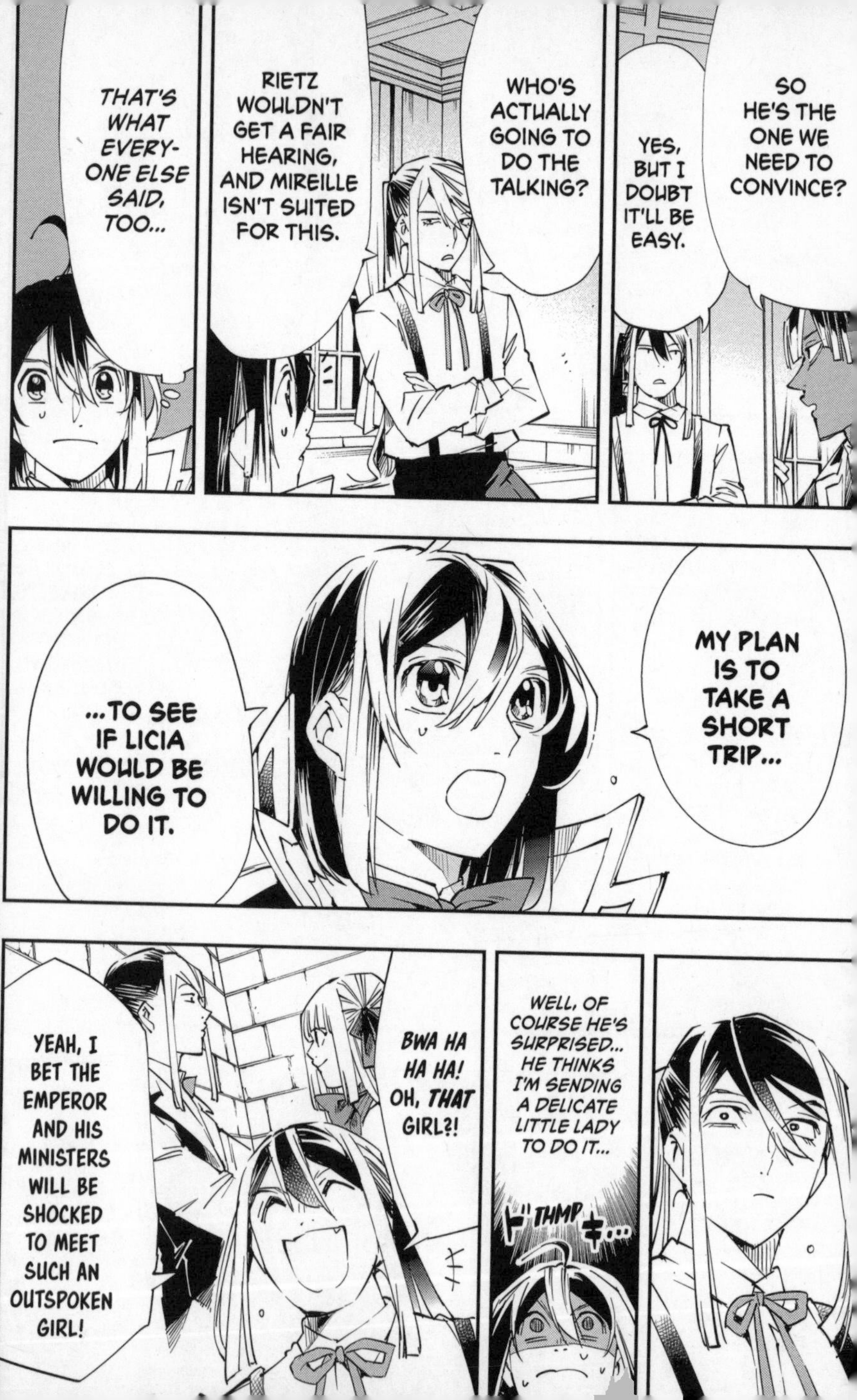
SO HE'S THE ONE WE NEED TO CONVINCE?
YES, BUT I DOUBT IT'LL BE EASY.
WHO'S ACTUALLY GOING TO DO THE TALKING?
RIETZ WOULDN'T GET A FAIR HEARING, AND MIREILLE ISN'T SUITED FOR THIS.
THAT'S WHAT EVERYONE ELSE SAID, TOO...
MY PLAN IS TO TAKE A SHORT TRIP...
...TO SEE IF LICIA WOULD BE WILLING TO DO IT.
WELL, OF COURSE HE'S SURPRISED... HE THINKS I'M SENDING A DELICATE LITTLE LADY TO DO IT...
ド THMP キ...
BWA HA HA HA! OH, THAT GIRL?!
YEAH, I BET THE EMPEROR AND HIS MINISTERS WILL BE SHOCKED TO MEET SUCH AN OUTSPOKEN GIRL!

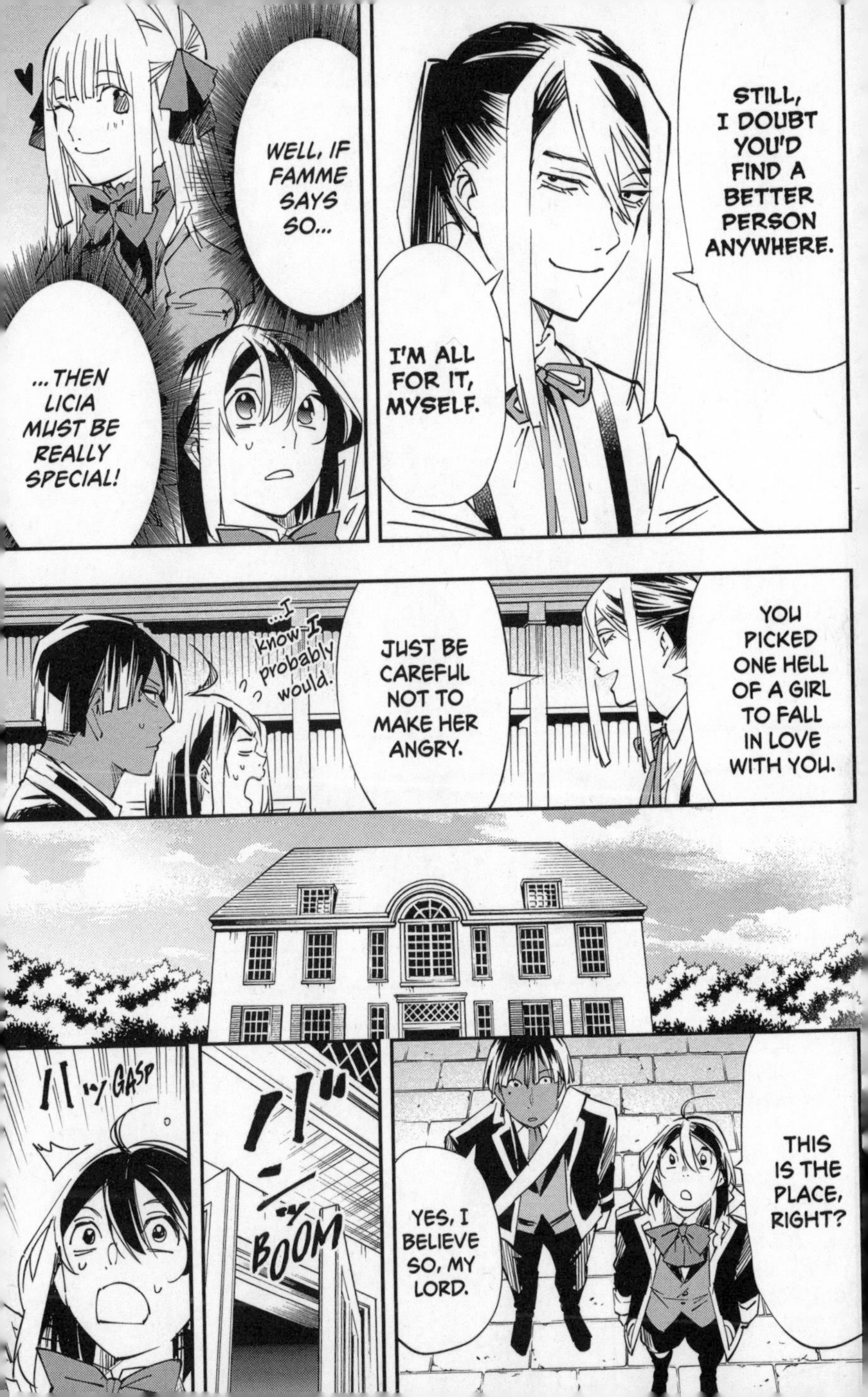
STILL, I DOUBT YOU'D FIND A BETTER PERSON ANYWHERE.
I'M ALL FOR IT, MYSELF.
WELL, IF FAMME SAYS SO...
...THEN LICIA MUST BE REALLY SPECIAL!
YOU PICKED ONE HELL OF A GIRL TO FALL IN LOVE WITH YOU.
JUST BE CAREFUL NOT TO MAKE HER ANGRY.
...I know I probably would.
THIS IS THE PLACE, RIGHT?
YES, I BELIEVE SO, MY LORD.
BOOM
GASP

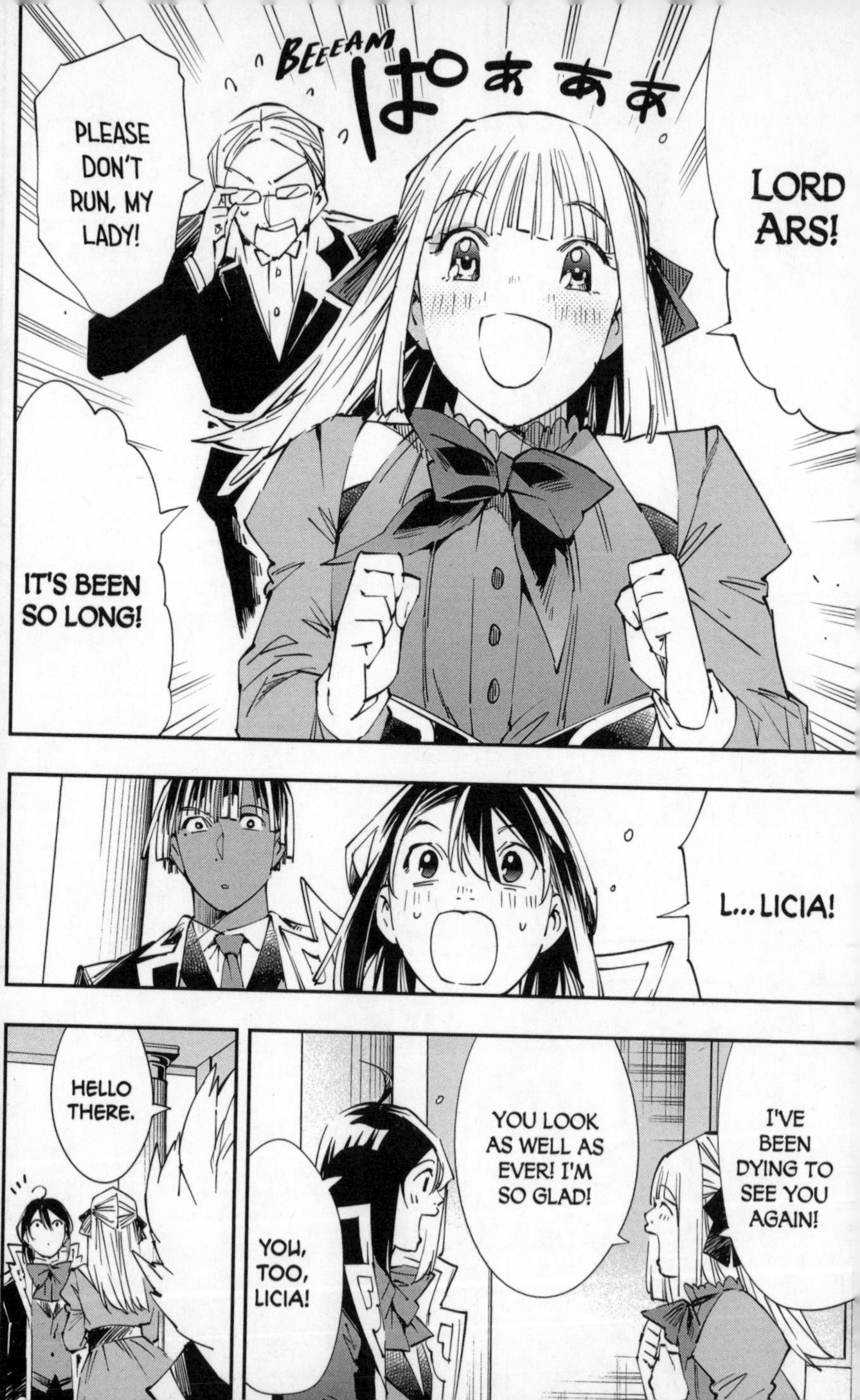
BEEEAM
ぱぁぁぁ
LORD ARS!
PLEASE DON'T RUN, MY LADY!
IT'S BEEN SO LONG!
L...LICIA!
I'VE BEEN DYING TO SEE YOU AGAIN!
YOU LOOK AS WELL AS EVER! I'M SO GLAD!
YOU, TOO, LICIA!
HELLO THERE.

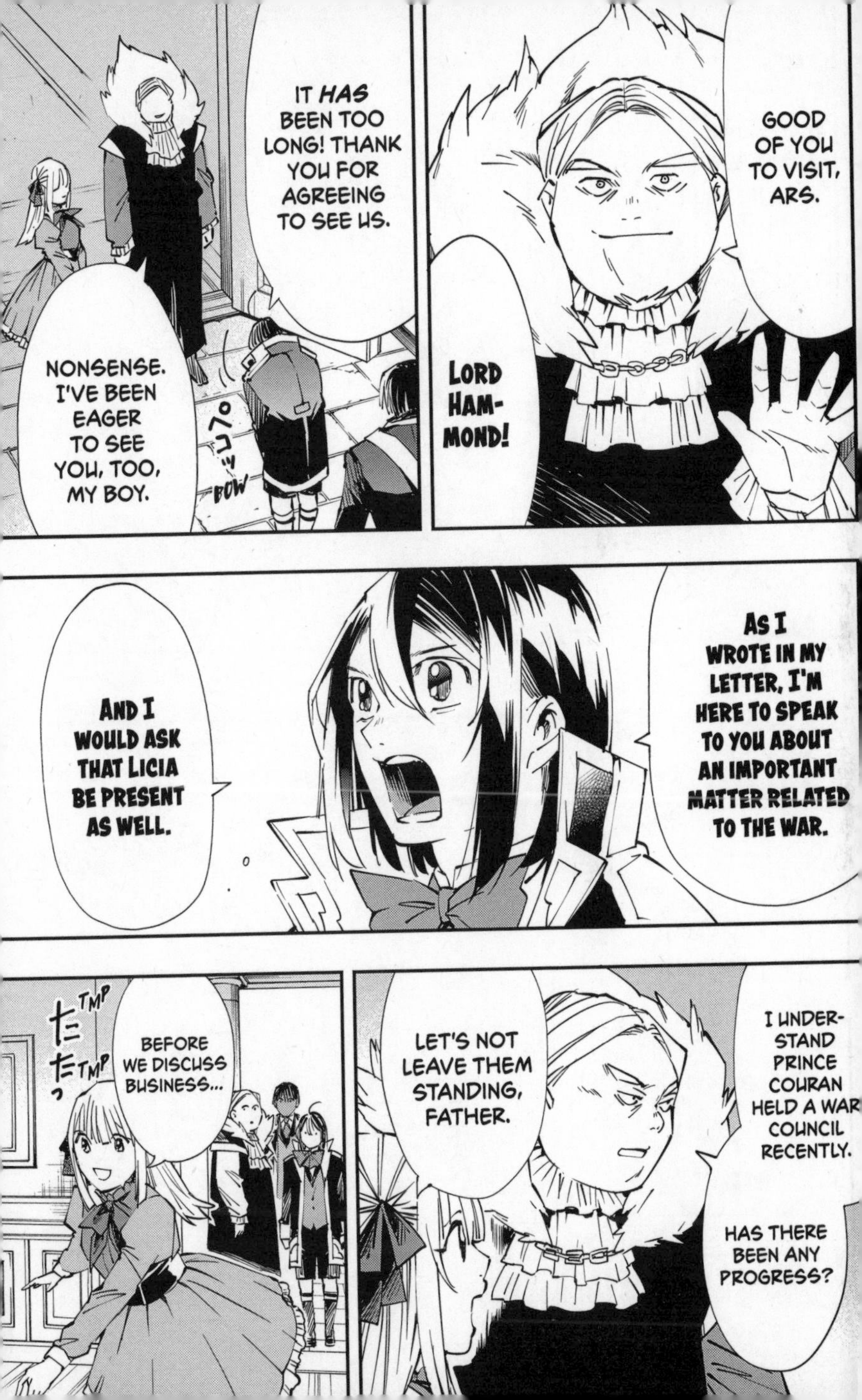

GOOD OF YOU TO VISIT, ARS.
LORD HAMMOND!
IT HAS BEEN TOO LONG! THANK YOU FOR AGREEING TO SEE US.
BOW
NONSENSE. I'VE BEEN EAGER TO SEE YOU, TOO, MY BOY.
AS I WROTE IN MY LETTER, I'M HERE TO SPEAK TO YOU ABOUT AN IMPORTANT MATTER RELATED TO THE WAR.
AND I WOULD ASK THAT LICIA BE PRESENT AS WELL.
I UNDERSTAND PRINCE COURAN HELD A WAR COUNCIL RECENTLY.
HAS THERE BEEN ANY PROGRESS?
LET'S NOT LEAVE THEM STANDING, FATHER.
TMP
TMP
BEFORE WE DISCUSS BUSINESS...

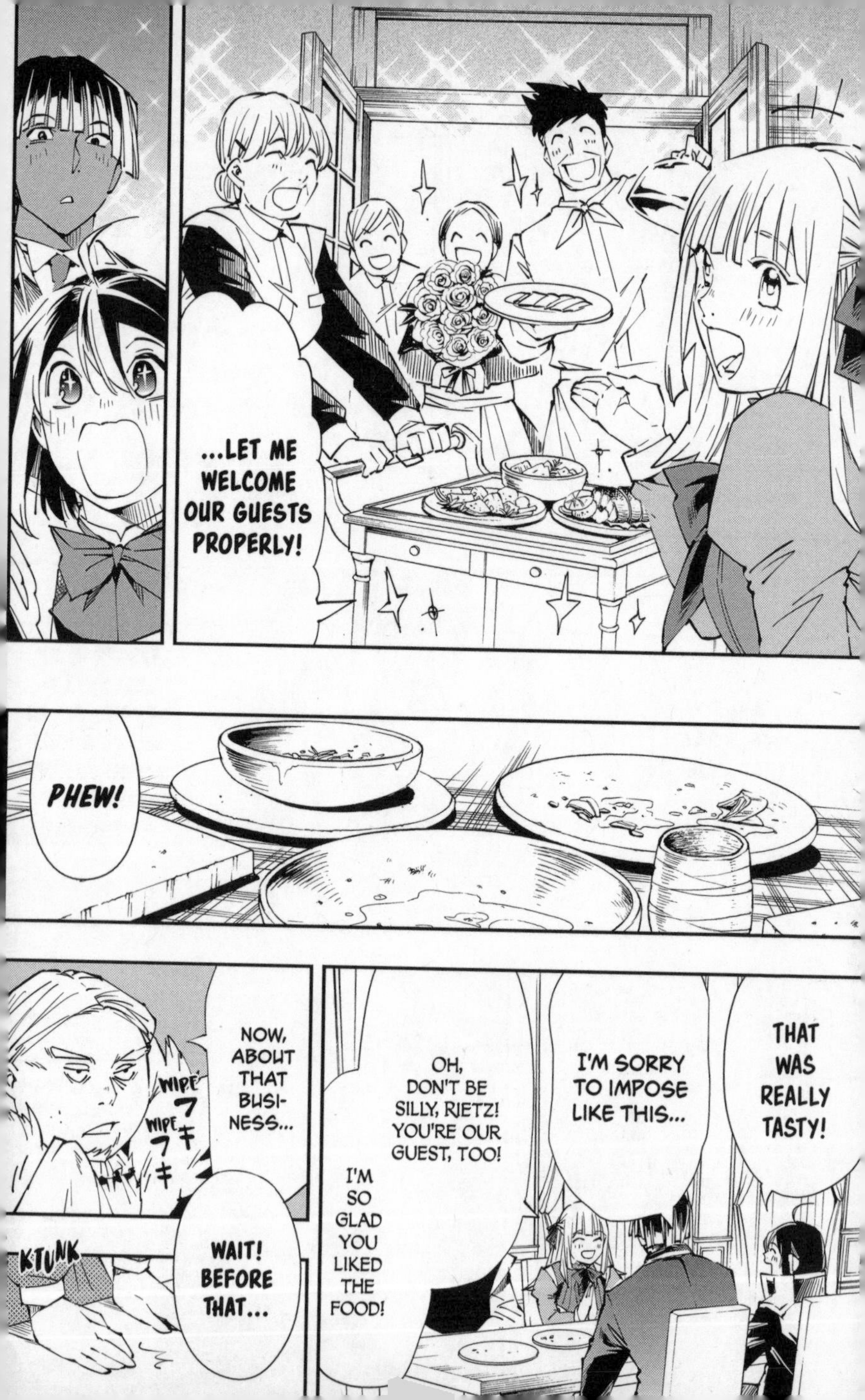
...LET ME WELCOME OUR GUESTS PROPERLY!
PHEW!
THAT WAS REALLY TASTY!
I'M SORRY TO IMPOSE LIKE THIS...
OH, DON'T BE SILLY, RIETZ! YOU'RE OUR GUEST, TOO!
I'M SO GLAD YOU LIKED THE FOOD!
NOW, ABOUT THAT BUSI-NESS...
WIPE フキ
WIPE フキ
WAIT! BEFORE THAT...
K-TUNK

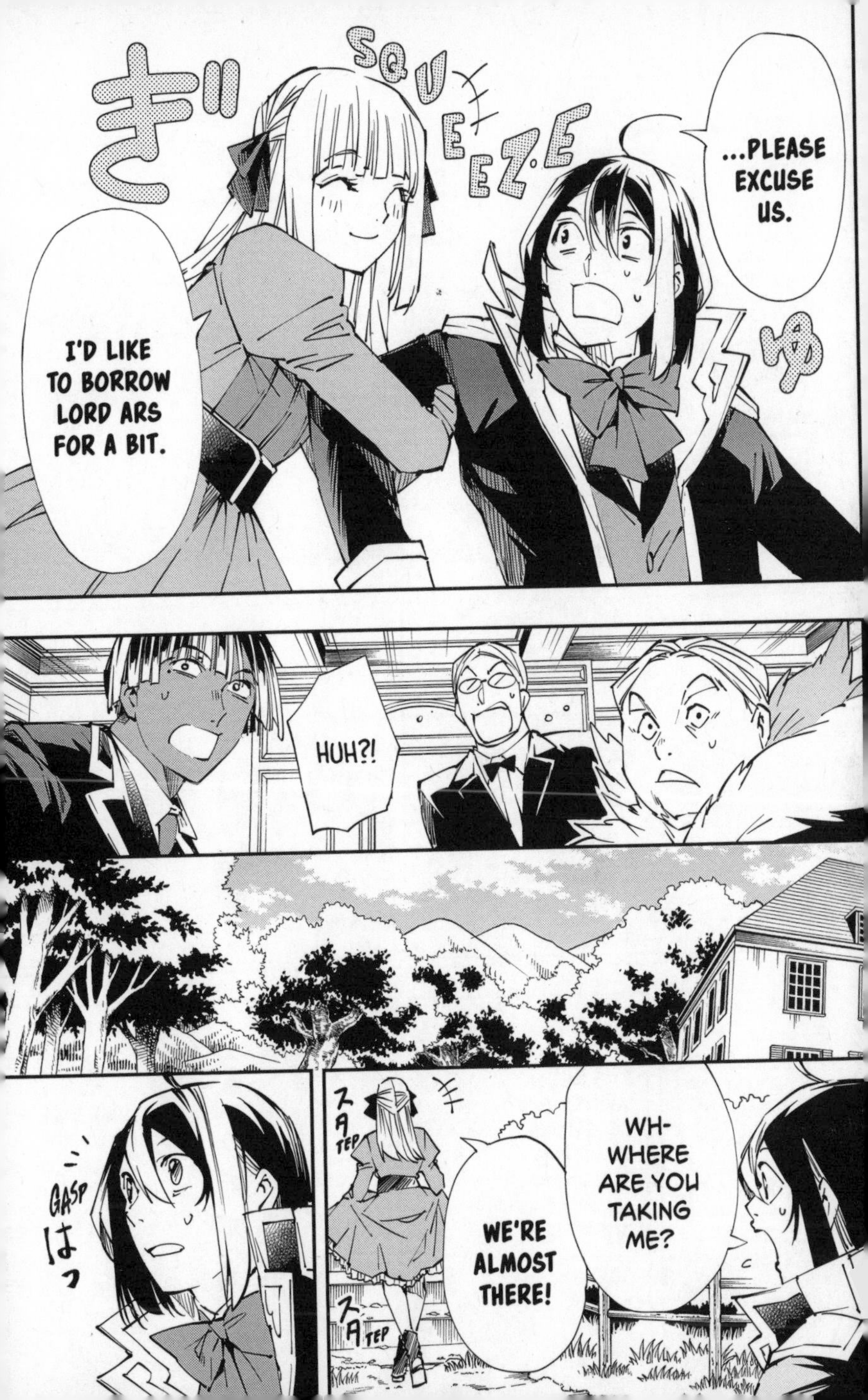
...PLEASE EXCUSE US.
SQUEEZE
ぎゅ
I'D LIKE TO BORROW LORD ARS FOR A BIT.
HUH?!
WH- WHERE ARE YOU TAKING ME?
WE'RE ALMOST THERE!
スタ TEP
スタ TEP
GASP
はっ

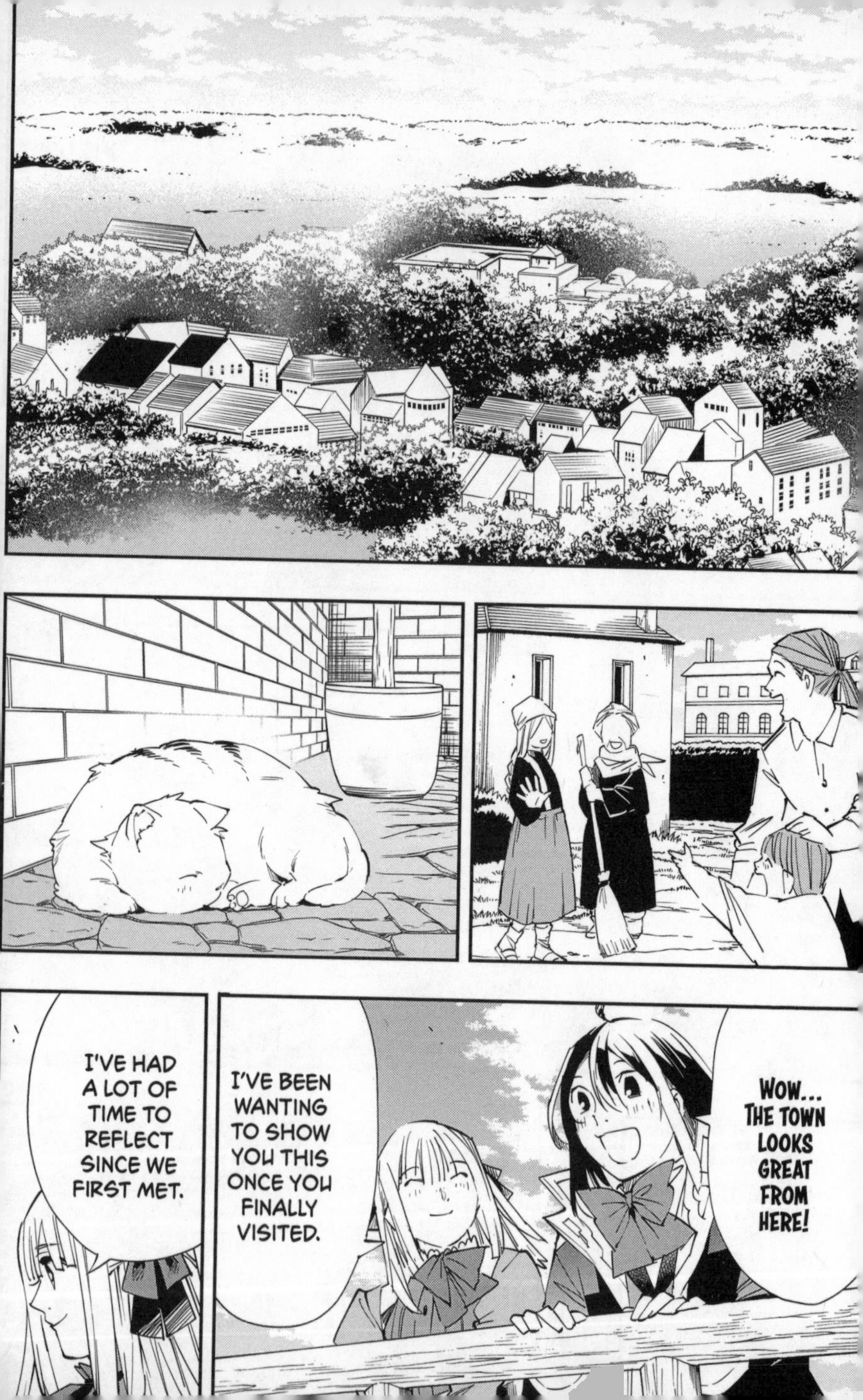
WOW... THE TOWN LOOKS GREAT FROM HERE!
I'VE BEEN WANTING TO SHOW YOU THIS ONCE YOU FINALLY VISITED.
I'VE HAD A LOT OF TIME TO REFLECT SINCE WE FIRST MET.

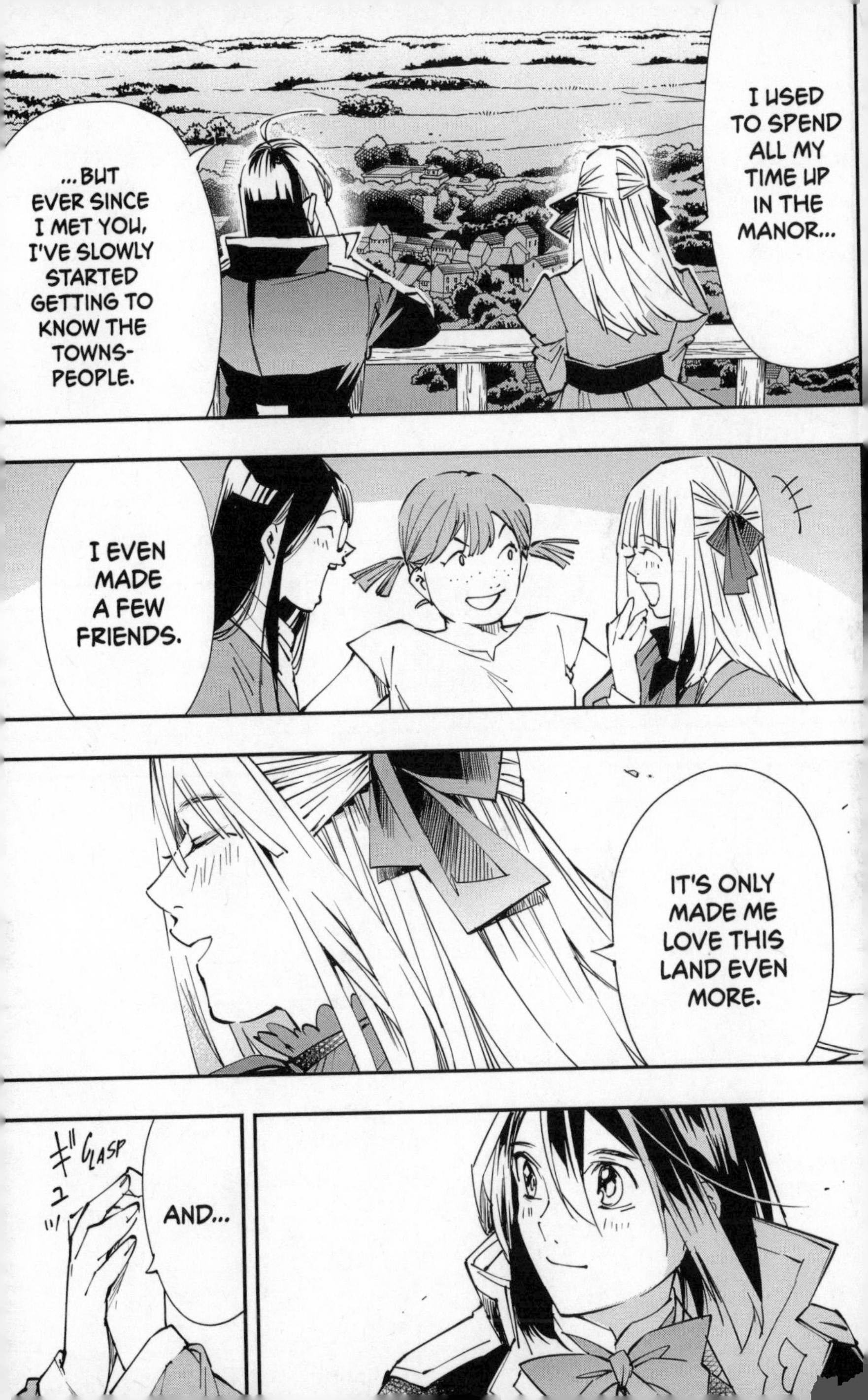
I USED TO SPEND ALL MY TIME UP IN THE MANOR...
...BUT EVER SINCE I MET YOU, I'VE SLOWLY STARTED GETTING TO KNOW THE TOWNS-PEOPLE.
I EVEN MADE A FEW FRIENDS.
IT'S ONLY MADE ME LOVE THIS LAND EVEN MORE.
CLASP
AND...

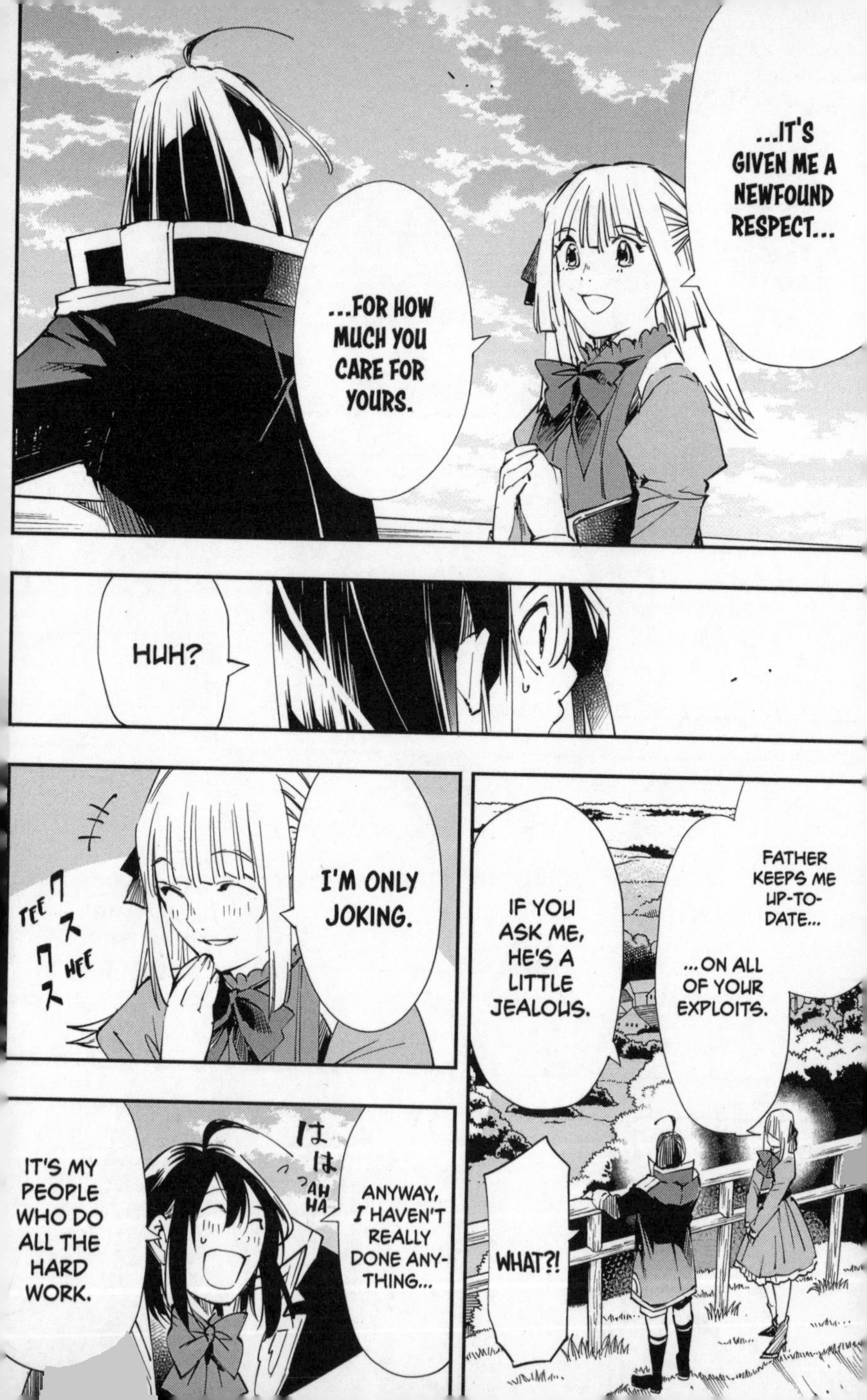
...IT'S GIVEN ME A NEWFOUND RESPECT...
...FOR HOW MUCH YOU CARE FOR YOURS.
HUH?
FATHER KEEPS ME UP-TO-DATE...
...ON ALL OF YOUR EXPLOITS.
IF YOU ASK ME, HE'S A LITTLE JEALOUS.
WHAT?!
I'M ONLY JOKING.
クスクス
TEE HEE
ANYWAY, I HAVEN'T REALLY DONE ANYTHING...
はは
AH HA
IT'S MY PEOPLE WHO DO ALL THE HARD WORK.

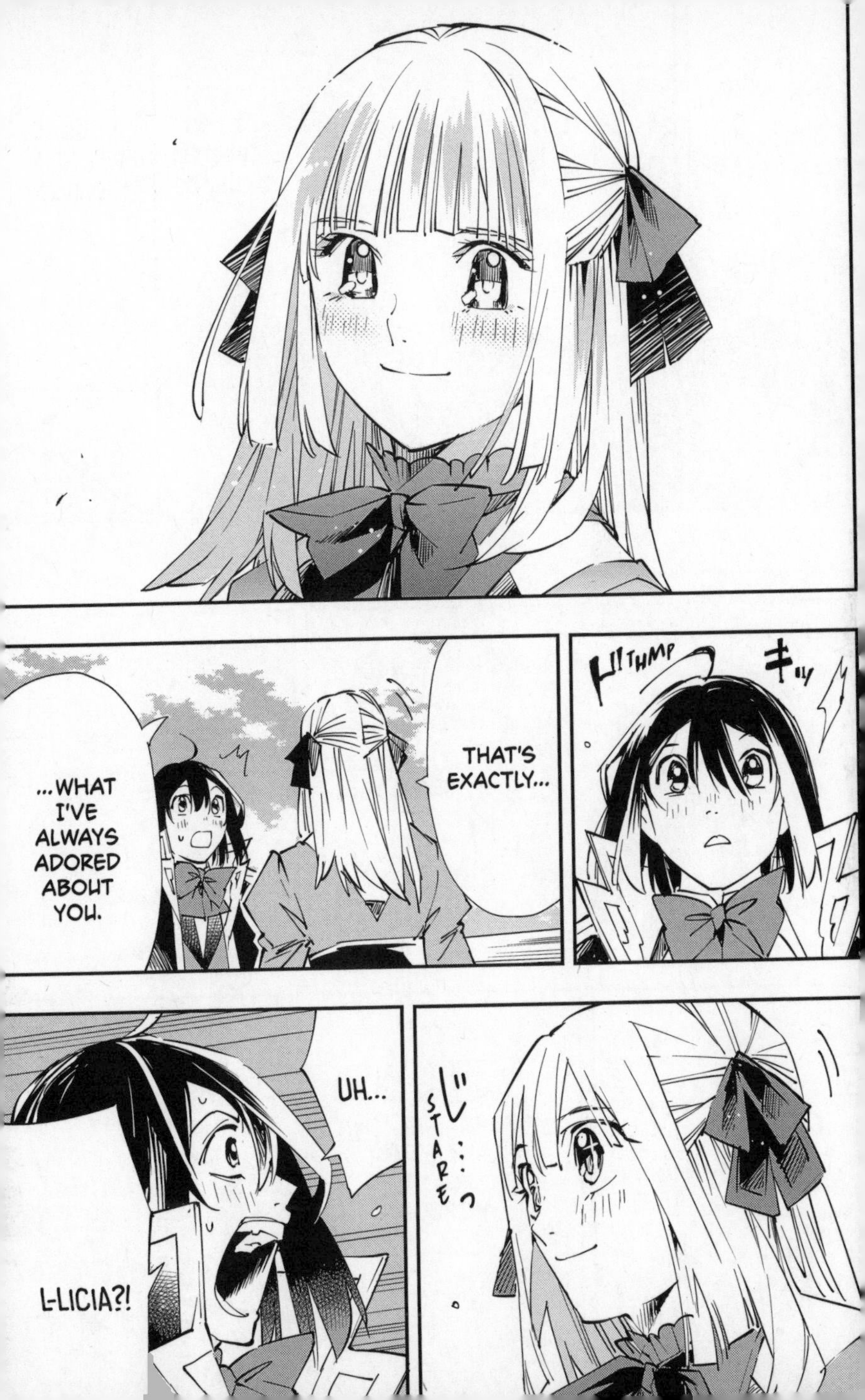
THUMP
THAT'S EXACTLY...
...WHAT I'VE ALWAYS ADORED ABOUT YOU.
STARE
UH...
L-LICIA?!

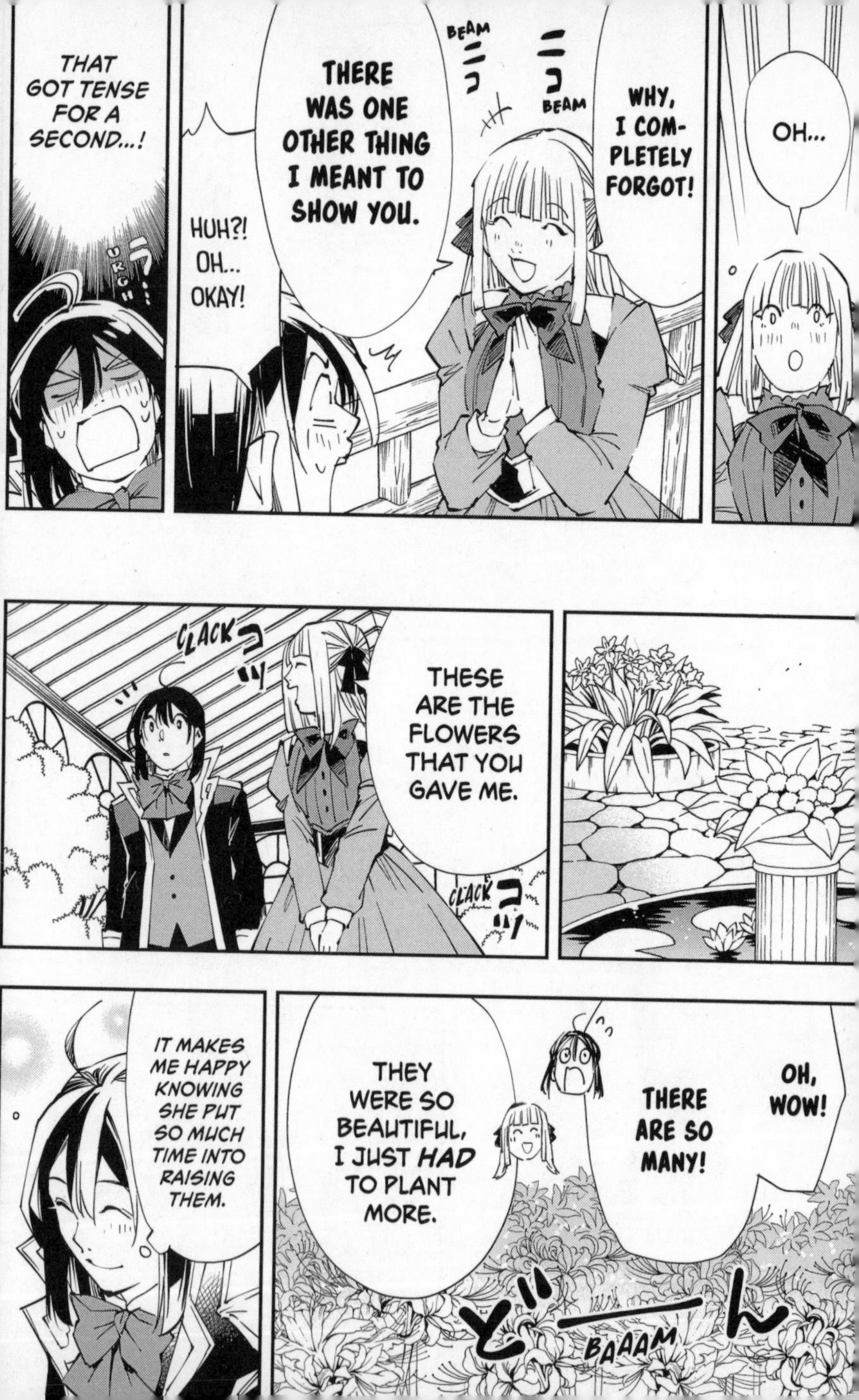
OH...
WHY, I COMPLETELY FORGOT!
BEAM
BEAM
THERE WAS ONE OTHER THING I MEANT TO SHOW YOU.
HUH?! OH... OKAY!
THAT GOT TENSE FOR A SECOND...!
URGH
CLACK
THESE ARE THE FLOWERS THAT YOU GAVE ME.
CLACK
OH, WOW!
THERE ARE SO MANY!
THEY WERE SO BEAUTIFUL, I JUST *HAD* TO PLANT MORE.
BAAAM
IT MAKES ME HAPPY KNOWING SHE PUT SO MUCH TIME INTO RAISING THEM.

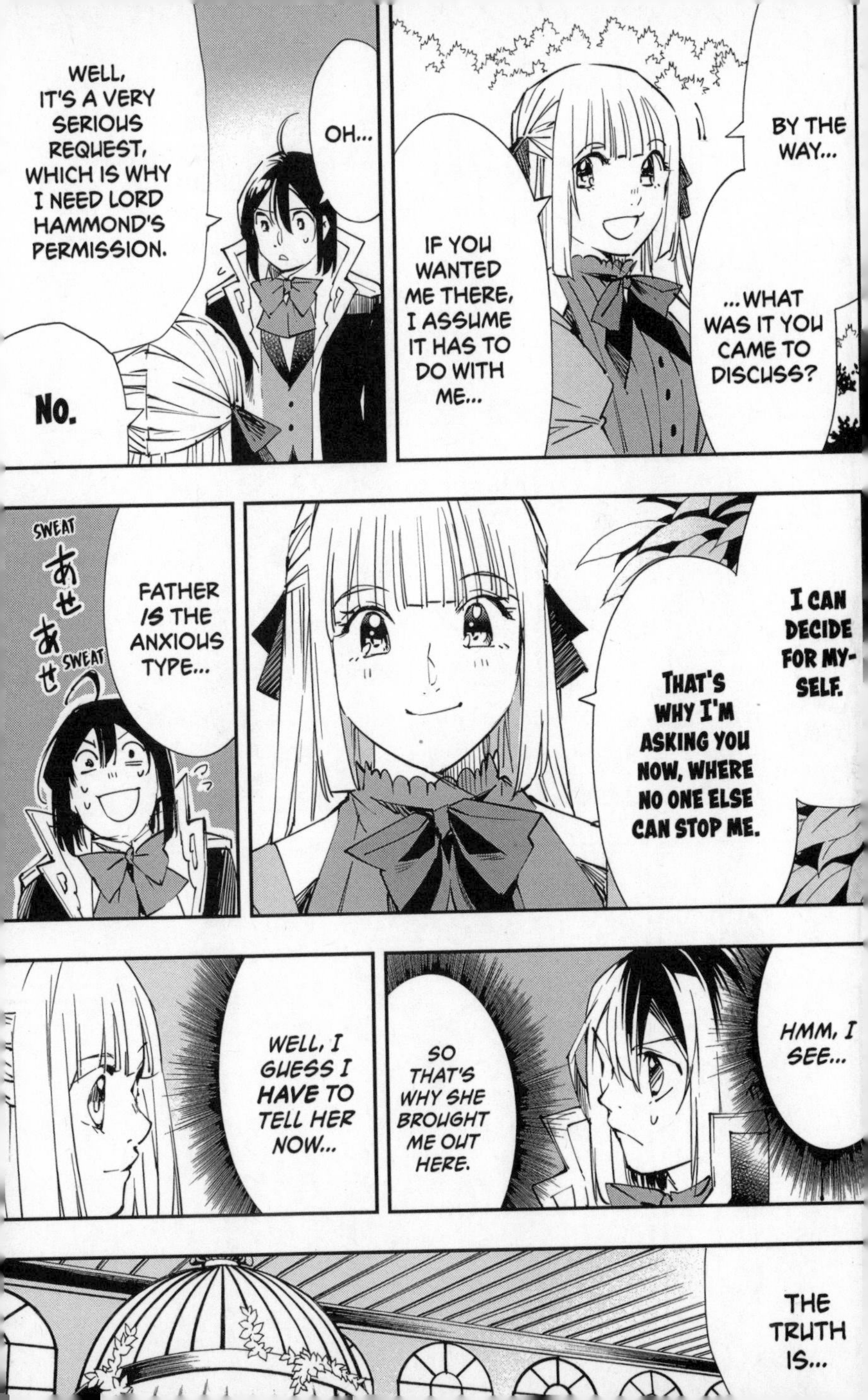
BY THE WAY...
...WHAT WAS IT YOU CAME TO DISCUSS?
IF YOU WANTED ME THERE, I ASSUME IT HAS TO DO WITH ME...
OH...
WELL, IT'S A VERY SERIOUS REQUEST, WHICH IS WHY I NEED LORD HAMMOND'S PERMISSION.
No.
I CAN DECIDE FOR MY-SELF.
THAT'S WHY I'M ASKING YOU NOW, WHERE NO ONE ELSE CAN STOP ME.
FATHER *IS* THE ANXIOUS TYPE...
あせ SWEAT
あせ SWEAT
HMM, I SEE...
SO THAT'S WHY SHE BROUGHT ME OUT HERE.
WELL, I GUESS I *HAVE* TO TELL HER NOW...
THE TRUTH IS...

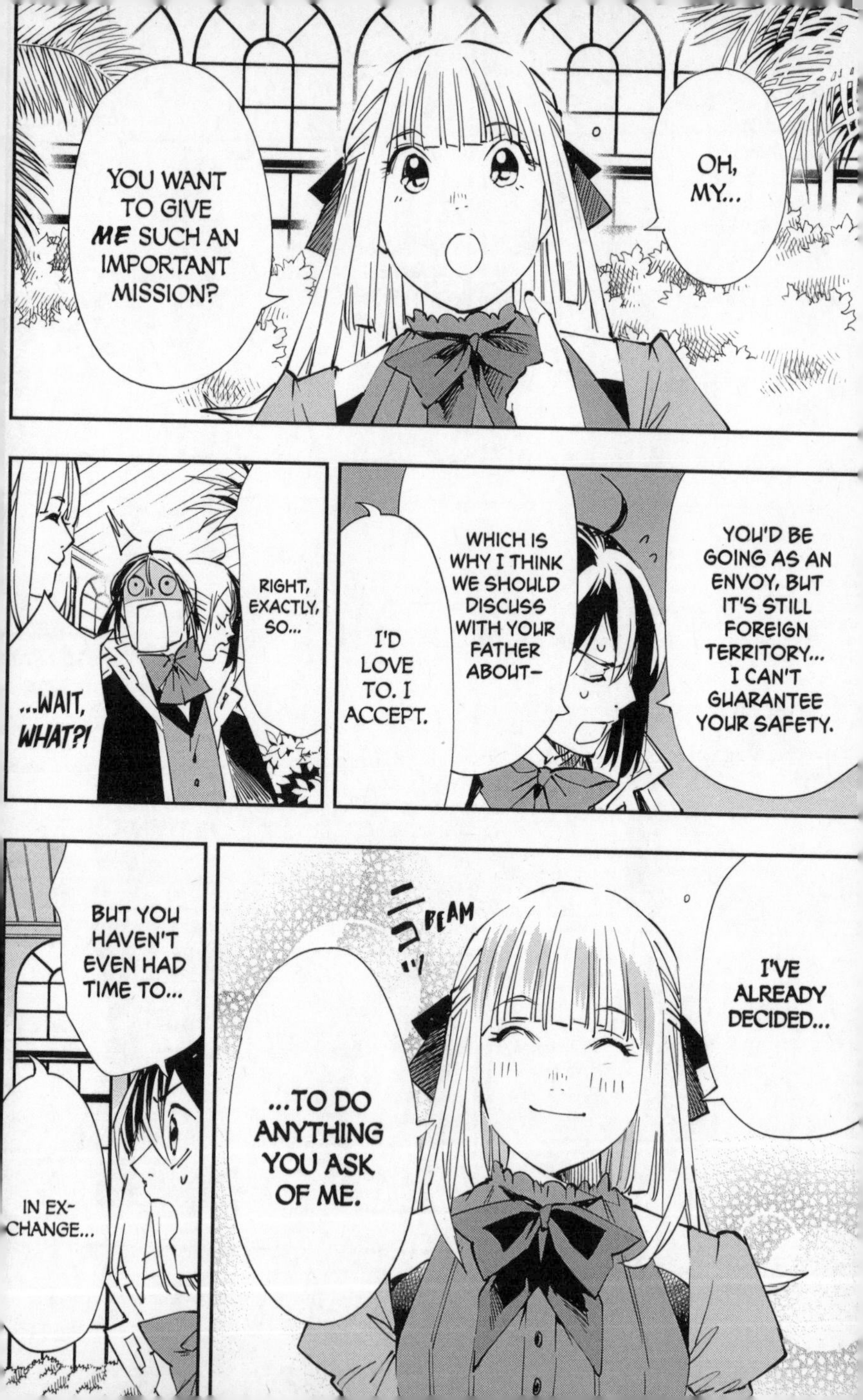
OH, MY...
YOU WANT TO GIVE ME SUCH AN IMPORTANT MISSION?
YOU'D BE GOING AS AN ENVOY, BUT IT'S STILL FOREIGN TERRITORY... I CAN'T GUARANTEE YOUR SAFETY.
WHICH IS WHY I THINK WE SHOULD DISCUSS WITH YOUR FATHER ABOUT–
I'D LOVE TO. I ACCEPT.
RIGHT, EXACTLY, SO...
...WAIT, WHAT?!
I'VE ALREADY DECIDED...
BEAM
...TO DO ANYTHING YOU ASK OF ME.
BUT YOU HAVEN'T EVEN HAD TIME TO...
IN EX-CHANGE...

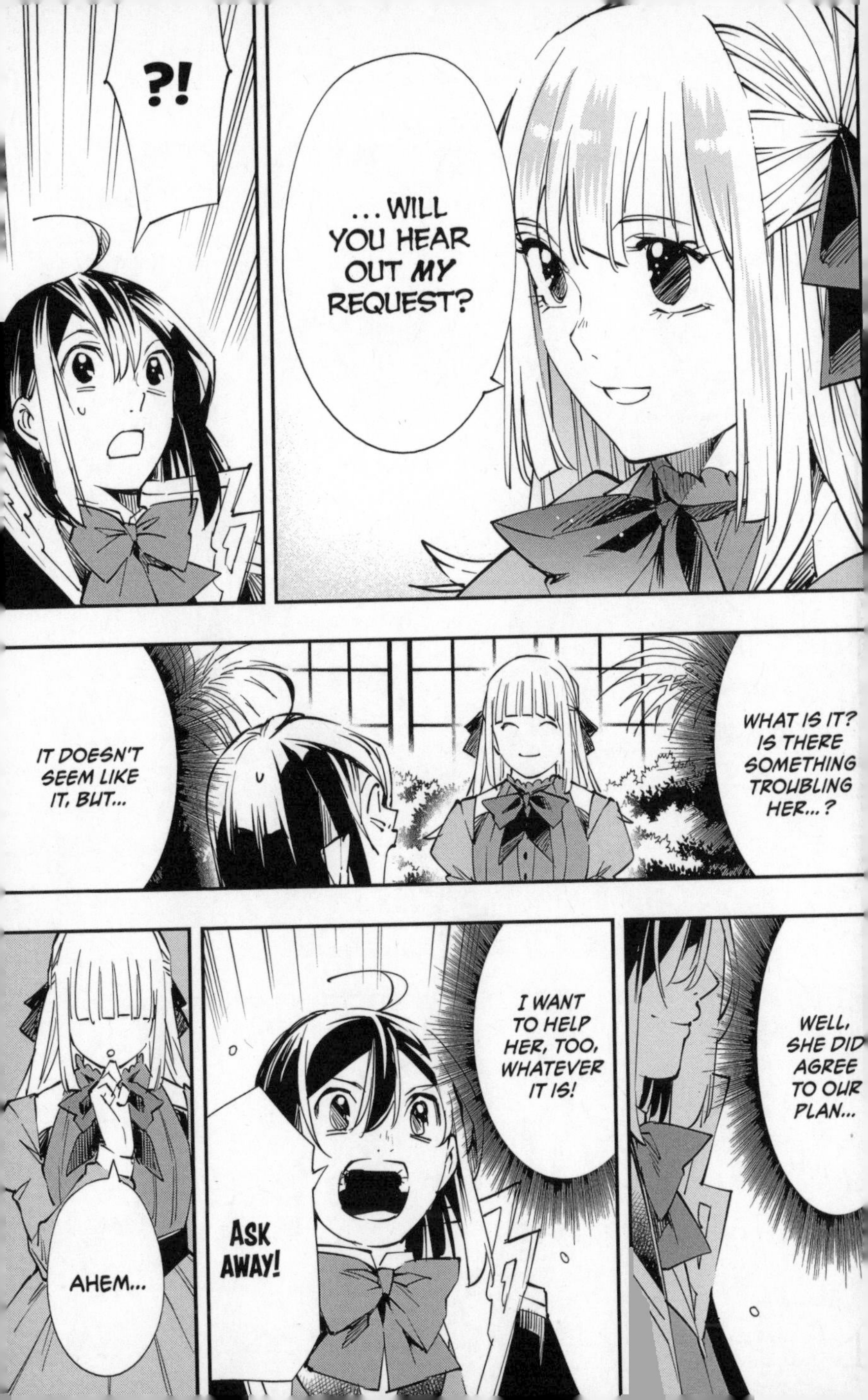
...WILL YOU HEAR OUT *MY* REQUEST?
?!
WHAT IS IT? IS THERE SOMETHING TROUBLING HER...?
IT DOESN'T SEEM LIKE IT, BUT...
WELL, SHE DID AGREE TO OUR PLAN...
I WANT TO HELP HER, TOO, WHATEVER IT IS!
ASK AWAY!
AHEM...

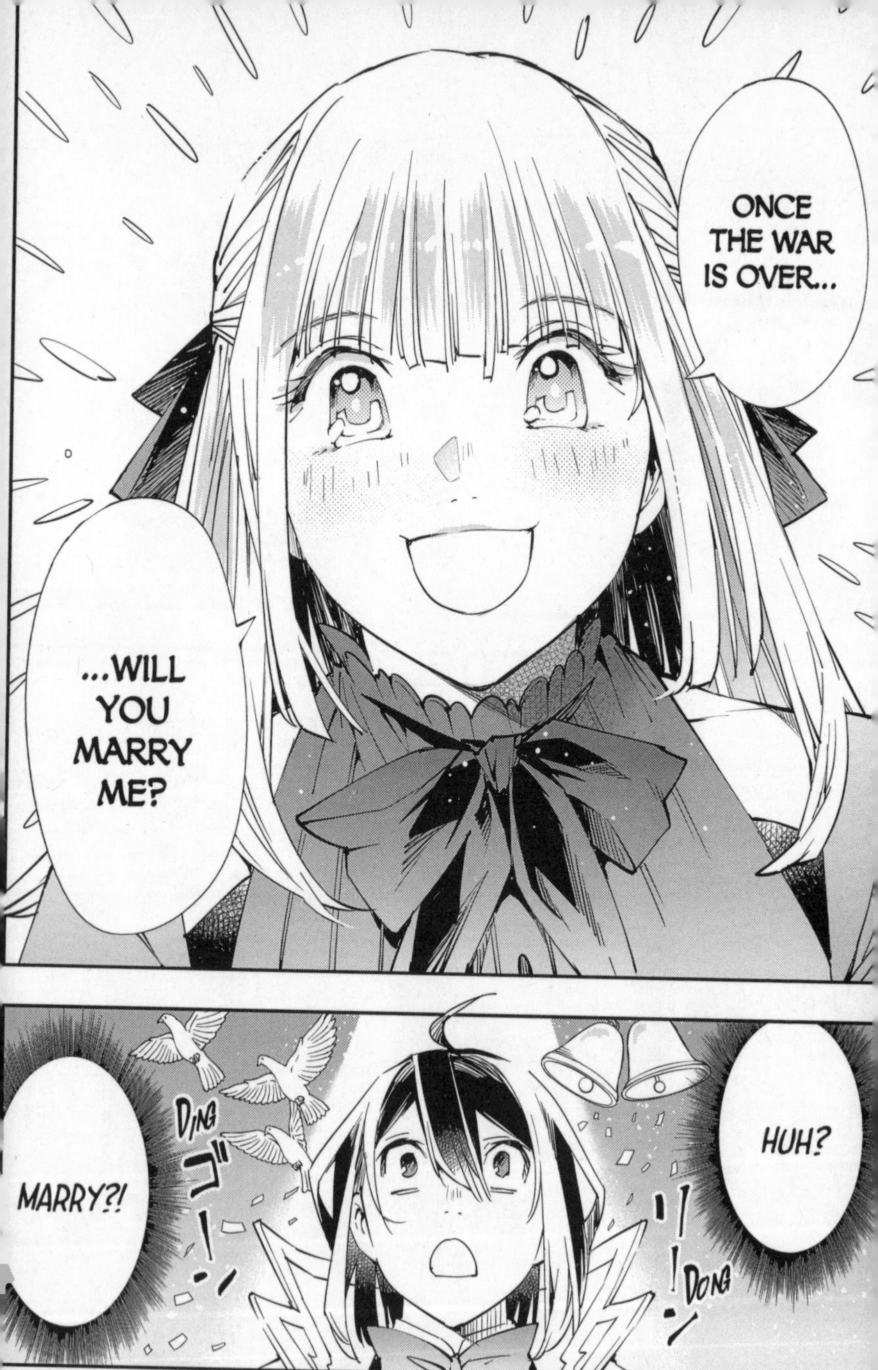
ONCE THE WAR IS OVER...
...WILL YOU MARRY ME?
HUH?
DING
DONG
MARRY?!

As a Reincarnated
ARISTOCRAT,
I'll Use My Appraisal Skill to
Rise in the World

As a Reincarnated ARISTOCRAT, I'll Use My Appraisal Skill to Rise in the World

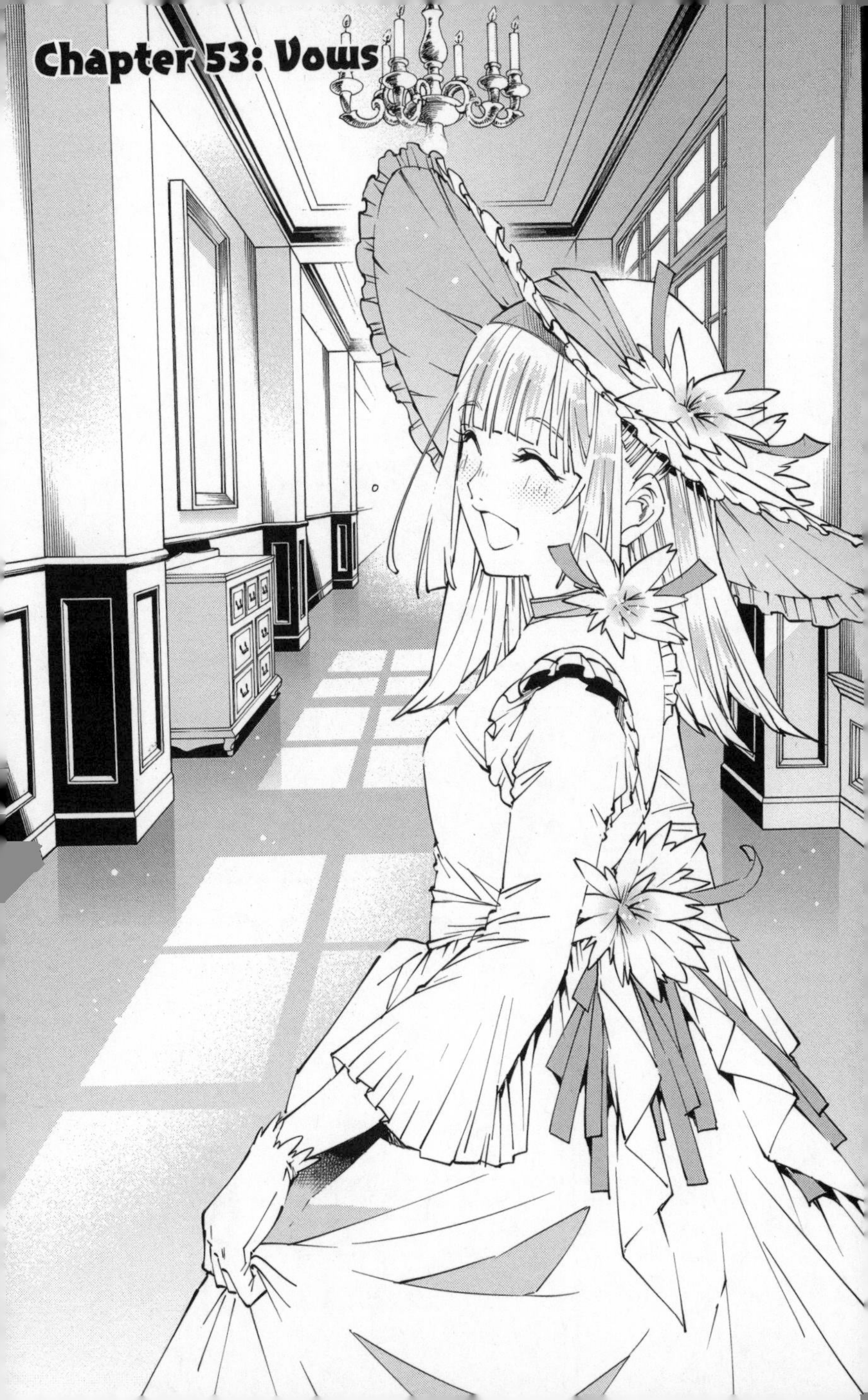
Chapter 53: Vows

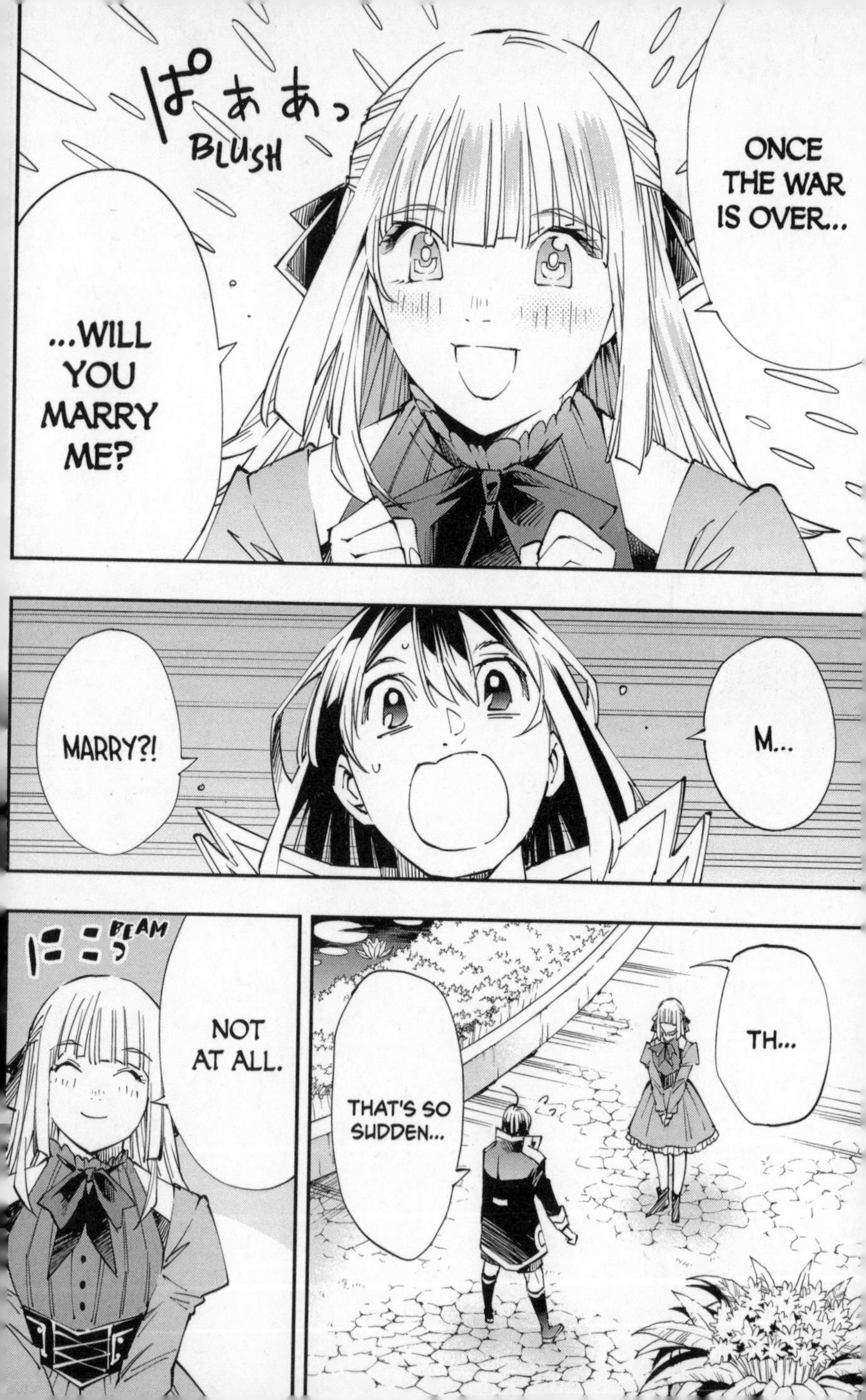
ONCE THE WAR IS OVER...
ぱぁあっ
BLUSH
...WILL YOU MARRY ME?
M...
MARRY?!
TH...
THAT'S SO SUDDEN...
にこっ
BEAM
NOT AT ALL.

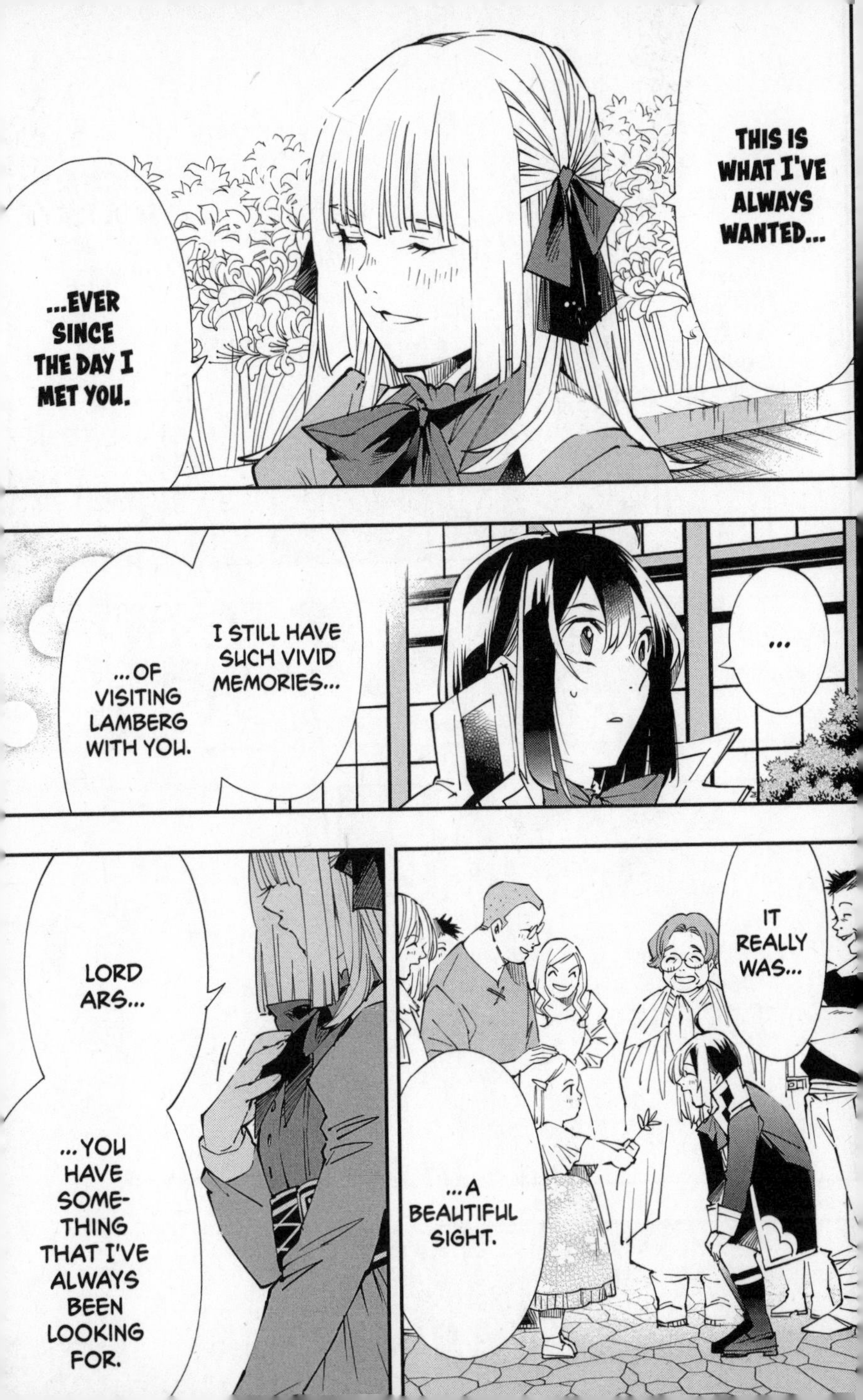
THIS IS WHAT I'VE ALWAYS WANTED...
...EVER SINCE THE DAY I MET YOU.
...
I STILL HAVE SUCH VIVID MEMORIES...
...OF VISITING LAMBERG WITH YOU.
IT REALLY WAS...
...A BEAUTIFUL SIGHT.
LORD ARS...
...YOU HAVE SOME-THING THAT I'VE ALWAYS BEEN LOOKING FOR.

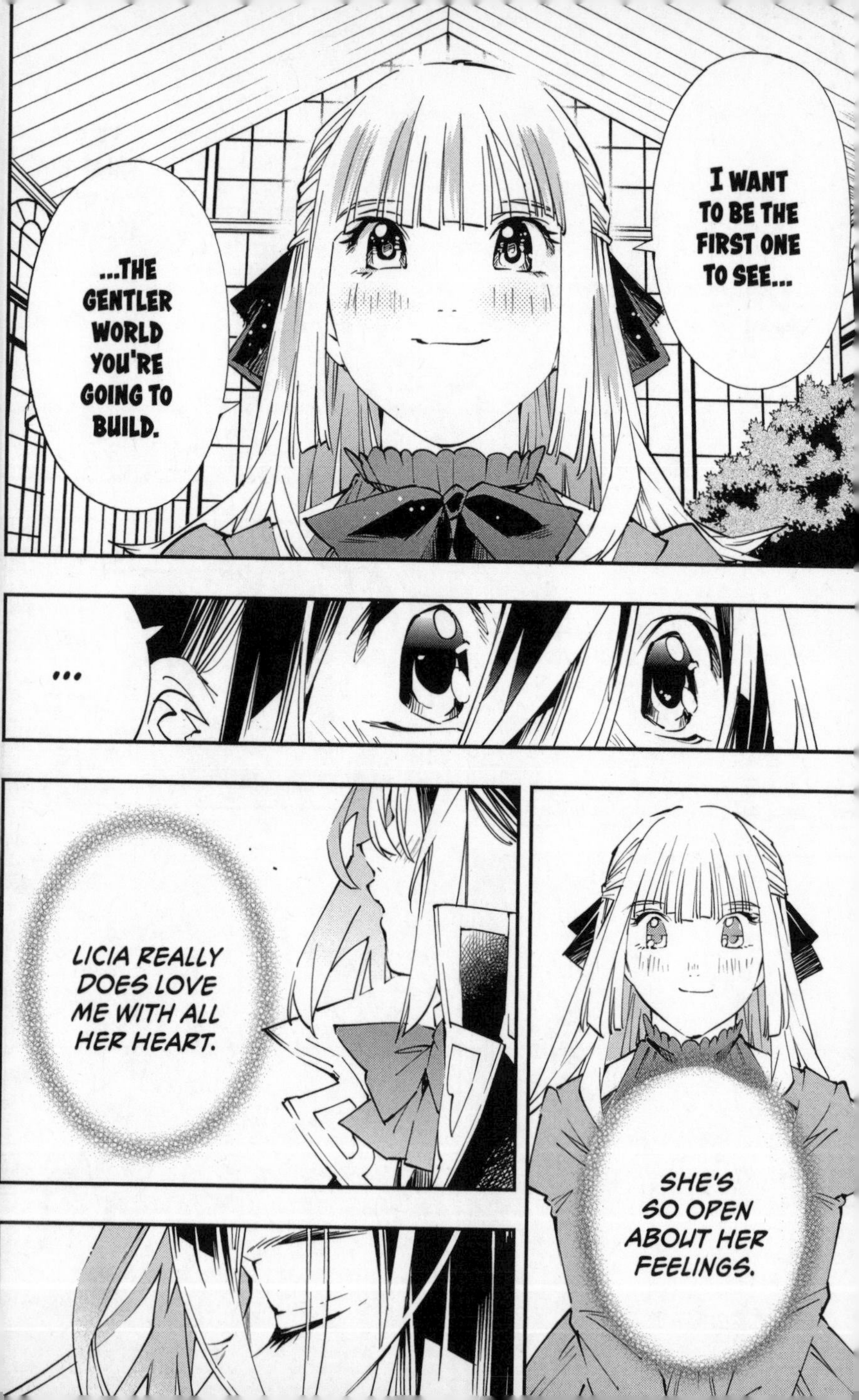
I WANT TO BE THE FIRST ONE TO SEE...
...THE GENTLER WORLD YOU'RE GOING TO BUILD.
...
SHE'S SO OPEN ABOUT HER FEELINGS.
LICIA REALLY DOES LOVE ME WITH ALL HER HEART.

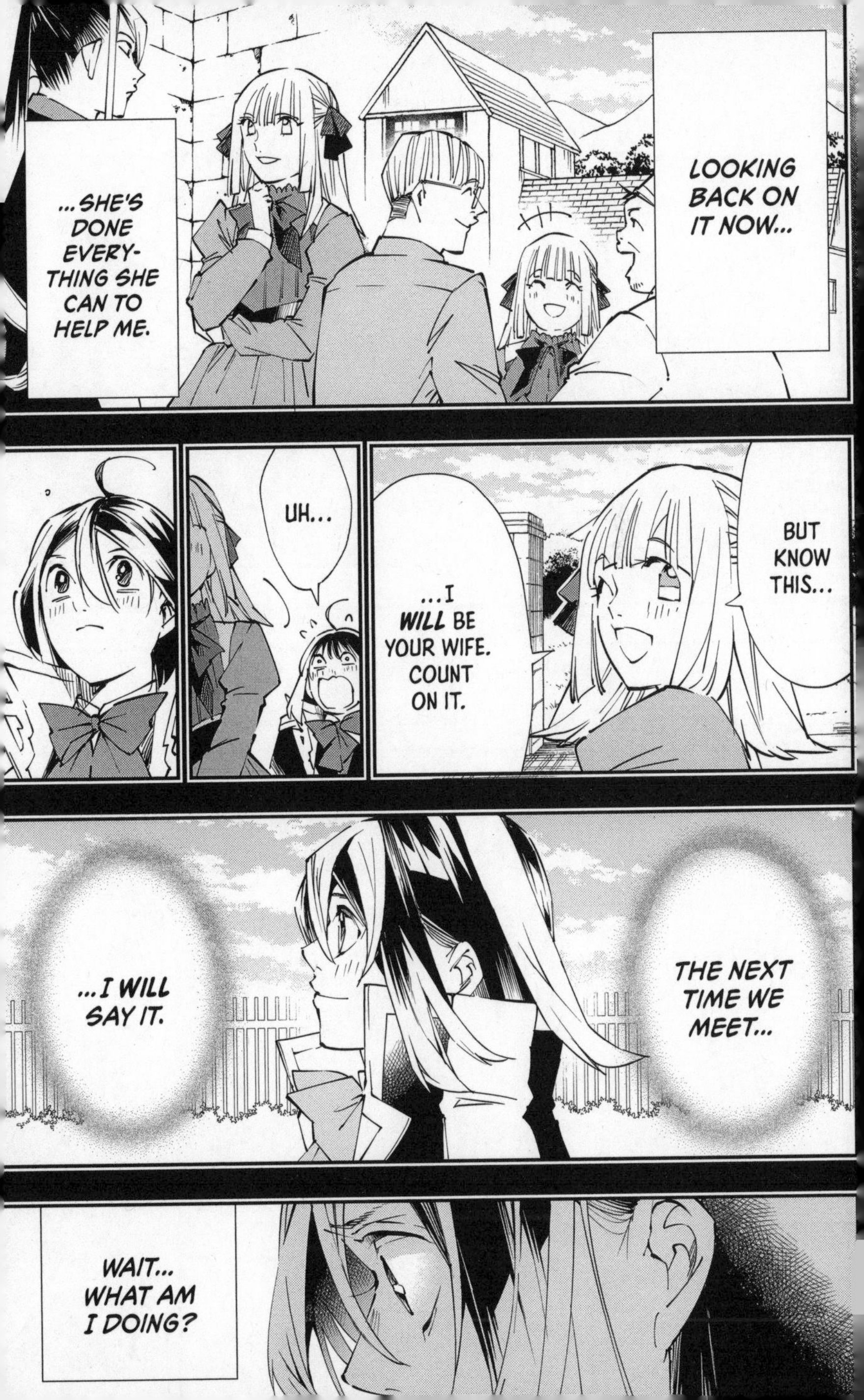
LOOKING BACK ON IT NOW...
...SHE'S DONE EVERY-THING SHE CAN TO HELP ME.
BUT KNOW THIS...
...I WILL BE YOUR WIFE. COUNT ON IT.
UH...
THE NEXT TIME WE MEET...
...I WILL SAY IT.
WAIT... WHAT AM I DOING?

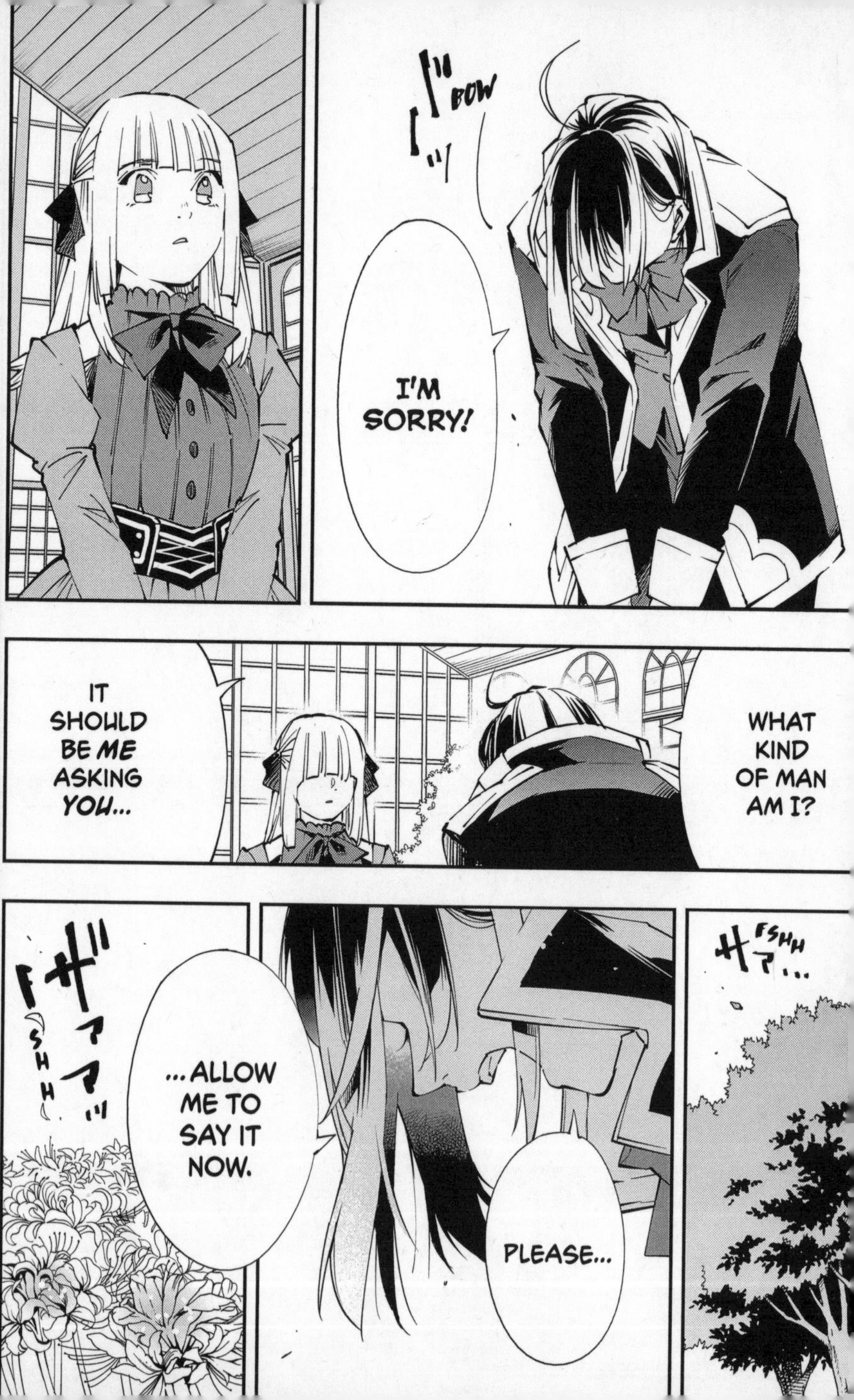
BOW
I'M SORRY!
WHAT KIND OF MAN AM I?
IT SHOULD BE ME ASKING YOU...
FSHH
サァ...
PLEASE...
...ALLOW ME TO SAY IT NOW.
FSHH
ザァァッ

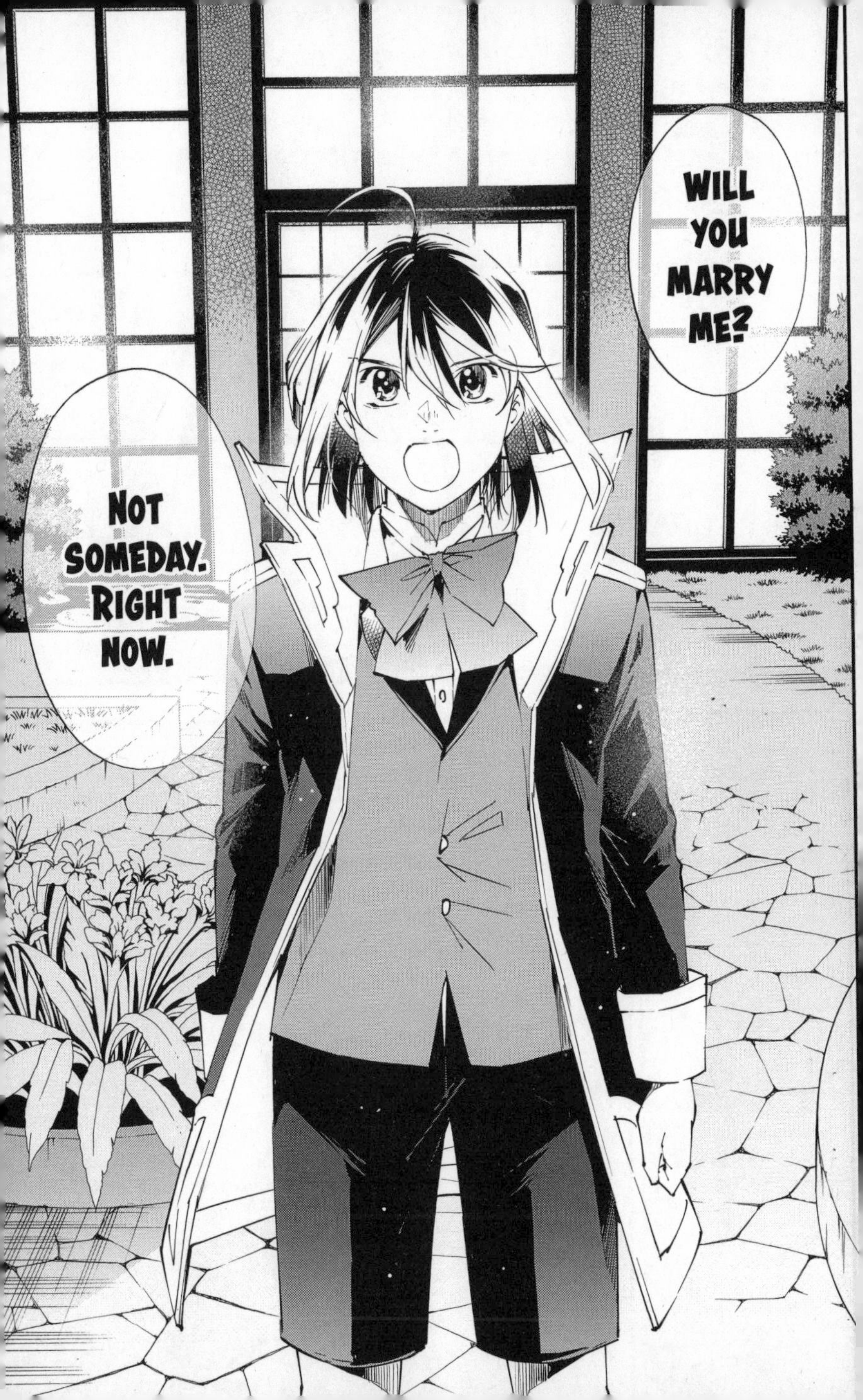
WILL YOU MARRY ME?
NOT SOMEDAY. RIGHT NOW.

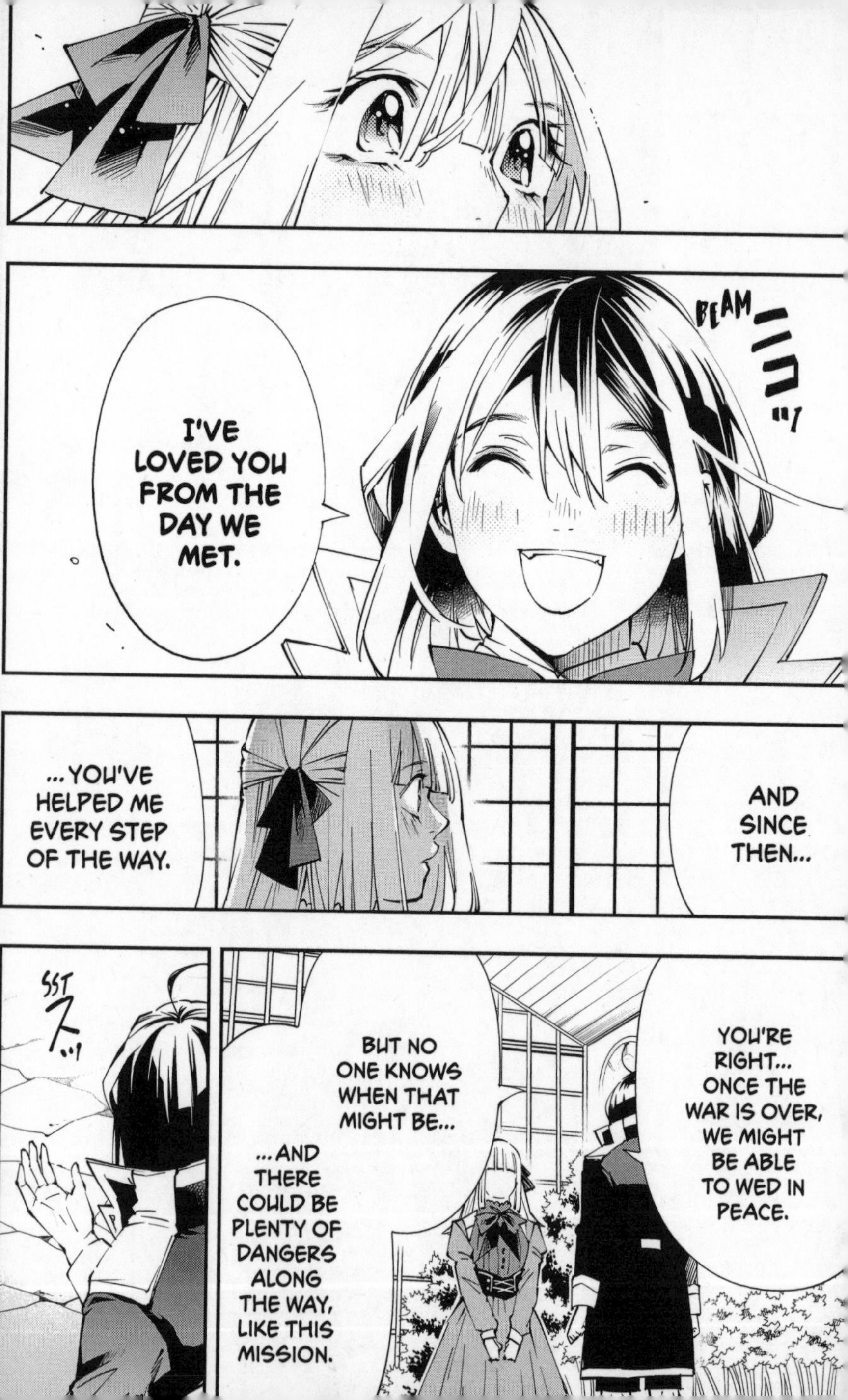
BEAM
I'VE LOVED YOU FROM THE DAY WE MET.
AND SINCE THEN...
...YOU'VE HELPED ME EVERY STEP OF THE WAY.
YOU'RE RIGHT... ONCE THE WAR IS OVER, WE MIGHT BE ABLE TO WED IN PEACE.
BUT NO ONE KNOWS WHEN THAT MIGHT BE...
...AND THERE COULD BE PLENTY OF DANGERS ALONG THE WAY, LIKE THIS MISSION.
SST

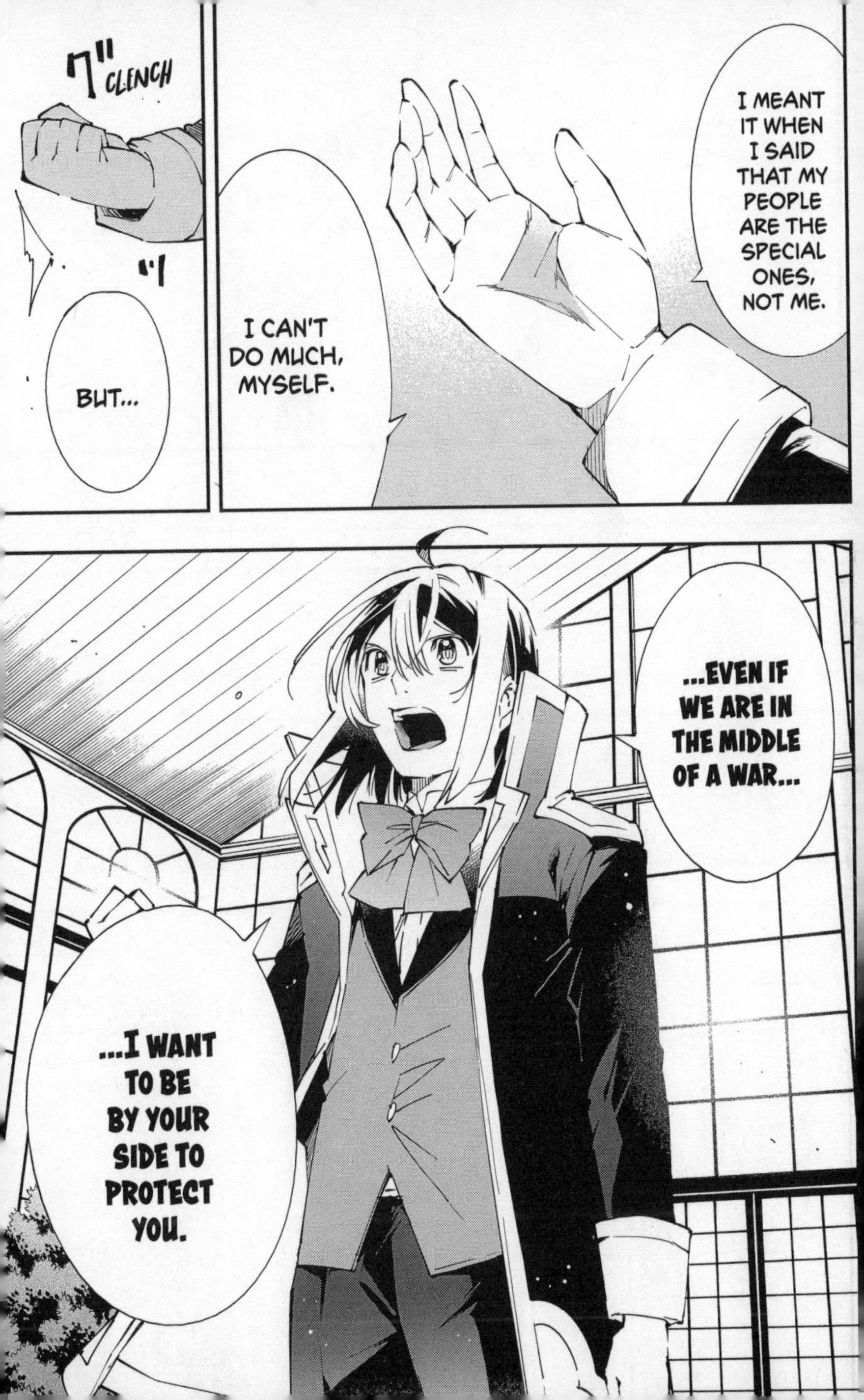
I MEANT IT WHEN I SAID THAT MY PEOPLE ARE THE SPECIAL ONES, NOT ME.
I CAN'T DO MUCH, MYSELF.
CLENCH
BUT...
...EVEN IF WE ARE IN THE MIDDLE OF A WAR...
...I WANT TO BE BY YOUR SIDE TO PROTECT YOU.

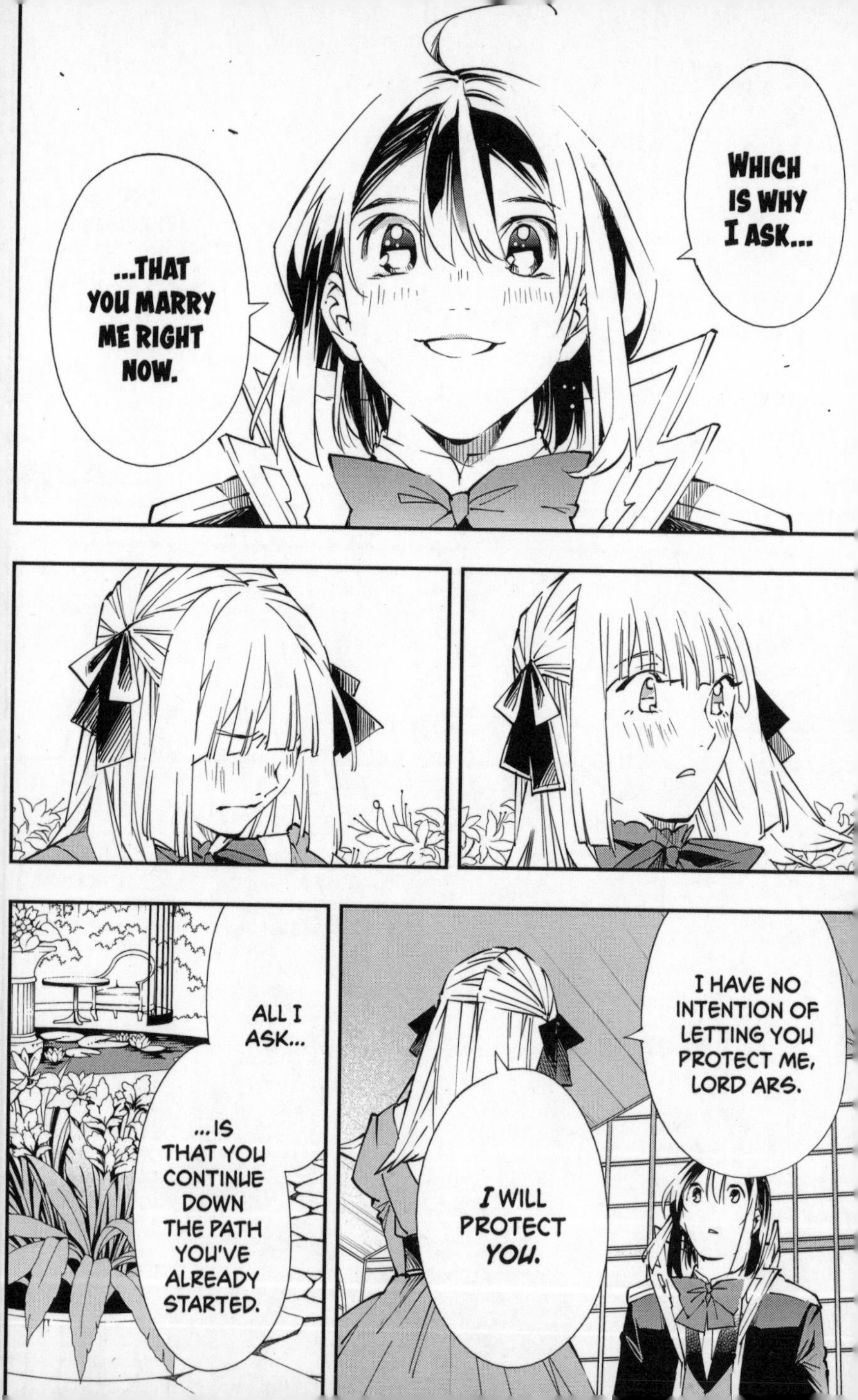
WHICH IS WHY I ASK...
...THAT YOU MARRY ME RIGHT NOW.
I HAVE NO INTENTION OF LETTING YOU PROTECT ME, LORD ARS.
I WILL PROTECT YOU.
ALL I ASK...
...IS THAT YOU CONTINUE DOWN THE PATH YOU'VE ALREADY STARTED.

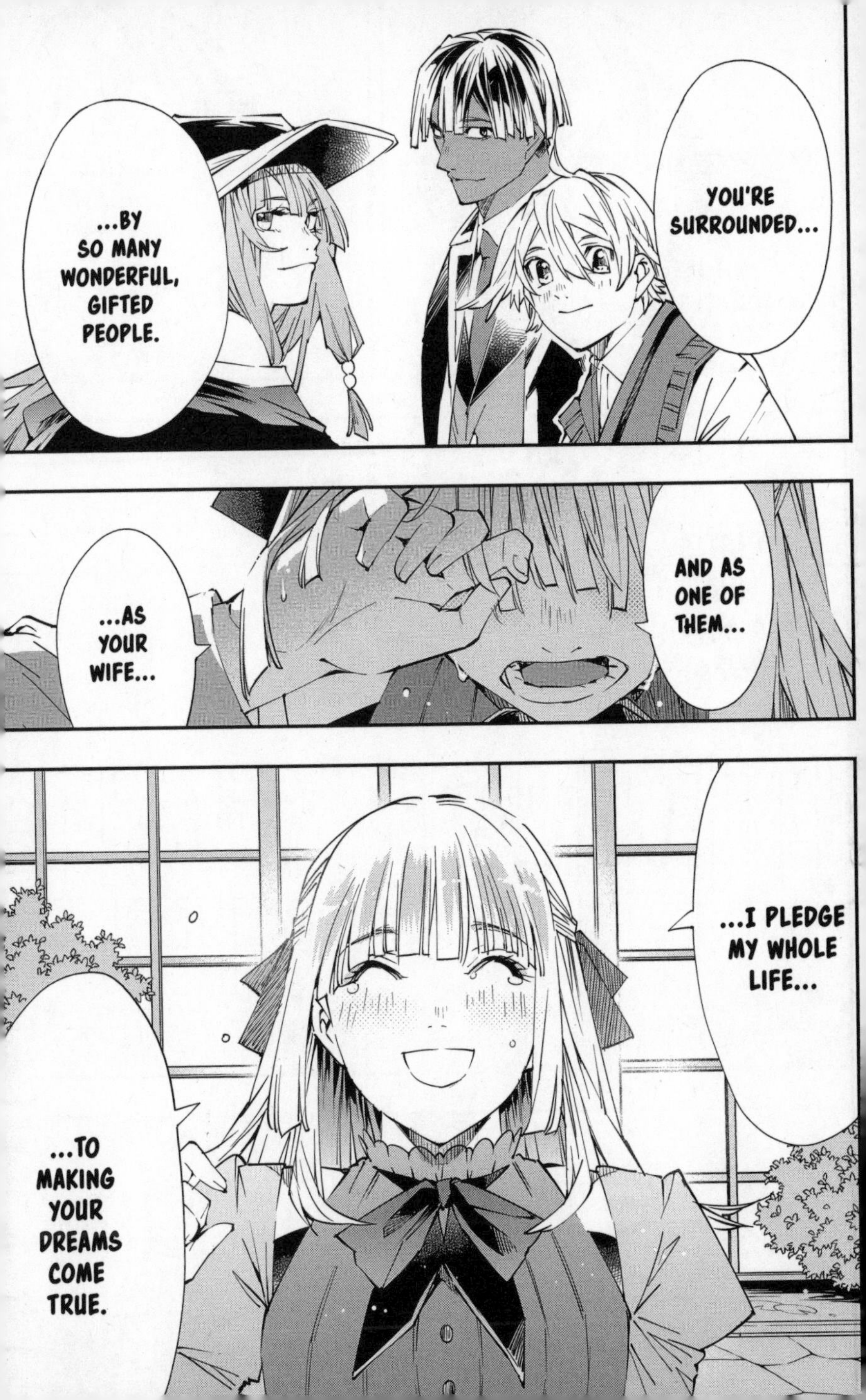
YOU'RE SURROUNDED...
...BY SO MANY WONDERFUL, GIFTED PEOPLE.
AND AS ONE OF THEM...
...AS YOUR WIFE...
...I PLEDGE MY WHOLE LIFE...
...TO MAKING YOUR DREAMS COME TRUE.

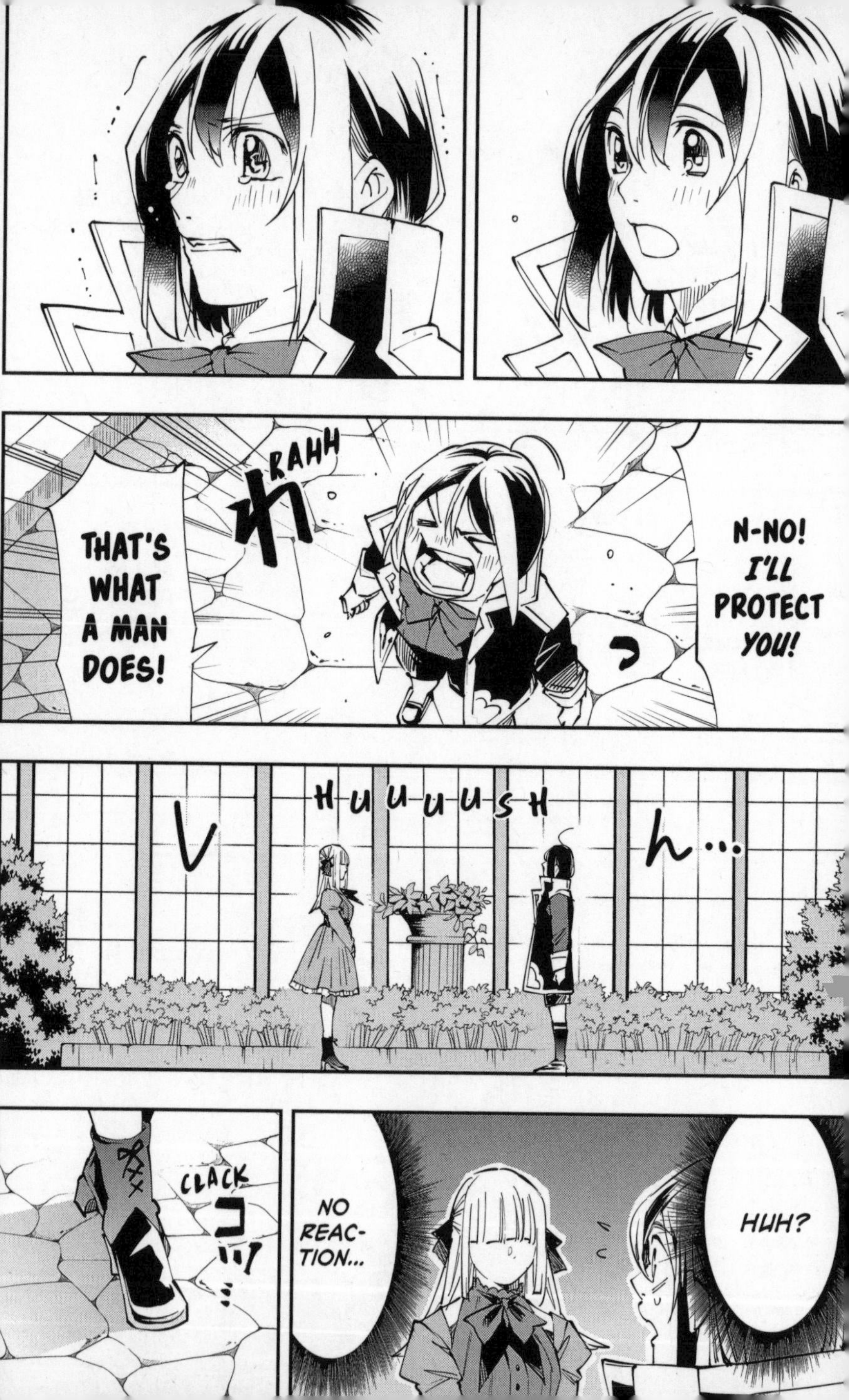
N-NO! I'LL PROTECT YOU!
THAT'S WHAT A MAN DOES!
RAHH
HUUUUUSH
CLACK
HUH?
NO REACTION...

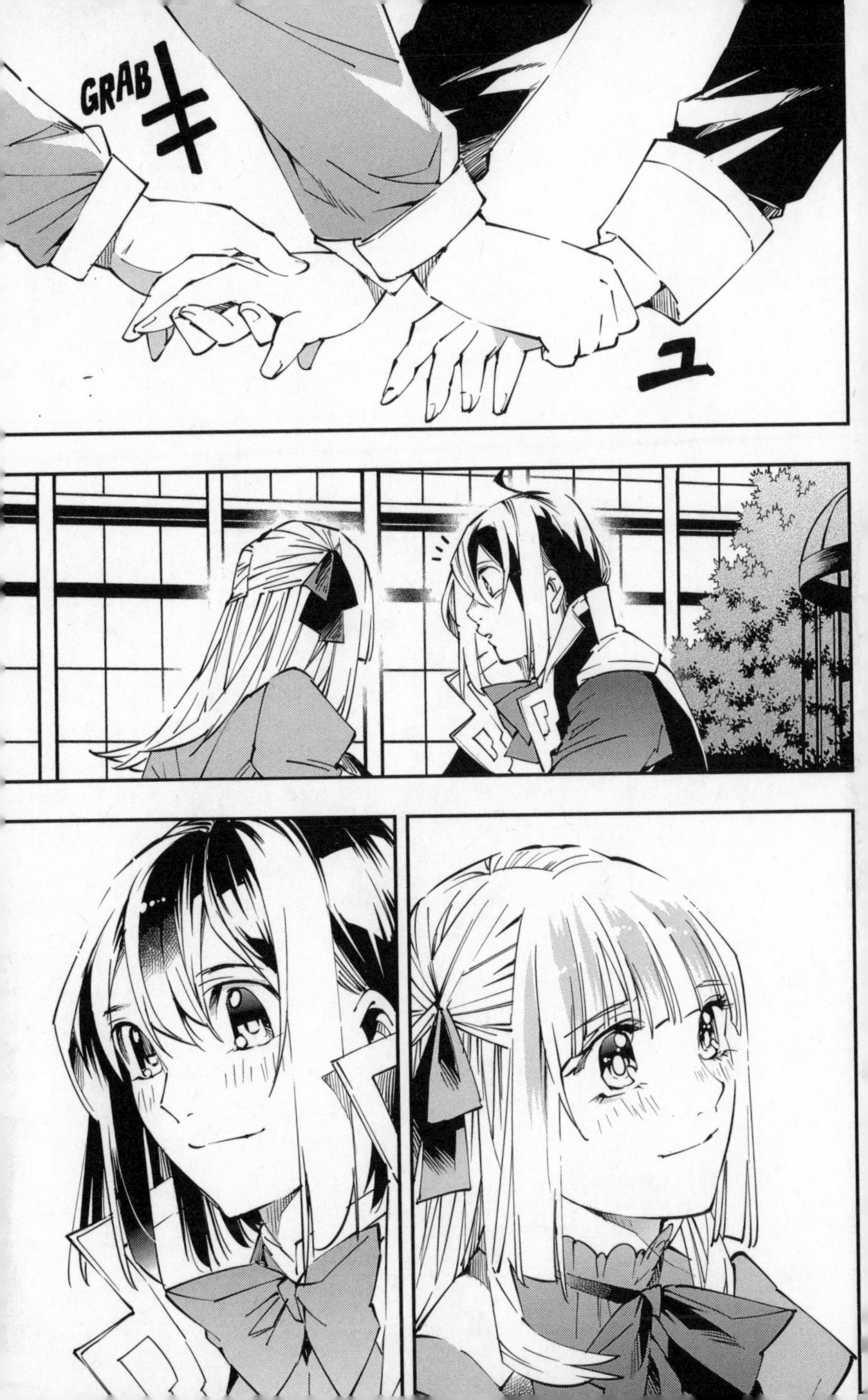
GRAB
キ
ュ

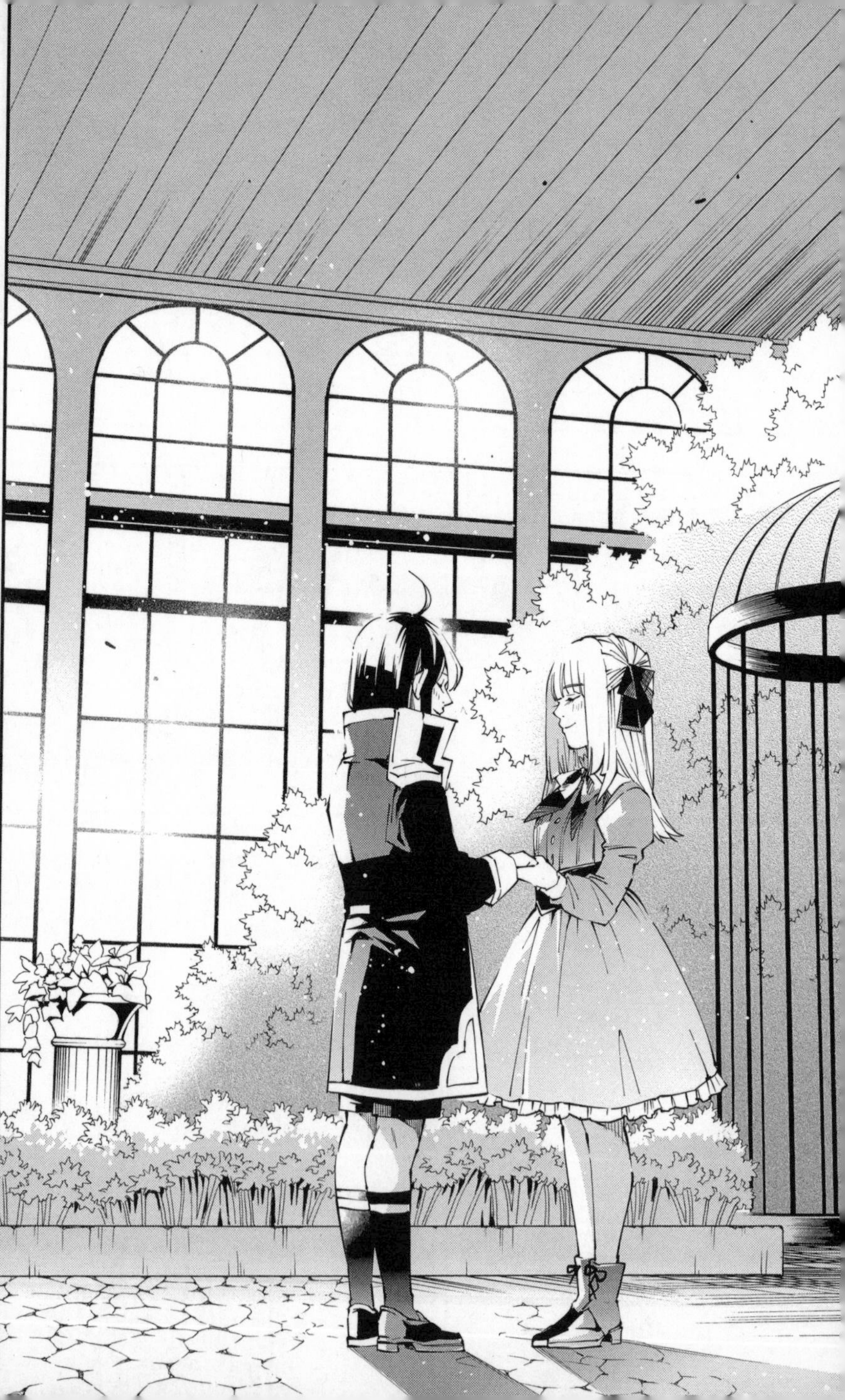

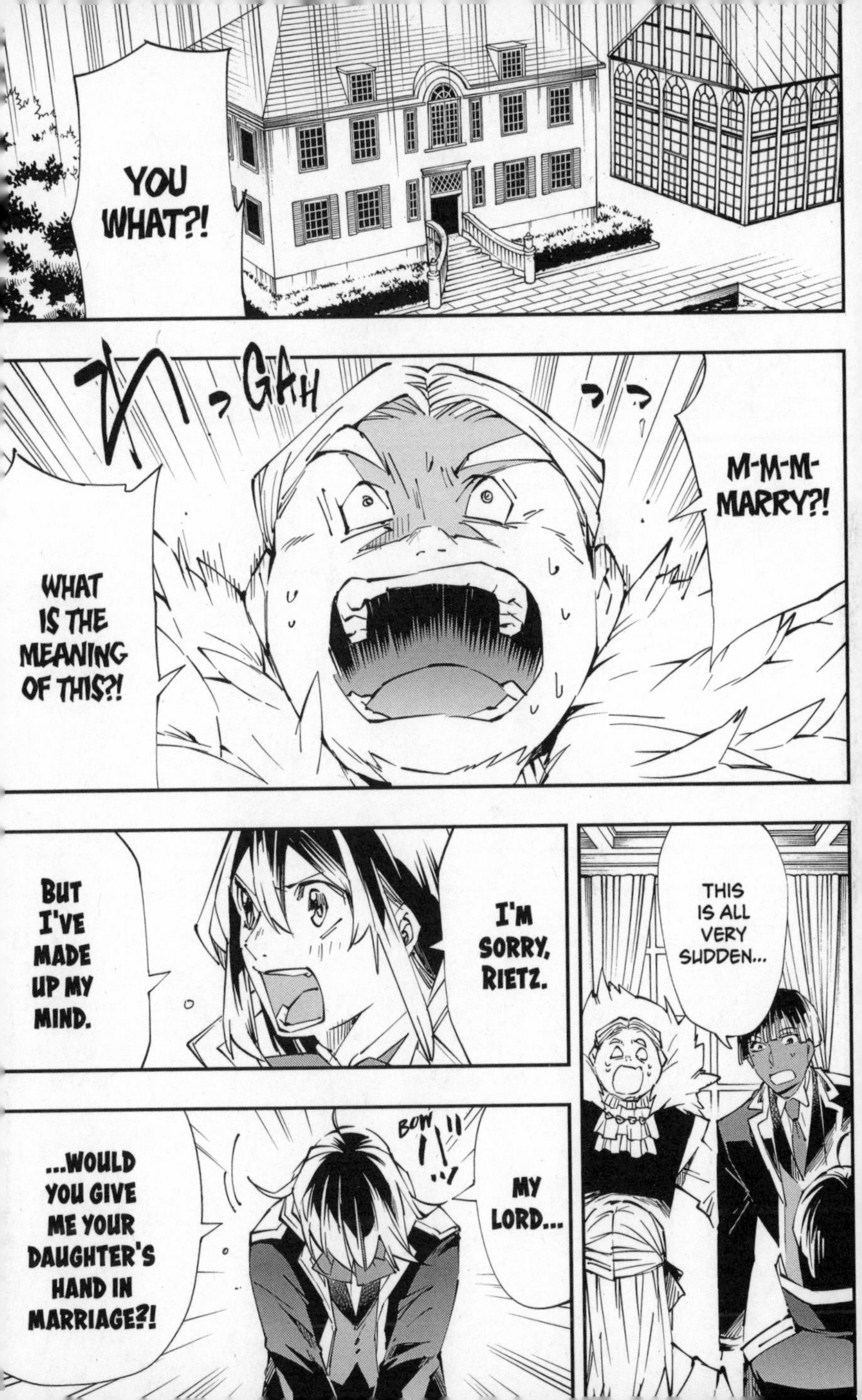
YOU WHAT?!
GAH
M-M-M-MARRY?!
WHAT IS THE MEANING OF THIS?!
THIS IS ALL VERY SUDDEN...
I'M SORRY, RIETZ.
BUT I'VE MADE UP MY MIND.
BOW
MY LORD...
...WOULD YOU GIVE ME YOUR DAUGHTER'S HAND IN MARRIAGE?!

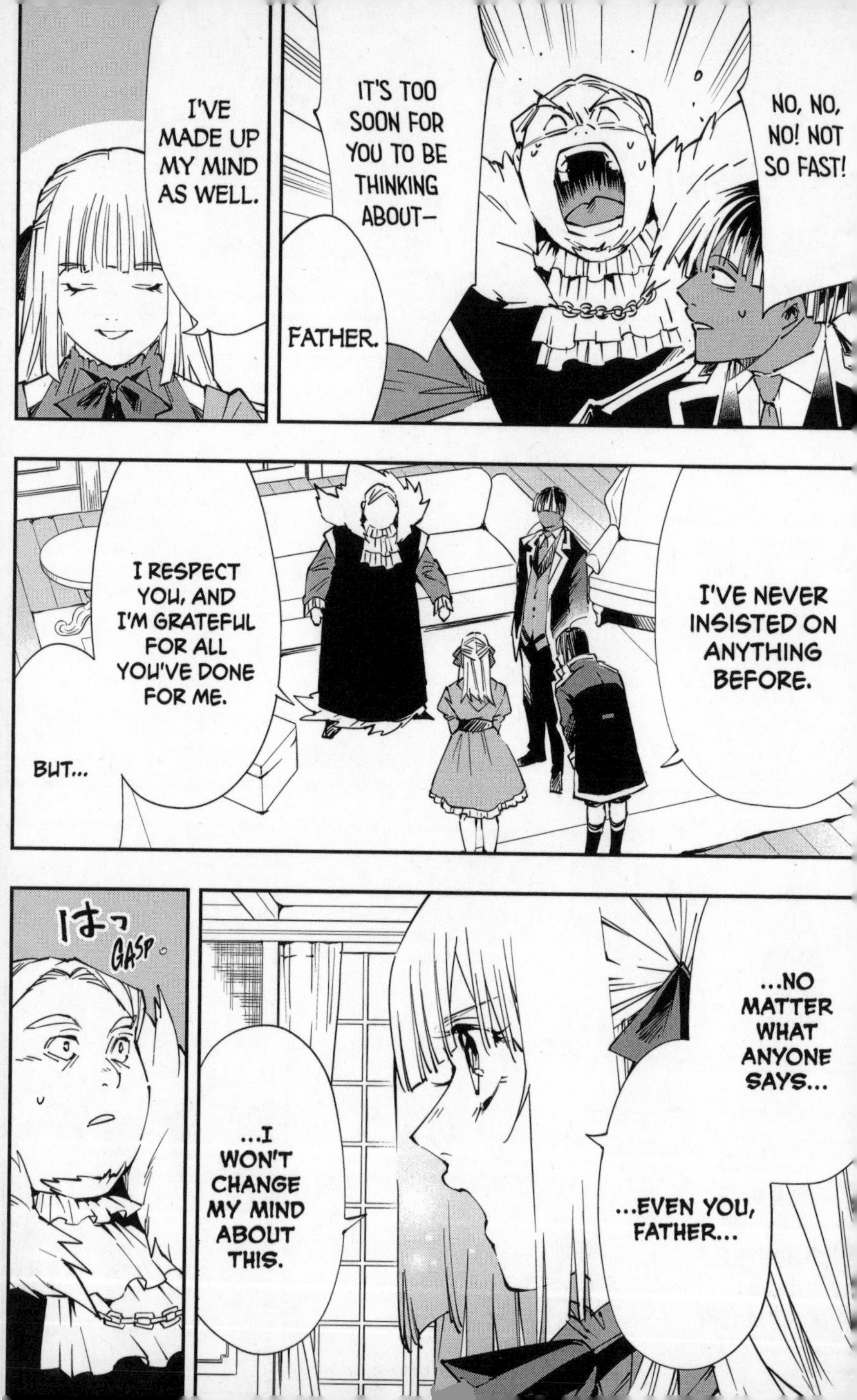
NO, NO, NO! NOT SO FAST!
IT'S TOO SOON FOR YOU TO BE THINKING ABOUT—
FATHER.
I'VE MADE UP MY MIND AS WELL.
I'VE NEVER INSISTED ON ANYTHING BEFORE.
I RESPECT YOU, AND I'M GRATEFUL FOR ALL YOU'VE DONE FOR ME.
BUT...
...NO MATTER WHAT ANYONE SAYS...
...EVEN YOU, FATHER...
...I WON'T CHANGE MY MIND ABOUT THIS.
はっ GASP

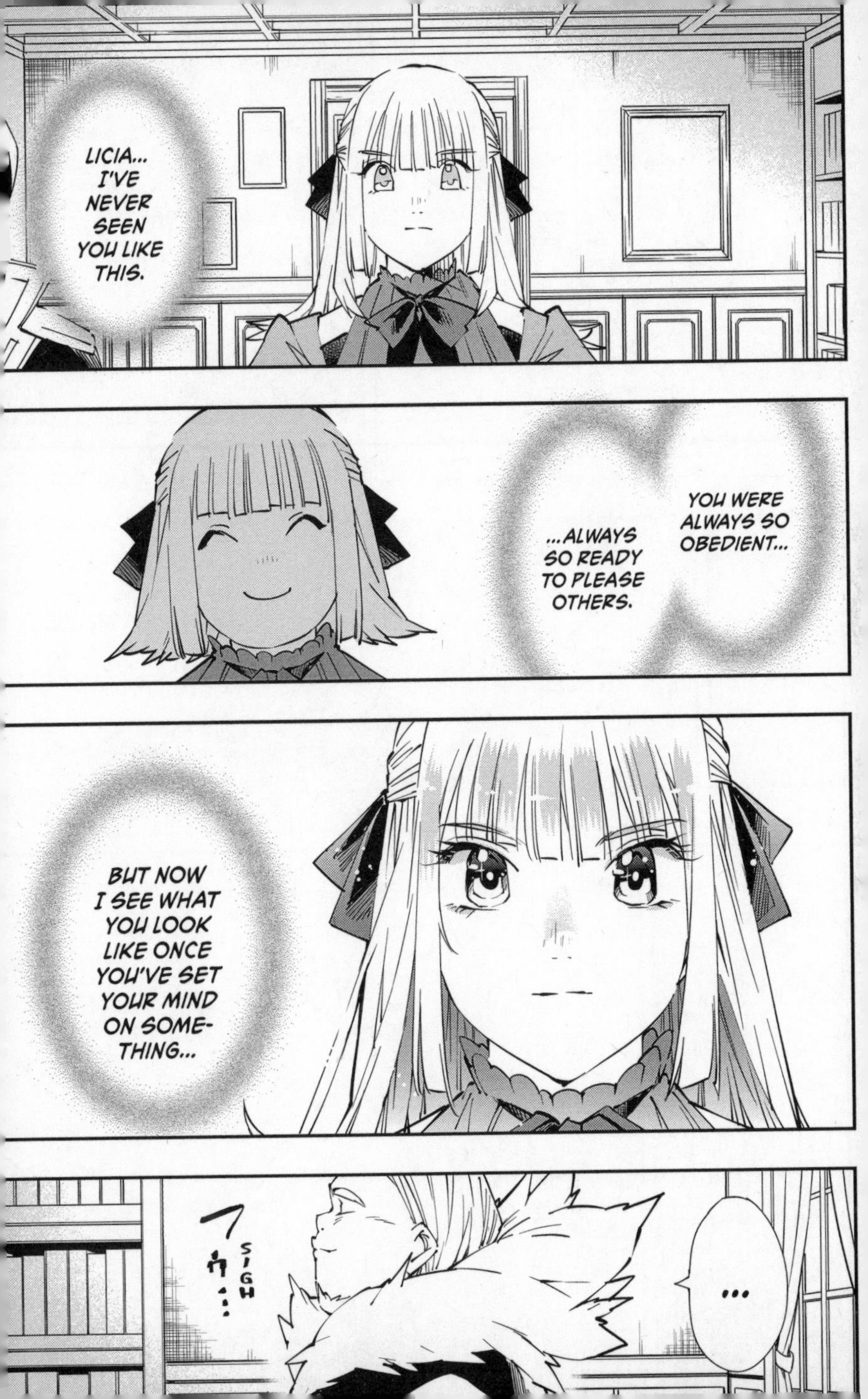
LICIA... I'VE NEVER SEEN YOU LIKE THIS.
YOU WERE ALWAYS SO OBEDIENT...
...ALWAYS SO READY TO PLEASE OTHERS.
BUT NOW I SEE WHAT YOU LOOK LIKE ONCE YOU'VE SET YOUR MIND ON SOME-THING...
...
SIGH

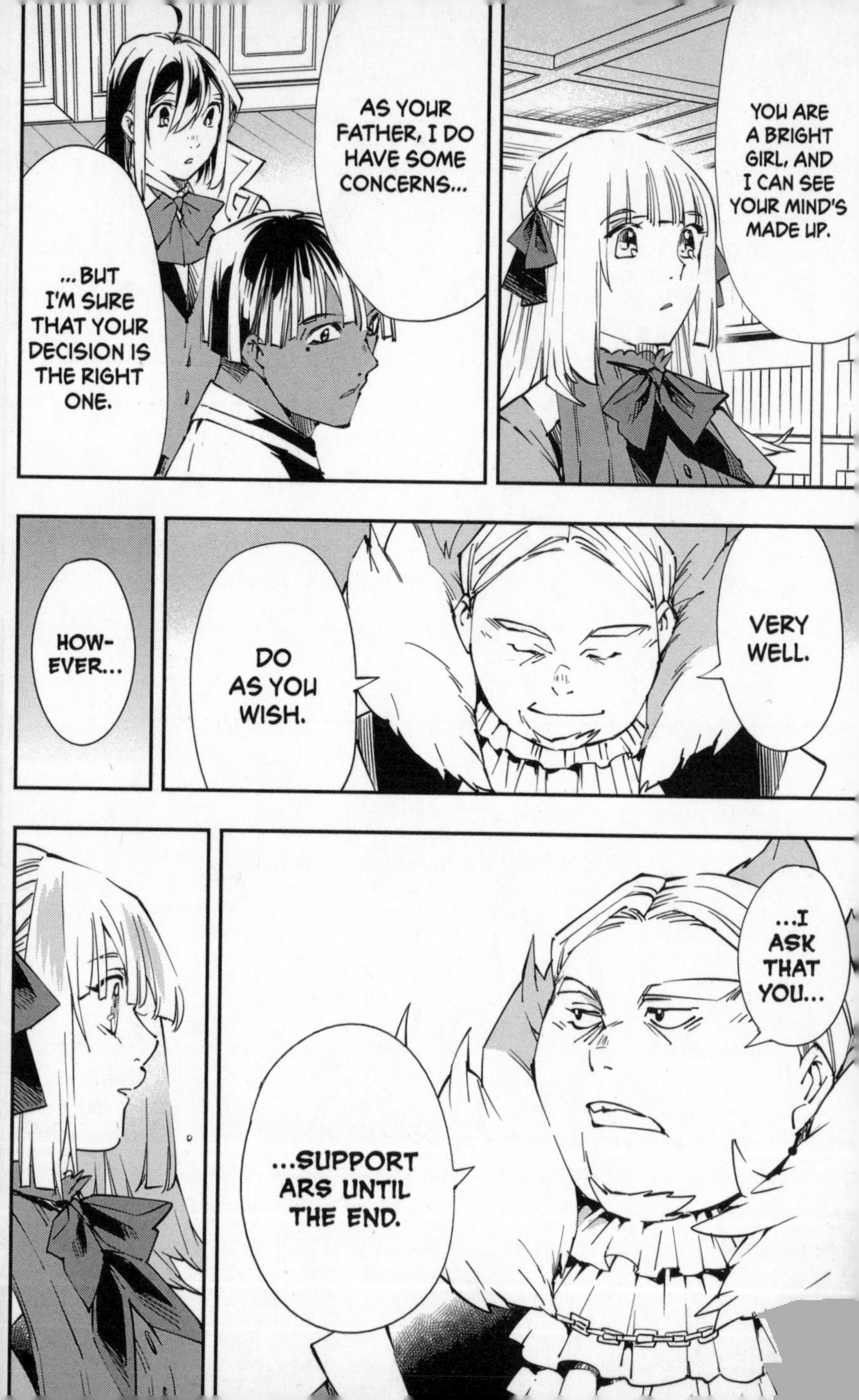
YOU ARE A BRIGHT GIRL, AND I CAN SEE YOUR MIND'S MADE UP.
AS YOUR FATHER, I DO HAVE SOME CONCERNS...
...BUT I'M SURE THAT YOUR DECISION IS THE RIGHT ONE.
VERY WELL.
DO AS YOU WISH.
HOW-EVER...
...I ASK THAT YOU...
...SUPPORT ARS UNTIL THE END.

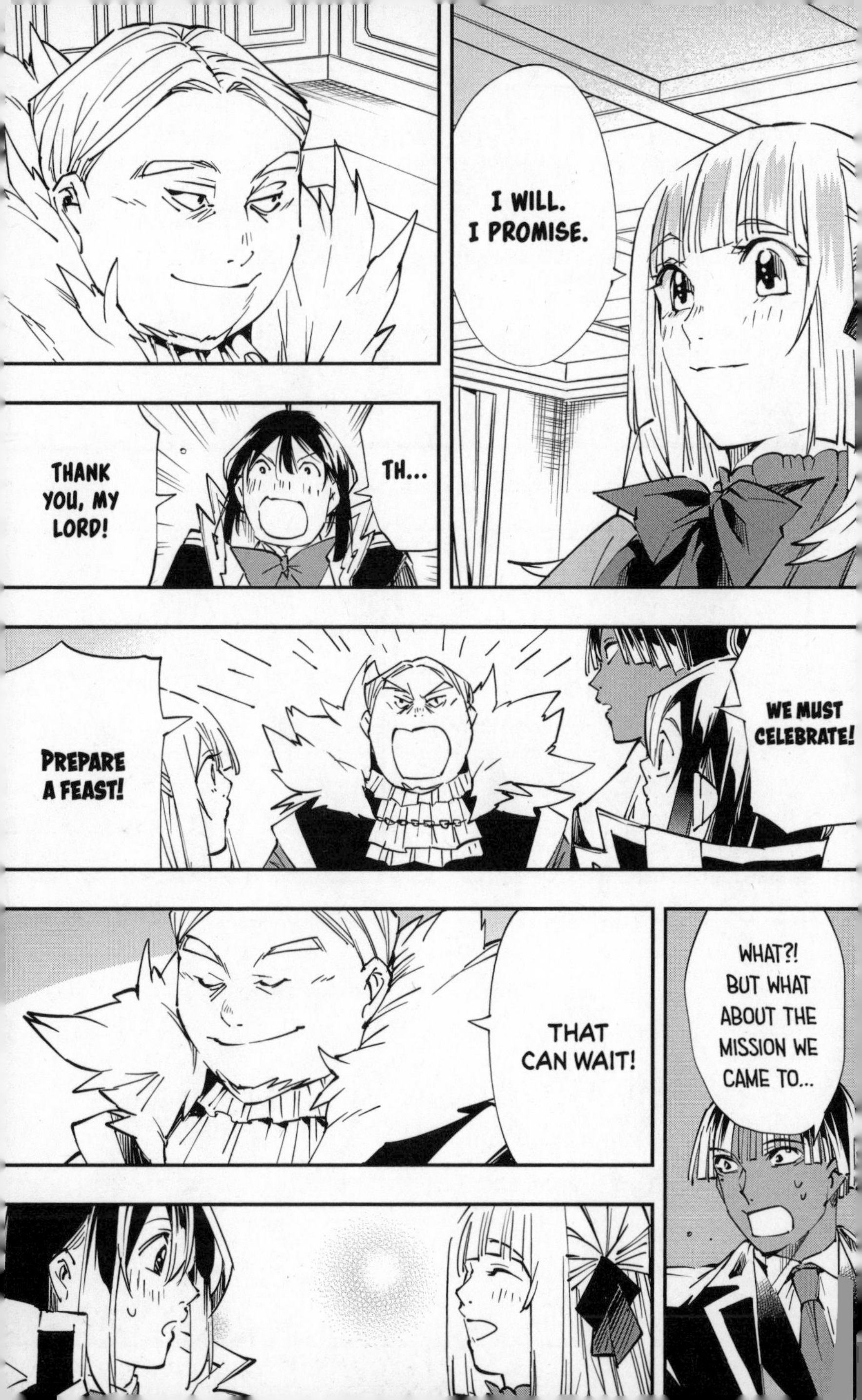
I WILL. I PROMISE.
TH...
THANK YOU, MY LORD!
WE MUST CELEBRATE!
PREPARE A FEAST!
WHAT?! BUT WHAT ABOUT THE MISSION WE CAME TO...
THAT CAN WAIT!

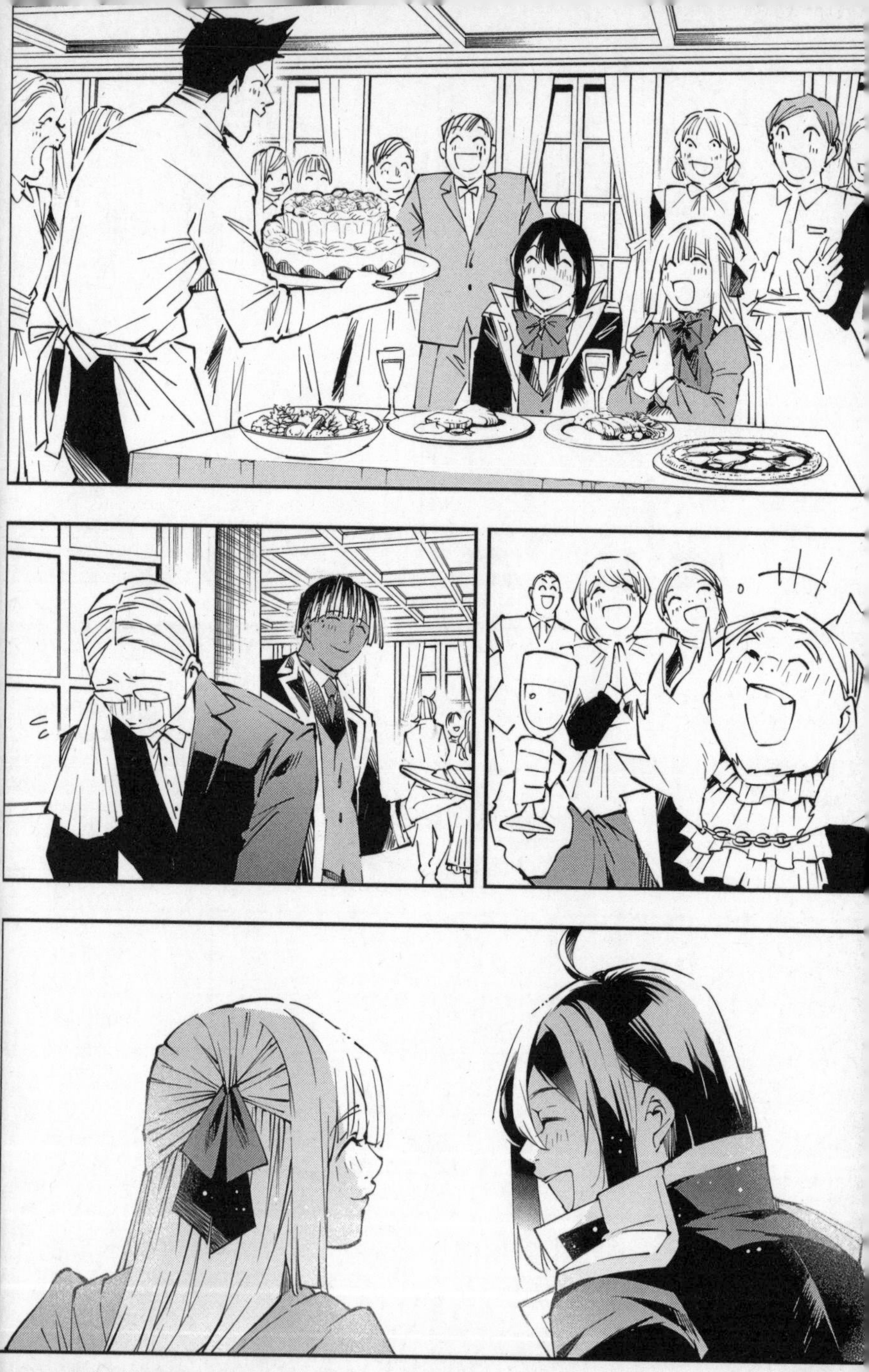

As a Reincarnated
ARISTOCRAT,
I'll Use My Appraisal Skill to
Rise in the World

As a Reincarnated
ARISTOCRAT,
I'll Use My Appraisal Skill to
Rise in the World

Bonus Story

by Miraijin A

Ars was paying a visit to the library in the manor of House Louvent. He had started spending a little more time on his studies ever since becoming the new baron. After all, knowledge was essential for any great lord. He might have vassals to help him manage the barony, but he wanted to be able to do more on his own.

As usual, Ars entered the library to find Rosell reading and taking notes. *That boy always has his nose in a book*, Ars thought. *I admire his dedication, but it's good to take breaks every now and then.* Even so, Ars didn't want to be the one to interrupt Rosell's studies, so he picked up a book and joined him instead.

Several hours later, Ars had managed to get through a couple of books. Heaving a weary sigh, he decided to take a break to rest his eyes. He glanced over at Rosell and saw that, sure enough, he was still absorbed in his studies. The boy's concentration was admirable, but Ars was starting to worry.

Hmm... Rosell's still a child, and children should be able to have fun. Then again, he isn't really the type to play outside. And in this world, there's only so much you can do for fun indoors...

Then a thought struck him. If there were no indoor games, then why not just *make* some? Even in this world, it should be possible to craft a deck of cards, or board games like chess, *shogi**, and Othello. They wouldn't be as nice as the ones you could buy in Japan, but you didn't need a deluxe set to have fun.

And I'll bet Rosell would love games that make you use your brain, Ars thought as he retired to his room for the night. The next day, he enlisted the help of several vassals to craft the needed materials, and several weeks later, they had produced a deck of cards and a *shogi* board.

Though the cards lacked any designs on the back, they did have numbers on the front, so they would serve for card games. Unlike Japanese *shogi* pieces, which had *kanji* written on them, these used the letters of the parallel world. They also varied slightly in size, but not enough to make it impossible to play. As for the board, it was a slab of polished wood with a grid pattern etched onto it.

Ars carried the *shogi* board and cards to the library. Rosell was already there studying, and Ars struck up a conversation.

"Hi, Rosell. Do you have a minute?"

"Oh... Lord Ars? What is it?" Rosell asked dazedly. He had been so absorbed in his book that it took him a moment to disengage himself.

---

*A traditional Japanese strategy game akin to chess. Using a set of 20 flat, pentagonal pieces, players attempt to capture the opponent's pieces and checkmate their king.

"Why not take a break with a little game?" Ars asked.

"A game? You know I'm not good at sports..."

"No, this is a game you can play indoors," Ars explained, placing the *shogi* board on the table. "You have to use your head. I think you'd like it."

Rosell eyed the board dubiously. "We're going to play with *this*?"

"Yes. I'll teach you how."

Ars proceeded to explain the rules. He had played quite a bit of *shogi* himself in his previous life, so he knew enough to be able to explain the finer details.

"I see," said Rosell. "You said it's called *shogi*? What a fascinating game..."

"I only went through the rules once. Are you sure you got them?"

"Yes, I remember what you said."

"About where the pieces go and how they move, too?"

"Yes."

Ars could only shake his head in wonder. Rosell really was an incredibly quick learner.

"Did you come up with this game yourself, Lord Ars?" Rosell asked. "That would really be something."

"Uh, no, I didn't. Let's just say I heard about it from an old man who lived in Canarre a few years ago," Ars lied. It wasn't as though Rosell would have understood even if he told him the truth.

"Well, then," Ars continued. "Want to try playing

a game?"

"Okay."

Ars and Rosell began setting up the board. Despite having only heard the rules once, Rosell knew exactly where all the pieces went. Next, they determined the order of play: Rosell would go first. As soon as the game was underway, Rosell's lack of experience became apparent. Ars had once been a fairly strong player, so he quickly gained the upper hand. However, as the game progressed, Rosell became better at anticipating his next move, and he began making up some of his early losses. Still, he had dug himself too deep at the start, and Ars eventually succeeded in checkmating his king.

Wow. I wonder if he could already beat me if we played another round, Ars thought anxiously. He knew Rosell was bright, but even he hadn't expected him to be this good after just one game.

"Oh, I see..." Rosell murmured. "So that's why you did that at the beginning. And that move *I* made was clearly wrong..." Apparently, Rosell could remember every single move he and Ars had made. He continued analyzing the game under his breath. When he had finished, he turned back to Ars. "You're very good, my lord. Have you played this *shogi* game much?"

"Yes, quite a bit. For about, oh, ten years?"

Rosell chuckled. "That means you would have picked it up when you were just three!" Clearly, he assumed that Ars was joking, when in fact Ars had been playing for over a decade in his past life. Ars could only shoot back a wry grin.

"This *shogi* really is fun," said Rosell. "Let's play again. This time, I'll win!"

"R-right..."

The normally quiet, mild-mannered Rosell was looking uncharacteristically animated. Determined not to lose the second round, Ars turned all his attention to the board. The resulting match proved quite the contest, with Rosell's declaration ultimately proving true.

"I resign..." Ars groaned.

"Yay, I won!" Rosell cheered.

His ability to think ahead is so far beyond me. If Rosell had been born in Japan, he could have been a pro shogi player, Ars mused, reeling under the disparity in their skill.

"*Shogi* is so fun!" Rosell exclaimed.

"I'm glad you're enjoying it..."

"Let's play again!"

"Umm... How about a different game this time?" Ars suggested, sensing that any further contests would only result in him being thoroughly embarrassed.

Ars brought out the deck of playing cards he'd had made. "How about this instead?"

"What are these?"

"They're called *cards*. You can play all kinds of games with these."

"Like what...?"

Ars considered what game they should start with. Tycoon and Old Maid weren't ideal for two players. Poker, maybe? He didn't remember all the different hands. Maybe they could play Blind Man's Bluff. Settling on this last option, Ars began exlaining the rules.

"I see," said Rosell. "So you hold the card up so only the other player can see it... and the player with the higher number wins. It seems simple, but I'm guessing it can get pretty tricky."

They started playing, Rosell and Ars each holding a card to their forehead. The moment Rosell saw Ars's card, his face sank.

"Let me guess," said Ars, "my card's really high?"

"Huh?! How did you know?! Oh, wait..." By the time Rosell had worked it out, it was too late; he ended up losing the round. In each subsequent round, Rosell kept inadvertently letting his emotions spill over onto his face, making it all too easy for Ars to win.

"I... I lost..." Rosell moaned.

If he's going to be a tactician, this might be something he should work on, Ars thought. It wouldn't do to let your enemy know when you were rattled. Rosell was still a child, though; no doubt he would learn to hide his emotions better as he grew older.

"Blind Man's Bluff was hard," said Rosell, "but I liked *shogi*. I'd like to try playing with other people.

May I borrow the set?"

"Of course. Do whatever you like with it, Rosell."

"Thank you!"

From that point on, Rosell would pull out his *shogi* set whenever he needed a break from studying.

The End

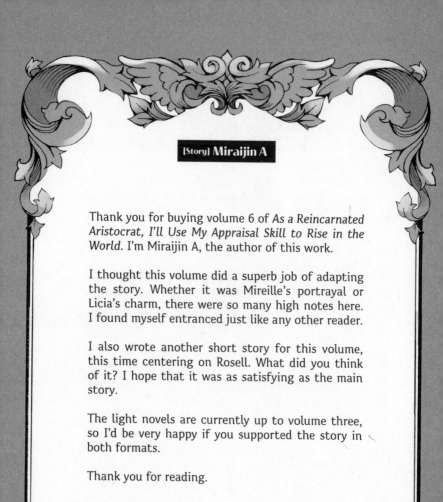

[Story] Miraijin A

Thank you for buying volume 6 of *As a Reincarnated Aristocrat, I'll Use My Appraisal Skill to Rise in the World*. I'm Miraijin A, the author of this work.

I thought this volume did a superb job of adapting the story. Whether it was Mireille's portrayal or Licia's charm, there were so many high notes here. I found myself entranced just like any other reader.

I also wrote another short story for this volume, this time centering on Rosell. What did you think of it? I hope that it was as satisfying as the main story.

The light novels are currently up to volume three, so I'd be very happy if you supported the story in both formats.

Thank you for reading.

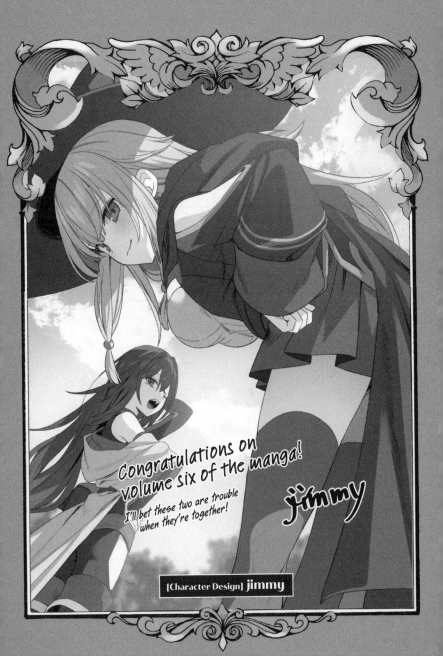

Congratulations on
volume six of the manga!

I'll bet these two are trouble
when they're together!

jimmy

[Character Design] jimmy

★★★★★★
Mazak - Age 22 ♂

Stats

	CURRENT	MAX
Command	3 3	4 4
Prowess	9 1	9 2
Intellect	8 7	9 0
Diplomacy	2 2	2 3

Ambition	4 5

Aptitude

Fighter	A	Cavalier	C	Archer	S
Mage	A	Engineer	C	Armorer	A
Mariner	D	Pilot	C	Tactician	B

A Kodansha Trade Paperback Original

As a Reincarnated Aristocrat, I'll Use My Appraisal Skill to Rise in the World 6
copyright © 2022 Miraijin A/Natsumi Inoue/jimmy
English translation copyright © 2023 Miraijin A/Natsumi Inoue/jimmy

Published in the United States by
Kodansha USA Publishing, LLC, New York.

Publication rights for this English edition arranged through
Kodansha Ltd., Tokyo.

First published in Japan in 2022 by Kodansha Ltd., Tokyo
as *Tensei kizoku, kantei sukiru de nariagaru*, volume 6.

ISBN 978-1-64651-684-1

Printed in the United States of America.

9 8 7 6 5 4 3 2 1

Translation: Stephen Paul
Lettering: Nicole Roderick
Editing: Andres Oliver
Kodansha USA Publishing edition cover design by Abigail Blackman

Publisher: Kiichiro Sugawara

Director of Publishing Services: Ben Applegate
Director of Publishing Operations: Dave Barrett
Publishing Services Managing Editors: Alanna Ruse, Madison Salters,
with Grace Chen
Production Manager: Claire Kerker

KODANSHA.US

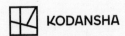

KODANSHA